Animal Matter

OXFORD STUDIES IN THE ARCHAEOLOGY OF ANCIENT STATES
Series Editors
Friederike Fless, Li Liu, Deborah L. Nichols, and D. T. Potts

Animal Matter: Ritual, Place, and Sovereignty at the Moon Pyramid of Teotihuacan
NAWA SUGIYAMA

The Syro-Anatolian City-States: An Iron Age Culture
JAMES F. OSBORNE

The Ancient Highlands of Southwest China: From the Bronze Age to the Han Empire
ALICE YAO

Urbanization and Religion in Ancient Central Mexico
DAVID M. CARBALLO

The Origins of Ancient Vietnam
NAM KIM

OXFORD STUDIES IN THE ARCHAEOLOGY OF ANCIENT STATES

Animal Matter

Ritual, Place, and Sovereignty at the Moon Pyramid of Teotihuacan

NAWA SUGIYAMA

OXFORD
UNIVERSITY PRESS

Oxford University Press is a department of the University of Oxford.
It furthers the University's objective of excellence in research, scholarship,
and education by publishing worldwide. Oxford is a registered trade mark of
Oxford University Press in the UK and in certain other countries.

Published in the United States of America by Oxford University Press
198 Madison Avenue, New York, NY 10016, United States of America.

© Oxford University Press 2024

All rights reserved. No part of this publication may be reproduced, stored in a retrieval system, or transmitted, in any form or by any means, without the prior permission in writing of Oxford University Press, or as expressly permitted by law, by license or under terms agreed with the appropriate reprographics rights organization. Inquiries concerning reproduction outside the scope of the above should be sent to the Rights Department, Oxford University Press, at the address above.

You must not circulate this work in any other form and you must impose this
same condition on any acquirer

Library of Congress Cataloging-in-Publication Data
Names: Sugiyama, Nawa, author.
Title: Animal matter : ritual, place, and sovereignty at the Moon Pyramid
of Teotihuacan / Nawa Sugiyama.
Description: Oxford ; New York : Oxford University Press, [2024] |
Series: Oxford studies in the archaeology of ancient states |
Includes bibliographical references and index.
Identifiers: LCCN 2024009009 (print) | LCCN 2024009010 (ebook) |
ISBN 9780197653395 (paperback) | ISBN 9780197653388 (hardback) |
ISBN 9780197653418 (epub)
Subjects: LCSH: Teotihuacán Site (San Juan Teotihuacán, Mexico) |
Animal remains (Archaeology)—Mexico—San Juan Teotihuacán. |
Human-animal relationships—Mexico—San Juan Teotihuacán. |
Political customs and rites—Mexico—San Juan Teotihuacán. |
Indians of Mexico—Mexico—San Juan Teotihuacán—Antiquities. |
Indian architecture—Mexico—San Juan Teotihuacán. |
Excavations (Archaeology)—Mexico—San Juan Teotihuacán. |
San Juan Teotihuacán (Mexico)—Antiquities.
Classification: LCC F1219.1.T27 S838 2024 (print) |
LCC F1219.1.T27 (ebook) | DDC 972/.5201—dc23 /eng/20240403
LC record available at https://lccn.loc.gov/2024009009
LC ebook record available at https://lccn.loc.gov/2024009010

DOI: 10.1093/9780197653425.001.0001

In memory of Kumiko Sugiyama
For Kai Orion Cebollero

CONTENTS

ACKNOWLEDGMENTS	ix
1. RITUALIZATION OF ANIMAL MATTER	1
2. PLACEMAKING: TEOTIHUACAN'S *ALTEPETL*	19
3. ANIMAL POLITICS	53
4. THE ZOOARCHAEOLOGICAL DATA	86
5. ISOTOPE EVIDENCE OF CAPTIVITY	135
6. ANIMAL BIOGRAPHIES	164
7. ANIMALS INHABITING THE *ALTEPETL*	181
8. EPILOGUE: A THICK DESCRIPTION OF BURIAL 6	205
APPENDIX	225
BIBLIOGRAPHY	229
INDEX	263

ACKNOWLEDGMENTS

AS A WORK THAT SPANNED a significant temporal span from initial conception (admittedly as a dissertation project), germination, and reflection, I would like to recognize the generous guidance of many human and nonhuman actants (people, institutions, and funding sources). First and foremost, I have to give due credit (and blame) to Saburo Sugiyama, as my father, mentor, and now colleague, for leading me down this path to exploring Teotihuacan's ritualized landscape. His dedication and passion have, and will continue to, fuel, inspire, and challenge my research. As co-director of the Proyecto Pirámide de la Luna (Moon Pyramid Project) with the late Rubén Cabrera Castro, their joint support and guidance were seminal in my ability to conduct research. Prof. Rubén's generosity and expansive knowledge have greatly influenced my perspective. Alejandro Sarabia, the director of the Programa de Conservación e Investigación en el Complejo Arquitectónico de la Pirámide del Sol (Sun Pyramid Project), facilitated my involvement with excavations and faunal analysis of the materials from the Sun Pyramid. I thank him for his generous support and the opportunity to work with him and his team.

As enigmatic emblems of Mexican national patrimony, the corporeal animal forms discussed in this manuscript continue to build relationships and intra-actions among countless collaborators, international institutions, a broader readership, and myself. Burial 6 materials were analyzed in collaboration with Raúl Valadez, Alicia Blanco, Gilberto Pérez, Bernardo Rodríguez, and Fabiola Torres at the Laboratorio de Paleozoología at the Universidad Nacional Autónoma de México (UNAM). The Laboratorio de Arqueozoología Ticul Álvarez Solórzano at the Instituto Nacional de Antropología e Historia of Mexico (INAH) with Oscar

Polaco, Felisa Aguilar Arellano, Maria Teresa Olivera Carrasco, and Norma Valentín Maldonado excavated and conducted preliminary analysis of the corporeal animal forms from Burial 2, 3, and 5 before I reanalyzed the collection under their guidance. Isotope work was conducted at the Paleodiet Laboratory at the University of California, San Diego, in collaboration with Andrew Somerville and under the guidance of Margaret Schoeninger. I would also like to acknowledge all the support provided by the Arizona State University Teotihuacan Research Laboratory staff and researchers, especially Lulú Caballero Mejia, Oralia Cabrera, and Michael Smith. Each lab sprouted many friendships and future collaborations and trained me in precious methods and techniques I am grateful for. I am indebted to INAH, who authorized all stages of this research. I continue to engage with this collection, some of which is briefly mentioned in passing, including new ancient DNA work on the fauna with Courtney A. Hofman, Robin Singleton, and Karissa Hughes and their team at the Laboratories of Molecular Anthropology and Microbiome Research at the University of Oklahoma.

I am very grateful for the collaborations, friendships, and professional guidance of many great minds and hearts that have influenced my career and research. I would particularly like to extend my appreciation to my dissertation committee, William Fash, Richard Meadow, David Carrasco, Rowan Flad, and Raúl Valadez, for their mentorship during my time at Harvard University as well as the countless faculty and graduate students who shaped my thinking and research during my time there. I'd like to acknowledge several people that through their research, friendships, and conversations, have influenced my own thinking; Alfredo López Austin, Leonardo López Lujan, Oralia Cabrera, Sergio Gómez, Julie Gazzola, Luis Rogelio Rivero Chong, Linda Manzanilla, David and Jennifer Carballo, Sarah Clayton, Ben and Margaret Nelson, Deborah Nichols, Emily McClung de Tapia, Tatsuya Murakami, Miguel Aguilera, Colin McEwan, Yen-Shin T. Hsu, Clarissa Cagnato, Jose Luis Ruvalcaba, Luis Barba, Verónica Ortega, Matthew Des Lauriers, Erin Thornton, Christine France, Ronald Bishop, Erin Sears, Torben Rick, Jade D'Alpoim Guedes, Lauren Santini, Christina Warinner, Qiaowei Wei, Janling Fu, Dylan Clark, Jeffrey Dobereiner, Wengcheong Lam, Alexandre Tokovinine, Ajita K. Patel, Emily Hammer, Michele Koons, Mikael Fauvelle, Elodie Dupey Garcia, Diana Magaloni, Maria Teresa Uriarte, David Stuart, Oswaldo Chinchilla, Maria Fernanda Martínez, and Richard Cooke.

I finalized this manuscript at my new academic home at University of California, Riverside, where I have found myself inspired anew in a stimulating environment of colleagues, friends, and students, including Karl Taube, Travis Stanton, Kenichiro Tsukamoto, Chieko and Somei Tsukamoto, Sara Becker, Elizabeth Berger, Sang-Hee Lee, Juliet McMullin, Jennifer Syvertsen, Fatima Quraishi, Xóchitl Chávez, Luat Vuong, Ilya Brookwell, Kim Frost, Annie Ditta, Kim Yi Dionne, Ryohei Takatsuchi,

Yun Ge, Ariel Texis, Yolanda Perez, Edsel Robles, Esther Aguayo, Rafael Cruz, and Diana Mendez Lee.

I sincerely thank Claudia Garcia-Des Lauriers and Andrew Somerville who provided comments on earlier drafts of the book. David Freidel and David Carbaollo's supportive mentorship have continued to influence my thinking throughout this process. Saburo Sugiyama, Karl Taube, Alejandro Sarabia, and Robert Cebollero provided image permission. A focused seminar at the School of Advance Research on *Imperial Matters*, organized by Tamara Bray and Lori Khatchadourian, has greatly influenced this manuscript. I would like to thank the session organizers and participants for their vibrant discussions. Likewise, productive conversations on matter and materiality during the graduate seminar with students and co-instructor Christina Schwenkel resulted in additional reflection. I would also like to thank Stephan Vranka, an editor at Oxford University Press, and two anonymous reviewers who have provided generative feedback that has positively impacted the work.

The NSF (BCS-1028851), the Fulbright Hays Doctorate Dissertation Research Abroad Program, the Dumbarton Oaks Research Library and Collections, and Harvard University funded the dissertation work. Many extended trips back to Mexico and reengagements with corporeal animal forms continued during my postdoctoral and assistant professor positions at the Smithsonian Institution, George Mason University, and now at the University of California, Riverside. During this second phase I received support from the Smithsonian Institution Peter Buck Fellowship, the National Science Foundation (BCS 1638525, BCS 2114021), and the National Endowment for the Humanities (RFW-279331-21).

Finally, I have indescribable gratitude for my family, who bore the brunt of my labor to complete this volume. My husband, Robert Cebollero, has provided critical edits to many sections of the book and continues to challenge my intellectual pursuits. Our nonhuman family, Goro, Tokio, and Morocco, provided first-hand experiences imposed by feline vitalities. Kai Orion, I dedicate this book to you because you reintroduced Mommy to the vibrant and intimate relations you seamlessly engage with nonhuman persons. Your entry into this world has taught me so much I didn't know about myself and the world. I want to thank my brother and sister, Yosei and Masano, their families (Cindy, Aki, Ella, Eric, and Koji), and Tokiko, who have harbored this road to be full of endless procrastination, joy, and love. Belén Chávez, Jesus Alfonso Ballesteros, and Lenora Chávez Ballesteros, who might as well be family, assured my well-being. And finally, I write in memory of my mother, Kumiko, who taught me courage, love, and forgiveness.

CHAPTER 1

RITUALIZATION OF ANIMAL MATTER

I WANT TO TALK ABOUT animal matter. Specifically, I want to feature corporeal animal forms as a potent type of animal matter. These are the subject of study for zooarchaeologists who examine fragmentary remnants of animal bodies and their by-products. Witness to the highly productive discourse on animism, relational ontologies, and new materialism in the greater anthropological literature, I explore how zooarchaeologists may be able to apply, even contribute, to these concepts precisely because we rely on rigorously quantified primary zooarchaeological, isotopic, spatial, and iconographic data. My job is to let the narratives derived from the bodies and secondary remains of nearly two hundred animals offered at the Moon Pyramid of Teotihuacan (1–550 CE) speak of their experiences, relationships, and spatiotemporal positionalities. I argue the involvement of animal matter in the ritualized co-production of one of the most influential ceremonial landscapes of Teotihuacan intimately entangled corporeal animal forms with the politics of sovereignty formations (defined as contextually contingent, fluid, and pluralistic processes, see Chapter 2). Co-production, in this context, alludes to the conjoining of human and nonhuman persons in the cooperative process of creation, such as in dedicatory acts analyzed in this volume.

The life histories of jaguars, pumas, wolves, rattlesnakes, and golden eagles provide the earliest evidence of mass animal sacrifice and wild carnivore management in captivity (Sugiyama et al. 2015), a feat unknown in this region for ten centuries until it appeared in lurid and marvelous colonial descriptions of "Moctezuma's zoo" (Blanco Padilla, Pérez Roldán, et al. 2009; Nicholson 1955). State-sanctioned ritualized performances staged the consecration of apex predators into direct *mediators*, not mere symbolic projections, of sovereignty formations. Perfected through sacrifice into the heart of the Moon Pyramid, their essence animated the pyramid into the material nexus of state authority and sovereignty, the *altepetl* (water mountain) of Teotihuacan.

Two key arguments form the foundation for the volume: First, Amerindian cultures recognized corporeal animal forms as active persons within a relational ontology precisely because of their animal-derived material vitalities. Second, the dedication rituals conducted at the Moon Pyramid were ritualized performances organized by the Teotihuacan state that became active arenas for producing, embodying, and maintaining an ultimate form of authority. Interpreting animal matter as active participants in ritualized performances allows archaeologists to retrieve the social transactions among humans, animals, and other agentive persons during sovereignty formations at Teotihuacan.

Animal Matter

Corporeal Animal Forms in a Relational Ontology

An archaeological exploration of ancient human-animal dynamics must begin with the fundamental question Ingold (1988a) proposed, "What is an animal?" While it is impossible to completely recreate an emic approach from material traces of the past, recent anthropological discourse on animism, relational ontologies, and new materialism provides a good starting point to explore Mesoamerican human-animal interactions through a relational ontological approach. This literature introduces animals (and generally nonhuman beings) as conscious, intentional agents, ontological subjects that require negotiating and establishing meaningful relationships (Armstrong Oma 2010; Bird-David 1999; Descola 2012; Hendon and Harrison-Buck 2018; Ingold 1988b, 2006; Losey et al. 2011; Pitarch Ramón 2010; Viveiros de Castro 1998; C. Watts 2013). In Hallowell's (2002) exemplary study of Ojibwa ontology, other-than-human or nonhuman[1] beings such as animals and stones are described as active agents with potential for personhood. Personhood is defined by the "ability of reciprocity where social identity is a mutually constituted relationship" (Harrison-Buck and Hendon 2018: 4). Thus, though many humans and nonhumans could act as agents, not all interacted in socially significant ways as persons (Hill 2018).

Bird-David (1999) explains that Nayaka hunter-gatherers in southern India understand *devaru* (spiritual superpersons) within a relational epistemology,

---

[1] Though the term other-than-human avoids the binary and biased nature of term nonhuman, here we use the latter with an explicit understanding that these are relational, not oppositional categories.

whereby performances raise people's awareness of 'persons' and functions to clarify one's place in an interlinked relational environment. She explains, "the devaru are present *as* they move, talk, make gestures, etc. They are present *as* they communicate and socially interact with Nayaka" (Bird-David 1999: S76). Conceptualizations of animal persons are not simply imposed but discovered and modified through corporeal experiences predicated upon variables (species, age, sex, gender, and status) (Hill 2018). As Ingold put it, "beings . . . continually and reciprocally bring one another into existence" (2006: 10). During these transactions, human-animal "eco-contracts" designate mutual rights and obligations that are constantly renegotiated (Armstrong Oma 2010; V. Watts 2013). Others have characterized this "humanization" process as a way of creating a "sentient ecology" built by reflexive actions between human and animal persons (Anderson 2000: 129–130). In a sentient world, a human moving through the encultured landscape is necessarily interwoven within a web of conscious interpersonal relationships and cannot be isolated from these entangled, or socially and materially interdependent, landscapes (Hodder 2012).

A key attribute relevant to the current case study is that agency is unequally and usually hierarchically distributed (Harrison-Buck 2018). Human and animal categories are produced by a culture-specific system actively negotiated through differential access to potent persons, such as powerful animals. In Chapter 3, I discuss how daily practices, hunting and subsistence strategies, and ritualized performances produce, maintain, reinforce, and modify (often hierarchical) relationships into being. Such relationships are not fixed but are constantly in flux and negotiated through interpersonal interactions (Descola 2012).

As subsistence hunters maintain strong bonds with their prey, hunter–animal interactions provide excellent comparative parallels to understand the material correlates of this intimate exchange. Hunting is a social process by which hunters must navigate the landscape by establishing interpersonal dialogues (involving acts of reciprocity and respect) with their prey that are usually characterized by mutual sentience, linkages in the form of kinship, and shared personhood (Hill 2018; McNiven 2010; Pitarch Ramón 2010). As these interpersonal exchanges are physical, archaeologists are well positioned to consider the materiality of these encounters. Hunters manipulate corporeal animal forms such as hides, bones, and teeth to develop and maintain interdependent bonds with these beings (Hill 2011, 2013; McNiven 2010).

Brown and Emery (2008) have demonstrated that large bone caches at hunting shrines in a modern Maya village of San Pablo La Laguna, Guatemala, were material testament to the negotiated relationships maintained with various agents—the animal guardian, the live prey, notable outcroppings, rock shelters, caves, hunting dogs, weapons, and the skeletal remains of the catch. Their informants explain because animals can regenerate from each returned bone, reuniting bones with the animal guardian in the hunting shrine maintains a resilient subsistence ecosystem. Detailed prescriptions on how to interact with the bones and teeth were part of the conditions of this exchange; they should not have butchering marks, and some Maya took care to boil, clean, and retain their whiteness (Brown and Emery 2008: 314). The ritualized actions at hunting shrines were "active sites of engagement" (sensu Todd 2014) where humans and animals navigated the social contracts embedded within an entangled landscape.

Recognizing the potential personhood of animals transforms the empirical natural environment into a complex relational landscape in a constant process of reconfiguration. Evidence of relational ontologies abounds in ethnographic literature of Amerindian cultures throughout South, Central, and North America (Bassett 2015; Brown and Walker 2008; Descola 2012; Ingold 1988b; Pitarch Ramón 2010; Reichel-Dolmatoff 1975; Todd 2014; Viveiros de Castro 1998; C. Watts 2013; V. Watts 2013; Zingg 2004) and have been argued for various Old World cases (Anderson 2000; Brightman et al. 2012; Kimura 1999).

In interpreting zooarchaeological vestiges of a relational ontology, I find it productive to distinguish physical animal bodies and their body parts from their representation (e.g., mural iconography) because the latter is predicated on physical encounters with the animal's corporeality. Though a figurine of a jaguar may be a potent agent and likely also an engaged person embodying rulership, it is fundamentally the encounter with the feline beast in the forest that establishes the baseline eco-contracts under which the figurine is forming and negotiating their interpersonal encounters. New materialists would likely argue that the material constituents of teeth and bone itself (discussed later) were part of the "vitalities" that afforded their "thing power," the efficacy of matter to affect, act, produce, and reassemble (Bennett 2010). It may very well be the physical matter at hand, in this case, apex predators, in their vitalities, such as their biology, behavior, and ecology, that affected their social positionality through interpersonal encounters (see Chapter 3).

Thus, I distinguish living animals as well as animal-derived products (flesh, pelts, claws, etc.) and artifacts produced from animal bodies that had the ability to engage in interpersonal relationships as corporeal animal forms. This category fits within animal matter, which includes corporeal animal forms and their representations, which have the potential for personhood, though with distinct materialities. From this perspective, the deposition of corporeal animal forms in the Moon Pyramid dedicatory caches, like the hunted bone assembled in Guatemala (Brown and Emery 2008) and seal bone caches among Yup'ik and Inupiaq Eskimo (Hill 2013, 2018), should be interpreted as material correlates of deliberate interpersonal engagements between humans and corporeal animal forms to maintain a salient ecology. This definition recognizes the generative and transformative possibilities of corporeal intra-action, such as the encounter between human and deer antlers at the Mesolithic English site of Star Carr generating a "corporeal transformation" of the human to deer (Conneller 2004).

In this conversation, the material properties and dispositions of animal-derived products, particularly bones/teeth, need to be mentioned as they will be the primary dataset for this study. The unique attributes of bone (and somewhat different properties for teeth discussed in Chapter 5) make them particularly prone to materialize interpersonal encounters. First, bone is alive during the organism's life, growing and molding experiential narratives into the physical properties of bone (e.g., bone size and growth lines indicate health and diet, chemical properties reflect diet and environment, and pathologies define disease and trauma). Second, zooarchaeological methods can usually distinguish residues of interpersonal relationships while the organism was alive (often at different points of development) from those that occurred postmortem (after the animal's death). Additional and often distinct relationships may flourish postmortem due to significant material transformations, resulting in a different physical experience during the interaction. Confronting a live jaguar presents quite a different experience from manipulating its skull. Bones/teeth and other associated animal-derived products have diverse functions (as artifacts, food, medicine, etc.) with disperate tactile and visible affordances to create, maintain, and redefine relationships with the animal's corporeal form.

In essence, bone/teeth provide opportune canvases to record synchronic (spatial) and diachronic (life history of an animal as well as across building phases) patterns in human–animal interactions. The durability of bone/teeth reinforces their survivability from the taphonomic process. Meskell (2008) picks up on this material deficiency of flesh and argues that plastering allowed human and animal skulls to be re-fleshed enabling their participation in 'tradition' (defined via durability, continuity, and resilience) at Çatalhöyük. These inherent properties of bone and teeth make them a particularly effective matter to apply an archaeometry reconstruction of human–animal interpersonal encounters.

The zooarchaeological record can distinguish the body parts endowed with potency and personhood. The fixation on plastered skulls into architecture at Çatalhöyük (Meskell 2008) or the curation of dugong ear bones in Torres Strait, Australia (McNiven 2010) demonstrates distinct vitalities attributed to specific body parts. In dedication and funerary contexts at the Maya site of Copan, Honduras, multispecies agents were active persons in negotiating stately power animated through the comingling of corporeal animal forms (Sugiyama et al. 2019). In one case, a necklace containing thirty-eight toothless deer mandibles were accompanied by thirty-three isolated crocodilian teeth, which was interpreted as the matter that brought the Starry-deer-crocodile into being. Intimate relationships between humans and animals are detectable in material correlates of faunal products and their bodies. Diachronic changes in human–animal dynamics directly affect social and economic engagements between human and corporeal animal forms in ritualized contexts. For example, Betts and colleagues (2012) analyze shifts in human–shark interactions in the Maritime Peninsula of the Northeastern United States through the abundance and spatial distribution of specific species of shark teeth over time.

Decentering the human in the archaeological past allows us to access innovative perspectives on the entanglements of humans, animals, and the environment (like mountains) as a socially rich ecosystem (Hendon and Harrison-Buck 2018; Hill 2011, 2013). However, we must be acutely aware of the pitfalls of postcolonial critique of cherry-picking and decontextualizing temporally and spatially specific indigenous ontologies that are diverse and dynamic (Harrison-Buck 2018; Motta and Porr 2023; Todd 2016). As archaeologists, we are well situated to engage in a more contextually embedded, historically contingent, data-driven, and interpersonally centered (not solely human centered) reconstruction of the past (Harrison-Buck and Freidel 2021). Such a reconstruction requires identifying specific material residues of how humans physically and symbolically interacted with corporeal animal forms. A life history approach facilitates retrieving narratives of interpersonal encounters with apex predators, which can elucidate how animals participated in the concretion of dominant ideologies at Teotihuacan. Within this premise, ritualized performances are particularly effective "sites of engagement" (sensu Todd 2014) wherein interpersonal relationships are publicly displayed and embodied.

Ritual: Definitions and Interpretive Paradigms

Defining ritual is a challenging task. There are as many ways to define ritual as there are contexts where ritualized activities take place. Some researchers who value historical and contextual specificity reject broad definitions, claiming that any universal definition would be too general or all-encompassing to be useful (Bell 1997; Insoll 2004). In this view, each ritual should stand in its own "thick context" (Insoll 2004: 12), defined by the society that practices it. Nevertheless, contextually specific definitions of ritual can be too narrow to be utilized anywhere else and thus meaningless for broader anthropological discourse (Taylor 1998). I do not propose a comprehensive universal definition of ritual but rather describe the particular context in which ritualized activities contributed to the production of the Moon Pyramid, one of Mesoamerica's iconic monumental forms. Only one type of ritual—those associated with state-level ritualized activities—and one set of actants—animal matter that participated in these activities—are analyzed.

I echo other archaeologists who argue that definitions and approaches to ritual (and religion) are restricted by the availability and type of data retrievable (Kyriakidis 2007a). We must accept a multiplicity of definitions while acknowledging their delineation within specific theoretical paradigms and contextual frameworks that can provide baselines for a comparative approach (Kyriakidis 2007b). Thus, instead of providing a historical overview of definitions of ritual and religion (see Bell 1992, 2005; Fogelin 2007), I briefly summarize broader theoretical approaches to define rituals to formulate an appropriate definition for the present study.

The inspiration for this research is an exceptional zooarchaeological assemblage of the numerous complete and partial skeletal remains from animals buried deep in the nucleus of the Moon Pyramid. This rich dataset extracted through meticulously refined methodologies provided a window for reconstructing specific decision nodes that shaped the preparation and execution of ritualized acts. For this reason, this study does not inquire about aspects of ancient ideologies but interrogates material residues of ritualized action. However, as these acts materialize a worldview, to decipher their patterns is to sketch a diagram of the grand plan behind the underlying processes that create, maintain, and materialize ancient cosmologies[2]. Following Astor-Aguilera (2010: 23) cosmology is a relational understanding of self to the material and nonmaterial surroundings. Therefore, while ritualized practices are the central interpretive unit, it is with the explicit recognition that these state-sponsored ritualized practices are arenas for creating and embodying (often hierarchical) relationships (Bell 1992; Rappaport 1979).

The theoretical stance frames the scale of analysis, the assumptions utilized, what data are analyzed, and the definition of the ritual itself (Fogelin 2008: 11). Structuralists are intrinsically interested in long-term symbolic meanings that are, to some degree, static (Geertz 1973; Lévi-Strauss 1955). They frequently rely on historical and ethnographic datasets and relate them to archaeological correlates to decipher ancient symbolic systems (e.g., iconographic analysis) that reflect the underlying ideological systems in operation (Busatta 2007). Here, ideology encompasses the, "the philosophical and political interrelations of a people, their

---

[2] See Fowles (2013) for critique of the term religion, especially when interpreting ancient Amerindian cultures. Thus, I chose to use cosmologies that is more in line with the relational ontological approach applied here.

societal institutions, and their cultural values" (Astor Aguilera 2010: 23-24). In contrast, practice theorists focus on individualized actions and how ritual practices reflect and enact sociopolitical transformations, such as the rise of hierarchical societies (Bell 1992; Turner 1977).

Unfortunately, this dichotomy has many pitfalls for understanding rituals. On the one hand, some structuralists don't recognize the underlying assumption of ritual stagnation under the guise of ritual stability wherein meanings are unaffected by the dynamic sociopolitical context of the time. Conversely, practice theorists may qualify rituals as "hyperactive," sometimes undermining the consideration that they operate within the "durable, adjusted dispositions" or habitus (DeMarrais 2004: 12). Habitus represents the underlying structuring mechanisms that give permanence, at the same time allowing for creative innovation and variability, making them effective forms of action to consider within ritualized contexts (Bourdieu 1977; Wacquant 1992: 18-19). The reality is that most researchers are not partisans, preferring to sample from the wares of both theoretical frameworks for insights that align with their particular research goals, circumstances, and available resources. However, as Fogelin (2007: 64) pointedly observes, this is usually a consequence of sidestepping fundamental theoretical constraints. A more explicit attempt to attain a more nuanced perspective is necessary.

One way to overcome this dichotomy is by interpreting the ritual act as a performance: a culturally constructed symbolic communication system experienced through the physical body (Rappaport 1979; Tambiah 1981; Turner 1986). Performance theorists focus on the active and communicative aspects of rituals, permitting scholars to view them as both a form of action and thus a process, while recognizing that they express meaning (Bell 1997; Inomata 2006; Inomata and Coben 2006a). A performative approach to state rituals permits a dialectic interaction between ideas and practice into an effective ideology. This study interprets rituals as performances that transform cosmologies into social actions.

Ritualized Performances

Several characteristics of ritualized performances make them a productive approach to apply to archaeological case studies:

1. They communicate meanings.
2. They include participants (actors and observers).
3. They take place in a particular setting.
4. They are embodied acts that materialize meanings and structures onto the sociopolitical landscape.

Each feature facilitates the direct connection of the theory to the methodology applied in this study.

Archaeologists are interested in how rituals *communicate meanings* and how to retrieve these meanings through material residues. While performance theorists do not simply assume that preexisting symbolic values are transmitted—they argue that new and revolutionary values can form—they also acknowledge the underlying traditions from which such ritual actions are formulated (Inomata 2006). In such contexts, "key symbols" summarize and elaborate concepts that orient the sociocultural value systems, which are most vividly displayed in ritualized acts (Ortner 1973). Key symbols are intricately tied to power dynamics, encoding messages of social difference that are created, manipulated, maintained, contested, reified, and embodied through ritualized actions (Rappaport 1979; Tambiah 1985; Turner 1986).

In addition, performance theory brings the *participants* of the spectacle—human and nonhuman actors and audience—into the forefront. Participants actively reinterpret value-laden symbols that are, at the same time, communicated to—and by—the participants (Bell 1997:73; Inomata 2006). Awe, fright, revulsion, and other emotive responses solidify messages into memories of the participants. Such collective experiences of strong sensual stimuli create an effervescence (sensu Durkheim 2001) that provides individuals with power generated from the assembled group (Fowles 2013: 190). At the same time, performance theory permits emotional variance among the actors, ranging from indifference or resistance to active participation (Bell 1997; Inomata and Coben 2006a: 15). Such a perspective allows for individual autonomy while generating a sense of community that maintains social (usually hierarchical) positionalities. The physical presence of the participants, as the ritualized body moves within the specially constructed stage, at the same time defines (imposes) and experiences (receives) the values ordering the environment (Bell 1997: 82; 2005). Because interpersonal encounters are much easier to document within the highly choreographed ritual theater, they provide an opportunity to reconstruct ancient relational ontologies.

Performance theorists are invariably concerned with the *setting*, that is, the materiality of space and associated objects, in which these practices occurred (DeMarrais et al. 2004). Particular landscape features, both natural and artificial, effectively materialize institutions because of their scale, visibility, and permanence (Earle 2001; S. Sugiyama et al. 2013). Creating ritual spaces—monuments, plazas, palaces, and other public spaces—was integral to this process (Inomata and Coben 2006b; Inomata and Houston 2000; Joyce 1992). The construction of these ordered spaces defines the physical properties and the communicative potential of the performances: the scale, the centrality, the trajectory (route), the acoustic properties, the lighting, the visibility, and the permanence —not unlike theatrical stages (Moore 1996a, 1996b; Tsukamoto and Inomata 2014).

At the same time, as a constructed space, it can be meaning-laden and often materializes dominant ideologies (Broda 1988; DeMarrais et al. 1996; Fash and Fash 1996; Fash and López Luján 2009; Sugiyama 2010b; Wheatley 1971). We can argue that the dedicatory act and the cosmologies they embodied physically co-constituted part of the material vitalities of the Moon Pyramid through their placement within the earthen mound. The setting itself was an eminent part of the ritualized act. More on this later in Chapter 2, when I discuss the ritualized production of place.

An effective strategy to anchor a community's social identities, traditions, and value systems to tangible images and actions is to have participants embody and engrain these concepts into their memories through *ritual experiences* (Inomata 2006; Joyce 2005; Valeri 1985). The public embodies rituals through emotive and somatic means, and these multifaceted sensory experiences reinforce and authenticate the underlying values (Dornan 2007). Some archaeologists analyze the inner workings of the brain, exploring cognitive archaeology approaches and neuroscientific methodologies to understand human experiences (Dornan 2007; Renfrew and Zubrow 1994; VanPool 2009). Others analyze bodily movement, directionality, and spatiality of the natural or built environment as critical features structuring ritual experiences (Moore 1996a, 1996b; Parkin 1992). Iconographic and epigraphic studies can also provide an in-depth perspective on how participants observed, came into contact with, heard, smelled, and felt the presence of ritualized bodies (Houston et al. 2006). In this case study, animal life histories permit us to construct narratives of human–animal encounters, bringing to life the physicality of facing live apex predators (as persons) during the ritualization process (see Chapter 8).

A performative approach to ritual requires attention to the embodiment process, material and spatial contexts, and physical interactions between diverse participants (human and nonhuman persons) (Inomata 2006). Importantly, these characteristics can be linked to features retrievable in the archaeological record. It allows us to analyze the materialization of the body (participants-actors) and space (physical location-stage) as the active arenas that define and are defined by ritualized actions. As an example, Fowles (2013) analyzes Pueblo "doings" in the Southwestern US as effervescent practices that facilitate the community to experience the entanglements of its constituent parts (people, things, and cosmos). An ecology of Pueblo "doings" entangles young boys sent from the village to retrieve water from distant lakes and springs at the edges of the cosmos with the directional waters that are conjoined at the village center into a single vessel, allowing the community to not only perceive the cosmos but bring the cosmos into being (Fowles 2013). As stages for constructing and communicating social boundaries, ritualized performances not only delineate and impose power, but are the generative forces that bring power structures into being.

Ritualized Matter and Sovereignty

Rituals generate and reinforce new social boundaries, such as the rise of new sociopolitical forms, across diverse historical, regional, and social contexts (Bell 1992; Kertzer 1991). State-sanctioned spectacles specifically create and integrate communities within the backdrop of negotiating asymmetrical power relations, often institutionalizing and empowering the state. In this way, institutional facts are ruled into existence and presented to the public for consumption, consolidation, and normalization through its repeated engagement (willing or enforced) in various acts of ritual prescription (Renfrew 2007). As the gatekeepers of access to participation itself, the governing officials orchestrating the rituals mete out privilege, esoteric knowledge, wealth, and a sense of belonging (Bell 1992). Inomata (2006) has shown that state-sponsored mass theatrical events held in large open plazas authenticated and solidified cohesion among Classic Maya communities. Similarly, the dedicatory rituals that would have accompanied the construction of the pyramids at Teotihuacan were one of the attractive mass-participatory forces that led to the success of Teotihuacan's highly differentiated social landscape (Sugiyama and Sugiyama 2021).

Kertzer (1991) argues that symbols are the only way organizations—such as church or state—can be "seen," becoming the medium for drawing social affinities. Rites embed symbols in emotionally charged actions, binding to the participants' identities. At the same time, these very same symbols define their world order (Kertzer 1991). A successful state ritual entangles empowered symbols with state authority, making the participants embody the newly created world order that inherently defines the symbols themselves.

Khatchadourian (2016), however, asserts identification of powerful symbols fall short of the "material turn", as things remain inert passive indices of symbolic projection. Things, in this regard, remain static *intermediaries* that "carry, transport, shift, incarnate, express, reify, objectify, reflect" meaning (Latour 2000: 18) but cannot participate in its production (Latour 2005: 37–42). New materialism highlights physical intra-actions (Barad 2007) as the processes by which matter can be co-constituted *mediators* of meaning-making and thus, as I would argue in Chapter 2, in placemaking. Once matter is afforded a "vitality" to "act as quasi agents or forces with trajectories, propensities, or tendencies of their own" (Bennett 2010: viii), we can begin to ask how nonhuman matter (in this case, animal persons) and humans engaged in deeply mutual and multifaceted entanglements that generated the conditions of sovereignty formations.

In this manner, we can recast clothed Inca serving pots not as "representations" of the Sapa Inca (king) but as the kingly body, "conceived as a container of vital ancestral substances" that engaged in the "propagation of life within the imperial domain ... created through a network of actors that included ceramic vessels, iconographic symbols, food and drink, architectural spaces and various categories of human persons" (Bray 2018: 253). Khatchadourian's (2016) analysis distinguishes between delegate, proxy, captive, and affiliate matter, providing a more direct inquisition of its role in shaping Achaemenid imperial formations. She emphasizes the inconceivably fluid temperaments of imperial matter as sources, not results, of sovereignty formations as they uphold and sometimes erode, displace, and reproduce imperial lifeways. Delegates, in particular, "share in the preservation of the very terms of imperial sovereignty through the force of both their material composition and the practical mediation they help afford" (Khatchadourian 2016: 68–69). In this regard, she argues that the multi-columned halls sourced from the northern highlands of Media and Armenia became delegates that recaptivated the Achaemenid sovereigns. These halls, through their stone, wood, and mud brick, held a firm grip on the experience of the congregation due to their performativity (such as restricted visibility and acoustic challenges).

Likewise, perhaps, we should understand that the wolves, eagles, falcons, hawks, pumas, and jaguars presented at the Aztec capital of Tenochtitlan were "dressed to kill" in ornate regalia (*atlatls*, darts, shells, and gold) as enigmatic militants on the battlefield (males) and in childbirth (females) (López Luján et al. 2022). These clothed apex predators sacrificed in Templo Mayor were not figurative expressions but were direct delegates of Aztec sovereignty. I have already mentioned relational ontologies afford particular credence to direct somatic encounters in establishing personhood, which here, through new materialism, also recognizes the physical properties to be at the center of its "thing power" (sensu Bennett 2010) to mediate political transformations. I see these two theories as not mutually exclusive. I think "thing power" contributed to the socialities of nonhuman persons. In both relational ontologies and new materialism, things (sometimes as persons) are experienced through their performative capacities.

A performative approach to rituals nicely complements the materially-focused relational ontological approach of corporeal animal forms applied in this study. This theoretical framework is directly linked to the analytical methods used to reconstruct the entanglement of these constitutive elements elements; persons persons (humans, animals, and others), places (pyramid as *altepetl*), and cosmos. The performance's form, context, and ritual process are retrievable in the archaeological record. This includes the performance's formal properties, the physical actants, and material and social settings (Inomata and Coben 2006b).

Corporeal Animal Forms as Ritualized Bodies

Throughout the human past, animals played integral roles in state-level ritualized performances; they partook in sacrificial rites, accompanied human burials, were killed in royal hunts, and became elaborate ritual paraphernalia (Goepfert 2012; López Luján & Moctezuma 2022; Russell 2012a). Animals sacrificed in dedication (complete, primary burials), as well as animal mediums deposited as offertory artifacts expressed by their body parts (secondary products), are analyzed in this zooarchaeological study. As discussed earlier, indigenous communities may regard both as corporeal animal forms with acknowledged personhood. As their material traces are analyzed, the production of the ritualized body will be the vantage point from which we survey the role and experience of corporeal animal forms in state-performative actions.

Catherine Bell defined the body moving across the symbolically structured environment in a ritually defined space and time as a "ritualized body" (1992: 93). Such bodies are invested with a 'sense' of ritual, internalizing and defining the principles of the delineated environment, becoming the site where power relations are deliberated, negotiated, and managed (Bell 1992: 197–204; Foucault 1980: 55). It is through the movement of ritualized bodies that a ritual landscape is conceived, co-produced, and transformed (Ingold 2013). From this paradigm, I analyze the materiality of apex predators at Teotihuacan by reconstructing the interpersonal relationships manifested during the ritualized performances that I argue accredited personhood to the corporeal animal forms as ritualized bodies.

In these performances, corporeal animal forms participated in two ways. Teotihuacan's "public" (defined further in Chapter 3 to include human and non-human persons) would have confronted apex predators as mediators of the Teotihuacan state in ritual spectacles as sacrificial persons par excellence. In addition, animal body parts—heads, wings, claws, pelts, feathers, isolated elements—entered the ritual stage as synecdochal objects that reference the source animal (*pars pro toto*). Cranial elements and sometimes claws represented the majority, likely manufactured into elaborate ritual paraphernalia to be offered to the monument. In continuation, I discuss how I approached each type of corporeal animal form (primary and secondary).

Animal Sacrifice

Like ritual, sacrifice is fraught with innumerable definitions (Carter 2003), where the balance between historical and social particularism, on the one hand, and flexibility to accommodate comparative interpretations, on the other hand, has yet to be successfully applied (Schwartz 2017). From studies that focus on the origins

(Carrasco 2005; Hamerton-Kelly 1987), the functions (as gift-debt exchange, sustenance, acts of communications, symbolism, and power) (Hubert and Mauss 1964; López Luján and Olivier 2010), to the moods and motivations (violence as human condition, ethics, human morality, foodways, and much more) (Keane 2018; Valeri 1985) of sacrifice, this subject is perhaps best approached as a polythetic class with "a wide repertoire of elements found in different members such that no single element defines all members and no single member contains all the defining elements" (Shipton 2014: S53).

Despite this broad range of applications, I confess that I hesitated to apply the term "sacrifice" to describe the primary burials deposited in the offerings at the Moon Pyramid. I find it particularly problematic because several principal assumptions of its constituent parts are not always applicable to studies exploring a relational ontological understanding of animal beings. For example, recognizing the personhood of the bear raised in the Ainu village of Japan during the Iyomante ceremony, Kimura (1999) criticized J. Z. Smith's (1980) interpretation of the sacrifice of the bear as a ritualization of the perfect hunt, expressing direct control over this wild beast. Instead, Kimura (1999) describes the fluid and relationally driven transformation of the personhood of the bear residing in the forest, to the *Kamuy* (mountain) spirit greeted as a guest in the Ainu village, to the return of the *Kamuy* from the bear's corporeal form back into the wilderness. In gratitude for the hospitality during the *Kamuy*'s residence, the bear's corporeal form is gifted by the *Kamuy* to the community. In essence, the direction of exchange is the opposite of that proposed (the *Kamuy* is the one carrying out the sacrifice) and debunks arguments that *only* "domesticated" animals or those under human control can be sacrificed (Ingold 1986; Smith 1987a).[3] In fact, this suggests that humans may not be the only persons who sacrifice! Ownership and domination are paramount to interpretations of sacrifice as a gift or debt payment and are associated with, and sometimes even regarded as exclusive to, hierarchical systems (Carrasco 2008; Hubert and Mauss 1964; Smith 1987a).

I want to question another central element of sacrifice: the kill. Whether the inherent violence or substitution is a component of the kill, the objective and the material manifestation of the act are assumed (admittedly by scholarship) to be

---

[3] Most of zooarchaeological evidence deals with animal sacrifice of domesticated animals (Clutton-Brock 1989; Russell 2012b; Yuan and Flad 2005). However, plenty of cases document wild animals being subjects of sacrifice (Fiskesjö 2001; Ikram 2005; López Luján and Matos Moctezuma 2022; Polaco 1991; Sugiyama et al. 2019). Wild animals captured specifically for sacrifice (Blanco Padilla, Pérez Roldán, et al. 2009; Elizalde Mendez 2017, 2022; McKusick 2001; Pohl 1991; Sugiyama, Fash, et al. 2018) represent one of the major acquisition strategies of wild species for sacrifice.

a lifeless being (human, animal, plant, or other persons). Nevertheless, we know native ontologies regard life forces as cyclical and do not necessarily abide by life/death binary. In Siberia, bears (like humans) retained potency after death, requiring careful treatment and disposition as the bear maintained awareness of its body parts, which led to proper regeneration (Losey et al. 2013). In Brown and Emery's study mentioned earlier, informants from the Maya village describe how the animal guardian "makes a new animal from each bone you return—even the smallest toe bone. That is why you have to return them all" (2008: 313). Thus, can we assume the corpses of carnivores offered into the pyramid indicate these animals were "killed"? What utility does the term *sacrifice* retain if we cannot be sure that the kill was a component of this ritual?

These hesitations are why I find definitions that emphasize the total ritualization process rather than just the instance of the kill to be more productive. I elaborate upon Henninger's (2005: 7997) attempt to align the process of ritualization with the objective of sacrifice, not just its commitment, by recalling the Latin origin of the term itself: *sacer* meaning "holy" and *facere* referring to the act "to make." The defining moment of sacrifice is the consecration of the object/subject, which I argue is achieved through establishing its personhood. Sacrifice is thus the consecration of persons (e.g., animals), "set apart," and ordained for a specific purpose evoked through the ritualization process. A native ontological approach may require us to keep the possibility open that the placement of ferocious beings into this newly constructed pyramid-*altepetl* was not to kill them but to consecrate their personhood as resident guardian animal spirits (Chapter 7).

So how can archaeologists capture this consecration process? Smith (1987a) would argue that domestication/ownership destined the animal for selective killing. By acknowledging the personhood of the animal, the ritual practitioner establishes a relationship of dominance, equivalence, or subordination to the sacrifice. To understand why these animals, as persons, were chosen for sacrifice, without assuming this connection a priori, we need to trace the nature and processes of human–animal socialities. Such an investigation necessitates a "thick description" (sensu Geertz 1973) of exemplary ritual processes and ensembles. Luckily, zooarchaeological investigations are particularly effective for defining the type and extent of human–animal relationships, with material remnants of these interpersonal relationships exposed through patterns signifying varying degrees of animal management during the consecration processes.

Faunal assemblages reflect how animal taxa or categories were evaluated (see Chapter 3). Age, sex, and other visual cues may illustrate the primary motivations behind the selection and record the origin and modifications in the sacrificial practices (Russell 2012b). Moon Pyramid faunal data are rich in contextual documentation that enable us to reconstruct the complete life histories of individual animals. In Chapter 6, I detail the biographies of four sacrificed carnivores to bring the experiences of this consecration process to life. These animals were set apart, consecrated, as persons within the social landscape of Teotihuacan (in part) through captivity and confinement.

Animal Artifacts

Animals and animal guardians are highly aware of their corporeal elements, sensing the treatment and distribution of their body parts (Hill 2011, 2013; Losey et al. 2013). In this manner, procuring, using, and depositing particular corporeal animal forms proceeded according to prescribed societal norms within their spatial and temporal constraints (Descola 2012). As durable subjects, they are material testimony and mnemonic devices for groups and individuals to recall and reexperience specific human–animal eco-contracts through revisitation and reengagement.

Furthermore, corporeal animal forms were mediators of communication and incorporation (transubstantiation) with animals and animal spirits. I have already introduced Conneller's (2004) work documenting how red deer antlers permitted the wearer to experience the corporality and perspective of a red deer at Star Carr. Such transformations determined the outcome of the hunt. In Maine and the Canadian Maritime Peninsula, possessing shark teeth enabled access to the potent supernatural abilities of the predator (Betts et al. 2012). Like these subsistence hunters, the bravest warriors in the Aztec Empire would take to the battlefield adorned in elaborate regalia derived from corporeal forms of local revered predators, investing themselves with the cunningness of the jaguar and the swiftness of the eagle (Careta 2001; López Luján and Matos Moctezuma 2022).

Corporeal animal forms also protected and animated distinguished structures, marking them as historically contingent and culturally significant places (not mere locations) on the landscape. In Jones's (1998) study of species variability among Neolithic Orkney midden and burial deposits, he argues that patterned deposition of remains from symbolic large-bodied carnivores was central to the co-production and definition of place. This process "involved the appropriation of certain powerful and special animals which were part of the lived and encultured landscape, and indicates the highly specific identities constructed between people, the landscape and animals, which in some cases involved redefining the ontological and spatial relationships associated with the bones of the dead through the medium of the topography of the landscape" (Jones 1998: 319). Corporeal animal forms are often literally embedded within places, as seen by the whale and cattle remains which fill junctures and voids between walls, passages, and roofs at Scottish sites of Skara Brae and Pierowall Quarry. At Çatalhöyük, Meskell (2008) described assemblages of animal skulls similarly installed on walls and features. By rigorously quantifying body-part and species distribution of corporeal animal forms in ritual spectacles at Teotihuacan, I explore how their material dispositions contributed to the ritualized landscape.

A Relational Ontological Narrative

In this chapter, I established the materially focused relational ontological approach to the study of zooarchaeological remains deposited in state-level ritualized performances at Teotihuacan. I would venture that not only is it feasible to apply a relational ontological approach to the past, but that the materiality of bone/teeth allows us to reconstruct fairly detailed physical experiential narratives that make the combination of pristine archaeological context and archaeometry data, interpreted in light of ethnographic perspectives, a productive avenue of research. The material properties of corporeal animal forms permit interpersonal interactions to be manifest through life history and temporal-spatial patterns in the faunal assemblage.

I also reviewed how archaeologists can recover ritual experiences and their abstract meanings through material correlates by interpreting rituals as performative acts, whereby participants engage in meaningful interpersonal actions. By generating a "thick description" (Geertz 1973) of the ritualized performances—the experiential narratives detailing the who, what, where, when, why, and how of the events within a stratified hierarchy of meaningful structures to extract inferences and implications (Chapter 8)—I unfold the meanings enveloped within the Moon Pyramid by highlighting one unlikely agent: carnivores par excellence considered active and potent persons on the landscape. I argue they were "set apart" as consecrated persons in state spectacles. They participated as delegates, empowered actants, captivated persons for sacrifice, animal products that embodied such identities, and mediators of sovereignty formations at Teotihuacan. The zooarchaeological dataset allows a reconstruction of the ritualization process of corporeal animal forms. It further provides a unique vantage into the entanglements of animal persons, human community, and sovereignty during the construction of the ceremonial landscape.

I will contextualize the sociopolitical landscape of Teotihuacan in Chapter 2. The paradigm applied in this study brings the production of the theatrical event, along with its stage, not as an epiphenomenal process but as the driving force that creates, concretizes, and transforms relationships (Inomata and Coben 2006a: 33). Such spaces are produced by—and for—the ritual spectacle, whereby they become places embedded in the asymmetrical cultural landscape. I introduce the concept of the *altepetl* (water mountain) as the entanglement of the life-sustaining resources, the persons that reside within (ancestors, deities, and animals), and the community within the greater landscape. The *altepetl* is the axis mundi that connects the upper, under, and terrestrial realms and is central to defining the ecology of the community, including the sociopolitics of power and authority. The *altepetl* was an expression of sovereignty for many Mesoamerican cities. From this, I hypothesized that the Moon Pyramid was ritually produced as the *altepetl* within Teotihuacan, mirroring the Cerro Gordo mountain.

To reconstruct animal personhood at Teotihuacan, I review each animal's social positionality in Chapter 3. In describing ethnographic, ethnohistoric, iconographic, and biological data pertinent to each prominent animal actor (felid, canid, eagle, serpent), I synthesize data on animal matter (both general distribution of corporeal animal forms and their representation) at Teotihuacan. Subsequently, the zooarchaeological remains and their isotopic values of corporeal animal forms (Chapters 4 and 5) are used to reconstruct individual life histories of the animals sacrificed/ritually produced in the ritual spectacle at Teotihuacan, illustrating diverse paths by which animals became active participants (Chapter 6).

The spatial and temporal distribution of the caches where these materials were typically found correlates with ceremonial intervals punctuating the progress of the monument's construction (Chapter 7). By revealing periodic changes in ritual fauna usage, these caches sketch a broad developmental arc of human–animal interaction that subtends the transformation of Teotihuacan's sociocultural landscape. In the city's earliest deposits, I return to my hypothesis that animal actors took center stage in ritual spectacles consecrating the Moon Pyramid as the *altepetl* of Teotihuacan. As centuries passed, animal actors yielded an increasing share of the ritual spotlight to human forms. However, their participation remained essential to harmonize and reconcile the roiling cosmopolitan ebullience of a city exploding into regional domination. Finally, I end with a thick description of the ritual spectacle of Burial 6 at the Moon Pyramid (Chapter 8) to enliven this ritual theater, albeit out of a plethora of possibilities.

CHAPTER 2

PLACEMAKING: TEOTIHUACAN'S *ALTEPETL*

IN THIS CHAPTER I INTRODUCE the natural and cultural features of Teotihuacan to understand the processes that contributed to the Moon Pyramid's place within the cosmos. Following the performative approach to rituals defined in the previous chapter, placemaking is understood within the context of its ritualized production. I argue the monument was co-produced through the conjoining of human and nonhuman persons (in dedication rituals) in a cooperative process of placemaking — or more precisely, the continuous remaking of place—as each generation impressed their ideological, economic, and political values into the dynamic landscape.

Placemaking is a continued process that requires maintaining a relationship with the animate landscape, fraught with ambitious incentives when new sociopolitical entities, like the Teotihuacan state, enter the stage. This perspective on placemaking recognizes that sovereignty at Teotihuacan was never a fixed entity but was fluid, contested, and reconfigured through a process of imperial formations (sensu Stoler 2008). Sovereignty formations, in this context, recognizes the nascent and ongoing negotiations between human and nonhuman persons that possess different temporalities and perspectives.

The mountain is a seminal place for many Mesoamerican cities, with the *altepetl* centralizing to both celestial and subterranean forces encompassing the community. The *altepetl* was a busy place hosting animals, ancestral spirits, and deities. These were the agents that controlled the vital source of water stored within. As artificial mountains, the pyramids were the means to develop a direct link to these life-sustaining beings on the landscape. As I explain later, the Postclassic usage of the term *altepetl* most vividly encapsulates the direct entanglement of these powerful entities on the landscape to human sociopolitical systems, intimately linked to sovereignty and hegemony (Hirth 2003; López Austin and López Luján 2009).

I argue dedicatory rituals cannot be interpreted as unrelated events but within the framework of the ritualized production and maintenance of the Moon Pyramid as an *altepetl* of Teotihuacan. There is thus no finality in the production of the Moon Pyramid as the *altepetl* (as a singular entity), and was a major participant in the very process of sovereignty formations.

Given my position that ceremonial landscapes are cosmograms, built to enhance sensually stimulating encounters with the cosmos, the second half of the chapter presents the chronological, spatial, and sociocultural backdrop of Teotihuacan by guiding you along the Avenue of the Dead to convey some of the phenomenological attributes of the site. I introduce the dedicatory rites that animated this trio of pyramids anchoring the axis of the ceremonial precinct. Venturing into the archaeological tunnels, we will encounter offerings as we peel back the layered structures and burrow into the passage of centuries to reconstruct the origins of this potent landscape. This narrative highlights the Teotihuacan Valley as a city-scale palimpsest: a multilayered landscape upon which each generation continuously imprints its decisions to preserve, construct, overbuild, and destroy natural and cultural features.

The Teotihuacan state fueled an endless and tremendously costly public works program that retained the populace as active agents in the process of placemaking. The successful orchestration of these labor-intensive monumental works synthesized a diverse array of individualized actions—from a laborer carrying a heavy load of fill material to a ritual practitioner burying a screeching eagle into a pit—into a force of collective commitment to empower and sustain the state. As I narrate our entry and traversal through the material nexus of this ingeniously engineered landscape, I hope to convey how the Moon Pyramid's presence distills over two millennia of active placemaking into the lived experience of Teotihuacan. This chapter sets the stage for understanding how sacred actors participated in the ritualized production of the Moon Pyramid in subsequent chapters.

Place and Ritual

Teotihuacan's imposing landscape was a materialization of their cosmogram, encoding their conceptions of time, space, history, and world order most conspicuously in monumental structures (López Austin et al. 1991; Šprajc 2000; Sugiyama 2010, 2017b). Such a powerful state ideology, graphically materialized into the ceremonial landscape, is said to be one of the main drivers behind Teotihuacan's expansion into one of the largest metropolitan centers of its time (Cowgill 2015; Sugiyama 2010). Thus, paying particular attention to how these ideologically charged monuments were co-produced through a multiplicity of human and nonhuman persons is critical for understanding what made this ceremonial center so impactful. To this end, I interpret the theatrical events marked by the dedicatory caches as part of the ritualized production of place, animating the monument within a dynamic sociopolitical landscape. To explain this process, I define place, examine the ritual production of place, and argue that dedicatory performances executed during large-scale construction programs were an integral component of placemaking.

Places are endowed with value and significance, situated within the complex sociopolitical landscape as a historically contingent process (Knapp and Ashmore 1999; McAnany 1998; Smith 1987b). As part of the encultured landscape, places convey how subjective human experiences transformed the landscape into a nested web of meanings, a canvas with layers of social, political, and cultural histories. Such loci can be considered place-thought, "the non-distinctive space where place and thought were never separated because they never could be separated" (V. Watts 2013: 21). Landscape anthropologists/archaeologists examine city planning, urbanization, and architecture as processes embedded within sacred geography that organized the sociopolitical order through the materialization of the cosmologic order (Brady and Ashmore 1999; Broda 1988; Fash and López Luján 2009; Joyce 2020; Reese-Taylor et al. 2001; Vogt 1981; Wheatley 1971). They identify vital places on the landscape that make them historically contingent, recording political (especially dynastic) histories that are meaning-laden and linked to social identities (Fash and Fash 1996; Houston 1998; McAnany 2008). They are cosmograms, materializations of worldviews in three-dimensional space, aligning monuments to specific astronomical phenomena (Aveni and Hartung 1986; Šprajc 2000), and even their dimensions can be referents of highly significant numerical cues (Morley and Renfrew 2010; Sugiyama 2010). They often replicate myths that encode social norms and underlying structures and are apt to be recounted and remembered through the theatrical reenactments at these locations (Basso 1996; Matos Moctezuma 1999).

In this manner, the Huitzilopochtli (patron deity of war) temple that stands at the core of the Aztec capital of Tenochtitlan is a materialization of the mythical mountain of Coatepec, birthplace of this god (Carrasco 1988; Townsend 1982). At this mountain, Huitzilopochtli sprung from his mother's womb, where he ferociously sacrificed his sister (goddess Coyolxauhqui) and his brothers (star gods) as his first act of life. From this mythical mountain, sacrificial victims were slain and tossed down the temple steps in the same vein that Coyolxauhqui met her fate, as materialized by her sculpture at the temple's base (Matos Moctezuma 1999). Repeated mythical reenactments recounting the apocalyptic origin continued to fuel the imperialist Aztec sacrificial ceremonies that regained order, stability, and a place within the cosmos (Carrasco 1988).

Landscapes are nested places, embodying concepts of time, identities, events, and actions at varying scales (Hirsch and O'Hanlon 1995; Knapp and Ashmore 1999). As a built environment, cultural landscapes organize space, time, meaning, and communication (Rapoport 1994; Smith 2003). Places are dynamic entities (persons) that serve as mediators, rather than just containers, for action (V. Watts 2013). In discussing Mesolithic/Neolithic monuments, Tilley (1994) traces the transformation to an encultured landscape, where megaliths become recentered as places—from the monument being set in the landscape to the landscape being the setting of the monuments.

Places become endowed with meaning through creation, maintenance, transformation, and destruction. Each of these processes is marked by individual actions, by the events and activities that serve to "make place" (production) (Brück and Goodman 1999), "take place" (occurrence/maintenance) (Smith 1987b), and "change place" (transformation) (Carrasco 1991).

The link between places and ritualized performances is apparent, as the spectacles assembled powerful persons into multisensorial joint experiences (Joyce 2020). At the same time, the ritual performances transform and renew the cognitive space within the participants' memories as places are created, maintained, transformed, and destroyed (Mills and Walker 2008). The physicality of place—its size, location, orientation, acoustics, visibility, and so on—contributes to the experiences that reflect the intentions and ideas of the creators (Inomata 2006; Inomata and Coben 2006b; Moore 1996b) and define the social relations of the participants (Bradley 1998). Therefore, material characteristics of the place, tangible in the archaeological record, can capture the meanings and intentions of the dominant ideology. One type of place, pyramids, and one type of ritualized performance, dedicatory rituals, exemplify this well. I will thus explore both in tandem to elaborate the process of ritualized production and maintenance of pyramids as sacred places at Teotihuacan.

Ritualized Production and Monumentality

The pyramids that dominate the horizon of Teotihuacan's majestic landscape are central icons standing as key symbols of state power. They are defined by the quality of monumentality: a vivid, active, and imposing presence and perseverance over the *long durée*. Nonetheless, they are transformative and reinterpreted within the sociopolitical landscape of each generation (S. Sugiyama et al. 2013). The creation of this ultimate performative stage was the mechanisms by which sovereignty formations was materialized and experienced (DeMarrais et al. 1996).

Monuments are particularly effective in expressing unambiguous messages of authority/power and establishing a cosmological order and a social identity (DeMarrais et al. 1996; Fash and Fash 1996; Moore 1996b; S. Sugiyama et al. 2013). These main bearings of the axis mundi, emplacements of the intersectional medium between cosmic layers, embodied and channeled the veneration of powerful ancestors (Freidel and Schele 1989; López Austin and López Luján 2009; McAnany 1998; Wheatley 1971). Even through the process of ruination, they maintain a "mound power" that attends to the "deep histories and slow processes as they animate social positionality and hope" (Bloch 2020: 520). In this manner mounds in the US South enroll descendants of Muskogee ancestry for companionship, acknowledgment, and care by "migrating" through deliberate mining for dirt fill and by "healing" their wounds of settler colonialism through breathing new life into ancestral relationalities (Bloch 2020). The ceremonial center of Teotihuacan, energized by its monuments, would have likewise staged ritualized performances to co-produce, maintain, and transform the vitalities of these nested places.

So how are monuments produced? The technologies and methodologies involved in the creation of these agentive matters are themselves often loaded with ideological meaning (Costin 2016; Inomata 2001; McAnany and Wells 2008), and reconstructing the way human and nonhuman persons co-produce and interact with these monuments is an effective first step. Here, production encompasses not only the physical properties of the building project, such as the procurement of resources and the organization of labor (Murakami 2019), but also its *ritualized production*. Ritualized production includes performative acts (e.g., like magic, chants, prayers, dances, feasts, and sacrifices) seemingly not related to the technological requirements, yet are considered essential for its production (Hruby 2007: 70; Monaghan 1998).

In this framework, African metal smelting technology in Malawi was ritually produced. Smelting technology is complex, necessitating a series of "magical" acts (like chants and offerings) not directly linked to the physical properties of the metal or smelting procedures that were essential to the success of a smelting episode (van der Merwe and Avery 1987). The reciprocal engagement of the smelting furnace and smelter in the co-production was a generative and sexual act of production; proper smelting had much wider social consequences (Schmidt 2009). Likewise, frustrated Spanish chroniclers documented the numerous Nahua incantations and rituals involved in every act, from cutting wood, making lime, and sowing fields to hunting animals (Ruiz de Alarcón 1984). Dialogues with the wood, the axe, the fuel, the field, the snares, the deer, among other actors, were requisites to each seemingly mundane task.

Analysis of the ritualized production of monuments from a relational ontological framework requires us to acknowledge that ancient Mesoamericans may have interacted with temples, palaces, monuments, and architectural features as animate beings with potential personhood. As Harrison-Buck explains, production is not "a one-way process of engagement, it is the mutual work or co-production between relational beings that defines their personhood, and through their generative act of production an animacy or life force is spawned" (2018: 267).

According to Vogt (1998), the construction of a new thatched-roof, wattle-and-daub house at Zinacantán required the performance of two rites, the "binding of the head and roof" (*hol chuk*) and "holy candle." A complex set of actions was required to inaugurate this structure and safe to cohabit: ritual meals, animal sacrifice, dedication rituals, and other performative acts (prayers, music, and processions). Epigraphic evidence from the Maya region also documents the animation of structures, with most texts serving a dedicatory function directly and visibly engraving ritualized events onto the structures (Stuart 1998: 19). For example, the panel of Structure 23 from Yaxchilán records dedicatory ceremonies (known as *och-k'ak'*) brought Lady Xook's structure into being (McAnany 2008; Plank 2004: 51).

Monaghan (1998: 50) categorizes dedication ceremonies as part of this production process, arguing that we must conceptualize these rites and practices as partaking in creating and maintaining the conditions of their existence without isolating these as a phenomenologically distinct activity. I agree with Monaghan's (1998) framing of dedication as production, but add that we should conceptualize them within the process of ritualized production of place, of the significance of the built environment that must be activated and animated through cooperation with various persons.

Dedication rituals were required to animate a structure, making it safe to inhabit or use, and termination rituals were employed to deanimate and dispose (Joyce 1992; Monaghan 1998; Vogt 1998). Archaeological evidence affirms dedicatory rites were conducted at varying stages of construction for diverse architectural features, including domestic structures, monuments, plazas, stelae, and benches throughout Mesoamerica (Freidel and Schele 1989; Sugiyama et al. 2019; Vogt 1998). Offering caches at the Aztec capital of Templo Mayor ensouled and fed major ceremonial structures through blood, animal, and human sacrifice (López Luján 2005). These acts helped maintain an amiable relationship with powerful animate structures and beings that inhabit these places.

On the contrary, termination rituals ceremoniously "de-hearted" or deanimated structures (Joyce 1992; Stross 1998: n5). Evidence showing looters aggressively targeted the Feathered Serpent Pyramid (FSP) during abandonment (Sugiyama 1998b) or communities leaving material objects ritually "killed" and broken (Joyce 1992) are patterns of activity diagnostic of termination: archaeological correlates that reflect the processes of place deconstruction.

The association of ritualized production with strategies of power and control is apparent. Levels of esoteric knowledge are often restricted. Codified symbols are decoded to varying degrees by the participants (Inomata 2001; McAnany 2008; A. Smith 2003). Mapping degrees of access to this knowledge helps disentangle the underlying social structures and shifts in the sociopolitical landscape over time. Participants include individuals who are contributing to the physical production (architects, engineers, laborers, state personnel, etc.), those involved in the ritualized production who may or may not be the same as the former (sacrificed individuals, performers such as musicians, observers), and the community that maintains its place-ness through physical bodily interactions during and post construction. In the Moon Pyramid case, I argue that corporeal animal forms collaborated in significant ways in the co-production of the monument as the city's *altepetl*.

The Mountain: The Concept of *Altepetl*

Communities throughout Mesoamerica intentionally engineered the built environment, particularly at the ceremonial core, to entangle the natural landscape with the encultured landscape. Rulers position specific architectural elements—palace structures, monuments, altars, and temples—in relation to vital natural features such as caves, mountains, and water sources. For example, at the Maya site of Dos Pilas, three of the largest public architectural complexes were strategically sited near caves, linking their authority to sources of water stored within (Brady and Ashmore 1999). In particular, pyramids were conceptualized as artificial mountains (Bernal-Garcia 1993; Townsend 1982; Vogt 1981, 1983: 113–114), with ample ethnohistorical documents reporting indigenous communities understood pyramids as "mountains made by hand" (Seler 1986: 35).

For Mesoamerican communities, a mountain is a sacred entity linking the earth to the sky and a gateway into the underworld (Brady and Ashmore 1999; López Austin and López Luján 2009; Townsend 1982; Vogt and Stuart 2005). It is an axis mundi, a portal to celestial forces and primordial waters of the underworld housing the mountain gods who controlled lightning, thunder, clouds, and rainfall (Carrasco 2000:135; Vogt and Stuart 2005). The Post-Classic Nahuatl term *altepetl*, meaning watery hill, hill of sustenance, or water mountain (Sahagún 1956, Vol. III: 345), was based on an understanding of mountains as a life-sustaining source. The *altepetl* stores vital life sources, including water, which is why springs and rivers are found at the foot of mountains (Bernal-Garcia 1993; Sahagún 1956 Vol. III: 344–345; Tobriner 1972). Patron deities responsible for creating and protecting the community reside in the *altepetl* (López Austin and López Luján 2009).

FIGURE 2.1
Tlalocan mural painting from Tepantitla compound. Photograph: N. Sugiyama.

Aztec iconographic conventions often represented a mountain as a cavern or bowl full of water, suggesting a literal translation of the natural phenomenon of the origin of water sources (rain clouds, rivers, and springs) residing in its core (Broda 1989). A mural painting at the Tepantitla apartment complex at Teotihuacan depicting a bell-shaped hill with water inside or gushing out of it from a cave opening suggests a strong link among water, mountain, and cave (Kowalski 1999; Pasztory 1997; Tobriner 1972) (Figure 2.1). As a life-giving source, mountains were "alive," endowed with spirit through the actions of divine kings and ritualized performances (Freidel and Schele 1989; Helmke and Nielsen 2014; Stuart 1997; Vogt 1981).

Every community holds a close connection to mountains as they are the axis from which a sacred geography is created, linked to mythical/historical models of the cosmos, often consecrating dynastic histories and binding communities both physically and politically to the ritualized landscape (Freidel and Schele 1989; McAnany 1998; Townsend 1982). This explains why pyramid-mountains were such ubiquitous anchors of the ceremonial landscapes throughout Mesoamerica from the Early Formative period until the Spanish conquest (Broda 1989; Joyce 2020; López Austin and López Luján 2009; Ortíz and Rodríguez 2006; Townsend 1982). Taking an ontological and New Materialist approach, Monte Alban's "vibrant urbanity" can be understood as the assembling of the natural mountain with humans, rain, earth, maize, deities, masks, buildings, and bloodletters, among additional nonhuman entities into a mountain of sustenance, the *altepetl* that mediated "social differences and cosmic planes . . . over space and through time" (Joyce 2020: 88).

The mountain-pyramid analogy is strikingly appropriate as Mesoamerican indigenous communities describe mountains as stratified like the sky encompassing the heavens with thirteen layers ascending toward the celestial realm (Vogt and Stuart 2005). The main stairway leading up to the pyramid's pinnacle would have replicated the ascent into the heavens, where only designated actors would have had access to this restricted vertical space.

Interestingly, the *altepetl* not only stored water but also was the natural habitat of animals, ancestors, and deities (Gossen 1975; Hill 1992; Vogt and Stuart 2005). The guardian spirit corralled animal companions into the mountain at night, keeping them safe from harm (Vogt 1981). As the safeguard of the animal companions of the settlement, the *altepetl* protected and controlled the community. Colonial sources describing the Fiesta del Volcán that reenacts the Spanish takeover provide a glimpse into this concept. During the festival, a large papier-mâché volcano replica was built on the main plaza to host live deer, peccaries (wild pigs), tapirs, coatis, and other creatures through cave-like portals on its sides (Hill 1992: 1–6). Here, the replica volcano-mountain is animated by assembling live animals, with roles intimately linked to the community, in its interior.

The *altepetl* also reinforced social hierarchies. In Chapter 3, I describe indigenous communities' classification of animals into upper and lower levels, and the jaguar was often the most prominent "master" of the animals (Gossen 1975). They regarded the community within the mountain to be as hierarchical as their community outside of it. They linked the social landscape to the natural landscape, thereby "naturalizing" the "social speciation" of the community (McAnany 2008).

The *altepetl* was both synonymous with 'community' and 'kingship', directly tied to ultimate control of vital sources of power precisely because it referenced this conceptual link between cave-springs, mountains, and human settlements (Kowalski 1999; Seler 1986: 35). Rulers drew on the concept of mountain-*altepetl* for their political backing, as their intimate connection to these powerful entities on the landscape allowed them to access the vital sources and ancestral spirits stored within (Stuart 1997). As a social integrating unit, it encompassed "the ruler, his supporting population, and the geographic territory that supported them" (Hirth 2003: 69). The *altepetl* was a material expression of sovereignty, and I propose that Teotihuacan state already substantiated such a definition (see also Joyce 2020).

At Teotihuacan the primary north-south avenue, the Avenue of the Dead, is aligned with the center of the Cerro Gordo Mountain and the Moon Pyramid, configuring these two features into the axis from which the city's sacred geography originated. Cerro Gordo (650 m high), a highly conspicuous landform visible from nearly every corner of the Teotihuacan Basin, was probably regarded by the

Teotihuacanos as their source of sustenance, the *altepetl* (Kowalski 1999; Tobriner 1972) (Plate 1a). Several natural features of the Cerro Gordo make it a prominent candidate. The main advantage is the profusion of springs and streams that would have emerged from the mountain itself and the presence of caves at its base (Gamio 1922: 13). Like many extinct volcanoes the peak of Cerro Gordo is dimpled by a remnant caldera, forming a cleft known as a "quebrada," where some report that waters could be heard gushing in the mountain's interior (Tobriner 1972). Altars, shrines, and *marcadores* (pecked cross markers) (Aveni et al. 1978) scattered throughout the Cerro Gordo further confirm the importance of this mountain as a central feature in the ceremonial landscape.

The Moon Pyramid anchors the central axis of the ceremonial core, where its crisp prismatic slopes both occlude and restate the massive cascading shoulders of the grand *altepetl* beyond, whose form it seems to replicate in counterpart. Reconstructing the ritualized production of the Moon Pyramid—the growth of the monument itself as well as the dedicatory rituals that were part of its ritualized production—will be essential to distinguish whether the monument became the *altepetl* of Teotihuacan.

Setting the Stage

The Natural Environment

Ideational landscapes encompass not only cultural features such as the robust pyramids, axial avenues, neatly organized apartment complexes, and heavily terraced hillsides but also are necessarily an expression of the community's connection to the natural ecosystem: the imposing mountains, flowing springs, fragrant flora, and the dynamic fauna that cohabitate the area. As mentioned earlier, many indigenous communities respect the proprietary agency and even personhood of natural and cultural features, and recognize that their place within the living landscape is contingent upon continuous bilateral negotiation with it.

The Teotihuacan Valley is located within the Basin of Mexico, a temperate semiarid environment in the highland plateau at an elevation of 2,300 meters. It is one of many closed basins within the Volcanic Cordillera, a series of volcanoes that transverse between the Bajío region to the north and the Rio Balsas basin to the south. Volcanic mountains surround the Teotihuacan Valley, and major monuments were designed to model them. The Sierra Patlachique and the Sierra de Malpais (max elevation 2,800 m) are aligned along the south, and three extinct volcanoes—Cerro Chiconautla (2,550 m), Cerro Malinalco (2,580 m), and Cerro

Gordo (3,050 m)—loom to the north (Sanders 2000: 9). These mountainous ridges, with their seismic activities, created a heterogenous landscape. Some areas could be quarried for sharp volcanic glass in state-controlled obsidian mines. Other regions hardened into spongy volcanic tuff quarried as construction fill to manufacture the cityscape.

The duration and balance between the wet and dry seasons dictated annual crop yield to sustain and fuel the city. Successful transition from the cold and dry winters to the warm and wet summers, the latter responsible for more than 80% of the annual precipitation (Sanders et al. 1979: 82), was essential to rainfall agriculturalists throughout Mesoamerica. Average rainfall varies dramatically within the Basin of Mexico (450 mm to >1500 mm). The Teotihuacan Valley is one of the drier areas with annual precipitation averaging only ca. 500 mm (Sanders et al. 1979: 82; Starbuck 1975: 17), just within the lower limit for rainfall-dependent cultivation of maize (Evans 2016: 57). Around eighty permanent springs and floodwater irrigation systems helped feed the ever-growing populace in an area where annual rainfall alone would barely suffice and weather patterns could be extremely unpredictable (Evans 2016; Sanders 1965: 23–24).

Mexican fauna and flora are considered megadiverse due to extreme elevational and longitudinal variation that connects two major biogeographical zones: the Nearctic real encompassing northern Mexico, where Teotihuacan is located, and the Neotropical zone just south of the Mexican high plateau (Ramamoorthy et al. 1993). The Teotihuacanos thus had expedient access to approximately 540 vertebrate species in the Basin of Mexico, distributed along a variegated ecological gradient encompassing tundra, desert, and lake systems (McClung de Tapia and Sugiyama 2012; Valadez Azúa 1992: 101). In addition, completely distinct Neotropical flora and fauna would have been located only a stone's throw away. Gamio's (1922: 24–49) comprehensive taxonomic list captured this local floral and faunal diversity in the Teotihuacan Valley during the early twentieth century prior to the massive modern urbanization of Mexico City encroaching from 45 km away.

Ancient urban foodways reflected the biodiversity of resources available in this landscape. Teotihuacan residents practiced a broad-spectrum diet composed of agricultural products and domesticated animals supported by various locally available wild plants and animals (Starbuck 1975, 1987; Sugiyama and Somerville 2017; Valadez Azúa 1992). A compilation of published zooarchaeological reports tallied eighty-eight species and ninety-eight genera of fauna (Sugiyama et al. 2017). City residents enjoyed a variety of meat protein, including white-tailed deer (*Odocoileus virginianus*) and rabbit/hare (Leporid), alongside Mesoamerica's two domesticates: the dog (*Canis familiaris*) and the turkey (*Meleagris gallopavo*). Various species of birds, particularly waterfowl such as ducks, also contributed to their diet.

While it is true that Mesoamerica lacked large domesticated livestock, more studies have detected various levels of human–animal interaction along the wild–domestic continuum. Diverse animal management practices, including household-level breeding and taming, likely supplemented wild resources (McClung de Tapia and Sugiyama 2012; Sharpe et al. 2018; Sugiyama et al. 2018; Sugiyama, Martínez-Polanco et al. 2020; Valadez Azúa 2003). At Teotihuacan, for example, zooarchaeological and isotopic data revealed rabbits and hares were kept, possibly bred in captivity, providing a vital and reliable protein source. They make up roughly a quarter of the city's dietary protein, and their isotope values illustrate that up to 62% of the diet was composed of C_4 plants, likely from maize consumption (Somerville et al. 2016; Sugiyama et al. 2017). While we have not conducted isotopic work on waterfowl remains, colonial sources mention diverse tamed waterfowl in domestic spaces (Parsons 2006; Valadez Azúa 2003), and I suspect similar practices existed at Teotihuacan. Nonetheless, Teotihuacan foodways continued to incorporate a diversity of wild fauna from both local and foreign sources (Sugiyama and Somerville 2017).

The introduction of fine-screening excavation techniques amplified our perspective of imported foodstuff, including marine fish, consumed and processed at the neighborhood center of Teopancazco (Rodríguez Galicia 2010; Rodríguez Galicia and Valadez Azúa 2013). Up to twenty-four genera/species of nonlocal vertebrates have been identified in varying frequencies at Teotihuacan (Sugiyama et al. 2017). Imported foodstuffs potentially acquired from the marketplace augmented locally sourced fauna. We must also not dismiss the nontrivial role that invertebrates (insects and their larvae) as well as avian eggs (quail and turkey), difficult to retrieve in the archaeological record, likely played in urban food systems (Widmer and Storey 2017).

Though the Teotihuacan Valley is a semiarid highland biome, access to five extensive lake systems immediately southwest offered a bounty of aquatic-related foodstuffs and resources. Not only would these lakes have hosted thousands of wintering waterfowl, Spanish Colonial documents confirm the availability of fresh water and saline resources such as fish, waterfowl, migratory birds, crustaceans and mollusks, turtles, and even various aquatic insects and their larvae were exploited (McClung de Tapia and Sugiyama 2012; Parsons 2006). Zooarchaeological data from Teotihuacan support reliance on such freshwater resources (Sugiyama et al. 2017).

City and Sovereignty

Teotihuacan research has supplied data contributing to diverse models of ancient urbanism, state formation, governance, and cultural ecology (Carballo 2016; Cowgill 2004; Manzanilla 1997; Millon 1981; Parsons 2015; Sanders 1965). The city began to attract a large population around the first century BCE. Over the next five centuries, the gross scale of the city and its population increased to approximately 20 km^2 in size and 100,000 people respectively, becoming one of the largest urban centers in Mesoamerica. Teotihuacan is unique among contemporaneous Mesoamerican cities in its ability to implement a city-wide civic engineering project that organized city life around neatly structured apartment compounds oriented to an alignment of 15°30′ east of true north (Cowgill 2008, 2015; Millon 1981).

These residences were multiethnic, specialized, and stratified. They were as dynamic as the sociopolitical landscape at the time, expanding and contracting with the city itself. Household-level ritualized activities operated through inclusive and divisive mechanisms functioning to integrate households into larger social units, while also providing a means to define their boundaries (Carballo 2016; Clayton 2009). A constant stream of ethnically and socioeconomically diverse immigrants sustained this bustling city (Clayton 2005; Spence and Gamboa Cabezas 1999; Storey 1992; White, Storey et al. 2004). Ethnic enclaves dispersed throughout the metropolis suggest that many merchants, artisans, and laborers likely immigrated to pursue economic opportunities (Manzanilla 2017; Storey 2006). Teotihuacan's influence extended beyond the Basin of Mexico. Teotihuacan-style portable goods and architectural styles were distributed at sites as far southeast as Guatemala and Honduras, and northwest into modern Mexican states of Michoacán, Jalisco, and Zacatecas (Bove and Madrano Busto 2003; Gómez Chávez 2002; Hirth et al. 2020; Stuart 2000). Discoveries of Maya dignitaries visiting and perhaps even temporarily residing within Teotihuacan's ceremonial core likewise add to the growing evidence that Teotihuacan maintained active political alliances with regional powers (Gazzola and Gómez 2020; Sugiyama et al. 2016, 2022; Sugiyama, Fash, et al. 2020). While models defining the nature of this interaction range in basis from commerccial, religious and political, to outright military conquest (Braswell 2003; García-Des Lauriers and Murakami 2022; Hirth et al. 2020; Houston et al. 2021; Marcus 2020; Stuart 2000), ample archaeological data attest that Teotihuacan's governing groups oversaw foreign and local social, political, religious, and economic transactions.

Like many comparative states and empires, sovereignty at Teotihuacan was a contingent process (Stoler 2008). The nature of Teotihuacan governance remains an unresolved issue, with suggestions ranging from the gamut of autocratic rulership (Headrick 2007; Sugiyama 2005; Sugiyama and Sugiyama 2021), corporate sectors (Manzanilla 2001), to dual leadership (two rulers) models (Sanders 2008; Sanders and Evans 2006), while others talk of possible diachronic changes that muddle the evidence (Carballo 2020; Cowgill 2015). The city is enigmatic precisely because it provides some of the most apparent evidence of top-down centralized planning and coordination (Sugiyama and Sugiyama 2021). However, collective action was organized and practiced at different scales, ranging from domestic apartment compounds and neighborhood centers to major civic, administrative, and religious centers (Carballo 2020). However, I am not convinced these modalities are strictly mutually exclusive, as urbanism operates as a multiscalar process of social structure organization. In any case, apex predators may provide another line of evidence.

Apex predators played a propagandistic role as the main protagonists of ritualistic and military violence, and this is precisely why these taxa were associated with Teotihuacan governance. One often cited artifact in this debate is a Teotihuacan-style thin-orange bowl from Las Colinas, Calpulalpan, Tlaxcala (Linné 1942: 170–174) (Figure 2.2) that depicts four humans marching in ritual procession around a base depicting the Teotihuacan Tlaloc (Storm God). Their identities remain unclear, though each is identified with a distinct nonhuman person: a Tasseled Headdress, a canid, a Feathered Serpent, and a raptor. Whether the four marching figures represent military clans (Angulo 2006; Millon 1973), governing sectors of the city (Manzanilla 2001), or a mix of social categories of heterarchical or hierarchical distinction is still debated.

In this processional scene, bean-like elements demarcate a tasseled headdress, distinguishing the ensuing personage crowned by the same headdress who bears bold rings of the Storm God on his eyes. The tasseled headdress has been interpreted as an insignia of authority in office (Millon 1988a) or a reference to Teotihuacan as a place (Robb 2017). I suspect there was no separation between place and governing individual/body, not unlike Ramírez's (2005) explanation of how the Pachu Inka (ruler) was referred to as Cuzco, the capital, and his physical procession as

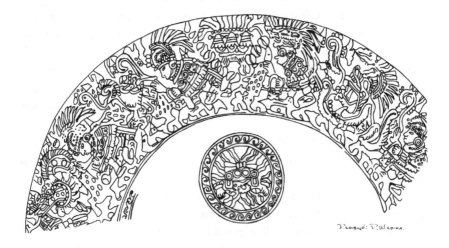

FIGURE 2.2
Drawing of Teotihuacan-style thin-orange bowl excavated from Las Colinas, Calpulalpan, Tlaxcala (Linné 1942: 170–174). Redrawn by R. Medina (2023).

el "Cuzco" across his imperial domain effectively produced territoriality and sovereignty of the Inka empire. By comparison, the three ensuing members of the Calpulalpan bowl wear a round headdress (resembling the Classic Maya *ko'how* war helmet) (Robb 2017). It seems that a leading personage of the entourage is distinguished by title (Tasseled Headdress) and markers of divine authority (Storm God) distinct from the other three humans indexed by an animal companion that may also personify a form of authority, be it religious, administrative, and/or military in nature. While I discuss the implications of this iconography in further detail in lieu of the Moon Pyramid faunal data from Burial 5 in Chapter 7, here it is important to emphasize that each apex predator indexes the organizational form of Teotihuacan governance and the social identities of the human actants. Therefore, reconstructing why specific taxa were elected to participate and the specific human-animal eco-contracts formulated with these corporeal animal forms in state ritual performances provide insight into how sovereignty was experienced at Teotihuacan.

Three distinct arcs in Teotihuacan's trajectory proceeding the Pre-Monumental period (prior to 150 CE) are vital to understanding its ritualized landscape: the Ceremonial Monuments period (150–250 CE), the subsequent Urban Renewal period that continued until 350 CE, and the Teotihuacan Expansion period that extended until the collapse of Teotihuacan circa 550 CE (Figure 2.3). The ceremonial landscape of Teotihuacan reflects centuries of occupation and use, abandonment, and rediscovery (Sugiyama et al. 2021). The reconstructed mounds, temples, and apartment compounds open to public visitation today reflect a small fraction of the cityscape extant at the close of major construction in the city's ceremonial core

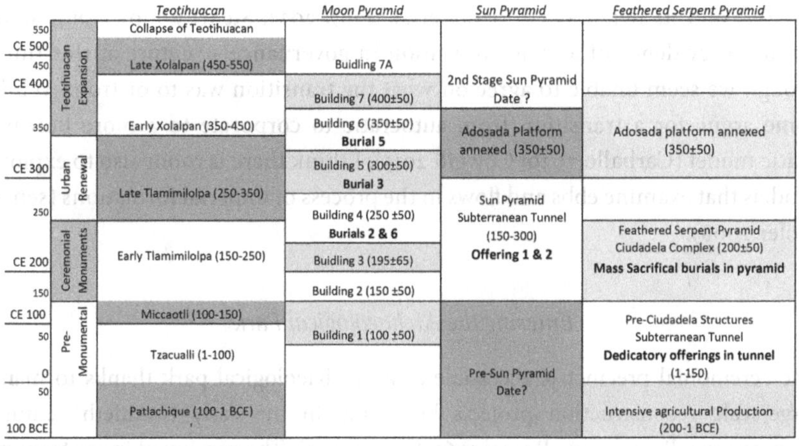

FIGURE 2.3
Chronology of Teotihuacan correlated with the building phases and offerings.

circa 350 CE that reflects the start of the Teotihuacan Expansion period (Cowgill 2015; Nichols 2015). The timing of the installation of these public structures is still debated. Some argue, based on the distribution of ceramics throughout the Teotihuacan Valley, that its namesake settlement grew dramatically during the Patlachique (100–1 BCE) phase, and by the Tzacualli phase (ca. 1–100 CE), the city had developed into a metropolitan state (Millon 1992). However, recent radiocarbon data from the three major monuments (the Moon Pyramid, Sun Pyramid, and FSP) suggest they reached a monumental scale around the same time (Sugiyama and Sugiyama 2021). The timeline of their construction, phrased and punctuated by strings of dedicatory spectacles, constitutes the streak of monumental growth from 150 to 250 CE that defines the Ceremonial Monuments period.

The Urban Renewal period is defined by a city-wide implementation of multihousehold apartment compounds during the subsequent century as Teotihuacan transformed from a tangle of scattered settlements into a gridded, orthogonal metropolis (Murakami 2019; Nichols 2015). I characterize the Teotihuacan Expansion period as beginning with the transition between Talmimilolpa to Xolalpan ceramic phases circa 350 CE and extending until the collapse of Teotihuacan. The city multiplied as the influence of Teotihuacan approached its maximum extent, which some would attribute to evidence of imperial formations (Montiel 2010; Smith and Montiel 2001). During this period, there was a return to rebuilding projects centered in the ceremonial center, most notably the concealment of the FSP's principal façade (Cabrera Castro 1998; Sugiyama 1998). It is also characterized by a sharp turn in the nature of Teotihuacan presence abroad, especially in the Maya region, where "arrival" scenes of Teotihuacan militants are epigraphically recorded at the Maya center of Tikal and its neighbors (Freidel et al. 2007, 2023; Stuart 2000). Some have discussed evidence of a major transition in governance structure at this time, though we seem unable to agree on what the transition was to or from. While some argue for a transition from autocratic to corporate to a more bureaucratic model (Carballo 2020; Cowgill 2015), I think there is room also to explore models that examine ebbs and flows in the process of imperial formations (sensu Stoler 2008).

Entering the Archaeological Park

The ceremonial precinct is accessible as an archaeological park thanks to many large-scale reconstruction projects beginning in the early twentieth century (Acosta 1964; Batres 1906; Bernal 1963; Gamio 1922). The continued importance of this UNESCO World Heritage site as a pilgrimage center and an icon of Mexican national identity is apparent every year when millions flock to the site on the spring equinox. On this day, it is easiest to imagine this site similarly thronged during its apogee. Observing the swarming crowds processing along the Avenue of the Dead, taking selfies at every turn in this highly Instagram-able landscape, I am astounded by how seamlessly the site continues to fulfill its original purpose: to impress large and vastly diverse crowds by directly confronting the timeless. With legs quivering from a smartphone-tracked 25,000 steps and 200 floors and arms heavy with souvenir-stuffed bags, visitors of every stripe depart this place enriched and awestruck by its scale and immutability. This domineering landscape has ingrained itself in the social memory of yet another generation of pilgrims. School children, young teens, families, global tourists, and even New Age religious groups can relate to this shared experience.

Visitors typically enter the site through Puerta 1, the principal gate at the park's southern sector where a highway connects Teotihuacan to Mexico City just 45 km to the southwest. Upon parking the car, visitors are cajoled by local independent artisans specializing in handcrafted Teotihuacan-style figurines, masks, magnets, and the like. It is fitting that this parking lot occupies the same graded quadrangle that formed the Great Compound (Plate 1b, #3), which served as the heart of the ancient market square. Then, as now, this area would have been the primary gateway greeting visitors, locals, merchants, and foreign dignitaries into Teotihuacan's ceremonial center. The market would have been a significant impetus for the economic growth of the city (Carballo 2013; Hirth 2020). Numerous craft workshops dedicated to obsidian, ceramic, shell, stonework, and other commodities operated at the household, neighborhood, and state levels (Cabrera Cortés 2011; Carballo 2007; Hirth 2020).

One of the best vistas of the site is at this southern tip of the archaeological park just outside the Great Compound along the Avenue of the Dead. From this vista, the gaze is directed via the precise arrangement of a series of temples and platforms along the grand corridor, homing in on the central monuments just to the north. The magnificent scale of state coordination can be felt at this vantage point, where every structure visible in the ceremonial center (150–250 ha large) is almost too perfectly aligned to the standard Teotihuacan orientation. The slightly northward inclination of the valley bottom emphasizes the looming presence of the Moon Pyramid and the Sun Pyramid. The refined silhouette of the Cerro Gordo Mountain seems to hover somewhere beyond and above the Moon Pyramid. The boundary between the artificial mountain in the foreground blends with its ghostly natural archetype in the background. At only a few paces into this sublime landscape, one's knees are already buckling before its vertiginous optics.

The Feathered Serpent Pyramid

To enter the Ciudadela complex directly opposite the Great Compound, one must cross the Avenue of the Dead and surmount the 7 m staircase that mantles the defensive wall enclosing the FSP. At over 16 ha, the Ciudadela encompasses a monumental expanse approximately twice that of St. Peter's Square in the Vatican. With an open floorplan interpreted as a ceremonial staging ground, Gazzola (2017) and Gómez (2017) have proposed ritual flooding of the complex recreated the primordial sea from which the sacred mountain, represented by the FSP, emerges.

The FSP, also known as the Quetzalcoatl Temple, occupies the eastern sector of the plaza. Flanked on its northern and southern sides by a pair of accessory compounds, a 12 m stairway beckons ascent to the platform atop its western face. Atop the platform, one can observe the arresting panorama as a fantastic sculptural menagerie yawns into view opposite the V-shaped channel, cleaving the corpus of the pyramid. A riot of decadently sculpted Feathered Serpents seems to leap from a watery backdrop studded with engraved mollusks and conch shells cascading down the terraced pyramid (Figure 2.4). What may not be apparent to our visitors is that these remarkable icons of the Teotihuacan state were displayed for only

FIGURE 2.4
The Feathered Serpent Pyramid's principal façade. Photograph by N. Sugiyama.

about 150 years. Indeed, the function of this platform, known as an *adosada*, was to extinguish it.

Manuel Gamio (1922) discovered this juxtaposition during his pioneering tunnel operations along the juncture between the main body of the pyramid and its *adosada* extension, exposing these extraordinary undulating sculptures for the first time in roughly 1,500 years. He observed these fantastical beasts in various conditions; some in situ, many burnt, and others dismantled and intentionally destroyed. Such evidence of iconoclastic demolition prior to the complete concealment of these powerful emblems of the state suggests a breakdown of Feathered Serpent symbolism in the southern sector of the city (Cabrera Castro 1998; Sugiyama 1998a,1998b). These contextual clues are compounded by evidence of looting targeting several dedicatory complexes housed in and around the pyramid; both allude to a religious and sociopolitical transformation that swept through the prevailing hierarchy at the start of the Teotihuacan Expansion period circa 350 CE (Sugiyama 1998a).

Though the *adosada* was the last architectural enlargement made to the FSP, it concealed the very elements that make this otherwise modest pyramid one of Mesoamerica's most emblematic structures. At 20 m high and a base of 66 × 66 m, the main body of the pyramid is the smallest of the monumental triad. However, the Ciudadela's construction was tremendously costly due to these stone sculptures and the large amount of earth moved to build its perimeter wall (Murakami 2019).

These sculptures remain a legendary archetype of the Feathered Serpent iconography in Mesoamerica (Sugiyama 2000). Each leering chimeric bust, faint splashes of pigment still winking from their porous surfaces, represents the apex of Teotihuacan artisanal masonry prowess. These once-vibrant beings are the material remains of a grand vision of state authority. According to López Austin and colleagues (1991), the sinuous back of each Feathered Serpent bears the Primordial Crocodile headdress (known as *cipactli* during Aztec times), proclaiming a "new era" (see also Taube 1992). Thus, S. Sugiyama (2000, 2005, 2017a) interprets this façade as a royal accession scene heralded by the arrival of a powerful being, the Feathered Serpent, thereby inaugurating symbolic imagery that would reverberate in Mesoamerican mythology for centuries after the collapse of Teotihuacan (Carrasco 2000).

To follow S. Sugiyama's hypothesis, we must venture into the tunnels explored by the Proyecto Templo de Quetzalcoatl, or Temple of Quetzlcoatl Project (PTQ, 1988–1989) directed by S. Sugiyama, Cabrera Castro, and Cowgill (Cabrera Castro et al. 1991; Cabrera Castro and Cabrera 1991; Sugiyama 2005). This project extends from essential contributions by the Proyecto Arqueológico Teotihuacan, or Teotihuacan Archaeological Project (1980–1982) that restored much of the FSP and adjacent structures in the Ciudadela Complex (Cabrera Castro et al.

1982a, 1982b). What archaeologists found in the esophageal windings of the FSP tunnel was the aftermath of an extravagant, violent spectacle that laid the foundation from which this ritually charged monument was constructed. The remains of approximately 137 individuals were arrayed in an orderly pattern of trenches intersecting the cardinal axes of the pyramid. Each of their hands were bound behind their backs. With many unexcavated burials remaining, this mass sacrifice represents the largest such single event excavated in Mesoamerica to date. It claimed the lives of approximately two hundred individuals circa 200 CE. Hundreds of projectile points were scattered across the bodies, and human, canid, and imitation shell maxillary pendants decorated their chests. Stable isotope analysis on the sacrificed individuals and the human maxillary pendants showed both were comprised of a population of foreigners, foreign-born migrants to the Teotihuacan Valley, and a few local individuals (Nado et al. 2017; Spence et al. 2004; White et al. 2002).

The mortuary pattern reflects a cosmic archetype whereby symmetries in number, orientation, and sex materialized a worldview. Militaristic accouterments of this predominantly male assemblage suggest preferential selection of warriors or war captives for this meticulously coordinated dedicatory event. Despite the Feathered Serpent iconography that bedecks this pyramid, there are hardly any feathers or serpents represented in its dedicatory assemblages. There is a distinct scarcity of corporeal animal forms altogether; rather, this pyramid has been animated almost exclusively by humans. The unprecedented scale of this sacrificial event, the victim's burial accouterments, and the pyramid's iconographic context constituted a material expression of human sacrifice, militarism, and rulership (Sugiyama 2005).

Álvarez and Ocaña's (1993) preliminary zooarchaeological report provides a rough taxonomic list with minimal body-part information (Appendix, Table A1). Most of the specimens seem to be from the fill of the offering or the tunnel, with some mention of disturbed contexts. Noteworthy samples from in situ dedicatory contexts include three rattlesnakes (counts in MNI-minimum number of individuals), a single incomplete golden eagle, two incomplete hawks, a partial juvenile puma, isolated elements of two white-tailed and two mule deer, and a canid maxillary pendant adorning a sacrificial victim (Burial 4A) (Appendix, Table A1).

The group of canid maxillae initially identified by Álvarez and Ocaña (1993) as representing six dogs was later reassigned by Valadez Azúa and colleagues (2002a, 2002b) as a compilation of fourteen canids composed of dogs and several hybrids (wolf-dog, coyote-dog, and coyote-wolf-dog). Animal parts from various species were fused to compose artificial corporeal animal forms that agree with a lush iconographic context teeming with fanciful hybrids.

So what factors predicated the construction of the FSP in its current location? Public pre-monumental structures discovered within each pyramid's nucleus indicate that the ceremonial precinct incorporated active legacy places (Gazzola 2017; S. Sugiyama et al. 2013). A visitor examining the austere quadrangle in front of the FSP would find it difficult to imagine the tangle of structures, narrow streets, canals, and small patios that once crammed this plaza around the first century BCE during the Pre-Ciudadela phase, contemporaneous with the Pre-Monumental period (Gazzola 2009, 2017). Gazzola (2009: 227) interprets the artifacts excavated within the structures, including a possible ball court, as a likely elite occupation. Many of the Pre-Ciudadela buildings not only date to a similar time frame as Building 1 of the Moon Pyramid but were also aligned 11 degrees east of true north, 4 degrees westward of subsequently established Teotihuacan orientations.

Two earlier architectural features anticipated the FSP's position. (1) Traces of a razed foundation within its nucleus are the vestiges of a modest structure upon which the pyramid currently stands (Sugiyama 1998b). (2) A sizable subterranean tunnel boring 14.5 m deep and 102.6 m long beneath the FSP (like the Sun Pyramid and its subterranean tunnel) likely predates the pyramidal construction (Gazzola and Gómez 2020). This subterranean tunnel, still under investigation by Gómez Chávez (2013, 2017), completely revolutionizes our understanding of the function and meaning of the Ciudadela Complex. Thousands of state-controlled goods, many imports spanning Greater Mesoamerica, have been dated to an early phase of Teotihuacan state formation. They include greenstone figurines, enormous conch shells with Maya and Mixtec-style inscriptions, rubber balls, precious stone artifacts, cacao pods, and amber, among many others that are still undergoing restoration, curation, and analysis (Gazzola and Gómez 2020; Grube and Gómez Chávez 2017). At the time of writing, no publication of the vertebrate remains was available, but no doubt this find will add to the substantial evidence of ritualized animal remains at Teotihuacan.

Preliminary interpretations by Gómez Chávez (2017) suggest the Ciudadela Complex was the material manifestation of the origin place and axis mundi of Teotihuacan where the primordial sea (Ciudadela plaza), the sacred mountain (FSP), and the passage to the underworld (subterranean tunnel) all convened during ritual reenactments at this underground passage. Even after it was filled and sealed, evidence of reentry into this tunnel suggests it continued to be ingrained into the Teotihuacanos' social memories (Gómez Chávez 2017).

Gazzola (2017) identified a fourth and oldest intensive agricultural production period when she uncovered two large canals dating to circa 100 BCE. These Pre-Ciudadela architectural features constitute some of the earliest evidence of occupation within the ceremonial core.

In summary, at least four major phases, in chronological order from most recent to oldest, characterize the Ciudadela Complex: the concealment of the Feathered Serpent sculptures via the addition of an *adosada* annex circa 350 CE during the turbulent transition between the Urban Renewal to Teotihuacan Expansion period, the completion of the FSP and Ciudadela Complex consecrated by a mass sacrificial ritual (150–250 CE) during the Ceremonial Monuments period, the use of Pre-Ciudadela structures during the Pre-Monumental period when the subterranean tunnel would have been active (1–150 CE), and finally an intensive agricultural production phase (200–1 BCE) (Figure 2.3). Each period reflects the intentional decisions to construct, destroy (sometimes intentionally demolish), reutilize, and rediscover these fundamental features of the landscape.

The Sun Pyramid

Visitors experience the same ritual procession along the Avenue of the Dead as those who traveled to this legendary pilgrimage destination over 1,500 years ago throughout the 1.2 km walkway toward the Sun Pyramid from the Ciudadela (Evans 2015, 2016). The continuous stream of tourists submerging and reemerging along six sunken patios almost reenacts the serpent's undulation. On both sides of the avenue, giant stairways invite the curious to visit some of the "palatial" complexes, some excavated and restored, like the Street of the Dead Complex, and others left as abandoned mounds. These compounds were prime real estate for elite residences, palaces hosting governing individuals, and/or civic-administrative compounds where public work projects would have been designed and implemented (Sanders and Evans 2006).

This civic engineering endeavor's meticulous precision and massive scale are felt at every corner of the city. Take, for example, the San Juan River that runs perpendicular to the grand avenue. Most visitors do not realize they have crossed this now-seasonal river before reaching the first sunken plaza. The Teotihuacanos artificially aligned its naturally meandering course for a stretch of roughly 3 km to match the Teotihuacan grid layout (Evans and Nichols 2016; Sugiyama 1993: 114). For the Teotihuacanos, there was a single model for "vibrant urbanity" (sensu Joyce 2020), and even natural features needed to obey construction regulations.

While it is intimidating to stand in the footsteps of the third largest pyramid in the world (originally 215 × 215 × 63 m), the ceremonial center's position along the valley bottom facilitated direct observation of these monuments from any point in the city, its domineering presence always felt even in the remote insubstantial structures inhabited by farmers and artisans (Cabrera Cortés 2011). Like the rest of Teotihuacan, the pyramid's size, orientation, form, and decoration were carefully crafted to reflect their cosmos (Sugiyama 1993, 2010). The pyramid faces west, oriented 15°30′ east of magnetic north to align with sunset along the western horizon on August 12 and April 29, separating the year into the 260-day calendar when the sun passes to the south of that alignment and the 105 days when it passes to its north (Aveni 2000; Drucker 1977; Šprajc 2000).

Gazing up to confront the towering mountain, it is now swarming with tiny ant-sized tourists striving to reach its pinnacle.[1] Many chant their school rally or yell the names of family members who withheld their inclination to suffer through the 63 m ascent. These voices echo to the base of the plaza and can be heard in adjacent complexes as they ricochet along the avenue. The Sun Pyramid's elevated visibility and favorable acoustic properties enabled select state-level authorities to propagate official messaging from this ancient broadcast platform to the crowds below.

Under the auspices of President Porfirio Díaz, the Sun Pyramid was the first ancient edifice reconstructed in the modern era for the 1910 Mexican independence centennial celebration (Batres 1906; Sarabia González 2008). Having served as a backdrop for countless events hosting foreign diplomats, artists, and distinguished guests, it stands as an enduring national symbol. As with the FSP, its massive central prism was built in a single phase, while the *adosada* platform was later annexed. Architectural features and offering deposits excavated within the Sun Pyramid have helped refine the construction sequence, meaning, and function of this renowned monument (Matos Moctezuma 1995; Millon et al. 1965; Millon and Drewitt 1961; Noguera 1935; Pérez 1935; Vaillant 1932). More recently, Sarabia González's (2002) project, the Programa de Conservación e Investigación en el Complejo Arquitectónico de la Pirámide del Sol, or Proyecto Pirámide del Sol (Sun Pyramid Project) (PPS, 2005–2011), with the integration of S. Sugiyama and N. Sugiyama in 2008, began to reexplore two architectural features (Sarabia González and Núñez Redón 2017). First, the pyramid's interior spaces were excavated via additional pits within and new tunnels branching from Noguera's (1935) earlier archaeological tunnel. Second, the subterranean tunnel beneath the pyramid (similar to the one already described under the FSP) was mapped and small-scale surface cleaning and test pits were performed (Figure 2.5) (N. Sugiyama et al. 2013).

Serendipitously discovered in 1971 (Heyden 1975), this subterranean tunnel opens via a 2.7 m vertical shaft sinking about 6.5 m from the surface into the bedrock. A sloping *talud* wall at the base of the opening would have allowed those descending into the dark fissure to release their grip from the rudimentary hollows carved into the chalky bedrock layer beneath this pyramid, easing the final approach into the

---

[1] This description was formulated before the COVID-19 pandemic. Now, tourists cannot climb the Sun Pyramid.

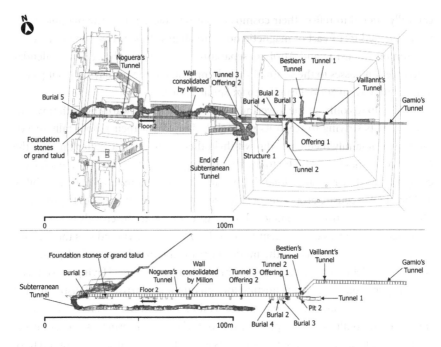

FIGURE 2.5
Plan (above) and profile (below) map of excavation units and key features in the Sun Pyramid. CAD drawing by Moon Pyramid Project © Saburo Sugiyama.

underground passage. This damp, lamp-lit passage narrows and widens in irregular pulses as its track meanders 97.4 m to the east before abruptly terminating in a spacious quatrefoil chamber. Though a series of partitions once segmented the tunnel into eighteen chambers, each wall was breached in a burst of determined looting activity. Unfortunately, documentation from the initial archaeological exploration remains scant. Subsequent test pit excavations by the Teotihuacan Mapping Project describe the presence of stone drainage channels caped by manhole-like covers (Millon 1992: 387). Findings of shells, tiny scales, and fish spines are the only faunal elements referenced in this report.

While some have applied Postclassic mythology to interpret this feature as the natural primordial cave from which humanity originated (Heyden 1981; Taube 1986), PPS mapping and exploration data indicate that the subterranean tunnel was as artificial as its FSP counterpart, entailing a similarly extensive and complex quarrying operation (see also Barba et al. 1990; Manzanilla et al. 1994; N. Sugiyama et al. 2013). Though comparatively fragmentary, these remnants of greenstone artifacts, shell beads, and slate discs recovered by PPS recall the exceptional deposits of ritual implements in the FSP's subterranean tunnel (Gómez Chávez 2017).

The Sun Pyramid's base is arrayed with a motley display of sculptural forms: felids menace with bared fangs alongside stylized human hearts and a large slab depicting a flaming structure with a twisted rope. Fash and colleagues (2009) argue that the latter sculpture represents the New Fire ceremony and propose that the *adosada* platform was a staging ground for cyclical renewal and accession ceremonies. For S. Sugiyama, the Sun Pyramid was the Moon Pyramid's dualistic counterpart, emphasizing "fire, warmth, the dry season, masculinity, and the sun" (Sugiyama 2017b: 36). More recent PPS discovery of in situ puma balustrades decorating the *adosada*, echoing the Feathered Serpent sculptures discussed at the FSP, further supports the monument's solar association (Sarabia González and Núñez Redón 2017) (Figure 3.3b).

In total, PPS excavations uncovered four burials and two offerings, [2] with all but two burials dating to the construction of the main corpus of the Sun Pyramid. Unlike the Moon Pyramid, PPS burials were characterized by isolated individuals, usually infants/children, in keeping with Batres's (1906) finds, buried with few or no associated artifacts (N. Sugiyama et al. 2013).

Offering 1 was a small cache found within the Sun Pyramid's fill near an earlier, preexisting structure. The offered goods included a large pyrite disc covering a configuration of organic fibers, an obsidian eccentric that would have stood upright on this disc, a large conch shell, and many projectile points. No vertebrate remains were associated with this cache.

Only Offering 2 contained corporeal animal forms. As a result of an elaborate consecration rite, Offering 2 would have inaugurated the ritualized production of the Sun Pyramid (N. Sugiyama et al. 2013). PPS found multiple superimposed layers of obsidian, greenstone, shell, pyrite, slate, ceramics, and animal bones throughout the cache (N. Sugiyama et al. 2013) (Plate 2). A greenstone mask with pyrite eye inlays and two greenstone anthropomorphic figurines exemplifies the exquisite lithic artistry of the state.

A complete golden eagle (sacrificed), a puma skull, a wolf skull, and the extremities of a red-tailed hawk were among the corporeal animal forms selected for dedication (Plate 3). The eagle placed on the eastern sector of the offering carried a small pyrite surfaced disc on its back. I have interpreted this assemblage as a material manifestation of the raptor's role as the bearer of the sun that carries the solar disc from where it rises in the east across the horizon (Sugiyama 2014; 2023). Reprising a pattern that we will further discuss in the Moon Pyramid

---

[2] Projects named caches with human skeletal remains as an "Entierro" (Burial), while caches lacking human skeletal remains were labeled an "Ofrenda" (Offering). These designations do not distinguish intent (dedication versus burial).

assemblage, this eagle consumed two rabbits immediately prior to its ritual slaughter. In addition to the sculpted pumas that line the Sun Pyramid's base, the inclusion of a puma skull and its phalanges with cutmarks, likely indicating the pelt was still attached to the disarticulated digits, further support the monument's solar affiliation.

Despite these significant findings, corporeal animal forms in the Sun Pyramid's ritual deposits were restricted relative to their abundance in Moon Pyramid caches. Only one of the six burial/offering contexts contained faunal material. Offering 2 animal remains correspond to the same primary animal actors found in Moon Pyramid caches. The lack of adult human remains in these elaborate offerings further distinguishes the Sun Pyramid offerings from those at the Moon Pyramid and FSP. Instead, human sacrifices were usually of children or infants and with little or no accompanying artifacts.

PPS results challenge conventional theories on the timing of the Sun Pyramid's construction, dated initially to a relatively early period of incipient urbanism, during the Tzacualli period (1–150 CE) or even earlier (Millon 1960; Millon et al. 1965; Noguera 1935; Vaillant 1932). New PPS radiocarbon dates establish the contemporaneous construction of the pyramid and the subterranean tunnel around 150–300 CE, a century later than initially proposed (N. Sugiyama et al. 2013, 2018; see, however, Sload 2015). Three phases were defined: a Pre-Monumental period before the Sun Pyramid construction, the erection of the Sun Pyramid during the Ceremonial Monuments period (150–300 CE), and the addition of the *adosada* platform during the start of the Teotihuacan Expansion period (circa 350 CE) (contemporaneous with FSP *adosada*) (Figure 2.3). Like the FSP, the Sun Pyramid's construction was a process of *remaking* place, requiring the dramatic ritual termination of Pre-Sun Pyramid structures before embarking on one of the most ambitious construction projects at Teotihuacan.

The Moon Pyramid

As visitors approach the slopes of the Moon Pyramid that presides over the northern terminus of this long ritual passage, the distant and looming bulk of Cerro Gordo gradually disappears beyond the monument's chiseled shoulders. This mountain was and continues to be a dominant marker that helps navigate the Teotihuacan Valley's spontaneous and extreme weather conditions. Many years of fieldwork have taught archaeologists that when the rain clouds hover over the Cerro Gordo, it is time to pack up as buckets of rainwater speedily approach the site. As mentioned earlier, this characteristically clefted extinct Pleistocene volcano likely was the natural correlate to an *altepetl*, the hill that stored water in its interior (Kowalski 1999; Tobriner 1972).

FIGURE 2.6
Moon Pyramid and Moon Pyramid Plaza with central altar. Photograph: S. Sugiyama.

The Moon Pyramid stands 46 m high and 168 m × 149 m at the base at the axis of a larger complex called the Moon Pyramid Plaza (Figure 2.6). This plaza includes several stepped platforms, two central structures (central platform and Building of the Altars), and a series of residential/palatial complexes, including the Quetzalpapalotl palace just to the southwest. The obsidian workshop adjacent to the pyramid would have been busily producing the finest obsidian eccentrics, bifaces, and the like used in dedicatory rites (Carballo 2007). Such attached workshops were essential factors controlling the production and distribution of state-controlled crafts (Carballo 2013; Hirth 2020).

Unlike the plazas visited thus far, the Avenue of the Dead bleeds right into the Moon Plaza. A central altar would have been a discernable and lively stage for music, dancing, and the like. Even today, this inviting plaza is where "Aztec dancers" rhythmically pace in a circle with *ayoyotes* (Aztec jingles made of hard shells of nuts) shingling on their feet, large plumed headdresses flowing through the air, and their brilliant white attire blinding from the sun's reflection. A crowd of spectators and passersby assemble around the dancers, some forming to consult the shaman-healer who cures patients bathed in potent incense smoke that lingers in their sinuses. Despite its open form, however, a spatial syntax analysis of the accessibility of the city showed that the Avenue of the Dead, especially the Moon Pyramid Plaza at its northern extreme, was one of the most restricted spaces in the

FIGURE 2.7
Southward view from the apex of the Moon Pyramid on the Spring Equinox. Photograph: S. Sugiyama.

city, requiring visitors to walk the entire length of the Avenue of the Dead to approach this space (Robb 2007).

Although visitors reach this temple fatigued and intimidated by the heavily inclined stairway, it is worth the climb as the summit of this pyramid projects my favorite vista of Teotihuacan. Raised above and along the axis of the central core of the cityscape, the Moon Pyramid's view is priceless (Figure 2.7). Due to the gradual slope of the terrain, the Moon Pyramid's summit (2,350 masl) is roughly at the same height as the Sun Pyramid (2,357 masl). From this central node, we can observe the Sun Pyramid's profile foreshadowing the Patlachique Mountain, the line of visitors crawling along the avenue, and even the low-lying dust accumulated from the crowds bustling through the Ciudadela Complex and Great Compound.

Two female megaliths found in the Moon Plaza may be telling of the meanings bestowed in this area. One of these still stands in its eroded state to the southeast of the central platform. The second, rediscovered behind Building 4 of the Moon Plaza, is suggested to have originated from the Moon Pyramid's summit (López Luján 2017). Both appropriately emphasize the Moon Pyramid Complex's association with lunar, female, rainy season, earth, and fertility symbolism (López Luján 2017; Sugiyama 2017b). As the function, meaning, and ritualized production of this monument are the central subject of the present study, let us examine in finer detail its production sequence and how massive ritual spectacles played an eminent role in its ritualized production.

The zooarchaeological remains analyzed in the present study originated from tunneling operations by Saburo Sugiyama and Ruben Cabrera (2007) during the Proyecto Pirámide de la Luna, or Moon Pyramid Project (PPL, 1998–2004). Project goals were to create a three-dimensional map of the Moon Pyramid Plaza and, based on this map, explore interior and exterior spaces in this plaza complex to define its construction sequence, and uncover associated burial/offertory deposits. They were also keen on establishing the timing and nature of public works dating to the earliest periods of state formation.

The Moon Pyramid grew over the course of seven building phases and minor architectural changes in the plaza (Sugiyama and Cabrera Castro 2000, 2007, 2017). Each of the pyramid's construction phases was labeled Building 1 through Building 7, Building 1 being the oldest and smallest mound at its core. Six burial/offering complexes were associated with several of these remodeling phases, either built along the bedrock at its base or in the nucleus of structures. Each dedicatory cache was named sequentially in the order of their discovery as Burials 1 through 6 (López Luján and Sugiyama 2017; Sugiyama and López Luján 2007). While all caches contained human skeletal remains, Burial 1 and 4 are not discussed in detail because they lacked faunal remains. Burial 1 was a neonate found in a pit in the northwestern corner of the mound (post-Teotihuacan), while Burial 4 was composed of seventeen severed human heads located between Building 5 and Building 6 without associated artifacts.

During the first three building phases, the Moon Pyramid was an insubstantial dirt mound that grew exponentially during Building 4, reaching a monumental scale during the Ceremonial Monuments period (ca. 250 ± 50 CE) and continuing to expand throughout three subsequent rebuilding episodes during the Urban Renewal and Teotihuacan Expansion phases (300–450 CE) (Sugiyama and Cabrera Castro 2007). Let us examine when these buildings were manufactured and what artifacts constituted the offertory assemblage.

The Moon Pyramid's Building 1 was one of the earliest public structures built at the ceremonial core (100 ± 50 CE), predating even the Sun Pyramid's construction. Contemporary with some of the Pre-Ciudadela structures mentioned above, the Moon Pyramid was initially also oriented 11–12 degrees east of magnetic north, just a few degrees short of the characteristic Teotihuacan orientation (Sugiyama and Cabrera Castro 2007). The subsequent two phases, Building 2 (150 ± 50 CE) and Building 3 (195 ± 65 CE), were modest alterations retaining Building 1's form and only grew from 23.5 m to 31.3 m at the base. They were square platforms with deteriorated or destroyed façades and lacked offertory caches. Significant public structures existed before the large-scale expansion of the city itself. These pre-monumental structures demarcate the pivotal nodes anchoring the massive engineering project; these important legacy structures had to be incorporated into the ceremonial precinct to retain their placeness, animacy, and interpersonal ties with the local community. These three initial substructures and subsequent Building 4 are architecturally distinct from later developments: they lack an *adosada* platform and are square with stepped *talud* (sloped) walls at the base. This contrasts with the usual *adosada* platforms decorated with *talud-tablero* façades (slope-and-panel wall) (e.g., FSP) characteristic of Teotihuacan in later periods.

One of the most notable features of Building 4's construction (250 ± 50 CE) is that it marked the establishment of state monumentalism. By this time, the well-known city-grid system, along with its unique orientation, was implemented, and it is roughly contemporaneous with the construction of the Sun Pyramid and the FSP (Figure 2.3) (Sugiyama 2013). Not only did the pyramid expand in size, extending nine times more in volume than the previous structure (measuring 88.9 m north-south and 89.2 m east-west), but its ritualized production became substantially complex. The earliest state-sanctioned dedicatory caches from the Moon Pyramid were integrated into the nucleus of this structure. Despite tunneling into Buildings 1–3's axial locations, corresponding caches were absent in these early structures. These ritualized dedicatory acts entailed producing and displaying highly elaborate offerings of exceptional quality and quantity, carefully placed into prime loci. Burial 2 was located along the pyramid's central axis at its base, and Burial 6 was embedded roughly at the three-dimensional core of the structure. During this phase, there was a radical change in the extent of state control and legitimation. The fact that this major rebuilding program coincides with two of the earliest dedicatory chambers in the Moon Pyramid and the richest faunal assemblage found to date at Teotihuacan cannot be a mere accident. It reflects the direct measures the Teotihuacan state took in negotiations with the cosmic landscape.

A man seated along the eastern wall of Burial 2 was discovered bound as a sacrificial victim (Plate 4) (Spence and Pereira 2007). Diverse animals also met their fates here. Two complete pumas, one wolf, nine eagles, and six rattlesnakes were discovered as primary burials, while other faunal products were scattered throughout the cache (Polaco 2004; Sugiyama 2014). Most notably, the wooden post holes surrounding the two pumas and wolf provide the most convincing evidence that these animals were buried alive, reinforced by the remains of coprolites in the cages themselves. Besides these ossuary remains, obsidian eccentrics, bifaces and projectile points, shell pendants, and Tlaloc vessels accompanied the cache (Sugiyama 2004; Sugiyama and López Luján 2006a). Two greenstone figurines, two slate disks, obsidian projectile points, a shell necklace of imitation human maxillae, and worked and unworked shell artifacts assembled near the center. At the base of each of the two central greenstone figurines were nine sacrificial knives in radial configuration (eighteen total).

Burial 6 is the largest dedicatory chamber inside the Moon Pyramid, delimited by vertical stone walls 5 m (north-south) by 4.5 m (east-west) and 2 m high. Strikingly, ten decapitated human skeletons were piled up on the northern sector of the cache, while two complete humans were crouched (flexed) near the center; all had their hands tied behind their backs (Plate 5). Of the twelve sacrificed individuals, those whose sex could be determined were males, two of which had associated greenstone and/or shell artifacts and osteological alterations such as cranial deformation or dental decoration suggesting they were of high status (Spence and Pereira 2007). The magnitude of faunal remains in a single context is unprecedented in Teotihuacan, with over one hundred individuals, including thirty-three complete animals. The faunal remains were among an equally rich and unique array of dedicatory artifacts such as obsidian eccentrics and weaponry, jade figurines, and Tlaloc vessels. Like Burial 2, eighteen radiating eccentrics, this time carved in the form of Feathered Serpents and undulating knives, were arranged around a greenstone mosaic figurine that stood atop a pyrite mosaic disc (Sugiyama and López Luján 2006b). Similar artifact types and numerals across Burial 2 and 6 reference a coherent message. These ritual paraphernalia were state-regulated implements of power and authority.

Building 5's architecture incorporated, for the first time, an *adosada* platform connected to the central structure and the adoption of a typical Teotihuacan *taludtablero* form (evidence is unclear in Building 4) (Sugiyama and Cabrera Castro 2007: 120–121). This addition caused an elongation of the north-south axis to 104 meters, while the east-west axis stayed the same. This building was probably constructed around 300 ± 50 CE, at which point Burial 3 (2.2 × 2.5 × 1.5 m) was integrated into the back façade. Three individuals in extended and one in flexed position carefully lay with their hands tied behind their backs (Plate 6). Rich offerings surrounded and adorned their bodies, including many prepared animal skulls. The osteological and isotopic data concur with the scenario that these males were likely captive warriors (Spence and Pereira 2007; White et al. 2007). Each individual possessed body ornaments, such as shell and greenstone ear spools, greenstone nose pendants and beads, and a shell necklace made of imitation human maxillae. Deteriorated fibers found on the cache's northwestern corner likely represent a mat upon which Individual 3-D could have sat. Worked shell ornaments, obsidian projectile points and blades, a pyrite disk, greenstone figurines, and small anthropomorphic figurines were scattered around the human sacrificial victims.

Located in the three-dimensional center of Building 6, Burial 5 simultaneously marked the termination of Building 5 and the consecration of Building 6 (Sugiyama and Cabrera Castro 2007). Radiocarbon samples date this deposit, measuring 6 m² and 3.5 m deep, to 350 ± 50 CE. By this time, the pyramid would have had the same form and size as the modern reconstruction appreciable in the archaeological park. This cache is contemporaneous with Burial 4 mentioned earlier, consisting of seventeen decapitated heads buried within the structure along the base.

In Burial 5, three humans sat cross-legged facing west, adorned with regal ornaments that point to the highly elevated status of these individuals (Plate 7). Unlike all the sacrificial victims from the other caches, these prominent figures did not have their hands tied behind their backs. Instead, their hands were crossed in front; two individuals had their hands overlaid atop animal skulls (Spence and Pereira 2007: 151). Whether their hands were tied or just placed in that configuration remains to be determined. Personal paraphernalia included atypical and highly controversial Maya-style greenstone objects, including jadeite "pinwheel" ear spools and pectorals usually found in Maya sites that may indicate these burials/victims were of foreign dignitaries (Sugiyama and López Luján 2007). Each person was associated with an animal (puma, wolf, and raven/eagle). In addition, scattered remains of numerous rattlesnakes and animal skulls were found throughout the cache. A seated greenstone figure with associated greenstone beads, worked and unworked shells, obsidian points and blades, and woven fibers were also presented. Unfortunately, the large boulders that filled this cache caused extensive taphonomic damage to the osteological remains, probably due to water filtration, making this collection the most degraded samples analyzed.

The Moon Pyramid, as it currently stands, dates to Building 7, likely built around 400 ± 50 CE, which continued to function until the city's collapse circa 550 CE (Sugiyama and Cabrera Castro 2007: 122). Even after the decline of the Teotihuacan state, the monument continued to be used, reoccupied, worshiped, and looted in subsequent periods. The presence of Burial 1, placed by the Aztecs (1300–1521 CE) just outside of its northwestern corner, further emphasizes the longevity of the Moon Pyramid as a sacred place even after the collapse of Teotihuacan as a sociopolitical entity. All fauna from dedicatory offerings from the Moon Pyramid were analyzed in this study, a sample that spans Building 4 to Building 6, ranging from 250 CE ± 50 to 350 ± 50 CE. This allows us to look at diachronic changes in animal use during the materialization of a revolutionary and monumental cityscape and the subsequent expansion brought about by its success.

These four offering caches in the Moon Pyramid represent the largest quantity of potentate fauna offered from a single loci at Teotihuacan thus far. One hundred eighty-eight animals were offered as sacrificial victims or secondary corporeal animal forms. The only comparable dataset within Teotihuacan is the copious remains of animal parts recently uncovered by Gómez Chávez (2013, 2017; see also Gazzola and Gómez 2019) in the subterranean tunnel under the FSP, though detailed zooarchaeological study is still underway. The unprecedented quantity of fauna alludes to the singular role these highly symbolic animals played as active and fundamental actors in the process of placemaking at the Moon Pyramid.

Producing Monumentality at Teotihuacan

By framing the analysis of the animals who participated in the dedicatory spectacles at the Moon Pyramid as part of the ritualized production of a sacred place, I open a path to retrieve the underlying messages communicated through interpersonal interactions between ritualized bodies (human and nonhuman persons) and the physical properties of the ritual stage. Pyramids, in particular, are a monumental testament to their place within the cosmos; they are a material embodiment of the nested social actants participating in its ritualized co-production.

The concept of the *altepetl* as the sacred water mountain I presented earlier is not novel to Teotihuacan. Water mountains have been salient in Olmec iconography since the Early Formative period (e.g., Cerro Manatí, 1250–900 BCE) (Ortíz and Rodríguez 2006). I focus on the execution of the ritualized production of the Moon Pyramid through the entanglement of place, community, and social structure, which made it embody a distinct expression of *altepetl* closely aligned with sovereignty. This co-production required the active participation of human and nonhuman persons, especially the potentate corporeal animal forms analyzed in this study.

In the journey through the archaeological site, I recognized how each monument was not built in a vacuum but entailed the ritualized production of an integrative ceremonial landscape based on a cosmic blueprint that structured a powerful experiential narrative. I demonstrated what monumentalism *does*; it solidifies a radically distinct way of interacting with and experiencing the landscape. Generations of experiential narratives superimposed on the landscape still confer on Teotihuacan's status as a pilgrimage site for Mexican and international communities to this day. Local residents, specialists, and tourists may catch, to differing degrees, particularities such as orientation and size, architectural form and decoration, and esoteric knowledge about the meaning and historical caveats of each structure, but we can all appreciate what it is like to walk down that grand corridor.

I also summarized relevant archaeological data to create a chronologically situated narrative of when and how these structures were ritually produced. Pre-monumental structures sleeping in the nucleus of each major pyramid demonstrate that the precinct's cosmic blueprint was presaged on the distribution of localized animate places. The constant modification, sometimes even destruction, and rediscovery of specific structures continuously renegotiated, redefined, and reinvigorated significant places on the landscape. By characterizing each dedicatory cache within the building phases, I demonstrated how Burials 2 and 6 of the Moon Pyramid reflect a quintessential period during a city-wide monumental construction program (Ceremonial Monuments phase). Subsequent dedicatory caches, Burials 3 and 5, characterize periods of Urban Renewal and Teotihuacan Expansion, respectively. These dedicatory spectacles were seminal for imposing prevailing state ideologies to an unprecedented scale. Thus, they provide an opportunity to reconstruct some of the social processes during the definition of these monuments as essential *places* that conspicuously encoded new forms of authority into public works.

For the remainder of the book, I concentrate on reconstructing animals' role in the ritualized production of the Moon Pyramid. I ask why these animals participated in the ritualized spectacle and how they contributed to the placemaking of the Moon Pyramid. As I hypothesize animal matters were seminal delegates of Teotihuacan sovereignty formations, authenticated by the interpersonal negotiations publicly broadcasted during ritualized performances, I begin by reviewing how animal matter (both their corporeal forms and their representation) is distributed at Teotihuacan in the following chapter before presenting the raw zooarchaeological data from the Moon Pyramid.

CHAPTER 3

ANIMAL POLITICS

NOT ALL ANIMALS ARE ADEQUATE persons for sacrifice. Recall that we're examining the archaeological vestiges of a state-controlled selection process to assemble a cohort of animals that manifest as quintessential sacrifices. There is a reason why the turkey was not the victim of choice here (no offense to the turkeys), and it has to do with how animals are socially and often hierarchically classified. In this regard, animals are as political as the humans who draw from and engage in animal politics to authenticate their social positionality. In the case of Teotihuacan, Headrick rightfully asserts animals did the "dirty work" (2007: 85) of the state.

While the general social classification of the animals—based on preferences, behaviors, and negotiated eco-contracts of reciprocity and exchange—were understood at the categorical level (e.g. species), individual encounters (e.g., in dedication rituals) merited stages for refined negotiation (Hill 2018). Human–animal interactions were experienced through representations of animals that usually relate to the social values and concepts attributed to the animal in question and physical human–animal encounters with individual "persons" through corporeal animal forms.

In this chapter, I provide a general review of the social values attributed to the main participants in ritualized performances at Teotihuacan: the felid (jaguar and puma), the wolf, the golden eagle, and the rattlesnake. Their iconographic proliferation, in contrast to the distribution of corporeal animal forms, conveys why and how individuals were "set apart" and transformed into active persons within Teotihuacan society. I suggest particular taxa may have helped authenticate specific human actants and embed them within the governing structures of the city. This review will help contextualize the zooarchaeological and isotopic results presented in subsequent chapters, which comprise the raw data to generate individual life history reconstructions (Chapter 6). I present relevant biological (ecological and

Animal Matter. Nawa Sugiyama, Oxford University Press. © Oxford University Press 2024.
DOI: 10.1093/9780197653425.003.0003

behavioral) and cultural (zooarchaeological and iconographic data) traits used to decode the factors weighting on each decision node (e.g., how many and what species, age, or sex to sacrifice) during the ritualization process. These factors help establish why these particular species became active delegates of Teotihuacan sovereignty and how the public experienced animal persons in state spectacles (Chapter 7).

Animal Hierarchies

In this chapter, I lay the groundwork to discuss how animal matter engaged in the politics of sovereignty formations at Teotihuacan. I draw on Bauer and Kosiba's work to define animal politics as the entanglement of animal matter in the "practices and processes by which people established social differences and ties as they constitute a collective body, a 'public' oriented toward a specific problem or concern" (2016: 116). This approach calls for understanding the situated action of animal matter as part of the public in mediating (not representing) cultural values and intentions. To begin, I introduce the social positionality of animals within native classificatory systems that are highly stratified and often perceptive to human–animal interactions.

Animal classificatory systems explicitly address attitudes, motivations, and reciprocal relationships between and among humans and animals in a given social context (Leach 1964; Tambiah 1969). They are indexical categories referencing unique modes of perception and interaction with the world (Urton 1985; Viveiros de Castro 1998). Animal classification systems are instrumental in the structuring of human social organizations. As encultured subjects, animals submit to, reinforce, or modify the rules and norms prevalent in society (Chen 2012; Hill 2013; Taube 2003). Their natural ontology can bootstrap the hierarchies and roles that classify humans and illuminate the underlying structures organizing human social dynamics (Douglas 1957; Lévi-Strauss 1966). As with the human world, not all animals are made equal, and the diversity in the taxa's morphology, behavior, and ecology provides the basis for indigenous zoological systems.

Tzotzil Maya informants explain that companion animals inhabit the sacred mountain (Gossen 1975). This mountain is stratified like the heavens, with its thirteen levels containing specific types of companion animals. Distinctions between predator/prey and domestic/wild strongly influence the animals' hierarchical position; wild carnivores occupy the upper strata, while herbivores and small animals inhabit the lower levels (Gossen 1975; Pinzón Castaño 2002; Vogt 1981). The concept of "the master of animals" as predators that control animals and natural features on the landscape seems to be pan-continental (Fausto 2012; Gossen 1994;

Hill 2011; Ingold 1986; Ulloa 2002; Viveiros de Castro 1998) . Such dominant animals were also highly praised as mediators with other spirits, gods, and ancestors.

The apparent dominance of the predator role legitimizes inequality, and eco-contracts bind these potent animals to their human counterparts. As preeminent hunters, indigenous communities describe carnivores as teachers/elders from whom humans learned the art of hunting and are responsible for maintaining ecological order. In these transactions, differential access by select individuals within a community directly impacts their social positionality. For the Huichol communities in northwestern Mexico, the wolf is their elder brother who taught them how to hunt deer (Valadez 1996). Yet only selected shamans can transform into wolves, acquiring the ability to hunt, heal, and control rain (Fikes 1985: 249).

Similarly, not everyone can have a jaguar as their soul companion; the master of animals would only permit the most potent elites/shamans who occupy the highest echelon of society as their counterparts (Vogt and Stuart 2005). Hunters, warriors, shamans, and royalty have always depended on maintaining a close affiliation with the jaguar, as the ethno-zoological classification system authenticated the underlying ridged social stratification (McAnany 2008; Saunders 1989). In this manner, the harmonious gift exchange between society and animals/animal spirits often utilizes elites as interlocutors in human–carnivore eco-contracts (Busatta 2007).

One of the ways human–animal relationships are classified is by their relative positionality within a spectrum of wild, managed/tamed, herded, to domesticated. Domestication is characterized by biological and social interdependence, whereby human groups intentionally alter the morphology and behavior of a species but also their own livelihood and lifestyle (Clutton-Brock 1994; Zeder 2015). Domestication is a process with greater or lesser degrees of direct biological and relational adjustments to both the animals/plants and humans that affect not just single species but the way human communities interact with the interrelated landscape (Sugiyama, Martínez-Polanco, et al. 2020; Zeder 2006). Animal taming involves the social incorporation of the animal into the household, and herding can be defined by keeping animals as property (Russell 2012b). Management refers to any deliberate practice to maintain or alter the population, including selective hunting, restricted usage, or habitat manipulation. While many of these categories are not mutually exclusive, only domestication assumes that breeding took place within the domestic sphere, often radically modifying animal phenotypes that enhance the symbiosis of the relationship with humans.

The domestication process reinforces the humanity of the animal and creates a new perspective on the animal hierarchy, establishing a relationship based on subordination and control. Ingold (1986) draws a parallel between the dominant position animal guardians exhibit over the domain of wild animals and the position humans acquire through the domestication process. Others describe that when a ruler, shaman, or warrior "domesticates" an animal, they establish a direct connection with or understanding of the animal, allowing them to acquire specific properties, often derived from the attributes of the animal in question (better sight, hunting instincts, strength) (Pinzón Castaño 2002). I argue similar realignments in human–animal interpersonal contact when select individuals (likely governing elites) directly managed influential animal persons buried in the Moon Pyramid. I focus on reconstructing specific human–carnivore dynamics to identify how early evidence of animal management contributed to the animal's corporeal form and its place within the social landscape of Teotihuacan.

By centering animal matter in the sociopolitics of placemaking and power, their materiality provides important clues about the processes of sovereignty formations at Teotihuacan. The emphasis on physical encounters with corporeal animal forms implies that documenting material residues of such encounters in the form of skeletal features, body-part representation, pathologies, and additional life history markers, as well as internment practices, can inform how each "person" mediated the socially differentiated landscape and how personhood was constructed in the past (Hill 2018).

I begin by reviewing the taxonomic list of the fauna uncovered in the offertory caches at the Moon Pyramid as species diversity and abundance pinpoint the primary actors of a ritual spectacle. A total of 21 species/genera of mammalian, avian, and reptilian fauna composed of 188 minimum number of individuals (MNI) were identified from the dedicatory caches (Table 3.1). While minor variations in taxa are present in each offering, state rituals consistently conjured a core set of prominent actors. Shaded columns in Table 3.1 signal primary burials (complete articulated individuals), while shaded rows indicate high species abundance. The cells with overlapping tones represent species interred as primary burials that were also most consistently (found in multiple contexts) and abundantly represented in the faunal record ($n = 134$, accounting for over 70% of MNI). They constitute apex predators of the sky (golden eagles), the earth (wolves, pumas, and jaguars), and liminal spaces (rattlesnakes); the carnivores I argue became ritualized bodies. Though a single complete raven was identified in Burial 5, these animals were not regular participants in Teotihuacan state rituals (total MNI 3) and are seldom found in Teotihuacan iconography. Additional secondary deposits (with disarticulated and/or incomplete bodies) amplified species diversity. Notably, high raptor diversity (owls, hawks, and falcons) among secondary deposits indicates that parts of the feathered extremities supplemented primary participants. Small game found in the stomach content of the sacrificed animals (rabbit, hare, mouse) or as fill debris (vole, squirrel, lizard, etc.) were also extant.

We can observe at least two distinct tactics of animal politics applied in ancient Mesoamerica. Compared to the remarkable consistency in species representation

TABLE 3.1
Species Distribution of Zooarchaeological Remains from the Moon Pyramid

		Burial 2			Burial 6			Burial 3		Burial 5			Total		
		P	S	MNI	P	S	MNI	P	S	P	S	MNI	P	S	MNI	%MNI
Aves																
Aquila chrysaetos	Golden eagle	9	—	9	9	9	18		—	1	—	1	19	9	28	15
Bubo virginianus	Great horned owl	—	2	2	—	—	—		—	—	—	—	0	2	2	1
Buteo sp.	Hawk	—	3	3	—	—	—		1	—	1	1	0	5	5	3
B. magnirostris	Roadside hawk	—	—	—	—	2	2		—	—	1	1	0	2	2	1
B. jamaicensis	Red-tailed hawk	—	1	1	—	—	—		1	—	—	—	0	1	1	1
Colinus virginianus	Bobwhite quail	—	—	—	—	2	2		—	—	—	—	0	2	2	1
Columbidae	Dove/pigeon	—	—	—	—	—	—		—	—	3	3	0	3	3	2
Columbina inca	Inca dove	—	—	—	—	1	1		—	—	—	—	0	1	1	1
Corvus corax	Common raven	—	2	2	—	—	—		—	1	1	1	1	2	3	2
Falco mexicanus	Prairie falcon	—	1	1	—	—	—		—	—	—	—	0	1	1	1
UnID Bird		—	2	2	—	3	3		1	—	—	—	0	6	6	3
Mammalia																
Ateles geoffroyi	Spider monkey	—	—	—	—	—	—		—	—	1	1	0	1	1	1
Canis sp.	Canid	—	—	—	—	—	—		—	—	1	1	0	1	1	1
C. lupus baileyi	Mexican wolf	1	—	1	1	7	8	17 or 18*	1	1	2	3	26	29	15
C. latrans	Coyote	—	—	—	—	2	2		—	—	—	—	0	2	2	1

(*continued*)

TABLE 3.1
Continued

		Burial 2			Burial 6			Burial 3		Burial 5			Total			
		P	S	MNI	P	S	MNI	P	S	P	S	MNI	P	S	MNI	%MNI
Felidae	Feline	—	3	3	1	—	1	—	—	—	3	3	1	6	7	4
Cf. Panthera onca	Jaguar	—	—	—	1	5	6	—	—	—	2	2	1	7	8	4
Puma concolor	Puma	2	1	3	3	4	7	1	8	—	10	11	6	23	29	14
Leporid	Rabbit/hares	—	1	1	—	—	—	—	—	—	—	—	0	1	1	1
Lepus sp.	Hare	—	2	2	—	—	—	—	—	—	1	1	0	3	3	2
Sylvilagus sp.	Cottontail	—	3	3	—	1	1	—	—	—	—	—	0	4	4	2
S. audubonii	Desert cottontail	—	1	1	—	3	3	—	—	—	—	—	0	4	4	2
S. floridannus	Eastern cottontail	—	1	1	—	1	1	—	—	—	—	—	0	2	2	1
Microtus mexicanus	Mexican vole	—	1	1	—	—	—	—	—	—	—	—	0	1	1	1
Peromyscus sp.	Deer mouse	—	—	—	—	1	1	—	—	—	1	1	0	1	1	1
P. maniculatus	Deer mouse	—	—	—	—	1	1	—	—	—	3	3	0	3	3	2
Sciurus aureogaster	Mexican gray squirrel	—	—	—	—	1	1	—	—	—	—	—	0	1	1	1
UNID Mammal		—	1	1	—	2	2	—	—	—	—	—	0	3	3	2
Amphibia/Reptilia													0	0		
Crotalus sp.	Rattlesnake	6	—	6	18	—	18	—	—	9	—	9	33	0	33	18
Anura/Lacertilia	Frog/lizard	—	—	—	—	—	—	—	—	—	1	1	0	1	1	1
TOTAL		18	25	43	33	41	74	13	29	29	42	64	124	188			

MNI: minimum number of individuals; P: primary burial; S: secondary burial.
*Totals are calculated based on MNI of 18 wolves.

at Teotihuacan (five primary agents), later Aztec dedicatory caches with mega diversity of over 250 local and foreign species attest to the Aztec Empire's long arm traversing incredibly diverse ecosystems (López Luján et al. 2012, 2014; López Luján and Matos Moctezuma 2022; Polaco 1991). Spanish conquistadors marveled at how Moctezuma's "House of Beasts" and aviary specialized in captive rearing of not only the apex carnivores like those found at Teotihuacan but also exotic marine, freshwater, and tropical species, all curiosities to newly arrived soldiers from the Old World (Blanco Padilla, Pérez Roldán, et al. 2009; Díaz del Castillo 2003; Elizalde Mendez 2017, 2022; Nicholson 1955). In contrast, the Teotihuacan state consistently assembled the same faunal actors as state symbols. These protagonists in ritualized performances are the exact figures lavishly imprinted in the mural paintings and stone sculptures that are the hallmarks of Teotihuacan art (Berrin 1988; Fuente 1995a; Miller 1973). They are portrayed amid acts of ritualized violence, hunting and consuming victims, marching in military regalia, and processing along the walls city-wide.

As iterated in Chapter 1, I find merit in distinguishing physical traces of human–animal interactions materialized by their corporeal animal forms from encounters with the animal's representation in the visual art of Teotihuacan. I explain the contextual and spatial distribution of the two material expressions of human–animal encounters for each sacred actor: the restricted access to corporeal animal forms reserved for stately functions versus the iconographic abundance of their imagery throughout the city and beyond. This latter pattern is particularly relevant in the discussion of rulership at Teotihuacan, as the body of known state art—famous for its conspicuous absence of explicitly denoted ruling figures and indeed any indication that conventional forms of ruling office existed—has been a significant basis for challenging autocratic models. Instead, apex predators stand in as protagonists in acts of state militarism, ritual procession, and sacrifice across Teotihuacan and beyond. In a dynamic piece, likely from the Technantitla apartment complex, a feathered feline whose speech scrolls are replete with precious flowers and water droplets marches in decadent military regalia, menacing flames emanating from sharp protruding claws (Pasztory 1988: Plate 32) (Figure 3.1). Prominent feline soldiers are featured among Teotihuacan "arrival" scenes in the Maya region. They were direct delegates of the Teotihuacan state and imposed major disruptions in local Maya sociopolitics.

Felids (Felidae): Jaguars and Pumas

From Formative Olmec cave art (c. 1200–400 BCE) lavishly displaying lords with menacing felid fangs emerging from the underworld cave to Aztec-period

60 ANIMAL MATTER

FIGURE 3.1
Feathered feline mural fragment, 500–550 CE, earthen aggregate, stucco, and mineral pigments, 26 × 40 in (67.5 × 102 cm). Fine Arts Museums of San Francisco, bequest of Harald J. Wagner, 1985.104.6. Photograph: Randy Dodson. © Fine Arts Museums of San Francisco.

(1300–1521 CE) depictions of brave jaguar warriors marching to battle that led a war-driven empire to military success, felid symbolism has been a potent emblem of Mesoamerican iconography across time and space (Coe 1972; Grove 1972; Saunders 1989). While space limitations prohibit a comprehensive discussion of the variance across ethnographic and archaeological cases of felid use (see Benson 1972; Furst 1968; Olivier 2016; Saunders 1989; Sugiyama et al. 2019), I want to emphasize their quintessential position as a pan-Mesoamerican symbol of power and authority. Their intricate and well-established association with power made them appropriate delegates of the Teotihuacan state.

Several felid species reside in Mexico: the jaguar (*Panthera onca*), the puma (*Puma concolor*), the jaguarundi (*Felis yogouaroundi*), the margay (*Leopardus wiedii*), the bobcat (*Lynx rufus*), and the ocelot (*Leopardus pardalis*). So far, the puma and jaguar are the only two felids chosen as central participants in stately dedications at Teotihuacan. As the apex predator, its size, cunning hunting ability, and regal characteristics are all emphasized in Mesoamerican mythology and iconography.

Jaguars, the most prominent and strongest felines in the Americas (1.57–2.41 m long), are known to kill and move prey heavier and larger than themselves. Their unique pelts, usually formed by black rosettes over an orange-yellow or tan background, are key phenotypic characteristics that help distinguish jaguars from the solid cinnamon/reddish brown coat of the puma in Pre-Columbian art. Jaguars mostly prowl at night, and their unique adult pelage resembling the starry sky explains their close association with the nocturnal underworld. The brilliant coat of the puma, almost blinding from its solar reflection, is regarded as a dual counterpart representing the diurnal sun (Sugiyama 2016). As I explain later, puma/jaguar cub pelage significantly differs from adults as the majority of the sacrificed individuals were young, with jaguar cub pelage heavily marked with black spherical spots separated by a yellow netted design and puma cubs having black spots distinct from the iconic golden sheen (Figure 3.2).

Jaguars possess light-gathering cells (*tapetum lucidum*) in their pupils for nocturnal vision (Saunders 1990). Their effervescent mirror-like eyes can be spotted in the dark underworld, prowling for prey. A jaguar skull bearing golden pyrite mirrors as its eyes, discovered at the Maya site of Kaminaljuyu, materially illustrates this feature unique to felid vision (Miller and Taube 1993: 102). The Aztec deity Tezcatlipoca (Lord of the Smoking Mirror) manifested his reflective jaguar-like foresight that was "omnipotent, omniscient and omnipresent" (Saunders 1990: 167), wielding his all-seeing mirror to gaze into people's souls (Olivier 2004). Though pumas avoid contact with water, jaguars are excellent swimmers, reiterating their connection to the watery underworld.

Ethnohistoric and ethnographic data concur with the regal, powerful, and prestigious association of jaguars, regarded as masters of the animals, standing at the highest order of *nagual* (spiritual animal companion) (Gossen 1975: 452). High elites, shamans, warriors, and rulers throughout Mesoamerica drew on felids to legitimize their domain, negotiate the agricultural cycle, and bring fertility and abundance to their reign. Jaguars controlled vital life sources, most notably water. Young males from Acatlán, Guerrero, secure agricultural success by engaging in ceremonial combat, wearing elaborate jaguar masks and costumes and spilling their blood in the petition for rain (Saunders 1989: 162).

Jaguar body parts, especially the skin, canines, paws, and ears, proclaimed direct affinity with this powerful beast. Shamans, priests, rulers, warriors, and even deities are depicted as jaguars or adorned with jaguar accouterments. The military selected the bravest Aztec warriors to join the *quauhtli-ocelot* (eagle-jaguar) order. In battle, they wore elaborate jaguar and eagle regalia that instilled bravery, cunningness, and foresight in their bearers (Saunders 1994: 108; Seler 2004: 33). Similarly, ornaments made of jaguar pelts, bone, and teeth are essential implements for shamanistic vision quests. At the Maya site of Copan, a total of sixteen jaguars and pumas (sacrificed and secondary corporeal forms) were dedicated to each of the sixteen kings, endorsing the dynastic record on Altar Q placed above the offering

FIGURE 3.2
Felid cub pelage patterns: (a) jaguar (*Panthera onca*) and (b) puma (*Puma concolor*). Photo credits: (a) "One of the Jaguar Cubs," photograph: Becker 1999; CC BY 2.0; (b) "Puma Cub Looking a Bit Afraid," photograph: Tambako the Jaguar; CC BY-ND 2.0.

cache (Sugiyama et al. 2019). Tangible corporeal animal forms were embodiments of specific deities, drew social affinities, obtained animistic qualities, and defined their position within the cosmos.

Puma and jaguar iconography at Teotihuacan displayed felids as main protagonists, marching in military regalia and conducting acts of sacrifice. Here, too, felids likely stood at the pinnacle of the animal hierarchy as the master of animals, as principal icons of power and ritual violence. They participated in Teotihuacan's sovereignty formations elaborately framing public and private spaces in mural, sculptural, and portable forms. Teotihuacan murals depict naturalistic rendering of jaguars (like "Mythological Animals") (Fuente 1995b: Plate 1) and pumas ("Gran Puma" on platform 16, mural 2) (Fuente 1995c: Figure 7.1), as well as anthropomorphic depictions.

Felid corporeal forms were integrated into human costumes, as can be observed by the large felid helmets adorning two individuals performing seed scattering on the Teopancazco mural. Chimeric characteristics are common. Serpentine bifurcated tongues protruding from gnarling feline heads that may convey the feline war serpent (Cabrera Castro 1998; Taube 2012) are rendered in mural and ceramic forms (discussed further in Chapter 7).

Perhaps the flamboyant netted jaguar war serpent devouring a human heart (Figure 3.3a) is referencing the jaguar/serpent's aquatic attributes, but specifically indexing the netted pelage characteristic of jaguar cubs (Figure 3.2a). As all the jaguars found zooarchaeologically are juveniles, local artisans likely encountered live jaguars with netted pelage. The presence of spotted and netted jaguars in Teotihuacan art implies age was potentially a socially relevant category. The depiction of the felid ingesting a trilobed object is an iconographic trope repeated on the Sun Pyramid façade and may allude to heart sacrifice and consumption (Figure 3.3b). Interestingly, this scene of felids in the midst of heart sacrifice is replicated in later Epiclassic (600–900 CE) illustrations at the Highland Mexican site of Tula and the lowland Maya site of Chichen Itza. Sarabia and Núñez (2017) draw parallels between the puma balustrades adorning the principal façade of the Sun Pyramid to the Feathered Serpent sculptures decorating the FSP, suggesting felids were likewise closely associated with the Teotihuacan state. The puma balustrades and their corporeal animal forms in Offering 2 (N. Sugiyama et al. 2013) strengthen the Sun Pyramid's long-held solar association.

Zooarchaeological and Biological Considerations

Compared to the distribution of puma and jaguar iconography, their limited distribution in the zooarchaeological record at Teotihuacan indicates that felid corporeal forms were reserved for specific contexts, with the majority found only within the

64 ANIMAL MATTER

(a)

(b)

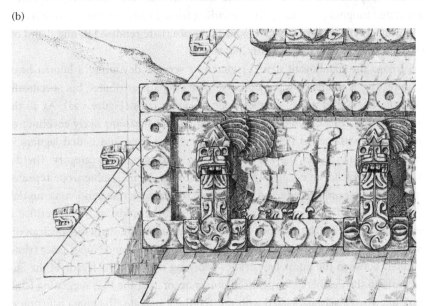

FIGURE 3.3
Jaguar and puma iconography at Teotihuacan: (a) netted-jaguar warrior from Atetelco (Photograph: A. Texis), (b) hypothetical reconstruction of the sculptures on the Sun Pyramid's adosada platform. Taken with permission from Sarabia González and Núñez Rendón (2017: Fig 7.6). Drawing by Victor Álvarez and Alejandro Sarabia González.

monuments. The PTQ recovered three pumas represented by one deciduous tooth, one semi-complete individual, and one cranium in the nucleus of the FSP (Álvarez and Ocaña 1993). Inside the Sun Pyramid's Offering 2, the skull and phalanges of a puma were assembled alongside additional ritual objects (N. Sugiyama et al. 2013). Only an isolated puma bone/tooth was identified at the Teopancazco apartment complex (Rodríguez Galicia 2006).

As jaguars are not local to the semiarid highlands of Central Mexico, the discovery of primary and secondary remains in the Moon Pyramid caches is notable. Outside the pyramids, there is only one instance of a canine from the Oztoyohualco apartment compound (Valadez Azúa 1992). Jaguars are primarily distributed in the tropical lowland region, though they extend along the Sierra Madre Occidental into Northern Mexico (Chihuahua and Sonora) and are even reported in Nogales, Arizona (Hall 1981: 1037). While jaguars were foreign to Teotihuacan, their geographic source could not be determined. Conversely, pumas are widely distributed throughout North and South America (Currier 1983; Rosa and Nocke 2000) and would have been available in the Teotihuacan Valley.

Isolated jaguarundi and lynx bones in Merchant's barrio and Teopancazco compounds respectively are noteworthy but rare finds at Teotihuacan (Rodríguez Galicia 2006; Starbuck 1975). The lack of jaguar and puma elements from other contexts at Teotihuacan is staggering, considering their prominence in the iconography. I caution, however, that reaching species-level identification with felid post-crania is extremely difficult. The subadult and juvenile-dominated assemblage at the Moon Pyramid prohibited using body size as a primary identifier. Instead, I relied on a mixture of morphometric characteristics on the head, dentition, and feet following pertinent literature (Isidro Luna 2007; Montserrat Morales-Mejía et al. 2010; Sugiyama et al. 2019).

Native classificatory systems pay close attention to the physical characteristics of the animal in question, such as their phenotypic features, behavioral traits, and environmental connotations (Hunn 1982). Specific renderings of netted jaguars, for example, may refer to certain ages that were particularly relevant to jaguar social positionality. Biological factors relevant for species designation, parameters used for age and sex, and behavioral traits all contribute to interpreting the physicality of the ritualization process of the animal during its acquisition, management/manipulation, and deposition.

Birth season and other biological characteristics of jaguar/puma cubs helped calculate seasonality and understand kill-off patterns. Jaguar cub birth patterns vary by location and circumstance (in captivity, recorded year-round) but are usually reported from July to September, with litters ranging between one and four cubs in Mexico (Seymour 1989: 3). They reach sexual maturity by two to three years among females and between three to four years for males. Jaguar cubs may continue to suckle for five to six months, staying with the mother for about one-and-a-half to two years before becoming solitary (Rosa and Nocke 2000: 32).

Most puma births are distributed over a much wider span, between April and September, and can occur year-round with litters between one to six cubs (average of two) spaced every two to three years (Currier 1983: 3). At birth, puma cubs weigh around 8–16 ounces and wean for four to five weeks or longer. Their coats at birth are spotted (Figure 3.2b), the dark brown spheres begin to fade at twelve to fourteen weeks, and by one year of age, are barely discernable, resuming their characteristic pure golden sheen. As pumas are rendered without spots, it seems contrary to netted jaguars, young or adult pumas are depicted in Teotihuacan art. The young usually travel with their mother for one-and-a-half to two years. At two to four years, pumas reach sexual maturity and full body size (Currier 1983).

Age determination relied on published dental eruption and wear sequences for puma (Currier 1983; Gay and Best 1996) and jaguars (Rabinowitz and Nottingham 1986; Stehlik 1971). Bone fusion and relative body size were also helpful, especially because abnormal wear patterns due to captivity. Once felids reach adult stature, morphometric traits can help designate sex (Currier 1983: 3). However, as most felid skeletons represent juveniles and subadults, many remain unsexed.

Both pumas and jaguars are highly territorial solitary predators, only coming together for copulation. Home ranges vary significantly between jaguars and pumas but also within a species based on seasonality, environment, prey availability, and other intrinsic factors (age, sex, body size, etc.). Lower estimates of jaguars extend between 25–38 km^2 for females and 50–76 km^2 for males (Rabinowitz and Nottingham 1986), while upper estimates of pumas reach between 723 km^2 (males) and 541 km^2 (females) (Grigione et al. 2002).

Due to their territorial overlap, pumas and jaguars are direct competitors and retain a sympatric relationship. As hyperspecialized carnivores, an immense amount of meat protein was required to sustain in captivity. Jaguars enjoy feasting on terrestrial mammals over 1 kg in body mass (mainly peccaries, capybaras, pacas, agoutis, armadillos, caimans, and turtles) and consume an average of 1.2–1.4 kg a day (Emmons 1987: 277; Seymour 1989: 4). Pumas are opportunistic hunters that prefer deer (contribute up to 50%–90% of their diet), and require similar meat yields (Currier 1983; Leopold 1972: 480).

Given their highly territorial behavior, obtaining multiple live felids for sacrifice would entail logistical hardships. Felids above two years old needed to be acquired from disparate home ranges, and the proximity of various felids would have created hostile conditions for management. Provisioning these highly specialized carnivores adds significant costs, as does coordinating their transport. These biological features explain the motivations and restrictions to acquire, manage, and sacrifice these menacing predators. They can also be considered "thing power" (sensu

Bennett 2010) of animal corporalities that should be evaluated when interpreting their social positionalities.

Canids (Canidae): Wolves and Coyotes

The Moon Pyramid's faunal assemblage included three canid species: the Mexican wolf (*Canis lupus baileyi*), the coyote (*Canis latrans*), and possibly a wolf-dog hybrid (*Canis lupus-familiaris*). Mesoamerica's premier domesticate, the dog, featured prominently in household rites and as foodstuff but was primarily excluded from state spectacles. Wild versus domestic canids were symbolically and functionally distinct, and the abundance of wolves (not coyotes) in the dedicatory caches suggests the Teotihuacan state selected the wolf as a primary state agent. This is why I argue that the canids figured in Teotihuacan art, referred to as coyotes (Millon 1988b), were wolves. Previous interpretations were likely influenced by the lack of wolves in the Teotihuacan Valley during historical periods, the proliferation of coyote imagery and myth among the Aztecs, and cultural favoritism of coyotes as New World curiosities by Europeans.

Historical documents record that wolf populations were dramatically compromised after the Spanish conquest due to their appetite for domestic livestock. By the time Gamio (1922: 42–49) recorded local species in the Teotihuacan Valley, wolves were no longer locally available. Presently, the endangered Mexican wolf (Department of the Interior 2015) is only reported in the Sierra Madre Occidental, including the arid mountains of western Coahuila and eastern Chihuahua, and San Luis Potosí (Leopold 1972: 401). However, wolves once roamed the Sierra Madre mountain range and adjoining tableland region of Western Mexico through southeast Arizona, southwest New Mexico, West Texas, and southward into Central Mexico (State of Mexico, Puebla, and Tlaxcala) (Heffelfinger et al. 2017; Young and Goldman 1944). They would have been locally abundant during the Teotihuacan occupation. Coyote populations thrived as their direct competitors diminished (Hidalgo Mihart et al. 2004: 2027).

Colonial sources describe that the Aztecs regarded coyotes as astute, revengeful, but thankful, expressing sexual desires. As the feather workers' patron deity, coyotes loved music, dancing, and pleasure (Aguilera 1985: 18; Millon 1988b: 208). The coyote has direct associations with predating on deer, curing the dead, sexual intercourse, and agricultural yield. Various Uto-Aztecan tribes called the coyote an "elder brother" of humankind and described him as a cultural hero identified as the morning star (Kelley 1955: 397). While some identify distinguished warriors who achieved high rank in battle as coyote warriors known as "*caballero pardos*" (Millon 1988b: 208), Blanco and colleagues (2007) have argued that these militants wore wolf regalia. Interestingly, the zooarchaeological evidence from the Templo Mayor has featured wolves more prominently than coyotes, with evidence of captivity and decadent adornment, indicating they were central persons in Aztec imperial formations (Chávez Balderas et al. 2022; López Luján et al. 2022). However, ethnographic and ethnohistoric sources portray coyotes and wolves prominently often conflating the two species in a similar light. For example, Kelley (1955) describes the fascinating parallel between the Uto-Aztecan coyote symbolism and Huichol myths from northern Mexico.

The Huichol Indians describe the wolf as a vengeful trickster with sexual implications. Wolves are ancestor deities and referred to as "elder brothers" (*matzimama*), a kinship metaphysically expressed through mythological narratives of interbreeding and marriage (Fikes 1985: 268–268; Zingg 2004: 68–75). As master predators who taught man the art of hunting peyote and deer, wolves are custodians of ecological order (Fikes 1985: 253). They are revered social carnivores who astutely execute a hierarchically organized pack-hunting strategy. Shamanic wolf transformations are only attainable by specific family lineages. Wolf shamans master three abilities through reaching this uppermost heightened stage: hunting deer, healing, and control of rain (Fikes 1985: 249). Wolves support Huichol communities obtain the necessary blood from their hunt to feed the ancestor deities who, in turn, provide them with rain and maize (Valadez 1996).

In both Aztec and Huichol cosmology, coyotes or wolves are respected for controlling three main factors: fertility (through their sexuality), subsistence (through their association with the deer), and water (for manipulating agriculture, particularly maize). In both cases, humans interact with and transform into these beings, either through becoming warriors or through shamanistic transformations. Given the apparent biases against wolves and the conflated ethnographic/ethnohistoric sources, I rely on zooarchaeological and biological data to interpret canid iconography at Teotihuacan.

Canids are also central protagonists in Teotihuacan art. In some cases, quadrupedal canids roam along the room blocks in acts of ritualized violence (hunting or holding sacrificial knives), and in others, they walk upright in military uniform. Lacking a deciphered writing system, we cannot rely on conventional linguistic methods to define folk canid classification systems at Teotihuacan. Instead, we must decipher the iconographic indexes artists use to specify taxa.

Dog iconography is distinguishable by form and material type. Clara Millon (1973: 308) differentiates wild canids shown with body fur from spotted domestic dogs surrounded by an exceptionally thick, heavy outline. Dogs tend to be rendered as peripheral and still naturalistic figures, appearing more abundantly in figurines and ceramics but rarely in mural or sculptural art. Wild canids are usually in active anthropomorphic poses as main protagonists in murals, stone sculptures, and ceramic artifacts. It is challenging to distinguish between the two wild species: the wolf and the coyote.

Deciphering if the Teotihuacan classification system differentiated between wolves and coyotes would require identifying social and biological attributes used as taxonomic indices. For example, the "Coyotes and Deer" mural (Figure 3.4) depicts two canids devouring a deer. Previously, the bristling hair on necks and backs (as an act of piloerection) and the likelihood that it would take a pair of coyotes to attack larger mammals justified their identification as coyotes (Millon 1988c). However, neither attribute is exclusive to coyote behavior; in fact, they are more characteristic of wolves.

The two wild canids practice distinct social structures and prey choices. Coyotes usually live alone or in pairs and sometimes even hunt in larger groups, but unlike wolves, they never form packs (Gompper 2002: 21; Leopold 1972: 397). Due to their smaller size, coyotes often only approach small mammals and young or injured/sick large mammals and often scavenge the remains of larger wolf killings. Even though coyotes are traditionally associated with deer killings, they usually only prey on fawns and weakened individuals (Leopold 1972: 398).

In contrast, wolves' complex social organization makes them appropriate parallels to human groups. They live in varying pack sizes year-round, exhibit pair bonding, have extended family clans, and have strict leadership hierarchies (Fritts et al. 2003; Mech and Boitani 2003). Wolves commonly hunt in pairs or packs; adult white-tailed deer are the prime and favored prey.

Differentiating between coyotes and wolves is challenging because the locally available subspecies, the Mexican wolf, is among the smallest gray wolf subspecies in the Americas. Although still larger than coyotes, their coat color is very similar as fur coloration is heavily influenced by extrinsic factors like climate and alimentation (Young and Goldman 1944: 59). The Mexican wolf is distinguished by its large, broad nose and paws, rounded ears, darker highlights along the back, ends of their ears, and tail, and its mane-like longer fur along the shoulders and anterior part of the back (Figure 3.5a). In comparison, coyotes have a more gracile build and distinct pointed, long, and forward-facing ears, small, slender noses, and delicate feet (Jackson 1951) (Figure 3.5b). These subtle details that biologists use to arrive at a species designation help interpret the mural paintings at Teotihuacan (Sugiyama and Sugiyama 2007).

A canid depicted in profile at the Atetelco complex is marching in procession with a back mirror, likely representing a *Tezcacuitlapilli* (lower back disk/mirrors) used by warriors. Close by, at the Patio Blanco, Portico 2 (Cabrera Castro 2006a: Plate 9), a wild canid marches consuming trilobed hearts in acts of heart sacrifice like the felid mentioned earlier (Figure 3.6a). Several details, such as its protruding paws with impressive claws, exaggerated rounded ears with a black point on end, a large

FIGURE 3.4
"Coyotes and Deer" mural curated at the De Young Fine Arts Museum of San Francisco. Photograph: N. Sugiyama.

(a)

(b)

FIGURE 3.5
(a) Mexican Grey Wolf, *Canis lupus baileyi* (Carlos Galindo Leal/CONABIO CGL3360); and (b) coyote, *Canis latrans* (Miguel Ángel Sicilia Manzo/CONABIO MASM00799).

(a)

(b)

FIGURE 3.6
Canid imagery: (a) image of canid from Atetelco compound (photograph: A. Texis); (b) Aztec coyote warrior, from Sahagún S.XVI: fol.73r. Redrawn by N. Sugiyama.

rounded snout and nose, a long black-tipped tail, and explicit delimitation of a mane, are phenotypic characteristics specific to wolves.

Later Aztec/Colonial depictions of canids clearly labeled as coyotes are strikingly different. Figure 3.6b illustrates a coyote warrior with a very pointed and narrow snout, small ears, and uniform coat color, with little emphasis on the claws/paws. Stylistic conventions in art form from these two culturally distinct images aside, each artist intentionally exaggerates the relevant phenotypic attributes used for taxonomic identification.

The wild canids depicted in Teotihuacan mural art likely represented the Mexican wolf, the exclusive canid species regularly utilized in state-ritualized spectacles. Wolf corporeal animal forms were related to acts of ritualized violence: hunting, sacrifice, and militarism. Because of their cunning ability to hunt deer and as prominent social carnivores, wolves were hunters and warriors par excellence. They march the walls of Teotihuacan in military regalia with elaborate headdresses, carrying a bundle of darts and spear throwers, consuming trilobed hearts. Others roam the walls with sacrificial knives in hand. Wolves performing heart sacrifices were prominent warriors, while fallen war captives were metaphorically conceived as deer, the wolf's favorite prey (Millon 1988c) (Figure 3.4). Like *caballeros pardos* during later Aztec periods, wolves at Teotihuacan probably constituted a military sector.

Zooarchaeological and Biological Considerations

Like the felids, there is an incongruity between the prominence of wolves in mural art and the limited distribution of canid corporeal animal forms. Wolf remains were primarily restricted to state-level rituals, whereas domestic dog assemblages were eminent in nonritual refuse or household burials. Residential units hosted an MNI of 326 dogs (*Canis familiaris*), accounting for 11% of the Teotihuacan faunal assemblage (Sugiyama et al. 2017). The dog is the only species regularly intentionally buried (alone or accompanying human burials) in various residential contexts.[1] Throughout Mesoamerica, dogs are considered guides to the afterlife (Aguilera 1985: 21). Man's best friend held an intimate function in Teotihuacan's residential burial practices. However, dogs are mostly absent from dedicatory offerings at the ceremonial core during the Teotihuacan occupation (see Valadez Azúa and

---

[1] Rabbit skeletons were found accompanying burials at Oztoyohualco apartment compound (Valadez Azúa 1993), and isotopic work showed they were raised in this compound (Somerville et al. 2016). But this was a feature unique to this specialized rabbit-producing compound.

Rodríguez Galicia 2009 for post-Teotihuacan dog burials found in caves). They are also not depicted as abundantly in public art. The only exception is the canid maxillary pendant from the FSP, which intermixed dog bones. Coyote remains were conspicuously scarce in residential (MNI 2) and stately (MNI 2) contexts.

The low frequency of wolf remains from residential areas (MNI 2) contrasts sharply with their abundance within ritual offerings at the ceremonial core (Rodríguez Galicia 2006; Starbuck 1975). All three pyramids encompassed wolf corporeal animal forms. I have already described canid maxillary pendants adorning a sacrificed captive within the FSP (Chapter 2) (Figure 3.7), and in Burial 14 a wolf cranium and mandible were also uncovered (Álvarez and Ocaña 1993). A wolf skull placed in the Sun Pyramid's Offering 2 provides an additional data point to the growing evidence of wolves as seminal corporeal animal forms reserved for state rituals (N. Sugiyama et al. 2013).

Canid species identification is notoriously tricky. Based on morphometric traits defined in the literature (Blanco Padilla, Rodríguez Galicia, et al. 2009; Rodríguez Galicia 2000) the majority of the remains from the Moon Pyramid were wolves ($n = 29$), with only one coyote skull. Valadez Azúa and Rodríguez Galicia identified three of these individuals (two skulls and one primary burial) as a dog-wolf hybrid. As the teeth measurements of the third and fourth premolars still fit within wolf

FIGURE 3.7
Canid maxillary pendant from the Feathered Serpent Pyramid. Photograph: N. Sugiyama.

values, I have kept their species designation as tentative wolves in hopes to apply ancient DNA (aDNA) analysis in the future.

In the wild, wolves usually mate in late winter, producing cubs during the spring around March (Leopold 1972: 403). However, as observed by their domestic counterpart, prey availability is a decisive factor for reproduction, and wolves are known to breed year-round. Therefore, canids are less reliable for seasonality calculations. Like the felids, tooth eruption, wear, and bone fusion were used to determine age, while several metric and nonmetric characteristics helped determine sex (Blanco Padilla, Rodríguez Galicia, et al. 2009).

Golden Eagles (*Aquila chrysaetos*)

Indigenous Nahua communities of Central Mexico refer to sunrise as *cuauhtlehuanitl* (ascending eagle) and sunset as *cuauhtemoc* (descending eagle). For them, the solar pathway follows the flight of this raptor, who carries the radiating sun across the sky (Miller and Taube 1993: 82–83). A dominant predator of the upper world, these solar raptors were used as military, ritual, and stately paraphernalia to embody strength, bravery, and power (Aguilera 1985; Careta 2001; McKusick 2001). Today, the golden eagle graces the Mexican national flag, handsomely gliding with its outstretched wings, with talons grasping a serpent as it lands on a nopal cactus. This scene commemorates the legendary founding of the Aztec capital, Tenochtitlan. Like their jaguar counterparts, eagle warriors occupied one of the highest military orders and ventured into battle dressed in eagle regalia (Miller and Taube 1993: 183).

Not only were eagle corporeal animal forms used in ritual spectacles, but colonial sources document Aztec bird-rearing practices. The Spanish conquistador Bernal Díaz de Castillo (2003: 212) vividly recounts his experience encountering raptors, waterfowl, and tropical birds in this foreign land within the controlled confines of Moctezuma's aviary. At Moctezuma's House of Beasts, he and his comrades were intimidated by the passage of infernal growls and hisses emanating from ferocious carnivorous animals. Díaz del Castillo (2003) marveled at the impressive scale of operation involving dedicated caretakers who fed, placed eggs, and cleaned these New World curiosities (Blanco Padilla, Pérez Roldán, et al. 2009; Nicholson 1955). These animals were managed, raised, and likely even bred in captivity.

Ethnographies from the United States likewise document the ritual keeping of turkeys, eagles, ravens, and macaws for sacrifice. Modern Hopi and Hidatsa boys capture, feed, and raise eagle chicks until they are killed in sacrificial rites (Fewkes 1900; Lévi-Strauss 1966: 48–51; McKusick 2001). A series of photographs illustrates a tethered eagle perched on the rooftop of a Hopi home (McKusick

2001: Figure 25). After sacrifice, its feathers were plucked (particularly tail feathers) postmortem. These raptors were usually suffocated, and depending on the sex, a doll or bow was placed in front of the raptor buried in a designated eagle cemetery. One informant mentioned that families maintained up to seventeen captive eagles (McKusick 2001).

At the northern Mexican site of Paquime, archaeologists identified bird enclosures that would have housed birds captured, imported, bred, and raised during the twelfth–fifteenth century CE (Di Peso et al. 1974). Macaws, turkeys, hawks, and other birds were penned for feather extraction and sacrifice (Hargrave 1970; Hill 2000; McKusick 2001). The high frequency of pathologies, including diseases and injuries due to malnutrition, vitamin D deficiency, and fractured bones on the imported scarlet macaws, confirm an active breeding program in operation (Di Peso et al. 1974). Isotope work on this population further signaled a high degree of localized avian breeding and artificial feeding of C_4 (likely maize) products during captivity accompanied live importation of these colorful birds (Schwartz et al. 2021; Somerville et al. 2010).

Unsurprisingly, mural paintings from Teotihuacan teem with prominent avian forms. However, the species designation of what researchers call the "Teotihuacan bird" is debated. Some highlight their raptor-like attributes to argue that they represent owls (Von Winning 1948) or golden eagles, while others suggest their elaborate plumage resembles quetzals (Aguilera 2002; Miller 1967). I suspect these highly varied avian forms depicted several distinct species. Taxonomic identifications need to be evaluated for each variant, paying close attention to discernable phenotypic characteristics Teotihuacan artists used as referents to the specific bird category or species.

As a case in point, let us examine one of the anthropomorphic avian figures marching in profile with military regalia, each carrying an *atlatl* (spear thrower), a bundle of spears, and a fur element in the Atetelco complex (Figure 3.8a). It may be significant that this individual does not carry a shield with its *atlatl*, which differentiates this bird. Its thick, curved beak and sharp, bare claws are defining characteristics of a raptor's piercing weapons. Eagles, like most raptors, have prominent eye ridges and feathers that extend above and in front of the eyes that protect them, giving them an eyebrow-like appearance visible in this mural painting (Figure 3.8b). Four slightly rounded broad tail feathers are semispread. Horizontal lines along these tail feathers may represent two to three faint shades of brown waves that make up the eagle's tail. Small stubby fringes just above the claws may depict feathered tarsi, characteristic of golden eagles (Howell and Webb 1995: 205–206). Depicted in parallel form to the canid warrior image from the same compound (Cabrera Castro 2006a: Figure 18.2), it is likely that eagles also referenced a military order at Teotihuacan.

FIGURE 3.8
(a) Raptor warrior mural from Atetelco (photograph: N. Sugiyama); (b) tethered golden eagle (Carlos Galindo Leal/CONABIO CGL3175 *Aquila chrysaetos*); (c) bird mural from Tetitla (Photograph: N. Sugiyama); and (d) drawing of an owl in flight (drawing: R. Medina 2023).

In contrast, the frontal image in Figure 3.8c may represent an owl. It has distinctly large forward-facing rounded eyes illustrating a species with binocular vision, flattened face, large, broad, expanded wings, and highly flared tail feathers characteristic of owls in flight (Figure 3.8d). Two large frontal-facing feathered claws dangle during flight. Eagles, by comparison, have bare skin, and usually, a third claw is slightly visible during flight. Some images have very distinct rings on their face, with upright feathers surrounding the face and a triangular beak. Many frontal figures have their wings extended in a descending pose as if ready to catch their prey. Von Winning (1948) draws a connection between depictions of owls and weapons, often an *atlatl* and shield, that may be referencing the owls' close association with night, darkness, and death. The possibility that some of these avian forms, specifically those depicted with a spear-thrower and usually accompanied by a shield, reference a specific historical figure named "spear-thrower owl" (or more recently argued to be of an "eagle-striker") (Stuart, 2024) in the Maya hieroglyphic texts (Nielsen and Helmke 2008; Stuart 2000) is an interesting possibility that is beyond the scope of this brief description of the diversity in avian forms present at Teotihuacan. While there are reports of eagle and owl remains in the zooarchaeological record, there are no published cases of quetzals (Sugiyama et al. 2017). Thus, some avian representations, especially those in profile wearing ritual/military regalia, likely portrayed golden eagles, while other raptors (like the owl) may have also been depicted. These solar raptors were closely associated with military might.

Zooarchaeological and Biological Considerations

Besides abundant samples from the Moon Pyramid, PPS reported a complete golden eagle in the Sun Pyramid's Offering 2 (N. Sugiyama et al. 2013). The sacrificed eagle bore a pyrite disc representing the sun on its back (Sugiyama 2014, 2023). A complete golden eagle was also discovered sacrificed next to a spider monkey at the Plaza of the Columns (Sugiyama et al. 2022). Beyond these finds, eagle remains are scarce, with mentions of an MNI of 1 in the Teopancazco apartment compound (Rodríguez Galicia 2006) and vertebrae from Burial 14 in the FSP. Again, eagle corporeal animal forms seem to have been reserved for state-ritualized acts.

The low frequency of eagle bones is puzzling, given its local distribution. The golden eagle, *Aquila chrysaetos canadensis*, is distributed from Alaska, Canada, through the western United States, and extends into Central Mexico (Watson 2010: 43). They inhabit arid or semiarid areas, deserts, open grasslands, and even farmlands (Howell and Webb 1995: 206). These raptors form semipermanent pair bonds and maintain vaguely defined expansive home ranges (which vary based on prey availability but range between 12 and 152 km^2) that overlap common hunting grounds (Watson 2010: 92–93). At 79–91.5 cm tall and impressive wingspans reaching 183–213 cm, they were the largest raptors in Central Mexico. Their spectacular undulating display flights are evident and recognizable, making them avatars of the sky realm.

Eagles enjoy a variety of mammalian and avian prey, but leporids (particularly hares) and other small game (squirrels) constitute between 80% and 96% of the eagle's diet and foster an allopathic relationship with leporids (Herron et al. 1985: 46). Eaglets begin to eat on their own after one month in captive settings (Steenberg 1981: 111) by either tearing chunks of meat and bones off of the prey or swallowing whole. Eagle pellet studies found large, relatively unbroken bones with signs of corrosion (scouring, pitting, and thinning), polishing, and staining of the bone (Hockett 1996). These descriptions are consistent with the rabbit/hare bones described in Chapter 4 from the stomachs of these raptors.

Eaglets grow exceptionally rapidly from a hatchling weighing around 100 g to a fully grown bird weighing 3–4 kg in ten to twelve weeks (Watson 2010: 207). They live between twenty and thirty years (Watson 2010: 306) but survive longer in captivity, documented to reach up to forty-six years old (Gordon 1955: 36). Birds, unlike mammals, do not have epiphyseal growth plates, and bone porosity and length are the only indicators of infant and juvenile bones, making age estimates a challenging task for many avian specimens (see, however, McKusick 2001). Biologists usually use plumage for age designations once adult stature is reached. Plumage changes drastically throughout the life of an eagle, beginning with a "pre-pennae" white down for the first twenty-five days and transitioning into feathers with dark contours from twenty-five to fifty days. Its characteristic adult golden color plumage is established only after the fifth or sixth summer when they have completed multiple molts.

Methodological difficulties in aging is the primary cause of underrepresented young birds in the zooarchaeological record. However, when identified, they can be accurately aged. As one to three chick clutches hatch between late April and early May (Watson 2010), the presence of eaglets can indicate captivity, season of occupation, and selection pressures. For example, bones of very young macaws and turkeys alongside abundant eggshell fragments at the site of Paquime were instrumental in arguing that the site was a macaw breeding and trading outpost (Di Peso et al. 1974).

Not only are eagle remains hard to age, but they are also notoriously difficult to sex. Raptors exhibit reverse sexual dimorphism, with females reaching up to 10% larger wing spans and becoming as much as 40%–50% heavier than males (Watson 2010: 33). Many biologists rely on plumage (males have narrow, wavy grayish bands on the tails), behavior patterns, and genetic testing for sex designations (Wheeler

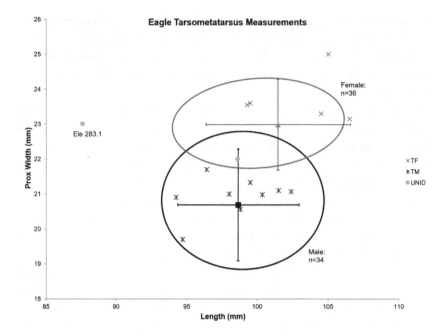

FIGURE 3.9
Eagle tarsometatarsus greatest length and proximal width distribution of Teotihuacan female (TF), male (TM), and unidentified (UNID) specimens plotted against McKusick's (2001) comparative data. 2σ error bars from the centroid (mean), circular outline of distribution for male (black) and female (gray) samples. Outlier E.283.1 is a juvenile.

and Clark 1995: 123–126). Harmata and Montopoli (2013) used a morphometric approach to statistically separate the populations based on head and hallux length. Females during reproductive stages can be confidently identified during medullary bone production (calcium clogging the marrow cavity released during eggshell formation) (Serjeantson 2009). This is seldom reported in the zooarchaeological literature for nondomesticated avifauna, and many sexually diagnostic elements (greatest breath of the cranium and synsacrum) tend to be difficult to find intact in the archaeological record. As females have generally longer and stockier tarsometatarsus, I used the greatest length (GL) to proximal greatest breadth (Bp) ratio (Von Den Drisch 1976: 129) to assign the eagle's sex following McKuisk's (2001) Table 9 (Sugiyama 2014: Table 5.7) (Figure 3.9).

Rattlesnakes (*Crotalus* sp.)

Snakes are associated with fertility, rebirth, and transformation because they shed their skin (Miller and Taube 1993: 149; Stone and Zender 2011: 86). Slithering along the ground, Mesoamerican communities compared their unique body movements to natural features like water and lightning that similarly meander (Seler 2004: 267). These multifaceted characteristics of serpents linked them to the sky, earth, rain, and the underworld (Garza 2001; Taube 1996). Another unique physiology was their detachable joints in the head, an adaptation to enable swallowing their prey whole (Miller and Taube 1993: 149). Maya cultures often illustrated vision serpents' disjointed jaws as passageways for deities/ancestors to emerge from this boundless opening (Miller and Taube 1993: 150; Schlesinger 2001: 269).

Rattlesnakes were called yellow lord (*tecutlacoçauhqui*) in Nahuatl (Sahagún 1963: 76) and were considered the master of snakes. They were associated with water because the acoustics of their rattling tails mimicked trickling water, and the snakes' emergence typically forecasted the arrival of the rainy season. Their trunks are often depicted with repeating symbols of round precious stones, *chalchihuitli*, emphasizing the rattlesnake's aquatic association (Bernal-Garcia 1993). Avian serpent bodies form floating sky bands in Olmec and Maya art, with gouts of water spilling from their mouths (Taube 1996: 92). Both the Aztecs and the Mayas considered these poisonous snakes as lightning thrust from the sky by the rain gods Tlaloc/Chac (López Austin and López Luján 2009: 154; Miller and Taube 1993: 150). In highland Mexico, the rattlesnake played a dominant role as *tecuhtlacozauhqui* (the principal yellow serpent). Many powerful deities like Coatlícue (Serpent Skirt) and Quetzalcoatl (Feathered Serpent) were identified by their rattlesnake attributes (Aguilera 1985: 73). Although the lowland Maya encountered many species of snakes both poisonous (e.g., fer-de-lance) and larger (*Boa constrictor*), the rattlesnake was associated with the mountain deities who dwell in caves and controlled all serpents. Serpents' meat was consumed, their skin was used, and they had curative functions (Aguilera 1985: 73).

Naturalistic rendering of snakes is rare at Teotihuacan, and most serpentine sculptures and murals reference the Feathered Serpent (also known as Quetzalcoatl, Figure 3.10a) (López Austin et al. 1991; Sugiyama 2000). Rattlesnake imagery proliferated in the iconic canon at Teotihuacan despite their scarcity in the zooarchaeological record. Their bodies frame the cityscape as they meander through the facades and along the panels of pyramids and room blocks with their unmistakable rattle-tipped tails (Figure 3.10b). Many chimeric forms integrate serpent features, such as the frontal-facing felids with bifurcated tongues (Kubler 1972; Taube 2012).

As described in Chapter 2, the Feathered Serpent iconography on the FSP façade likely expressed the arrival of enigmatic rulership, with a Primordial Crocodile mounted on its back (Sugiyama 2005) (Figure 2.4). This divine being was so potent that it propagated Mesoamerican iconography and mythology during and even after the collapse of Teotihuacan.

FIGURE 3.10
Rattlesnake imagery: (a) Feathered Serpent and Flowering Trees mural housed at the De Young Museum, and (b) sculpture of rattlesnake tail from the Sun Pyramid Plaza. Photographs: N. Sugiyama.

Zooarchaeological and Biological Considerations

Rattlesnake corporeal forms are scarce at Teotihuacan, with samples identified only at the FSP, Plaza of the Columns, and the Teopancazco apartment compound.[2] Vertebral and cranial elements from an offering cache (MNI 3) (Unidad 100, Cuadroo 87, Layer LXXIII), Burial 14 (MNI 1), and from the fill (MNI 1) were recorded from the FSP (Álvarez and Ocaña 1993). Nine rattlesnakes were reported in Plaza of the Column's Offering D4, where a spider monkey and eagle mentioned earlier were also sacrificed (Sugiyama et al. 2022). Only one individual composed of three vertebrae and one mandibular fragment was identified at the Teopancazco apartment compound (Rodríguez Galicia 2006: 89). Again, this species was primarily found in ritual contexts associated with the state, although the serpent's small bone size means recovery requires flotation and fine screening and their scarcity may be an artifact of screen-size bias.

Several rattlesnake species inhabit the Mexican Basin: the Mexican lancehead rattlesnake (*Crotalus polystictus*), the black tail rattlesnake (*C. molossus*), the Mexican dusky rattlesnake (*C. triseriatus*), the Mexican pigmy rattlesnake (*C. ravus*), and cross banded mountain rattlesnake (*C. transverses*) (Armstrong and Murphy 1979; Ramírez-Bautista et al. 2009). They cover diverse habitats, some along marshes and rocky or tall grasses, temperate pine-oak forests, and mesquite grasslands (*C. polysticutus*), while others prefer high elevations along the mountains (*C. molossus*). Their aggressiveness varies considerably by species and season. For example, the *C. transverses* are particularly non offensive. The *C. polystictus* emerges from hibernation relatively inoffensive in the late spring, resuming an aggressive posture only during the summer months.

While crania and mandibles may help derive species-level identification of the rattlesnakes, most zooarchaeological assemblages only contain ribs and vertebrae that are more abundant and larger than the thin, unfused cranial elements. Unfortunately, ribs are only diagnostic to the Suborder (Serpentes), and the vertebrae could only identify the family and genus (Walker 2003).

Animal Politics at Teotihuacan

Animals are socially differentiated (both heterarchically and hierarchically), just like human societies. Folk zoological classification systems often rely on their observed

---

[2] One rattlesnake was present on surface levels of Oztoyohualco apartment compound (Valadez Azúa 1992: Appendix 2.2), but all surface layers, when indicated, were not included in the MNI counts.

biological/behavioral traits, in terms of dominance/subordination, independence/ dependence, and predator/prey as a direct reflection of their social relationships and interactions among various types of humans (Hunn 1982; Urton 1985). Perhaps these properties of the animals may be considered part of their "vitalities" that contribute to their potential personhood. It follows, then, that defining intra-animal and animal–human interactions within the context of the vitalities of biology, behavior, and ecology is particularly pertinent in reconstructing the social positionality of animals in the past. Localized animal hierarchies can influence animal matter's spatial and temporal distribution in informative ways, providing a potential starting point for exposing ancient animal politics.

In this research, I hypothesize that animal matter was a potent mediator grounded in tradition entangled within a coherent world order and value system at Teotihuacan. Animal matter was highly political; they defined social differences vis-à-vis the collective public, which involved co-participation of animal matter, human communities, and nonhuman persons (like the *altepetl* described in Chapter 2). Animal matter took two forms, each with a separate distribution and experience. The distribution of their skeletal elements shows an explicit monopoly of corporeal animal forms to stately and ritual contexts. Offerings of apex predators were rarely outside the ceremonial core. In fact, except for dogs and rabbits, animals were usually not part of burial and dedicatory contexts at Teotihuacan (Valadez Azúa 1993). Instead, apex predators were prominently displayed as sacrificial victims and offertory paraphernalia (as secondary body-parts) during state dedication ceremonies within the city's ceremonial core.

On the other hand, these same apex predators were broadcasted through their representation across various media (mural, sculptural, and portable art) throughout the city and beyond, encouraging daily encounters with animal matter closely associated with the Teotihuacan state. The imagery along the city's vast public and residential spaces helped enliven the social memories of the legendary ritual spectacles where master animals, the apex predators of the landscape, roamed the city. These visual mnemonic devices reinforced into the social memory of Teotihuacan residents the participation of the apex predators as protagonists of ritualized violence, closely linked to militarism, hunting, and sacrifice.

Felids (jaguars and pumas), wolves, eagles, and rattlesnakes each possess important vitalities relevant to understanding their potential socialities at Teotihuacan. They were considered authorities presiding over other celestial, terrestrial, and chthonic species. Together the jaguar and puma ruled the day and night, their pelage marking their reign over the diurnal and nocturnal world (Sugiyama 2016). Their piercing gaze saw into the maw of the earth that manipulated elements of water and fertility stored deep within the mountains. As warriors prized for their organized hunting capacity, wolves predated on captives (deer) on the battlefield to fuel the city. The Golden Eagle was the bearer of the sun, creating seasonal changes as its pathway marked the transition from the dry to the wet season. The rattlesnake, as an element of the Feathered Serpent, was born at Teotihuacan as an ultimate mediator of state authority who meanders the watery underworld bearing the Primordial Crocodile on its back (Sugiyama 2005). It was a delegate so potent that there were attempts to "kill" it during the Teotihuacan occupation (as observed by the iconoclastic act on the FSP). However, it permeated well beyond the collapse of the city. The Feathered Serpent transcended regional and temporal boundaries as a potent person (often a delegate) across Mesoamerican cultures.

Animal matter facilitated Teotihuacan state personnel (elites, warriors, rulers, etc.) to gain strategic positionality as they engaged in animal politics described in this chapter. The zooarchaeological and isotopic data help reconstruct how corporeal animal forms were transformed into ritualized bodies, to participate in the politics of sovereignty formations.

CHAPTER 4

THE ZOOARCHAEOLOGICAL DATA

BONES ENCODE A TREASURE TROVE of information. The Teotihuacan assemblage is a testimony to the rich interpretive potential obtained from integrating zooarchaeologists from the onset of research design and excavation. The rigorous and contextually situated analytical data made it possible to reconstruct specific idiosyncrasies of the ritual spectacle, allowing me to generate the thick description narrated in Chapter 8. As the general methodological guidelines of a zooarchaeological study are readily available in the literature (Gifford-Gonzalez 2018; Reitz and Wing 2004), in this chapter, I directly apply standard zooarchaeological toolkits such as species abundance, age and sex profiles, element distribution, surface modification, and paleopathology to draw interpretations of ancient human–animal dynamics. Reconstructing the rich osteobiographies of each corporeal animal form as a ritualized body (sensu Bell 1997) helps identify continuity and changes in ritual performances across time and space. I have already iterated how bones/teeth materially embody the physicality of human–animal dynamics. My goal here is to extract from the descriptions of pathologies and tabulations of cutmarks the intimacies and perils of direct human–predator contact, as an eagle handler displaces the tendon controlling the sharp talons for his/her safety, and the artisan struggles to dislodge the pelt along the connection between the cumbersome tangle of small wrist bones and the phalanges. What implications do the patterns in preferences for specific age groups for some species, but not others, convey about their interaction with the Teotihuacanos? The raw zooarchaeological and isotope datasets, described in Chapters 4 and 5, should narrate their stories of how the predators arrived at the city, their experiences during management and captivity, how ritual practitioners manipulated their corporeal forms postmortem, and how they participated in the display, sacrifice, and deposition during their residence at Teotihuacan (Chapter 6).

Animal Matter. Nawa Sugiyama, Oxford University Press. © Oxford University Press 2024.
DOI: 10.1093/9780197653425.003.0004

I conducted the zooarchaeological analysis in collaboration with Oscar Polaco and specialists from the National Institute of Anthropology and History (INAH) (Burials 2, 3, and 5) and Raúl Valadez and his team at the Universidad Nacional Autónoma de México (UNAM) (Burial 6). I consulted modern reference collections at the Biological Institute at the UNAM and the mammalogy collection at the National Museum of Natural History, Smithsonian Institution. Chapter 3 described the standards applied for species, age, and sex designations for each key actor and more details, including coding sheets and raw metric data, are available in Sugiyama (2014: Appendix B–G). Each animal was assigned an "Element" number (E.#) in the field, though later laboratory analysis sometimes required splitting the Element number when multiple individuals were registered under the same number (e.g., E.1381.1, E1381.2) or combining them when the same individual had separate labels (e.g., E.192/189).

Felids

Primary Burials

The jaguar and puma have aroused more fascination, respect, and terror than any other animals in Mesoamerica. Ritual practitioners at Teotihuacan had an intimate knowledge of and acquaintance with these all-mighty predators. Felid corporeal animal forms were the most abundant animal represented in every context in the Moon Pyramid offerings (MNI 44, 22%) (Table 3.1). Felids were interred as primary burials (articulated and complete, MNI 8) or as prepared body parts composed of the skull (cranium and mandible) and their phalanges (MNI 36) (Table 4.1). Phalanges are challenging to separate from their skin, so bundled phalanges likely represent pelts fashioned into ritual paraphernalia or attire.

While the total felid MNI is impressive, acquiring live jaguars and pumas was a difficult feat obtained only in modest numbers. The five primary felids in Burial 6 (one jaguar, three pumas, and one unidentified large felid) constitute the largest concentration of sacrificed felids from a single context at Teotihuacan. In addition, two primary pumas were excavated in Burial 2, and one puma lay to rest in Burial 5.

The two pumas interred in the northern sector of Burial 2 convey the method of felid transport to the ritual scene. Postholes enclosing each puma delineate the stacked wooden cages (each 100 × 80 × 60 cm) that would have shielded the ritual practitioners carrying the ferocious felids into the dedicatory cache (Plate 8a). The puma in the lower cage (E.143) was a complete, well-preserved probable female (Plate 8b, c). Its full adult dentition but unfused skeleton identifies the felid as a young adult, between one-and-a-half to two years old. E.154, stacked atop the

TABLE 4.1
Summary of Felid Remains from the Moon Pyramid

Element #	Species	Bone	Age	Sex	Surface	Pat	Stom	Notes
Burial 2								
143	*P. concolor*	Complete	Y adult	F?	No	No	No	Caged animal.
151	*Felis* sp.	Phalanges	Infant/Juv	UnID	No	No	No	
154	*P. concolor*	Complete	Y adult	M	No	No	Yes	Caged animal. Coprolites in cage.
167.1	*Felis* sp.	Skull	Infant	UnID	Yes	No	No	Deciduous teeth, w/phalanges
167.3	*Felis* sp.	Isolated bones	Adult	UnID	No	No	No	Mixed frags. Not part of MNI calculation.
187	*Felis* sp.	Skull	Infant	UnID	No	No	No	Associated with human 2-A. Deciduous and permanent teeth (7–8 months of age).
192, 189	*Felis* sp.	Skull	Infant	UnID	Yes	No	No	Deciduous teeth.
270	*P. concolor*	Skull	Juv	UnID	No	No	No	Some deciduous teeth.
330	*Felis* sp.	Phalanges	Infant/Juv	UnID	Yes	No	No	Likely a pelt.
Burial 6								
1818.1	*P. concolor*	Complete	Y adult	F	No	Yes	Yes	Various pathologies, consumed cooked rabbits.
1887	*P. onca*	Complete	Y adult	UnID	No	Yes?	No	Possible infection on L forelimb.
1941	*P. concolor*	Skull	Y adult	M	Yes	No	No	Cutmarks
1960	*P. onca*	Skull	Infant	UnID	Yes	No	No	Deciduous teeth. Cutmarks.
1984	*P. concolor*	Complete	Y adult	F	Yes	Yes	No	Fused L ulna and radius.
1991.1	*Felis* sp.	Complete	Juv	UnID	No	No	Yes	Rabbit long bone frags in stomach.

2043	*P. onca*	Skull	Infant	UnID	No	No	No	Deciduous teeth with some permanent in alveolar cavity.
2044	*P. concolor*	Various	UnID	UnID	No	No	No	Isolated frags of phalange, tarsal/carpal bone, incisor, and ear bone. Probably from nearby skeleton.
2068	*P. concolor*	Skull	Juv	UnID	Yes	No	No	Cutmarks. Could not locate on plan drawing.
2071	*P. onca*	Skull	Infant	UnID	Yes	No	No	Deciduous teeth. Cutmarks.
2195	*P. onca*	Skull	Infant	UnID	Yes	No	No	Deciduous and permanent teeth erupting. Cutmarks.
2223	*P. onca*	Skull	Juv	UnID	Yes	No	No	Cutmarks.
2227	*P. concolor*	Probably complete	Juv	UnID	Yes	No	No	Missing the head and various long bones but field drawings of complete individual. Cutmarks on metacarpal and phalange.
2228	*P. concolor*	Skull	Juv	UnID	Yes	No	No	Cutmarks.
2245	*P. concolor*	Skull	Infant	UnID	No	No	No	Deciduous and permanent teeth erupting.
2253.2	*Felis sp.*	Phalanges	UnID	UnID	No	No	No	Likely a pelt.
-9999	*Felis sp.*	Various	UnID	UnID	No	No	No	Various frags of teeth and bone. No element number, likely part of other element.
N4.31	Cf. *P. onca*	Teeth and various	Juv	UnID	No	No	No	Teeth and blocks of unidentified degraded bone, possibly from E.1887.

(*continued*)

TABLE 4.1
Continued

Element #	Species	Bone	Age	Sex	Surface	Pat	Stom	Notes
Burial 3								
512	*Felis sp.*	Teeth	Adult	UnID	Yes	No	No	Two cut canines.
560.1	*P. concolor*	Skull	Adult	UnID	No	No	No	Could not locate in plan drawing.
571.1	*P. concolor*	Skull	Senior	M	Yes	Yes	No	Cutmarks, w/phalanges. Pathology on chin (mandible).
573.2	*Felis sp.*	Phalanges	UnID	UnID	No	No	No	Probably from nearby element.
574.2	*P. concolor*	Teeth	Juv/adult	UnID	Yes	No	No	Cut canine and other teeth.
575.2	*Felis sp.*	Phalanges	UnID	UnID	No	No	No	
576.2	*Felis sp.*	Phalanges	Juv/adult	UnID	No	No	No	
578.2	*P. concolor*	Teeth	Juv/adult	UnID	No	No	No	
579.3	*Felis sp.*	Phalanges	UnID	UnID	No	No	No	
597.3	*P. concolor*	Mandible	Adult	UnID	No	No	No	Only ventral region up to Pm3.
620.1	*P. concolor*	Skull	Adult	UnID	Yes	No	No	Cutmarks.
620.2	*P. concolor*	Teeth	Adult	UnID	No	No	No	Isolated tooth, R M1 superior.
632.1	*P. concolor*	Skull	Senior	M?	No	No	No	Completely fused sutures and dental wear, senior age.
632.2	*P. concolor*	Skull	Juv	UnID	No	No	No	No tooth wear.
691.1	*Felis sp.*	Skull	UnID	UnID	No	No	No	3 mandible and cranial frags, probably from another felid.
Various	*Felis sp.*	Phalanges	UnID	UnID	No	No	No	E.581, 605, 637, 643, 657, 703, 741. Various phalanges.

Burial 5

1054	*P. concolor*	Skull	Adult	UnID	No	No	No	
1318.2	*Felis* sp.	Phalanges	UnID	UnID	No	No	No	
1380	*Felis* sp.	Skull	Adult	UnID	No	No	No	Red pigment on mandible frag.
1381.1	Cf. *P. onca*	Skull	Adult	UnID	No	No	No	With phalanges.
1381.2	*P. concolor*	Skull	UnID	UnID	No	No	No	With phalanges.
1382.1	*Felis* sp.	Skull	Adult	UnID	No	No	No	
1382.2	*P. concolor*	Skull	Y adult	UnID	No	No	No	Teeth separate from E.1382.1.
1382.3	*Felis* sp.	Teeth	Y adult	UnID	No	No	No	Teeth separate from E.1382.1. Age not counted.
1382.4	*Felis* sp.	Skull	Juv	UnID	No	No	No	L maxillary canine and frag of L mandible with M1.
1382.5	*Felis* sp.	Tooth	Adult	UnID	No	No	No	Only L maxillary canine. Age not counted.
1422	*Felis* sp.	Phalanges	UnID	UnID	No	No	No	
1446.3	*Felis* sp.	Phalanges	Infant?	UnID	No	No	No	
1447.1	*Felis* sp.	Phalanges	UnID	UnID	No	No	No	
1500	*P. concolor*	Skull	Adult	UnID	No	No	No	
1505	Cf. *P. onca*	Skull	Y adult	UnID	No	No	No	
1506	*Felis* sp.	Phalanges	UnID	UnID	No	No	No	
1517	*P. concolor*	Skull	Y adult	UnID	No	No	No	With phalanges.
1565	*Felis* sp.	Phalanges	UnID	UnID	No	No	No	
1570	*Felis* sp.	Phalanges	UnID	UnID	No	No	No	

(*continued*)

TABLE 4.1
Continued

Element #	Species	Bone	Age	Sex	Surface	Pat	Stom	Notes
1584	*Felis sp.*	Skull	Adult	UnID	No	No	No	
1587.1	*Felis sp.*	Skull	Adult	UnID	No	No	No	
1587.2	*P. concolor*	Teeth	Adult	UnID	No	No	No	Teeth separate from E.1587.1.
1587.3	*P. concolor*	Teeth	Y adult	UnID	No	No	No	Teeth separate from E.1587.1.
1587.4	*P. concolor*	Teeth	Y adult	UnID	No	No	No	Teeth separate from E.1587.1. Age not counted.
1593	*P. concolor*	Skull	Adult	UnID	No	No	No	
1636.1	*P. concolor*	Skull	Adult	UnID	No	No	No	
1638.2	*Felis sp.*	Phalanges	UnID	UnID	No	No	No	
1639	*P. concolor*	Complete	Juv	UnID	No	No	No	Very degraded but was probably a complete ind.
S3E3.4	*Felis sp.*	Skull frag.	UnID	UnID	No	No	No	Probably from another element nearby.
S5E3	*Felis sp.*	Mandible	Adult	UnID	No	No	No	Probably from another element nearby. Age not counted.
Various	*Felis sp.*	Phalanges	UnID	UnID	No	No	No	E.1118, 1119, 1120, 1121, 1123, 1124, 1177, 1178, 1179, 1180, 1188, 1189, 1190, 1193, 1197, 1499, 1581. Various phalanges.

Surface: surface modification, Pat: pathology, Stom: stomach content, Y: young, Juv: juvenile, F: female, M: male, UnID: unidentified, Pm: premolar, M: molar. *P. concolor*: *Puma concolor*, *P. onca*: *Panthera onca*

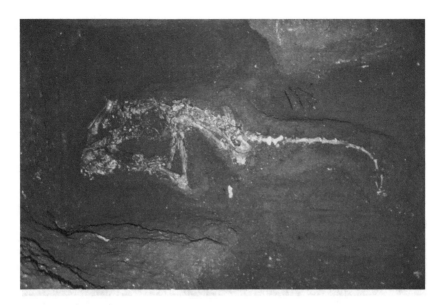

FIGURE 4.1
Puma E.154 in a cage from Burial 2. © Moon Pyramid Project.

former in its cage, was similarly a young adult (Figure 4.1). The coprolite adjacent to the felid indicated the animal was alive when it entered the ritual scene. E.154's coprolite detailed the remnants of its ultimate meal: isolated phalanges of a small mammal, bones of an unidentified small bird, and two teeth and three phalanges of a leporid, possibly of a cottontail (*Sylvilagus* sp.).

Out of the five complete felids in Burial 6, three expressed pathological markers of stress, disease, and malnutrition suggestive of prolonged artificial confinement. Overlapping and deteriorated skeletons of two felids, a canid, and two eagles sacrificed in the southwest corner of Burial 6 had restricted surface visibility. However, both of these felids exhibited pathologies (Plate 8d). Puma E.1984 was a young adult female roughly eighteen months old. The fused left radius and ulna, caused by an infection or injury, affected her entire left upper limb, significantly constraining her range of motion (Figure 4.2). A young adult jaguar (E.1887) lay atop E.1984. As most of the potential jaguar skeletons were of young individuals, these identifications are pending verification utilizing a comparative collection of young jaguar skeletons applying more rigorous morphometric study and, ideally, aDNA analysis. E.1887 exhibited inflammation of the left forelimb along the shaft of the humerus, radius, and ulna, likely reflecting an osseous infection.

Another juvenile puma, E.1991, was placed on the eastern sector of Burial 6 with overlapping limbs (Figure 4.3). Its location mirrored a western counterpart, the puma E.1818 whose trauma-driven osteobiography is narrated in Chapter 6.

FIGURE 4.2
Puma E.1984 from Burial 6, detail of fused left radius and ulna. Photograph: N. Sugiyama.

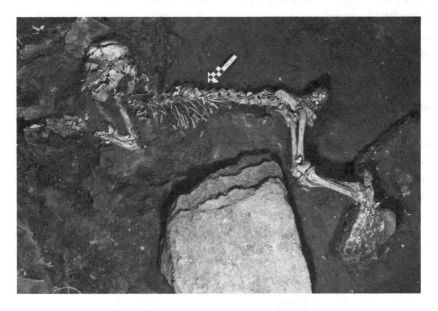

FIGURE 4.3
Puma E.1991 from Burial 6 with overlapping extremities. © Moon Pyramid Project.

Pathologies were absent on E.1991, who was offered between six to eight months old when some of his/her permanent dentition had formed within the alveolar cavity, about to erupt. The hind limbs of a young rabbit (*Sylvilagus* sp.) within its stomach cavity with clear signs of gastric etching were residuals of its last meal.

E.1639 was the only complete felid uncovered from Burial 5. The puma lay ventral to one of three humans sitting cross-legged (Individual 5-B), almost guarding its human counterpart. This juvenile had its full permanent dentition, unfused cranial and postcranial elements, and significantly smaller stature. The weight of the large boulders atop the bones and water leaching left a powdered and weathered-looking surface. Poor preservation permitted only partial dental reconstruction alongside a small skull and long bone fragments. Surface data could not be collected.

Some general conclusions on felid primary burials pertain to the selection process. In contrast to the hodgepodge of age ranges represented in secondary deposits, all primary burials were either juveniles ($n = 3$) or young adults ($n = 5$) under two years of age (Table 4.2). Biological factors during the felid's transition into adulthood undoubtedly played a role. As hyperspecialized carnivores, young adult felids consume

TABLE 4.2
Felid Age Distribution (MNI) for Each Offering

	Senior	Adult	Young Adult	Juvenile	Infant	Total
Burial 2						
Complete	—	—	2	—	—	2
Skull	—	—	—	1	3	4
Burial 6						
Complete	—	—	3	2	—	5
Skull	—	—	1	4	5	10
Burial 3						
Skull	2	3	2	1	—	8
Burial 5						
Complete	—	—	—	1	—	1
Skull	—	10	4	1	—	15
General pattern						
Complete	—	—	5	3	—	8
Skull	2	13	7	7	8	38
Total	2	13	12	10	8	45
Total (%)	4	29	27	22	18	

1.2–1.4 kg of daily meat, which is expensive for a city without domesticated livestock. Although they would not have reached sexual maturity nor full body size, the dark spots on the puma's coat fade by a year and a half, and its characteristic adult golden coat fully developed. Perhaps most importantly, this period is when felids (particularly males) begin establishing solitary habits, marking expansive territorial home ranges, and becoming aggressive toward other felids. As one recalls the behavior of even a house cat confronting a neighbor's felid, we can all relate to why it would have been considerably more dangerous to tame wild felids once they reached two years of age with their additional strength and size. The consistent preference for young adult felids (around one to one-and-a-half years old) across contexts spanning different periods suggests it was the optimal age when they had established adult pelage but would have coped with the presence of other felids in the vicinity.

Despite their young age, three of the seven primary burials exhibited pathologies indicative of disease, infection, or injury. It is noteworthy that some trauma hindered locomotion. In the wild, such injuries would have been fatal for these solitary predators, yet remodeling along the pathology suggests post-trauma survival. These are all notable features I will return to when discussing captive animal management.

Felid skeletal data also allude to the method of sacrifice. Ritual practitioners filled dedicatory caches with *tepetate* blocks, rocks, and earth. These were not empty cavities like the Egyptian tombs, and I propose live burial as a realistic cause of death. In fact, I think all the animals were in vivo burials. Burial 2's caged pumas (and the caged wolf from the same context described later) provide direct evidence that animals were brought to the ritual scene alive. The coprolites found within the cages imply their confinement for some time prior to concealment with earthen rubble. Where cages were absent, their overlapping extremities suggest they were bound. Humans interred in Burials 2, 3, and 6 also had their hands tied behind their backs, and physical anthropologists likewise interpret them as evidence of live sacrifice (Spence and Pereira 2007). The lack of perimortem trauma (inflicted at the time of death) on the felid bodies also supports this hypothesis. When present, the uniform preference for Leporids (rabbits/hares) as their final meal—a pattern consistent with wolf and golden eagle primary burials—indicates purposeful feeding was part of the ritualization process.

Secondary Burials

There were three types of felid secondary burials: isolated skulls (Figure 4.4), skulls accompanied by phalanges, or isolated phalanges. Bone deterioration and potential admixing made quantification of secondary burials challenging. A spatial overlap analysis following Marean and colleagues (2001; see also Abe et al. 2002; Fischer

FIGURE 4.4
Puma skull E.1941 from Burial 6 next to the ceramic vessel. © Moon Pyramid Project.

2007) mapped each bone fragment and surface modification to calculate total MNI and production patterns (Figure 4.5). Teeth, due to their high survivability as the densest and most easily recognizable elements, were essential for MNI calculations. I plotted age distribution taking into consideration total MNI counts and spatial proximity to bone concentrations (Table 4.2).

Age distribution of secondary deposits followed two patterns. Early deposits associated with Building 4 (Burials 2 and 6) displayed similar age preferences characterized by a predominance of infant (MNI 8) and juvenile (MNI 5) heads, with only one young adult skull found in Burial 6. Later deposits (Burials 3 and 5) favored more mature individuals, predominantly adults (MNI 13, 57%), with some young adults and senior individuals. Juveniles were only minimally represented, and no infants were identified from later deposits.

There were two processing techniques among felid crania: those that attempted to retain the cranium intact, extracting the encephalic mass from a small opening in the occipital region, and those that discarded most of the braincase, keeping only the frontal portion (Figure 4.6). Burial 2 and 6 skulls exhibited both processing techniques, while those from Burial 3 always lacked the neurocranium. Burial 5's preparation strategy is challenging to interpret, as teeth were often the only recognizable fragments. It is noteworthy, however, that most identifiable bone fragments pertained to maxillary and mandibular portions in line with a heavily processed

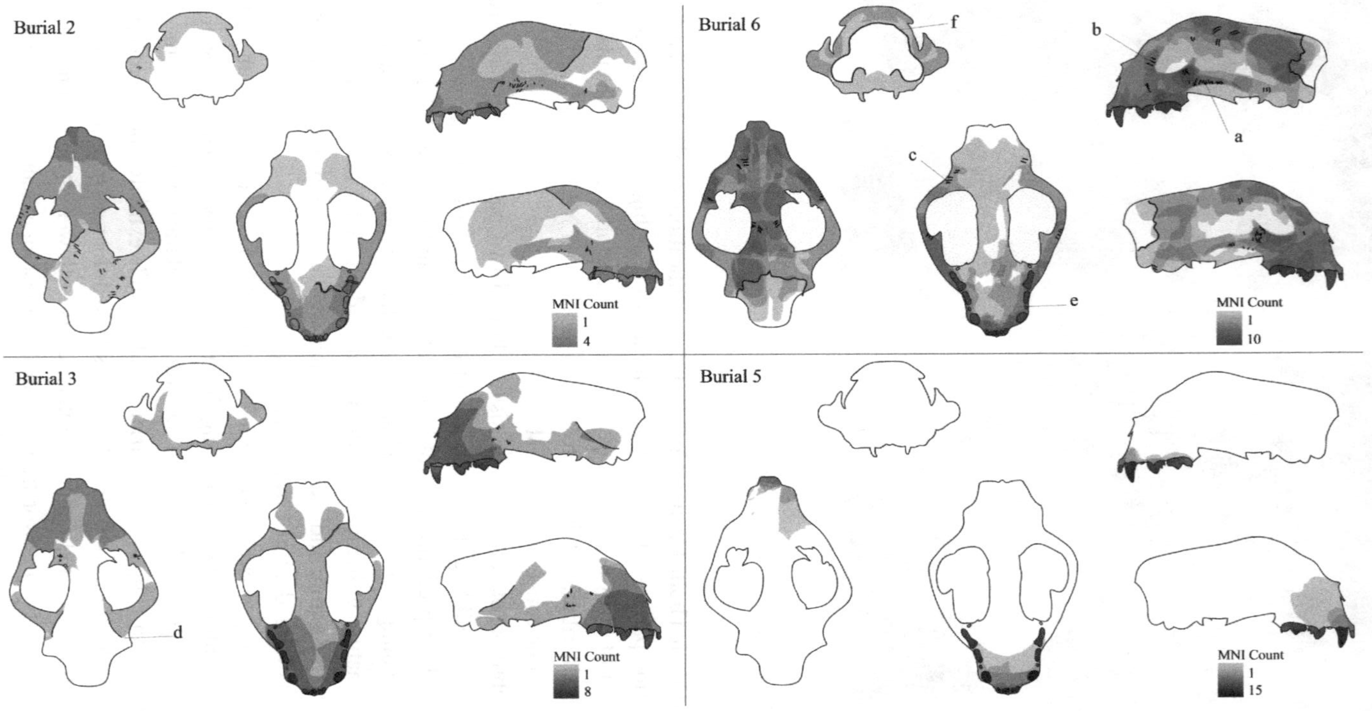

FIGURE 4.5

Overlap analyses (gray) of cranium and cutmarks/other modifications (black lines) of secondary felid remains from Burials 2, 6, 3, and 5. a. zygomatic bone, b. lacrimal bone, c. condyloid fossa, d. neurocranium, e. maxilla, and f. nuchal crest.

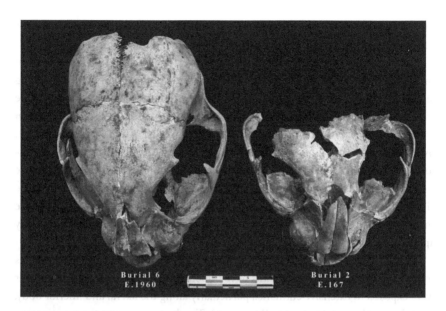

FIGURE 4.6
Two types of skull preparation techniques on puma skulls. Photograph: N. Sugiyama.

technique. Variability among Burials 2 and 6 skulls suggests the lack of standardized manufacturing technique during the earliest offering caches. In comparison, Burial 3 crania uniformly exhibits highly processed crania, lacking the majority of the braincase, a trend that likely continued into Burial 5's deposition.

The quantity of cutmarks on crania varied significantly, ranging from some with none, to others with numerous marks etched onto a single bone. Obvious preservation biases were present, with many bones left in a powdered state. For example, in Burial 5 teeth were often the only elements re-pieced, and only one mandible (E.1517) displayed cutmarks. Burials 2 and 6 exhibited the highest cutmark density and the total number of bones with cutmarks, while Burial 3 contained a relatively lower frequency of surface modifications (Figure 4.5).

When present, cutmarks on the cranium and mandible clustered around areas where the skin comes closest to the bone, indicating skinning prior to deposition. For example, a jaguar cub, E.1960, demonstrated parallel and superimposed cutmarks along the zygomatic bone (Figure 4.5a), conveying repeated scraping movements of the carver detaching the pelt (Plate 9). Cuts were even present on the lacrimal bone, likely inflicted during the extraction of the eye socket (Figure 4.5b). Deep grooves close to the condyloid fossa, where the mandible attaches to the cranium, recount added pressure as the practitioner struggled to remove the pelt from muscle insertions and attachment sites for tendons (Figure 4.5c). Mandibles were disarticulated from the cranium, facilitating usage as costumes and ritual regalia.

Prevalent marks along the frontal-parietal joint and the temporal line where the mastoid muscles attach to the cranium suggest pelt and meat extraction.

The size of the dorsal opening necessary to extract the encephalic mass from the braincase varied. Often, carvers took advantage of natural sutures, cutting along the edges of the frontal-parietal suture, the temporal-parietal suture, or the sphenoid-temporal junctures (Figure 4.5d). In some cases, only the occipital region was detached from the nuchal crest (Plate 9c, Figure 4.5f). This was accomplished by cutting into the bone, usually leaving striations or applying targeted blunt-force fractures. In the latter case, breakage patterns indicated green bone fracture (inflicted while the bone was still plastic near the time of death). In one instance (E.187, Burial 2), the fractured edges of the maxilla (Figure 4.5e) and areas of the mandible of a puma were discolored between dark brown and black with a flaky appearance. Heat exposure may have facilitated processing procedures.

Mandible processing took two forms. When carvers conserved only the mandible's frontal portion, hardly any cutmarks were inflicted, while more complete mandibles were exposed to extensive cutmarks, particularly along the lateral and inferior body, as well as on the angular process (Figure 4.7). The deep grooves on the superior surface of the coronoid process relate the difficulty in separating the cranial-mandibular articulation (Figure 4.7c). Like the cranium, the distribution of these marks coincides with areas where the skin would be closest to the bone, articular surfaces, and muscle attachment areas (e.g., the angular process where many muscles and tendons attach).

Despite the very minimal interpretation I can provide for Burial 5 secondary felid remains due to preservation limitations, it is worth mentioning that there was an apparent discrepancy between the high MNI count ($n = 15$) derived from dentition and the low volume of bone fragments. While differential preservation undoubtedly affected the assemblage, teeth of multiple felids may have been annexed onto mandibles and maxillae to create composite corporeal animal forms, much like the canid maxillary pendants mentioned earlier from the FSP (Valadez Azúa et al. 2002a, 2002b).

The inferior mandibular symphysis on the prepared puma skull from Burial 3 (E.571.1) was fused, and a bump on the chin identified this pathology as a blunt force trauma or some complication during the symphyseal fusion, causing abnormal bone remodeling in this area. Pronounced muscle markings also demonstrate that this was a robust male. It was one of the only three elements with cutmarks from this context.

Many phalanges were often deposited with the skull or as isolated bundles. In some instances, small sesamoid bones found with articulated digits confirm that the skin still adhered to the bones. A complete digit and its sesamoids from Burial 3 exhibited a pathology on the shaft of the first phalange with clear signs of remodeling (E.657) (Figure 4.8). This pathology parallels evidence for wounded and sick animals kept in captivity on primary burials. Cutmarks on the phalanges,

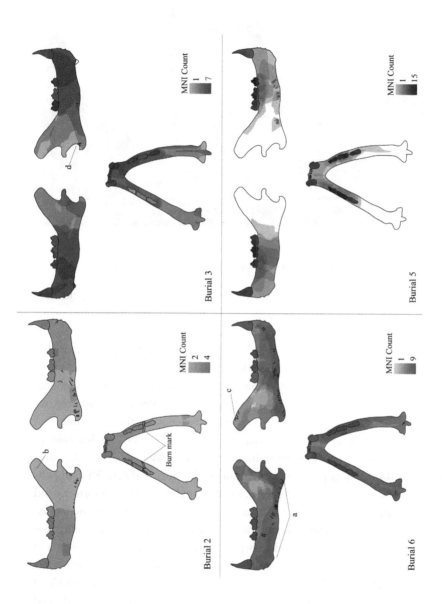

FIGURE 4.7
Overlap analyses (gray) of felid mandibles and cutmarks (black lines) from Burials 2, 3, 6, and 5. a. body of mandible; b. ramus; c. coronoid process; and d. angular process.

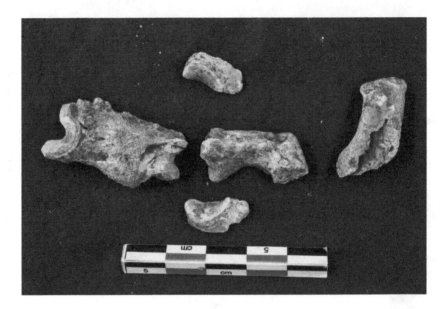

FIGURE 4.8
Puma E.657 from Burial 3, digit with a pathology. Photograph: N. Sugiyama

usually along the shaft, were likely inflicted during pelt extraction. Some pelts were interred as separate offerings, as suggested by isolated phalange bundles, while others were offered attached to or laid next to the skull.

Prepared felid bones/teeth have fewer restrictions imposed by their materiality as practitioners can acquire them at various moments, prepare them over a long time at different locations, and each bone/tooth represents diverse depositional histories. This likely contributed to the varied age/sex distribution and preparation techniques recorded among felid secondary remains. At the same time, secondary corporeal animal forms still functioned as referents of the complete animals deposited alongside them, perhaps utilized in the rituals as regalia and extensively traded and displayed as pertinent actors during the ritualized acts. Though pelts and other soft tissue are not preserved, overlap analysis of the bones/teeth and cutmarks provides valuable clues that many skulls were displayed skinned, often disarticulated from the mandible. While we cannot preclude the possibility that some skulls may have been affixed to organic materials to keep the cranium and mandible articulated, it is worth considering the reactions of the audience to the ritual display of bare skulls with shining white teeth accompanying the parade of live felids fated for sacrifice. Likely, the pelts of these impressive carnivores adorned the very practitioners carrying these skeletonized heads to the interior of the Moon Pyramid. Some may have even carried composite animal forms, much like the multispecies canid maxillae pendants adorning warriors interred in the FSP.

Canids

The canid assemblage was much more challenging to interpret because the heavily degraded bones often only permitted the reconstruction of its dentition. Unlike the felids, there was no indication of captivity and management. Capture of more statistically robust modern comparative metric traits and aDNA analysis of the possible hybrid specimens are still pending.

Wolves comprised most of the canids (MNI 29/32), with only two coyotes represented in the Moon Pyramid offerings (Table 4.3). Primary burials were exceptionally rare, with a complete wolf uncovered in Burials 2, 6, and 5 (MNI = 3). Though lacking primary burials, wolf crania are noticeably abundant in Burial 3, containing at least seventeen (likely eighteen) prepared crania scattered surrounding and directly on top of four sacrificed humans. Age preferences between burial types allude to distinct acquisition strategies. All three primary burials were juveniles (Burials 2, 6, and 5), while secondary internments represented the entire age range (Table 4.4). Adult (37%) and juvenile (34%) age groups were most abundant across the board.

Primary Burials

There were no telling markers of captivity on the three primary canid bodies, likely because preservation prevented observation of surface features, and wolves are adaptable to human cohabitation (facilitating domestication into dogs). Post holes outlined the wooden cage that confined the wolf in Burial 2 (E.213.1), mirroring the two caged pumas from the same context (Plate 10). This canid rested in a north-south orientation with its head to the south. The wolf was a juvenile between six and nine months old with full permanent dentition yet completely unfused bones. The *os penis* bone confirmed this individual as male. Like the felid burials, this wolf consumed a hare (*Lepus* sp.) and a cottontail (*Sylvilagus* sp.) before sacrifice. Discoloration on some of the rabbit bones reveals a cooked last meal. No additional surface features were identified.

Only one complete canid, E.2199, was buried in Burial 6. It was excavated in the southwestern corner of the dedicatory cache, where a concentration of primary burials of felids and eagles were superimposed. I will explain this individual's life history in Chapter 6.

A complete wolf (E.1636.2) rested on the right side of a human, Individual 5-C, in the northern sector of Burial 5 (Plate 11a). Like all bones in Burial 5, the canid skeleton was poorly preserved with no surface visibility. I was only able to determine the individual was a juvenile, between six to nine months of age, and the presence of the *os penis* bone marked it as male.

TABLE 4.3
Summary of Canid Remains from the Moon Pyramid

Element #	Species	Bone	Age	Sex	Pat	Surface	Stom	Notes
Burial 2								
213.1	*C. lupus*	Complete	Juv	M	No	No	Yes	Caged animal, 2 rabbits in stom, *os penis* male.
Burial 6								
1959	*C. latrans*	Skull	Juv	F	No	No	No	W/phalanges.
2072	*C. lupus*	Skull	Juv	UnID	No	Yes	No	Cutmarks, some deciduous teeth.
2079	*C. latrans*	Skull	Y adult	F?	No	Yes	No	Cutmarks, w/phalanges. Initial ID as wolf.
2194	*C. lupus*	Skull	Adult	F	No	Yes	No	Cutmarks, w/phalanges.
2221	*C. lupus*	Skull	Y adult	UnID	No	Yes	No	Cutmarks.
2224	*C. lupus*	Skull	Adult	UnID	No	No	No	
2229	*C. lupus?*	Skull	Juv	UnID	No	Yes	No	Initial ID as hybrid. Cutmarks.
2243	*C. lupus*	Skull	Juv	UnID	No	No	No	
2244	*C. lupus*	Skull	Juv	UnID	No	No	No	Permanent teeth erupting, w/phalanges.
2199	*C. lupus?*	Complete	Juv	F	No	No	No	Initial ID as hybrid.
2253.1	*Canis* sp.	Phalanges	UnID	UnID	No	No	No	Distal phalanges.
2225.2	*Canis* sp.	Phalanges	UnID	UnID	No	No	No	May be part of E.2224 or E.2221.
Burial 3								
570	*C. lupus*	Skull	Y adult	M	No	No	No	
572	*C. lupus*	Skull	Y adult	F?	No	No	No	
573.1	*C. lupus*	Skull	Adult	UnID	No	No	No	
574.1	*C. lupus*	Skull	Adult	UnID	No	No	No	

575.1	C. lupus	Skull	Juv/Adult	UnID	No	No	No	Could not locate in plan drawing.
576.1	C. lupus	Skull	Mature Adult	UnID	No	No	No	Heavily worn dentition.
577.1	C. lupus	Skull	Juv/Adult	UnID	No	No	No	
578.1	C. lupus	Skull	Adult	UnID	No	No	No	
579.1	C. lupus	Skull	Adult	UnID	No	Yes	No	Intentional breaks, cutmarks.
579.2	Canis sp.	Skull	Adult	UnID	No	No	No	Only represented by maxillary L I3.
580	C. lupus	Skull	Adult	UnID	No	No	No	
597.1	C. lupus	Skull	Juv/Adult	UnID	No	No	No	
597.2	C. lupus	Skull	Adult	UnID	No	No	No	
601.1	C. lupus	Skull	Adult	UnID	No	No	No	Could not locate in plan drawing.
601.2	Canis sp.	Skull	Juv/Adult	UnID	No	No	No	Three teeth.
606	C. lupus	Skull	Adult	M	No	No	No	
642	C. lupus	Skull	Juvenile	UnID	No	Yes	No	Some deciduous teeth, cutmarks.
746	C. lupus	Skull	Adult	UnID	No	No	No	Could not locate in plan drawing.
600	Canis sp.	Phalanges	UnID	UnID	No	No	No	
Burial 5								
1543	Canis sp.	Phalanges	UnID	UnID	No	No	No	One distal phalanx.
1508	C. lupus?	Skull	Juv	UnID	No	No	No	Initial ID as hybrid.
1636.2	C. lupus	Complete	Juv	M	No	No	No	Likely complete but badly preserved. Os penis male.
1447.2	Canis sp.	Phalanges	UnID	UnID	No	No	No	Intermediate and distal phalanx.

C.: Canis, Pat: pathology, Surface: surface modification, Stom: stomach content, Y: young, Juv: juvenile, F: female, M: male, UnID: unidentified, I: incisor, L: left.

TABLE 4.4
Canid Age Distribution (MNI) for Each Offering

	Burial 2		Burial 6		Burial 3		Burial 5		Total	
	MNI	%	MNI	%	MNI	%	MNI	%	MNI	%
Juvenile	1	100	6	60	1	6	2	100	10	34
Juvenile/adult	0	0	0	0	4	24	0	0	4	13
Young adult	0	0	2	20	2	12	0	0	4	13
Adult	0	0	2	20	9	59	0	0	11	37
Mature adult	0	0	0	0	1	0	0	0	1	3
Total	1		10		17		2		30	

Secondary Burials

Following the same analytical strategies employed for felid secondary burials, I found canid skulls were also deposited as bare bones with no skin or flesh. Notably, Burial 2 did not include secondary canid remains, and only one skull was present in Burial 5. Nine skulls, some with associated phalanges, were deposited throughout Burial 6. Zooarchaeological methods identified a single coyote from offertory contexts at Teotihuacan, excavated along the southern wall of the chamber (E.1959). Another skull (E.2079) was identified later as a likely coyote based on mtDNA genetic evidence (Hofman et al. 2023). Although the skull E.2229 was initially identified as a wolf-dog hybrid, *Canis lupus-familiaris*, their tooth measurements did not concur with this identification and remains labeled as a possible wolf until further analysis.

Burial 3 housed the most abundant canid assemblage, represented by an MNI of seventeen prepared cranial heads based on the overlap analysis of teeth (Figure 4.9). While seventeen is the minimum count, I suspect there were eighteen canid crania, as it corresponds to the number of Elements assigned during excavations (Table 4.3). Eighteen was significant in the Mesoamerican calendric system and is repeatedly represented by the numbers of offerings, including eagles, obsidian knives, and likely rattlesnakes in Burial 6.

Like the felids, canids were processed into two forms; one retained the complete skull, and the second highlighted only the snout and the mandible. Cutmarks, fractures, and intentional abrasion/wearing were recorded. Cutmarks were the most abundant modification type, and the frequency of surface modifications varied across offering contexts. While only two of the seventeen skulls from Burial

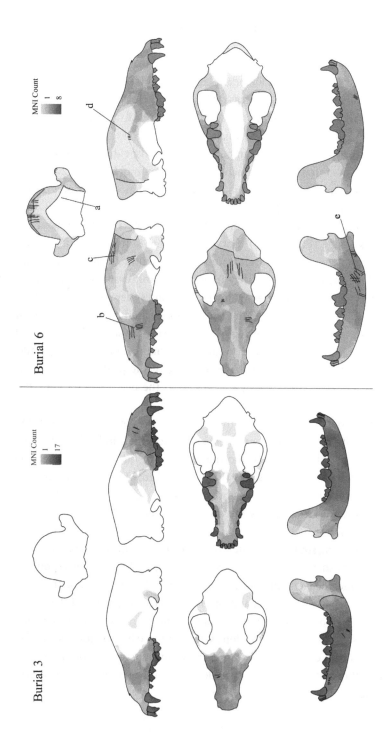

FIGURE 4.9
Overlap analyses of canid skulls (gray) from Burials 3 and 6. Cutmarks (black lines) distributed along (a) nuchal crest, (b) maxilla, (c) temporal region right by sagittal crest, (d) zygomatic bone, and (e) inferior body of the mandible.

3 exhibited surface marks (12%), Burial 6 displayed the highest percentage of canids with modifications (55%, $n = 5/9$).

Burial 6 applied both preparation techniques. Those that maintained the entire cranium intact tended to exhibit abundant cutmarks with apparent modifications along the dorsal opening of the braincase (Figure 4.9a). However, prepared snouts left scant cutmarks ($n = 3$). Overall, surface modifications from this context were more frequent in the number of individuals exhibiting cutmarks and, for the most part, the density of marks on each animal. Like the felids, cutmarks clustered on the maxilla near the infraorbital foramen, along the temporal bone, the zygomatic bone, and the inferior body of the mandible reflect production procedures during pelt extraction (Figure 4.9 b–e).

Take, for example, E.2194, a semi-complete skull of a female wolf between one and two years of age (Figure 4.10). Carvers kept this individual's cranium intact, taking advantage of the natural contours of the skull to dislodge the occipital region along the nuchal crest. They removed the soft tissue in the braincase from this opening. They also extracted the pelt, leaving sweeping cutmarks along the parietals near the sagittal crest, the left zygomatic, and on both mandibular bodies. A group of phalanges were deposited alongside the skull. The number of phalanges ($n = 24$) indicates at least two canid pelts in the offering. Deep parallel grooves on the medial and lateral shafts on three of the phalanges record the forced motions of the artisan struggling to detach the pelt along the muscles/tendons.

Skulls from Burial 6 were probably processed while the bone was still green and its soft tissue (pelt, meat, and tendons) were still intact. Three individuals retained the complete mandible, four were incomplete, and in one case, the dentition was all that remained. Only two skulls (E.2194 and E.2079) included the cranial-mandibular articulation, with the majority showing signs of disarticulation at the mandibular ramus, leaving only the mandibular body and tooth row in place alongside the cranium.

Burial 3's processing strategy consistently favored more compact forms, reducing the cranium to its snout. These crania were accompanied by the corresponding mandibles that included a mixture of complete mandibles ($n = 5$), some that were modified more extensively ($n = 7$), and yet others that only preserved their teeth ($n = 5$). The absence of the mandibular fossa (the cranial-mandibular articulation surface) on most skulls reveals deposition as disarticulated bare bones. The low frequency of skulls with cutmarks ($n = 2$) suggests acquisition usually occurred after the skin and other soft tissue had already degraded, although evidence of weathering was absent.

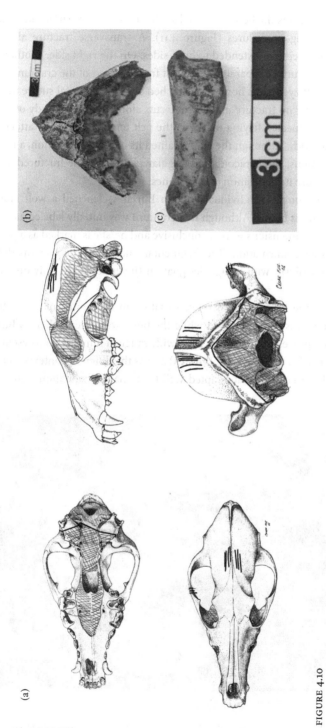

FIGURE 4.10
Wolf F.2194 from Burial 6, (a) coding sheet indicating cutmarks (black lines) and absent regions (gray), (b) photographs of cut along the nuchal crest, and (c) deep grooves along phalanx.

Burial 3's E.579.1 was the best-preserved skull with clear cutmarks and fractures denoting processing procedures (Figure 4.11). A transverse fracture along the fourth maxillary premolar extended to both sides. On the right side, another fracture on the lateral surface separated the snout from the rest of the cranium. At the same time, the left zygomatic bone was detached along the natural suture between the maxilla, leaving no fracture mark. Three cuts along the lateral body of the left mandible reflect repeated flaying marks as the pelt tends to be firmly attached to the mandibular body. Although the wolf retained its complete dentition, a fracture dislodged the ramus, the coracoid, and angular processes. The fractured surface was polished before its deposition as bare bones.

One of three humans (Individual 5-C) in Burial 5 clenched a wolf cranium (E.1508) between his hands. Although this cranium was initially labeled as a wolf-dog hybrid, teeth dimensions were inconclusive and he/she is marked as a possible wolf until further confirmation. The fragmentary nature of the remains did not permit further analysis, with its age designation (juvenile) based only on its preserved dentition.

Compared to the felids, there is more variation in the timing of access to the skull (Burial 6 seems to be accessed while the bone was green, whereas Burial 3 seems variable), processing technique, and wide range of numerical representation (only one in Burial 2, to eighteen in Burial 3) across the different contexts. Perhaps, as a familiar local favorite that adapted well to human cohabitation, acquisition

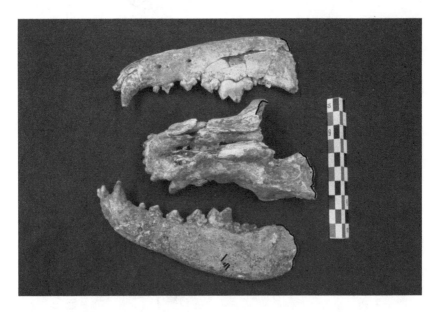

FIGURE 4.11
Wolf skull E.579.1 from Burial 3 with surface features outlined in black. Photograph: N. Sugiyama.

and processing methods could not be restricted to the Teotihuacan state, and thus remained less standardized across and within the various contexts.

Eagles

Eagles were the second most abundant species elected for sacrifice, with nineteen of the twenty-eight skeletons identified as primary burials (Table 3.1). Twelve males and nine females were identified after genetic tests adjusted original zooarchaeological sex designations (Table 4.5) (Singleton et al. 2023). Most eagles were of adult stature (MNI 14, 73% of the nineteen skeletons with age designations). However, this does not necessarily mean the raptors had reached sexual maturity (after five to six years of age). The overrepresentation of adults in raptor assemblages is likely an artifact of methodological restraints (see Chapter 3). Despite these biases, probable young were identified in Burial 2 (MNI 5, 26%). Ethnographic accounts record that birds are often ritually killed upon reaching prime plumage at around a year when adult stature has already been reached (McKusick 2001). Young are easier to tame and maintain in captivity and were likely optimal for sacrifice. Evidence of ritualized feeding is consistent with other species (see discussion in Microfauna: Stomach Contents section).

Distinguishing between primary burials and the deposition of secondary animal parts was not always easy. Primary burials were sometimes poorly preserved, and many of the secondary burials looked fairly complete and articulated but exhibited evidence of postmortem manipulation of the corpse (Table 4.5). After careful laboratory analysis, many raptors initially identified as primary burials were reassessed. I even argue that some were taxidermized. Due to this unclear boundary between primary and secondary burials and the similarities in surface modifications across deposition types, I discuss the results by context. In so doing, I argue that secondary burials underwent the same ritualization process as the live eagles participating in state ritualized performances.

Burial 2

All Burial 2 eagles were primary deposits and relatively well preserved. Despite scrutinizing bone surfaces in search of modifications, no osteological indicators of cause of death existed. Field drawings and photographs record that their wings and feet were likely tethered in place (Plate 11b). Thus, I suspect these complete eagles were also likely in vivo sacrifices.

Burial 2 was the only context with eaglets that suggests handlers acquired some eagles directly from the nest. E.165.1 miraculously preserved the thin interorbital

TABLE 4.5
Summary of Eagle Remains from the Moon Pyramid

Element #	Primary	Complete	Age	Sex	Path	Surface	Stom	Notes
Burial 2								
81.1	Yes	Yes	Juv?	M*	Yes	No	Yes	R tibiotarsus, diaphysis healed fracture. Rabbit and small bird in stom. G: UnID to M.
120	Yes	Yes	Juv?	M	Yes	No	No	Pathology on proximal L fibula (infection/fracture?).
121	Yes	Yes	Juv?	M	Yes	No	No	Lipping on several bones (phalanges and ulna).
144	Yes	Yes	Adult	F	No	No	No	
150	No	No	UnID		No	No	No	Claws of digit I or II from nearby individual, not part of MNI.
165.1	Yes	Yes	Y adult?	F	No	No	No	
191	Yes	Yes	Adult	UnID	Yes	No	No	Osteoporosis on ulna of both sides.
196	Yes	Yes	Adult	F	No	No	No	
209	No	No	UnID	UnID	No	No	No	L ulna and radius, probably part of Ele 120. Not part of MNI.
283.1	Yes	Yes	Infant/Juv	F*	No	No	Yes	One rabbit (burnt) and small bird remains in stom. G: UnID to F.
309.1	Yes	Yes	Adult	F	No	No	Yes	Two rabbits (burnt) in stom.
Burial 6								
1888	Yes	Yes	UnID	M*	Yes	No	No	Pathology on digit I, phalange 1. G: F to M.
1961.1	Yes	Yes	UnID	F	Yes	No	Yes	Pathology on L TM. Rabbit in stom.
1962	Yes	Yes	UnID	UnID	No	Yes	No	Cutmarks on L tibiotarsus distal articular surface.

1983	No	Yes	Adult	M	No	Yes	No	Many cutmarks on various extremities, fracture on head.
2010	No	Yes	UnID	M	No	Yes	No	Cutmarks on head, mandible, and L humerus.
2047	No	No	Adult	F	No	Yes	No	Cutmark on head, red pigment on bones. Taxidermized.
2069.1	Yes	Yes	UnID	M	Yes	No	Yes	Pathology on tarsometatarsus. Rabbit in stom content.
2070	Yes	Yes	Adult	M	Yes	No	No	Pathology on the L humerus, radius, ulna, and femur.
2192	Yes	Yes	UnID	UnID	No	No	No	
2193	No	No	UnID	M	No	Yes	No	Cut along head, axial skeleton extracted. Taxidermized?
2200	Yes	Yes	Adult	M*	No	No	No	G: F? to M.
2214, 1919	Yes	Yes	Adult	M	No	No	No	
2222	No	No	UnID	UnID	No	No	No	
2225.1	No	No	Adult	UnID	No	No	No	Possible feathered cape.
2226	Yes	Yes	Adult	F	Possibly	No	No	Possible pathology on R femur.
2239	No	No	Adult	F	No	Yes	No	Extremities only. Cutmarks on L TM and humerus. Taxidermy or feathered cape.
2246	No	Yes	Adult	M	Yes	Yes	No	Pathology on both TM and L humerus. Cutmarks/perforations on head, L coracoid, femurs, and L tibiotarsus.
2261	No	No	UnID	UnID	No	No	No	
Burial 5							
1638.1	Yes?	Yes	Adult	UnID	No	No	No	Likely primary burial, badly preserved.

Pat: pathology, Surface: surface modification, Stom: stomach content, Y: young, Juv: juvenile, UnID: unidentified, F: female, M: male, TM: tarsometatarsus, L: left, R: right, Sm: small, G: sex prior to and after genetic test.

*Sex designations have been revised based on genetic tests by Singleton et al. (2023).

tissue where the interorbital fenestra opening signaled its youth. The length and width ratio of the tarsometatarsus bone of E.283.1 determined it was still of nesting age, around one and a half to two months old. The remnants of rabbits—some burnt, some accompanied by distinct small mammalian and avian bones—were found in the digestive tract of three eagles.

A few eagles from Burial 2 also exhibited pathologies of trauma and nutritional deficiencies indicative of captive management. E.81.1, a possible juvenile identified by the generally smaller size of the skeleton, exhibited a pathology on its lower limb. This wound should have been detrimental to a wild raptor whose disabled leg would have restrained hunting ability. Nevertheless, new woven bone along the healed fracture reveals that the eagle survived this painful injury (Figure 4.12a). Gastric etching on the cottontail's hind limbs found within the eagle's abdominal cavity showed that the raptor enjoyed a lavish pre-sacrificial feast. Fragments of a nonidentified small bird and the left ulna of a hawk (*Buteo* sp.), where many of the precious wing feathers attach, were also mixed with the eagle bones. I suspect excavators accidentally combined the hawk bones with the eagle remains due to their proximity, as there was no sign of gastric etching.

Another injured male eagle (E.120) provides additional evidence of a highly stressed eagle population. A fracture or infection on its left fibula is peculiar, as this proximal shaft region is covered only by small tarsi feathers. An injury on the thin fibula, which can be easily fractured, would have facilitated handling significantly constraining the mobility of its precarious claws.

Overall, the health and nutrition of the population can be an indicator of captivity. Life under confinement and the resulting radical shift in the diet cause vitamin D deficiency and a nutritional strain often manifested through overall bone thinning, also known as osteoporosis. As long wing feathers attach to the ulnar shaft, considerable bone thinning on both ulnae on E.191 may reflect repeated nutritional strain caused by routine feather plucking (Figure 4.12b). This same pathological anomaly has been cited as evidence for captive confinement among tropical macaws penned at the site of Paquimé in northern Chihuahua, Mexico (Di Peso et al. 1974).

Burial 6

We must begin this discussion by considering the implication of the sheer quantity of eighteen eagles deposited in Burial 6. As already mentioned, this was likely a predetermined number based on its cosmological significance. Such a large population of eagles is unattainable from a single hunting party in the Valley of Teotihuacan given the territorial habits of the raptor. One can fathom why keeping some eagles in captivity was necessary to secure the requisite number of victims for

The Zooarchaeological Data 115

(a)

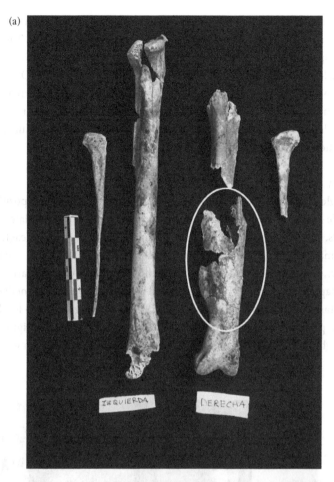

(b)

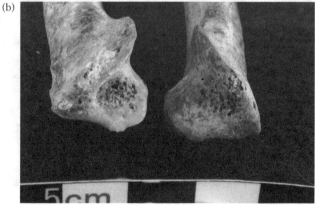

FIGURE 4.12
Examples of pathologies on eagles from Burial 2: (a) E.81.1 fractured right tibiotarsus bone (circle) and (b) E.191 ulnae showing bone thinning. Photographs: N. Sugiyama.

the ritual spectacle. This may also explain why the eagle population was split between primary (MNI 9) and secondary (MNI 9) deposits (Table 4.5). There was no apparent spatial arrangement of primary versus secondary deposits. Nine males and four females were sexed in Burial 6 through zooarchaeological and aDNA methods (Singleton et al. 2023). All raptors had reached adult stature, surviving beyond three months of age. Next, I describe the variable eagle life histories reconstructed via pathological indicators of captivity, distribution of surface features, and the composition of their stomach contents.

PRIMARY BURIALS

Nine eagles were sacrificed in Burial 6. Most primary eagles were positioned on their side with overlapping extremities, likely tethered in place (Plate 12a). Like the felids, pathological indicators of stress and disease on various eagles ($n = 5$, both primary and secondary burials) were telltale signs of long-term confinement. Moreover, multiple individuals exhibiting the same pathological marker indicate similar captive conditions. Three eagles had a deformation on the medial surface of their tarsometatarsus bone (lower limb). E.2069.1's (Figure 4.13a) left limb was rounded, porous, and inflated due to an infection, deforming the original smooth and straight surface. E.1961.1 manifests the same infection on its left tarsometatarsus

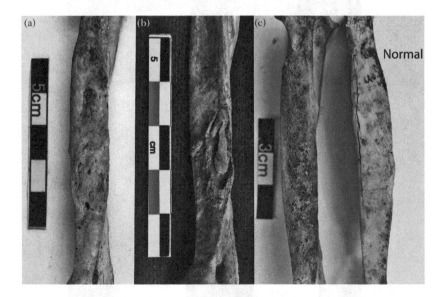

FIGURE 4.13
Medial view of eagle tarsometatarsus bones with pathology, (a) E.1961.1 left side, (b) E.2246 right side, and (c) E.2069.1 deformed right side next to normal left. Photograph: N. Sugiyama.

bone (Figure 4.13c). A third raptor presenting this same pathology was not of a primary burial, and his life history is presented in Chapter 6 (E.2246, Figure 4.13b).

I propose that the tethered confinement of the eagles at Teotihuacan resulted in repetitive and long-term friction along the medial shaft, resulting in the observed pathological condition. American kestrels (*Falco sparverius*) fitted with standard jesses in modern zoos caused "traumatic sloughing of the epidermal scales on the legs" (Brisbin and Wagner 1970: 29). Even leather jesses on screech owls (*Otus asio*) affected the tarsi-feathers due to the constant friction (Brisbin and Wagner 1970: 29). Golden eagles also have small tarsi-feathers that would complicate injury/infection as the feathers facilitate blood clots along cuts and abrasions. Ethnographic documentation of eagles tethered to perches in the Southwestern United States (Chapter 3) also supports the present explanation of the pathology.

The eagle's most lethal weapon is its sharp talons, and perhaps the pathology recorded on E.1888's first phalange on digit one helped reduce risk during handling. This male eagle placed on the southwest corner of the offering chamber lacked the distal end of the first phalange, and remodeling around the distal edge shows signs of healing where the cut was infected. The corresponding talon (third phalange) was absent despite the successful recovery of the rest of its phalanges. It appears eagle handlers intentionally removed the most prominent and dangerous talon.

Both tibiotarsi of E.1962 displayed deep cuts on the edges of the distal articular surface (Figure 4.14). The corresponding tarsometatarsus was intact with no

FIGURE 4.14
Eagle E.1962 left tibiotarsus distal articular surface with deep cutmarks. Photograph: N. Sugiyama.

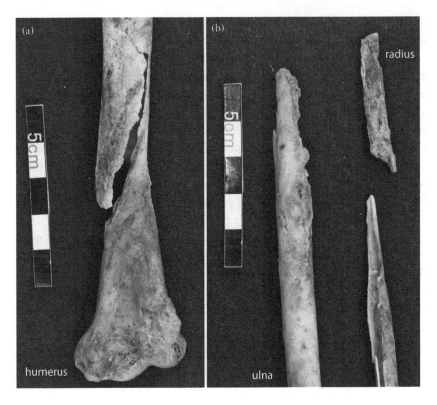

FIGURE 4.15
Eagle E.2070 pathologies: (a) humerus with bone thinning around spiral fracture; (b) ulna and radius with similar pathology. Photograph: N. Sugiyama.

surface modification. The distal tibiotarsus area is relatively bare, with only small tarsi-feathers, eliminating resource extraction as a viable explanation for the intervention. I propose the trauma was intentionally inflicted on the medial and lateral edges where tough tendons attach, disabling the eagle's keen and robust talons that would have facilitated handling. The absence of remodeling around the cutmarks suggests an injury relatively close to the time of death, although it was likely not the cause of death. No additional modifications were recorded on the skeleton, and I suspect it was a primary burial.

A spiral fracture ran along the humeral shaft of E.2070, where considerable bone thinning was observed (Figure 4.15a). As the corresponding radius and ulna exhibit similar bone thinning, the entire left wing seems affected by an infectious disease (Figure 4.15b). While the type of infection remains indeterminate, we can assume captive behavior increases risk due to alimental and nutritional stress, debilities caused by feather plucking, vitamin D deficiency, and mental and physical stress from restricted mobility. In particular, wings are susceptible to disease due to feather plucking, causing extensive energetic strain, and because flight is usually restricted, often by clipping their wings.

E.2226's right femur also displayed anomalies of discoloration and bone thinning on both epiphyseal shaft regions. While interpreted initially as a taphonomical cause, the parallels to E.2070's wings suggest it is probably also a pathology, likely an infectious disease that affected its lower limb joints.

While the surface modifications described earlier helped reconstruct complex life histories, some primary burials exhibited no alterations (E.2192, E.2200, and E.2214/1919). These eagles either represent a "wild" population or not all instances of captivity leave osteological traces. Skeletal isotopic data is need to supplement osteological markers of captivity to test this hypothesis (Chapter 5).

SECONDARY BURIALS

Next, I describe a heterogeneous secondary eagle population of Burial 6. Some were articulated complete skeletons with evidence of extracted secondary products (meat, tendons, soft tissue, and feathers). Others represented incomplete prepared artifacts, possibly feathered capes that emphasized their wings, while still others may have been taxidermically prepared. Like the primary offerings, some secondary eagles also demonstrated pathological indicators of captivity, yet others left no traces of such human–animal interactions.

Among the semi-complete secondary burials, particular portions of the eagle's body were repeatedly emphasized: the cranium/mandible, the wings, the digits, and the talons (Figure 4.16). The overlap analysis totals only eight individuals because E.2222's poorly preserved fragmented remains prohibited mapping onto the diagram. Unlike canid and felid secondary deposits that concentrated on their heads,

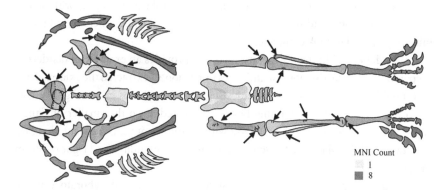

FIGURE 4.16
Overlap analyses (gray) and surface modifications (black lines) of secondary eagles from Burial 6.

sometimes including their phalanges, there was an emphasis on eagle heads and extremities. Wings were valued for their long feathers, and the iconic association with the eagle's greatest weapon, its prominent talons, is also expressed.

Surface modifications can be testimonies of preparation strategies, and six of the nine eagles exhibited extensive postmortem processing, many despite a complete and articulated skeleton. For example, E.2010 seemingly represented a primary burial, but skeletal reconstruction and careful examination of surface modifications revealed postmortem deposition. A large occipital orifice facilitated practitioners to extract the soft tissue from the brain case. They inflicted cutmarks along the left orbital margins and an accessory bone near the eye cavity while removing the eyeball. They also left very shallow cutmarks along the proximal shaft of the left humerus. While these marks signal postmortem modification of the corpse, the complete and articulated layout of the skeleton suggests that after extracting the soft tissue, meat, and/or feathers, they retained skeletal articulation up to its final deposition.

Cutmarks were generally distributed on the cranium, mandible, humerus, femur, tibiotarsus, fibula, and tarsometatarsus bones. These areas denote where dismemberment occurred and/or soft tissues were extracted (Figure 4.16). Consistent alterations on the occipital region of the eagle's cranium were to extract the encephalic mass from the braincase. Variations in the processing techniques included a round circular opening at the occipital region, a large orifice extending from the foramen magnum, and a transversal cut along the nuchal crest. Although many surface alterations concentrated near the ends of long bones, between the diaphysis and the shaft where many muscles and tough tendons attach, there were a couple of cutmarks along the medial shaft. Only one specimen exhibited cutmarks along the articular surfaces between the tibiotarsus and tarsometatarsus, signaling that very few animals were dismembered. These diverse patterns represent variations in preparation techniques; some individuals retained skeletal integrity with no dismemberment, some had secondary products removed, while others were taxidermically prepared to look complete.

E.2193, deposited in the northeastern corner, provides an example of taxidermic preparation. Skeletal distribution indicates practitioners extracted the axial skeleton and shoulder girdles, keeping the head, wings, and hind limbs intact (Figure 4.17a). However, they kept the remaining bones articulated, even the smaller phalanges and claws. They detached the braincase with a prominent transverse cut along the cranium. Additional cutmarks were placed on its left mandible and right radius by the proximal shaft.

A modern eagle taxidermy housed at the Paleozoological Laboratory in the Instituto de Investigaciones Antropológicas at the UNAM provided a comparative sample. Element distribution, as well as position and the type of surface

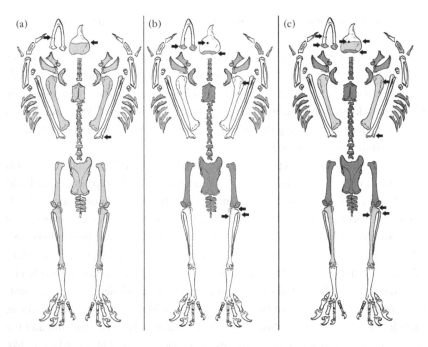

FIGURE 4.17
Element and cutmark distribution of eagles: (a) E.2193; (b) modern comparative eagle prepared by taxidermist; (c) overlap analyses of the two samples. Area in gray is absent; arrows highlight cultural modifications.

modification, were recorded. The axial skeleton (vertebrae, keel, and synsacrum), the shoulder girdle (coracoids, scapula, and furculum), the ribcage, and the upper hind limb (femur) were absent (Figure 4.17b). Taxidermists extracted these bones to remove the internal organ, stuffed its body, and used the remaining bones to maintain skeletal integrity. Additional modifications include a large transversal cut along the occipital region that extended to the basioccipital region, a perforation on the superior surface of the skull, a cut on both sides of the mandible at the angular area, a puncture on the humerus by the deltoid crest, a perforation on the proximal tibiotarsal articular surface, a cut on the proximal head of the fibula, and cuts on both ulnas at the articular surfaces.

The spatial overlap of the element distribution and surface modification of the modern taxidermy with E.2193 (Figure 4.17c) highlighted several striking parallels. Both preparation procedures resulted in the extraction of the axial skeleton, the ribs, the shoulder girdle, and part of the hind limb (presence/absence of tibiotarsus and fibula varied). Taxidermists discarded internal and cerebral organs by removing the entire braincase (E.2193) or extracting the occipital region (comparative sample).

Cutmarks and perforations signal areas that require additional support for body rigidity.

As a third comparison, golden eagles from Offering 120 at the Templo Mayor in the Aztec capital support taxidermy practiced during Post-Teotihuacan periods (Quezada Ramírez et al. 2010; Valentín Maldonado 2018). The authors describe five preparation techniques, but all display consistent patterns of extracting various axial elements and removing the encephalic organs from the braincase, similar to E.2193 and the modern comparative sample.

Like E.2193, E.2239 was represented only by its wings and hind limbs. While it is tempting to argue that this individual was also taxidermically prepared, its skull was absent. The eagle was likely prepared into a feathered cape or more extensively altered form. Deep grooves placed on the articular surface of the left tarsometatarsus bone and along the distal shaft of the left humerus mark areas of dismemberment.

Some individuals had no surface modifications but were designated secondary deposits because of incomplete skeletons. For example, E.2222 was represented by the wings, part of the axial skeleton, and parts of the mandible. E.2225.1 was similarly composed of the extremities, parts of the shoulder girdle, and tail vertebrae, including the last vertebra called the pygostyle. Lacking the axial skeleton and the head, this individual was a highly processed artifact, maybe a feathered cape (like E.2239). Retention of the pygostyle, the attachment site for the long tail feathers, suggests feathers were an integral part of the offering. Similarly, E.2261, located by the northern wall, was defined as a secondary burial because only fragments of the right humerus, left ulna, femur (both sides), phalanges, and talons were present. In the animal biography section (Chapter 6), I describe the life history of E.2246, which presented both pathological indicators of captivity alongside extensive modification, marking it as a secondary deposit.

Burial 5

Ritual practitioners placed an adult-statured eagle (E.1638) in Burial 5 between two animals; to its south lay a complete puma (E.1639), and to its east rested a complete crow (E.1637) (Plate 7). These complete animals are associated with humans. They arranged a complete eagle and crow before the central figure, Individual 5-A, while the puma lay next to Individual 5-B.

Unfortunately, extreme taphonomic damage resulted in very brittle and warped fragmentary bones, making it impossible to reconstruct fully. I was able to identify significant portion of the hind limb (fragments of the femur, tibiotarsus, tarsometatarsus, phalanges, and talons), parts of the wing (ulna, radius, and humerus), and fragments of the cranium and mandible. Despite the incomplete inventory, the distribution of bone scatter in field drawings and photographs suggests the eagle was a primary burial. No additional information concerning surface markings or pathologies was obtained.

Rattlesnakes

Rattlesnakes were the most abundant primary burial found in the Moon the Pyramid offerings (MNI 33, 36% of primary burials) (Table 4.6). Often deposited as a cluster, it was challenging to calculate total MNI. Furthermore, characteristic bones such as small cranial fragments are frequently destroyed or lost from archaeological records because serpents have a unique adaptation that allows them to dismount the jaw due to their never-fusing cranial elements. Good preservation and

TABLE 4.6
Summary of Rattlesnake Remains from the Moon Pyramid

Element #	MNI	Stom	Notes
Burial 2			
252	6	No	MNI count based on the number of mandibles.
Burial 6			
In Basket	18+	UnID	MNI count based on drawing from MRI images.
Burial 5			
1021	1	No	Semi-complete individual.
1022	2	Yes	MNI of 2 based on size difference, none are very complete. One had a rodent in stom. Vert of a third individual corresponds to E.1507, not in MNI count.
1037	1	No	One individual fairly complete, including cranial elements.
1063	1	No	
1489	2	Yes	MNI of 2 based on size difference. One had a rodent in stom. Some elements likely correspond to E.1568 and E.1569, not in the MNI count.
1494	1	Yes	Pathology, 2 dorsal vertebras fused together. MNI of 2 rodents in the stom.
1507	1	Yes	One rodent in stomach. Semi complete individual. Included materials from E.1022.
1552	—	No	Not complete. Likely part of E.1489 and E.1569
1568	—	No	Not complete. Parts of this individual in E.1489 and E.1569.
1569	—	No	Not complete. Parts of this individual in E.1489 and E.1568.

Stom: Stomach content.

meticulous excavation techniques in Burial 2 allowed the recovery of six pairs of mandibles, providing the only definitive MNI count. MNI calculations for Burials 6 and 5 are tentative as the number of vertebrae varies considerably by species and among individuals. Nonetheless, these counts are convincing due to the consistent use of significant numerals in Burial 6 and 5 (18 and 9, respectively). As each serpent bundle included all vertebral types (ventral, medial, and distal vertebrae), we assumed they were primary burials even if archaeological recovery of the entire skeleton was impossible. Serpent age and sex determination were unattainable.

At least two, and maybe three species of rattlesnake participated in the offerings based on the vertebrae's size and morphology. About five to six rattlesnake species inhabit the Mexican Basin (see Chapter 4), but species-level identification was impossible. Developing a comparative morphometric measurement standard for serpent vertebrae is necessary to designate species. A series of metric and morphometric traits were recorded for the archaeological collection following LaDuke (1991). Small rodent bones, particularly deer mice (*Peromyscus* sp.) mixed with rib fragments comprised their final meal before their sacrifice, paralleling ritual procedures of the mammal and avian persons.

Burial 2

Rattlesnakes concentrated near the center of Burial 2, just to the west of a large disk. The scattered vertebrae were assigned one Element number, E.252, and MNI calculations based on the number of mandibles were assigned later in the lab. No information about the age or sex of the individuals could be obtained. Consistent rattlesnake vertebral size suggested a preference for a single rattlesnake species, contrasting with the two size classes (and thus at least two species) represented in Burial 5's serpentine assemblage.

Burial 6

Near the center of Burial 6 lay an intact round basket with large concentric circles delimiting rows of woven fibers. This basket was excavated as a block to preserve this fragile find. Sampling of the vegetal material exposed small rattlesnake vertebrae and rib fragments stored within the basket. A magnetic resonance imaging (MRI) scan revealed that the basket contained many superimposed rattlesnakes (Plate 12b, c). As sampled vertebrae exhibited consistent morphology and size to rattlesnakes analyzed from Burials 2 and 5, I suspect all skeletons are of rattlesnakes. I generated a plan-view drawing via overlaying cross-sections of multiple MRI layers. MNI calculation was difficult because the MRI image resolution only distinguished the vertebral column, obscuring low-density bones such as ribs and crania. Taphonomic

(a)

(b)

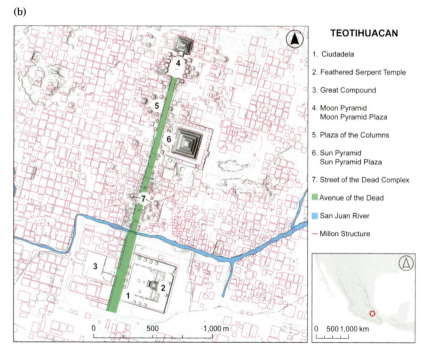

PLATE 1
(a) Vista of the Cerro Gordo, Moon Pyramid, and Sun Pyramid. Photograph: R. Cebollero.
(b) Lidar map of Teotihuacan overlaid with Millon's (1973) reconstruction of structures indicating sites mentioned in the text. © Project Plaza of the Columns Complex.

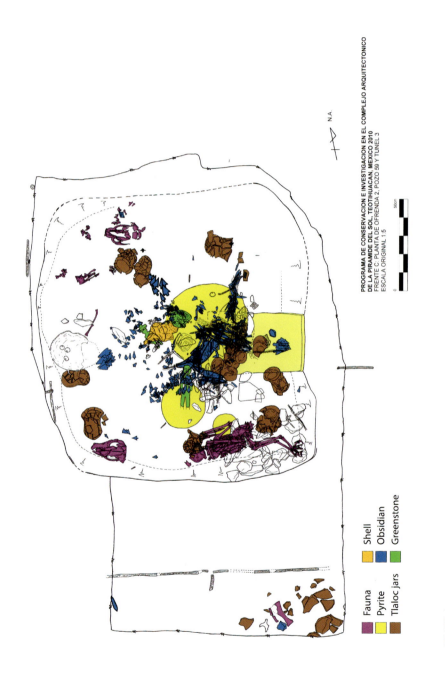

PLATE 2
Plan drawing of Sun Pyramid, Offering 2. Drawing by N. Sugiyama, O. Quezada, and S. Sugiyama.

PLATE 3
Animals from Offering 2, Sun Pyramid: (a) a complete eagle, (b) a wolf skull next to a Tlaloc vessel, and (c) a puma cranium. Photographs: N. Sugiyama.

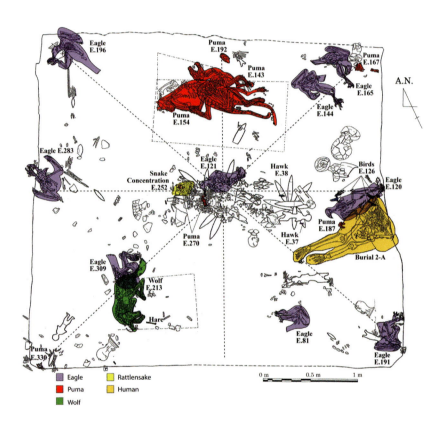

PLATE 4
Plan drawing of Burial 2. © Moon Pyramid Project.

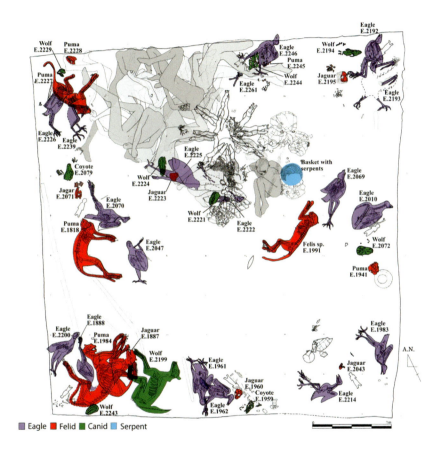

PLATE 5
Plan drawing of Burial 6. © Moon Pyramid Project.

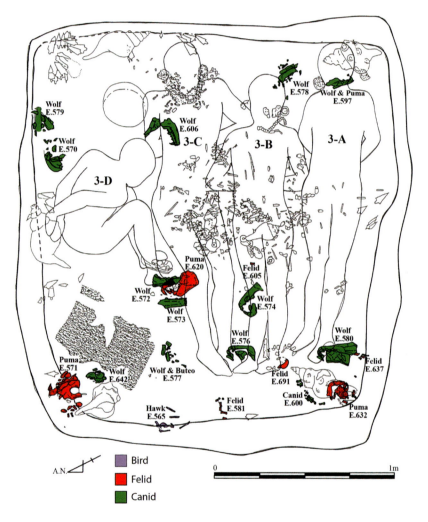

PLATE 6
Plan drawing of Burial 3. © Moon Pyramid Project.

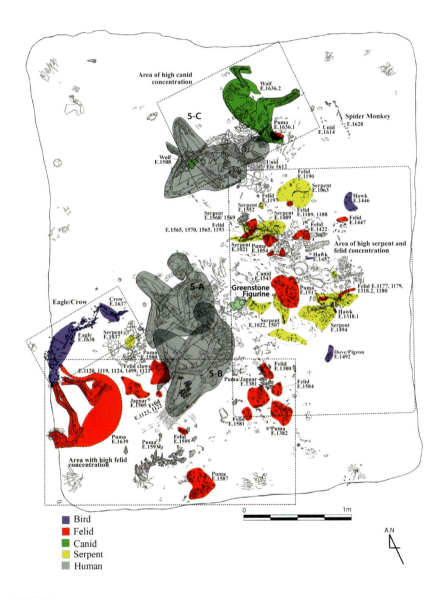

PLATE 7
Plan drawing of Burial 5. © Moon Pyramid Project.

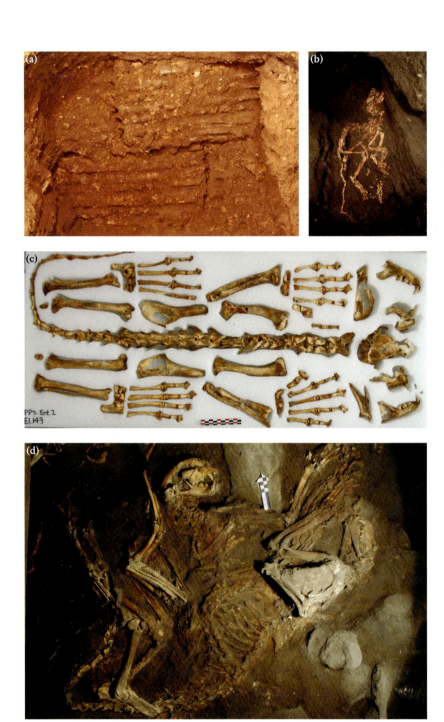

PLATE 8
Burial 2: (a) horizontal post holes of the two wooden cages, (b) puma E.143 in situ, (c) after cleaning and restoration, and Burial 6: (d) a puma (E.1984, left) and a jaguar (E.1887, right) in southwestern corner. © Moon Pyramid Project.

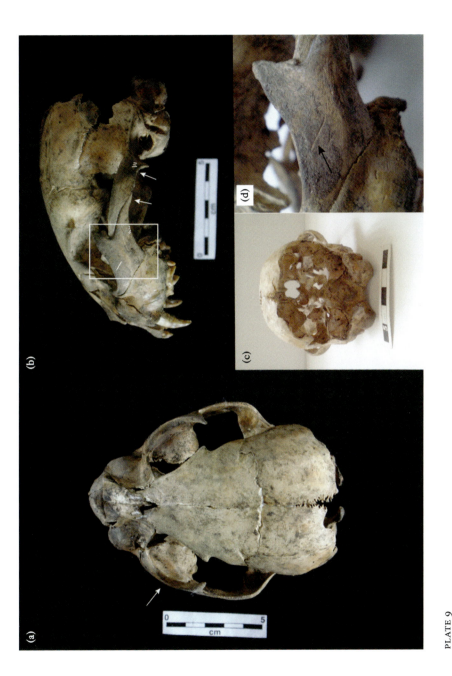

PLATE 9

Jaguar E.1960 from Burial 6: (a) superior view, (b) left lateral view, (c) dorsal view (with encephalic opening), and (d) detail of insert with cutmarks. White arrows and lines indicate the location of cutmarks.

PLATE 10
Burial 2: (a) wolf, E.213.1 and (b) post holes of wooden cage surrounding wolf. © Moon Pyramid Project.

PLATE 11
(a) Wolf E.1636.2 from Burial 5 and (b) Eagle E.196 from Burial 2 associated with a Tlaloc vessel. © Moon Pyramid Project.

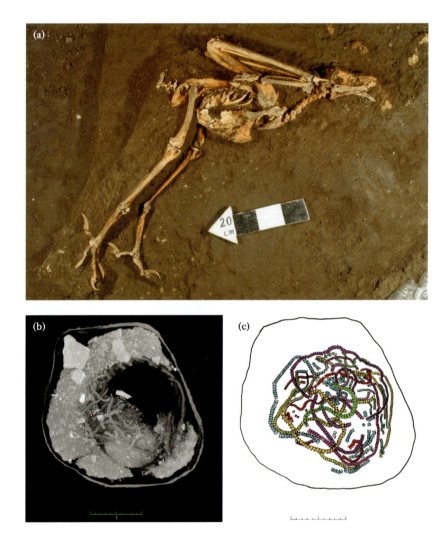

PLATE 12
(a) Eagle E.1983, Burial 6. © Moon Pyramid Project. Archaeological basket with at least eighteen serpents; (b) MRI image; and (c) line drawing. Scale 10 cm. Drawing: N. Sugiyama.

PLATE 13
Puma E.1818 from Burial 6: (a) in situ (note extremities superimposed) © Moon Pyramid Project; (b) left and right innominate (pelvis bone), the latter with pathology; (c) remodeling on right femoral shaft; (d) trauma on the occipital region; and (e) extreme wearing and loss of maxillary mesial dentition.

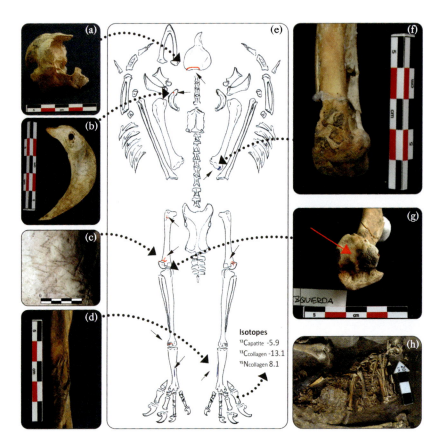

PLATE 14
Life-history data for eagle, E.2246: (a) dorsal view of the skull with a large opening; (b) furculum, left side with perforation; (c) microscope image of cutmarks on left femur; (d) pathology on left medial tarsometatarsus bone; (e) distribution of surface modifications (arrows) on complete skeleton (red = cutmarks, blue = pathologies) and isotope values; (f) pathology on distal humerus; (g) perforation on tibiotarsus bone; and (h) in situ photograph from Burial 6, © Moon Pyramid Project.

PLATE 15
Rattlesnake E.1494: (a) excavation photograph © Moon Pyramid Project, (b) after reconstruction (note white tape indicates fused vertebra), and (c) rodent remains found in the stomach content.

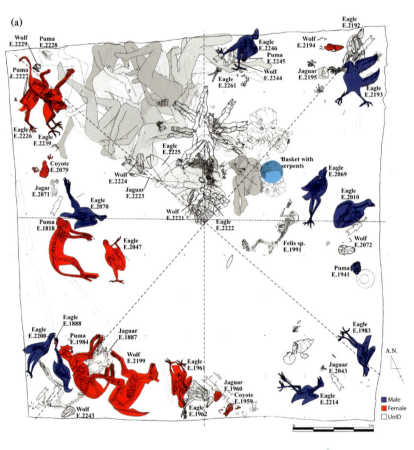

PLATE 16

(a) Plan drawing of Burial 6 labeled by animal's sex. Human bodies and artifacts drawn by G. Pereira and S. Sugiyama; animal outlines drawn by N. Sugiyama. (b) Photograph of militants raising their tethered golden eagles at the military march during the Mexican Independence. Photograph: Presidencia de la República, Creative Commons License CC BY 4.0, accessed 2023.

processes, the archaeological excavation, and the removal of a paleobotanical sample misaligned various elements, compounding quantification issues. The MNI estimate ranged between sixteen and twenty-two individuals, with eighteen providing a conservative estimate that matches general trends in the burial data. The potential eighteen serpents reiterate the importance of this number reflected in the quantity of eagles and eccentric obsidian artifacts.

While the MRI image analyses preserve the organic basket, small and low-density elements (including cranial fragments and stomach contents) remain unanalyzable, surface features undetected (including pathologies), and metric data irretrievable. I did, however, recognize two rattlesnake size classes similar to Burial 5, suggesting consistent usage of at least two species in both contexts. Because the MRI images demonstrate fairly complete vertebral columns swarming in an articulated position, I assume all rattlesnakes were complete and alive, buried in vivo.

Burial 5

Excavators grouped clusters of serpent remains from Burial 5 by Element number. When these groupings contained multiple individuals, zooarchaeological and contextual information assisted MNI tabulations. For example, E.1568 and E.1569, each composed of only a handful of vertebrae, were considered part of E.1489. Similarly, a few of the vertebrae of E.1507 that did not match in size were considered part of one of the three individuals identified in E.1022. An MNI of nine serpents were accounted for in Burial 5, a number repeatedly emphasized by the offertory objects. Consistent with other burials, rattlesnake remains represented two size classes. Besides the sheer quantity of primary rattlesnakes ($n = 33$) from the Moon Pyramid, the fused dorsal vertebrae on E.1494 are the only evidence for serpentine captivity and management as isotope work on serpents has not been carried out (see biography in Chapter 6).

Microfauna: Stomach Contents

A complete list of microfauna is presented in Table 4.7. Most small mammals originate from the abdominal cavity of the sacrificial carnivores. There was a preferential selection of two types of fauna: leporids (rabbits and hares) for the large carnivores (felids, canids, and eagles) and rodents (*Peromyscus* sp.) for the serpents. Isolated unidentified bird remains were also mixed in the stomach contents. A few additional small mammals (Mexican vole, Mexican gray squirrel, unidentified small mammals) were recovered from the offering fill and are likely unrelated to the dedicatory rite.

TABLE 4.7

Summary of Small Animal (Mammals and Birds) Remains from the Moon Pyramid.

Element #	Species	Age	Sex	Eaten by	Captive?*	Surface	Notes
Burial 2							
81.2	*Sylvilagus* sp.	Adult	UnID	Eagle	Yes	Gastric etching	Hind limbs only.
81.4	UnID small bird	UnID	UnID	Eagle	Yes	No	2 frags of unidentified diaphysis. Mixed in the stom of an eagle with another rabbit.
154.2	Leporidae	UnID	UnID	Puma	Yes	No	Mixed in with coprolites. 2 teeth and a phalange.
167.2	*Sylvilagus* sp.	Adult	UnID	—	No	No	With felid head E.1671. Can be fill or part of eagle E.165.
213.2	*Lepus* sp.	Y adult	UnID	Wolf	Yes	Discolored and gastric etching	Possibly burnt. Scattered elements of entire body.
213.3	*Sylvilagus* sp.	Adult	UnID	Wolf	Yes	Burnt and gastric etching	Greater degree of gastric etching.
217	*Lepus* sp.	Adult	UnID	—	—	No	Isolated tibia found inside cage of wolf E.213.
283.2	*Sylvilagus* sp.	Adult	UnID	Eagle	No	Burnt	Scattered elements of entire body.
309.2	*S. floridanus*	Y adult	UnID	Eagle	No	Burnt and gastric etching	Scattered elements of entire body.
309.3	*S. audubonii*	Juvenile	UnID	Eagle	No	Gastric etching	Scattered elements of entire body.
165.1	*Microtus mexicanus*	Juvenile	UnID	Eagle	No	No	Isolated ilium, unsure if stomach content or fill material.
283.3	UnID small bird	UnID	UnID	Eagle	No	No	2 cervical, 1 lumbar vertebra in stomach of an eagle.
218	UnID mammal	Inf/Juv	UnID	No	No	No	2 unfused thoracic vertebral frags. From fill.
Burial 6							
1818.2	*S. audubonii*	Infant	UnID	Puma	Yes	Burnt and gastric etching	Scattered elements of entire body. Second rabbit and bird in same stomach content.

					Burnt and gastric etching	
1818.3	S. audubonii	Infant	UnID	Puma	Yes	Scattered elements of entire body. Second rabbit and bird in same stomach content.
1818.4	UnID small bird	UnID	UnID	Puma	Yes	2 frag. of isolated long bones.
1961.2	S. audubonii	UnID	UnID	Eagle	Yes	Possibly cooked. Scattered elements of entire body.
1991.2	Sylvilagus sp.	Juvenile	UnID	Felis sp.	No	Mainly hind limb elements.
2069.2	S. floridanus	Adult	UnID	Eagle	Yes	Mainly hind limb elements.
2207	Sciurus aureogaster	UnID	UnID	No	No	7 cranial frags, 3rd metacarpus, 7 phalanges and 2 claws. Evidence of burning. From fill.
2077	UnID mammal	UnID	UnID	No	No	Spongy bone, unidentified medium mammal. From fill.
1982.3	UnID mammal	UnID	UnID	No	No	Sesamoid and spongy bone frags. From fill.
Burial 5						
E1S3.2	Lepus sp.	Adult	UnID	No	No	Metapodial frag, probably mixed fill refuge.
1022.4	Rodentia	UnID	UnID	Serpent	No	Skull frag, mandible and one long bone (humerus).
1489.2	Peromyscus sp.	UnID	UnID	Serpent	No	Cervical vert., pelvis and hind limbs.
1494.2	Peromyscus sp.	UnID	UnID	Serpent	Yes	Scattered elements of entire body.
1494.3	Peromyscus sp.	UnID	UnID	Serpent	Yes	Cranium only.
1507.2	Peromyscus sp.	UnID	UnID	Serpent	No	L tibia only.

See table 3.1 for common names. Surface: surface modification, UnID: unidentified, L: left. S.: Sylvilagus

*Captive? Implies if the carnivore that consumed the small game had pathological indicators of captivity. Many expressed isotope values of various degrees of anthropomorphic diet with heightened C_4 input.

TABLE 4.8
Leporid Age Distribution (MNI) for Each Offering

	Burial 2	Burial 6	Total #	Total %
Infant	0	2	2	13
Infant/Juvenile	0	0	0	0
Juvenile	1	1	2	13
Young Adult	2	0	2	13
Adult	6	1	7	48
UnID	1	1	2	13
Total	**10**	**5**	**15**	

Ritual practitioners most frequently fed eagles due to the abundance of primary burials. Seven eagles (37%, out of nineteen primary) were provided a meal prior to their ritual slaughter. In comparison, only one wolf (33%, out of three) and three felids (37%, out of eight) were fed. Five serpents (15%, out of thirty-three), in this case exclusively from Burial 5, also exhibited stomach contexts. Several predators consumed multiple animals prior to their slaughter. For example, a puma from Burial 6 (E.1818.1) ate two cottontails (E.1818.2 and E.1818.3) and an unidentified small bird (E.1818.4). Interestingly, some bones not only had gastric etching from the intestinal acids but also discoloration due to burning. The caged wolf from Burial 2 (E.213.1) consumed one hare and one cottontail with evidence of gastric etching, discoloration, and burning. At least six carnivores from both Burials 2 and 6 consumed cooked animals. The uniform assemblage of leporids and rodents as preferred foodstuff for the sacrificial victims demonstrates that ritualistic feeding was integral to the ritualization process. As discussed in more detail in the subsequent chapter, the leporid data also convey how Teotihuacan sustained a population of specialized apex predators and fed their city.

Leporidae (Rabbits and Hares)

We identified fifteen leporid remains from the offerings. The majority consisted of cottontails (*Sylvilagus* sp., $n = 13$), while hares (*Lepus* sp.) were the minority ($n = 2$). Cottontails are relatively smaller and easier to manage in captivity, which are optimal features for maintaining a constant protein source to feed these carnivores. Cottontails den easily and withstand co-habitation, whereas hares tend to require more open habitats (Somerville and Sugiyama 2021).

Leporids were consumed by sacrificed predators in Burials 2 ($n = 8$) and 6 ($n = 5$), but not in Burials 3 and 5. This is because primary animal burials were absent in Burial 3, and only serpents consumed microfauna from Burial 5. The majority of the leporids were adults (48%), while juvenile (13%), young adult (13%), infants (13%), and infant/juvenile (13%) were less abundant (Table 4.8). Leporid infants in Burial 6 imply access to a young population, which characterizes of a breeding population.

The representation of various fragmented bones throughout the entire body indicates that complete rabbits/hares were fed to the carnivores. In some instances, the presence of only the extremities suggested provisioning butchered sections. Bones discolored from heat exposure signaled artificial feeding.

Rodentia

Rodent remains found in rattlesnake's stomachs were very small and often incomplete, complicating age and sex designations. Most Burial 5 rodents were deer mice (*Peromyscus* sp.), optimal rattlesnake prey. Isolated bones were found disarticulated and mixed with the ribs. Since rattlesnakes tend to swallow their prey whole, these mice were probably fed whole. The rodents from the stomach cavity help prove the primary placement of rattlesnakes who underwent the same ritualized feeding process, even though the entire skeleton was not always recoverable. None of these rodents exhibited surface modifications. In one instance, one rattlesnake (E.1494) consumed two rodents. To date, evidence of rodent-fed rattlesnakes is exclusive to Burial 5. MRI image-based analyses of Burial 6 prohibited the detection of stomach contents.

The remains of one Mexican gray squirrel (*Sciurus aureogaster*), including seven cranial fragments, a third right metacarpal, seven phalanges, two claws, and incisors, were found burnt in Burial 6 (E.2207). It is unclear if these remains were part of the fill matrix or were consumed by sacrificed animals as no contextual data helped resolve this issue.

Other Avian and Nonlocal Fauna

In contrast to the redundant use of representative species in primary burials, several additional avian and nonlocal fauna were identified among secondary deposits. Such species diversified the offerings as secondary agents utilized in state rituals. They included various raptors (hawks, owls, and falcons), ravens, and other birds like the Columbidae (dove/pigeon) or the quail (Table 4.9). Furthermore, the discovery of the spider monkey in Burial 5 (albeit only represented by two incomplete arm bones) was unexpected and difficult to contextualize. Given the discovery of a complete spider monkey sacrificed at Plaza of the Columns Complex, nonlocal fauna may have been strategic gifts exchanged to form and display diplomatic ties (Sugiyama et al. 2022).

Most of these individuals represented semi-complete prepared skeletons or isolated elements, presumably to deposit not only their bones and teeth but also secondary resources such as pelts and feathers. Unsurprisingly, wing elements were most commonly represented among the avian remains. These additional species were

TABLE 4.9
Summary of Other Avian Remains from the Moon Pyramid

Element #	Specie	Age	Surface	Body Part	Notes
Burial 2					
38.2	*Bubo virginianus*	UnID	No	Isolated wing bone	Looks like E.126.3, but same element, MNI for *B. virginianus* is 2.
126.3	*Bubo virginianus*	UnID	No	Mixed incomplete	Various elements throughout the skeleton. Hard to determine if it was complete, but at least included both extremities.
126.4	*Buteo* sp.	UnID	No	Both wings	Wing elements on both sides, and possibly phalanges on the feet.
37	*Buteo* sp.	UnID	No	Isolated wing bone	R carpometacarpus.
81.3	*Buteo* sp.	Adult?	No	Isolated wing bone	Complete L ulna. Mixed with eagle, E.81.1 May be part of the stomach content or feathered wing.
38.1	*Buteo jamaicensis*	UnID	No	R wing elements	Looks like E.37, but larger. Maybe male/female difference.
126.1	*Corvus corax*	UnID	No	Mixed incomplete	Extremities, some cranial frags, and various axial elements. Probably was complete or semi-complete.
126.5	*Corvus corax*	UnID	No	Both hind limbs	Both distal tarsometatarsi. Much smaller Corvus specimen than E.126.1, may be of the common crow.
126.2	*Falco mexicanus*	UnID	No	Semi-complete	Frags of the head, extremities (wing and hind limb), and a few vertebrae.
91	UnID bird	UnID	No	UnID	Isolated bones associated with a shell. Looks like it might be a coracoid of an eagle, but might be too small.
Burial 6					
2056.1	*Colinus virginianus*	UnID	No	Mixed incomplete	Two L mandibles with MNI of two.
2056.2	*Colinus virginianus*	UnID	No	Mixed incomplete	Two L mandibles with MNI of two.
1982.1	*Columbina inca*	UnID	No	Both wings	

ID	Taxon	Age	Burned	Completeness	Notes
1982.4	UnID small bird	UnID	No	Mixed incomplete	Frags of vertebrae and long bone.
2060	UnID bird	UnID	No	Mixed incomplete	Unidentified laminar bone, may be from an eagle.
Burial 3					
565	*Buteo* sp.	Juvenile	Yes	Mixed incomplete	Wings not fully developed, thus juvenile. Some cutmarks on its extremities.
577.2	*Buteo magnirostris*	UnID	No	Isolated wing bone	R carpometacarpus bone found mixed with canid head, Element 577.1.
575.3	UnID small bird	UnID	No	Isolated eye piece	Sclerotic eye-ring piece. Because there are no eagles from this burial, may be from the fill or from the Buteo found in this burial.
Burial 5					
1446.1	*Buteo* sp.	UnID	No	Extremities only	R humerus, R wing phalange 1, and parts of tarsometatarsus and phalanges of both hind limbs.
1318.1	*Buteo magnirostris*	UnID	No	Isolated wing bone	R carpometacarpus.
1457	*Buteo magnirostris*	UnID	No	Isolated wing bone	L carpometacarpus.
1492	Columbidae	Adult	No	Semi-complete	Probably was a complete individual.
1446.2	Columbidae	UnID	No	R wing only	R carpometacarpus and ulna.
S3E3.3	Columbidae	UnID	No	Isolated wing and tail bone	R carpometacarpus and pygostyle. Both 1492 and 1446.2 have a R carpometacarpus so MNI is 3 for Columbidae.
1637	*Corvus corax*	UnID	Yes	Semi-complete	Probably a complete individual. Pathology on the feet (phalanges) and L digit 3 on the wing.

L: left, R: right

(a)

(b)

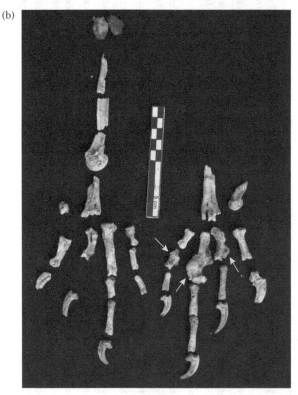

FIGURE 4.18
Raven E.1637 from Burial 5: (a) excavation photograph of head © Moon Pyramid Project and (b) photograph of feet after cleaning, white arrows indicate the location of pathologies.

most likely supplementary ritual paraphernalia accompanying restricted key corporeal animal forms. However, they also emphasize predatory/scavenging species of the day and night (owls, hawks, falcons, and ravens). Nonpredatory species include the bobwhite quail (*Colinus virginianus*) and the pigeon/dove (Columbidae), which may represent inclusions from the fill matrix that were not part of the offered assemblage.

Besides the eagle, the only other sacrificed bird was the common raven (*Corvus corax*) from Burial 5 (E.1637, Figure 4.18a). This raven was placed as the eagle's nocturnal counterpart in front of Individual 5-A on the western edge of the offering. Interestingly, it also exhibited pathologies of bone deformation on the left third digit of the wing and several of the phalanges of the feet (Figure 4.18b). This finding opens the possibility that bird handlers may have kept diverse birds in the city in addition to the eagle. Two ravens were also identified in Burial 2, though incomplete. Surface modification was absent. Very little age and sex data of the other avian fauna were retrievable.

Zooarchaeological Summary

There were notable patterns in the zooarchaeological data that reflect how each animal negotiated their place at Teotihuacan. Such negotiations were affected by the animal's vitalities, such as behavior and biology, including accessibility and adaptability to captive environments and their sociality (see Chapter 3). Felids, though highly abundant across all offertory contexts, were dominantly represented by skulls stripped of their pelts or as prepared pelts. Manipulation of felid corporeal forms was fairly standardized within each context and was conducted when the bone was still green (when preservation allowed assessment). Several pathologies among the primary felid bones indicate highly stressed and traumatic conditions under confinement, likely because these specialized solitary predators were quite challenging to maintain.

Canid corporeal forms contained very few primary individuals ($n = 3$), and none exhibited signs of captivity/manipulation. The secondary canid corporeal forms were much more varied in the timing of intervention and processing techniques, reflecting a more accessible local favorite. We must also remember that wolves are much more adaptable to human cohabitation, as they are the wild progenitor to dogs.

Eagle primary and secondary corporeal forms seem to have been regarded somewhat similarly as they both expressed evidence of manipulation, and there was an effort for eagle corpses to be presented intact with skeletal integrity, at least to the public during the ritual performance (including evidence of taxidermy). Thus, I hesitate to create the general binary of live sacrifice versus secondary deposit for eagles, a thought I return to in Chapter 6. Abundant pathologies and surface markings iterate the challenges of maintaining these raptors in captivity (regardless of being primary or secondary burials) and the safety precautions necessary to handle them.

Serpents are the only species represented exclusively by primary burials. This conclusion may be a product of the biases in knowing we cannot retrieve the entire skeleton intact. However, evidence of keeping them enclosed in a basket (Burial 6) and consistent representation of different body parts (cervical, dorsal, and caudal vertebrae, cranial parts, and ribs) suggest the rattlesnakes were complete and articulated. We recognized a pathological indicator of captivity only on a single rattlesnake from Burial 5. The sheer quantity of primary serpents ($n = 33$) from across the offerings suggests it would have been easier to attain with access to a captive population. Several serpents also participated in ritualized feeding (in this case, rodents).

Except for the eagles mentioned earlier, animal biographies differed substantially between animals selected for sacrifice (primary burials) versus those processed into secondary animal by-products (crania, skins, wings, etc.). Primary burials were likely buried alive. Evidence of disease and trauma mostly found on primary burials bespeaks not only their confinement under human care but some of the methods and perils of its acquisition, management, and mishaps during this experimental phase of carnivore rearing. Microfauna in the victim's stomach contents or coprolites indicate ritual procedures included a final meal. The primary burials tended to be young, probably brought into the city confines as cubs/chicks.

In contrast, practitioners hunted secondary deposits in the wild, their skulls, pelts, and plumed wings prepared into ritual artifacts. Diverse age groups participated as secondary burials, and golden eagles exhibited evidence of captivity even among secondarily prepared individuals. This pattern among secondary deposits is consistent with more diverse acquisition strategies of animals hunted in the wild and some even collected postmortem (e.g., canids). In continuation, I discuss the isotope data (Chapter 5) before proposing detailed animal biographies and reconstructing the ritualization process of animals chosen for sacrifice in Chapter 6.

CHAPTER 5

ISOTOPE EVIDENCE OF CAPTIVITY

INCREASINGLY, STABLE ISOTOPE RESEARCH IS integrated into zooarchaeological studies (Pilaar Birch 2013), allowing us to probe deeper into the entangled relationships between ancient human and animal diet, mobility, and environment (Emery et al. 2000; White 2004). Particularly relevant to this study is how carbon and nitrogen isotope ratios capture changes in dietary practices indicative of shifts in human–animal dynamics.

While I was fortunate to have clear pathological indicators of animal captivity, such pristine cases are few and far between as changes in animal management often do not leave osteological traces. Thus, the Teotihuacan dataset provides a valuable comparative baseline with osteological and isotopic signals of long-term animal captivity. Already, more recent isotope work in the Maya sites from Copan, Honduras (Sugiyama, Fash, et al. 2018) and Ceibal, Guatemala (Sharpe et al. 2018), as well as sites throughout Parita Bay, Panama (Sugiyama, Martinez-Polanco, et al. 2020), have utilized stable isotopes to tease apart varying degrees of human–animal interactions despite the absence of zooarchaeological markers of captivity.

As we have already published the raw data and methodology for the isotopic study elsewhere (Sugiyama et al. 2015), I present an overview of the results, highlighting how these data inform the zooarchaeological data. In addition, I plot the Teotihuacan isotopes onto simple and complex dietary models to further identify subsistence patterns across corporeal animal forms found in the dedicatory caches. Just as there were osteological distinctions between primary and secondary assemblages, the isotope data identified different dietary patterns among these two groups. Primary burials generally had isotopic values indicative of anthropogenically altered diets, modified from the predominantly "wild" signature of secondary deposits. The exception to this rule was secondary eagles, whose zooarchaeological signatures likewise demonstrated evidence of long-term captivity. I end the chapter by discussing life history reconstructions of the animals through examining teeth and both offsets.

Stable Isotopes as Paleodietary Proxies

I begin with an introduction to the fundamentals of stable isotope analysis to explain how I assessed the degree and duration of captive confinement from this data. Isotope analysis is based on the premise that you are what you eat. The isotopic composition of the organism's bones and teeth reflects ingested food and water sources. Particular isotope ratios of interest are expressed as delta values ($\delta^E X$) in parts per mil (‰):

$$\delta^E X = R_{sample} - R_{standard}/R_{standard} \times 1{,}000$$

(X = C or N, E = 13 or 15 respectively, and R = the ratios of $^{13}C/^{12}C$ and $^{15}N/^{14}N$)

Bone comprises organic (collagen) and mineral (carbonate/bioapatite) components; each provides information about different isotopes. Carbon and nitrogen isotope ratios are extracted from collagen, while carbon and oxygen isotopic ratios are read from carbonate. While we analyzed collagen and carbonate values from bone and tooth dentine, we could only gather carbonate data from tooth enamel because it is made primarily of hydroxyapatite with only negligible collagen content. We interpreted dietary patterns based on carbon and nitrogen isotope data. While oxygen isotopic values were obtained, they will largely not be discussed because of differential effects of body physiology, prohibiting interspecies comparisons.

The carbon isotopic ratio reflects a weighted average of three plant types, defined by its photosynthetic pathway, into the organism's diet (DeNiro and Epstein 1978; van der Merwe 1982). The Calvin cycle (C_3) photosynthetic pathway is characterized by a three-carbon molecule reduction process of atmospheric CO_2 found in most wild and cultivated plants of temperate, tropical, or subarctic regions (values range around −26.5‰) (Smith and Epstein 1971). A four-carbon molecule oxaloacetate found among tropical grasses is based on a Hatch-Slack cycle (C_4) mainly distributed in warm, arid to subarid regions (around −12.5‰). Crassulacean acid metabolism (CAM) plants are comprised of succulents found in hot and arid environments, such as agave, nopal cactus, and other cacti (their values range between C_3 and C_4 plants, overlapping more with C_4 values).

C_3 resources dominate the natural landscape in the Basin of Mexico, although a mix of CAM and C_4 resources is also available. While maize-based (C_4 dominated) diets are the hallmark of an artificial diet, statistically distinct dietary patterns are necessary to identify a captive versus a wild population because of natural prevalence of other local C_4 and CAM flora in the region (e.g., amaranth, *Amaranthus* spp., epazote, *Chenopodium ambrosodies*, and prickly pear cactus, *Opuntia* spp.) (Schoeninger 2009; Warinner et al. 2013).

C_3, C_4, and CAM plant signals enter into the carnivores' isotopic signature through two dietary pathways: direct consumption (i.e., puma eating corn) or as an indirect reflection of the vegetal composition of their prey (i.e., puma eating rabbit eating corn) (Ambrose and DeNiro 1986; DeNiro and Epstein 1978; Krueger and Sullivan 1984). As some carnivores tolerate some level of omnivory, it is critical to distinguish between these two sources of carbon input.

As nitrogen isotopes generally reflect the tropic level of the consumer, it can help separate the two consumption strategies. Nitrogen is incorporated into food webs from atmospheric N_2 in the soil, starting at a very low level (almost 0‰). N-fixing leguminous plants have much lower $\delta^{15}N$ values close to 0‰ while other plants process N through fractionation in their roots and stems, enriching the $\delta^{15}N$ values by 2‰–6‰ (Delwiche and Steyn 1970). The trophic level effect (TLE) results from the preferential preservation of heavy isotopes, with each trophic level recorded in both carbon and nitrogen values. This variation is subtle with carbon ratios (about 1‰ enrichment), but an average of 3‰–4‰ enrichment occurs with nitrogen at each trophic step (up to 6‰) (Kelly 2000; Schoeninger and DeNiro 1984). Thus, an herbivore's $\delta^{15}N$ value is around 3‰–4‰ more enriched than the plants they consume. It follows that a carnivore's $\delta^{15}N$ value is 3‰–4‰ more enriched than that of an herbivore, each trophic step indicating the trophic level of the consumer (Schoeninger and DeNiro 1984).

Mineral bioapatite-carbonate ($\delta^{13}C_{carbonate}$) and organic collagen ($\delta^{13}C_{collagen}$) phases yield slightly different information, with the former indicating the total diet (protein, carbohydrates, and lipids), while the latter is biased toward dietary protein (Ambrose and Norr 1993). Based on animal populations of known C_3 or C_4 diets, Kellner and Schoeninger (2007) derived a simple carbon model charting both $\delta^{13}C_{carbonate}$ and $\delta^{13}C_{collagen}$ on a pair of parallel regression lines, allowing researchers to visualize the relative contributing source (total diet or protein) of the C_3 or C_4 signal (see also Froehle et al. 2010).

While a simple carbon model effectively distinguishes $\delta^{13}C$ contribution from dietary protein versus whole diet, it is impossible to elucidate the dietary protein sources when samples fall between the two regression lines. It is also impossible to distinguish C_4 consumers from marine food consumers on the bivariate plot. This is why Froehle and colleagues (2012) developed a multivariate isotopic model to discriminate among five discrete dietary subgroups: (1) total diet 100% C_3 diet/protein; (2) 70% C_4 total diet, >50% C_4 protein; (3) 50% C_4 total diet, marine protein;

(4) 70% C_3 total diet, ≥65% C_3 protein; and (5) 70% C_4 total diet, ≥65% C_3 protein. A discriminant function analysis of their source datasets of known diets generated linear equations (functions):

"Carbon" F1= $(0.322* \delta^{13}C_{carbonate}) + (0.727* \delta^{13}C_{collagen}) + (0.219*\delta^{15}N) + 9.354$
"Nitrogen" F2 = $(0.393* \delta^{13}C_{carbonate}) + (0.133* \delta^{13}C_{collagen}) + (0.622*\delta^{15}N) - 8.703$

where Function 1 was most heavily influenced by $\delta^{13}C_{carbonate}$ and $\delta^{13}C_{collagen}$, while Function 2 was most strongly influenced by $\delta^{15}N_{collagen}$ (Froehle et al. 2012:357). This multivariate stable isotope diet model allows us to distinguish the dietary contribution of $\delta^{13}C_{carbonate}$, $\delta^{13}C_{collagen}$, and $\delta^{15}N_{collagen}$ sources into a two-dimensional plot. Applying these simple carbon and multivariate models among human populations has allowed researchers to assess dietary groupings across vast regions and chronological spans that reflect gender and status differences (Somerville et al. 2013; Yoder 2010). In this study, I apply simple and multivariate models to generate a holistic dietary reconstruction of the ritualized animals at Teotihuacan.

Hypothesis

Animals in confinement tend to alter their diet substantially from that of their wild counterparts. For example, domesticated dogs are omnivorous scavengers of human waste, and their diets provide informative proxies for human diets, often isotopically indistinguishable from their owners (Allitt et al. 2008). High C_4-based consumption patterns among Mesoamerican dogs showed they were fed almost exclusive C_4-based diets, presumably of maize (White et al. 2001; White, Schwarcz et al. 2004). A similar degree of dependence on C_4 input (up to 97%) in the diet of captive macaws and turkeys indicated that they were kept, even bred, in captivity (Rawlings and Driver 2010; Somerville et al. 2010). More recently, strontium and aDNA analysis shed light on the source population and how these captive populations were maintained (Lipe et al. 2016; Schwartz et al. 2021; Speller et al. 2010).

Some animals, like the peccary and deer, prefer disturbed vegetation, leading them to exploit milpas and agricultural products that heighten human–animal interactions (Pohl 1977; Reina 1967). Such secondary browsers from Maya sites were identified by a mixed diet of C_4 and C_3 grasses, with higher proportions of maize consumption than their wild counterparts (White 2004). In contrast, animals with a predominantly "wild" signature with very little C_4 input, including deer, peccary, and feral dogs, suggested they were hunted in more forested, nondisturbed habitats. Thus, isotopic analysis on diverse fauna spans a continuum in $\delta^{13}C$ values from wild, predominantly C_3 diets to domesticated/bred animals with C_4-dominated diets, and many intermediate values showing a spectrum of human–animal cohabitation in the domesticated landscapes of Mesoamerica (Sugiyama, Martinez-Polanco, et al. 2020).

Captive artificial feeding can also lead to increased levels of omnivory, detectable in the nitrogen isotopic ratios. Increased reliance on a C_4-based diet among dogs at the Maya site of Colha correlated with a decrease in nitrogen values, indicating lower levels of carnivory (White et al. 2001).

I use carbon and nitrogen isotopes to recognize artificial feeding in this paleodietary reconstruction of primary and secondary deposits of felids, canids, eagles, and rabbits. Based on available zooarchaeological evidence, I hypothesized two populations: primary burials composed of some animals kept in captivity for prolonged periods and secondary deposits prepared from wild, hunted animals. The captive-reared group would be discernable via two dietary patterns. Specialized carnivores (felids and eagles) would have tolerated only a diet of maize-stuffed small game (probably rabbits) raised within the city. More omnivorous carnivores (wolves) could subsist on a mixed diet of maize-fed small game combined with other vegetal staples such as maize. Each of these expectations should be detectable through distinct isotopic patterns in two elements: carbon and nitrogen. Increased maize consumption would lead to more enriched $\delta^{13}C$ values, while levels of carnivory are reflected in $\delta^{15}N$ values that increase along the trophic scale. Furthermore, changes in diet over the organism's lifespan can be captured by examining the tooth enamel, which mineralizes only once during the early stages of development, and the bone (and tooth dentine), which remodels continuously and fuses much later in life. A tooth and bone were sampled from the same individual when available.

Four hypotheses were tested (Figure 5.1). (H_0) wild animals were hunted (teeth and bone values = A); wild animals were captured and then kept in captivity by either (H_1) indirect consumption of C_4 resources acquired from maize-fed small game (teeth = A, bone = B) or (H_2) direct consumption of C_4 plants (teeth = A, bone = C); and (H_3) carnivores for ritual purposes were bred in captivity or were captured as cubs/chicks from the wild (teeth and bones = B or C). Different species likely required different strategies (e.g., H_1 for specialized carnivores; H_2 for those that can tolerate omnivory).

Teotihuacan Isotope Results

Isotopic research was conducted in collaboration with Andrew Somerville and Margaret Schoeninger at the Paleodiet Laboratory at the University of California, San Diego. Raw isotope data and details on the methodology are presented in Sugiyama et al. (2015) and Sugiyama (2014: Chapter 7). We sampled felid, canid,

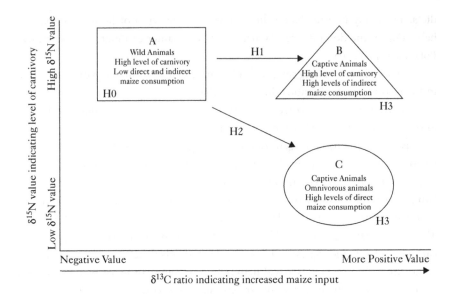

FIGURE 5.1
Model of hypotheses based on $\delta^{15}N$ and $\delta^{13}C$ values of wild (A) and captive (B and C) signatures.

eagle, and leporid remains systematically from Burials 2, 3, 5, and 6.[1] We attempted to standardize the bone/tooth selected for each species across contexts to prevent unintentional duplication of isotope data from the same individual and to account for differences in remodeling rates across elements. When feasible, we extracted a bone and tooth from the same individual. The number of individuals ($n = 80$), the percentage of the population of felids, canids, eagles, and lagomorphs represented (79% of MNI 101), the quantity of bones and teeth, and the sample size that passed diagenesis tests make this a representative sample (Table 5.1). Rigorous standards for diagenesis testing on collagen and carbonate samples (France et al. 2020) produced 100 (carbonate) and 46 (collagen) viable results.

Both carbonate and collagen results demonstrated a statistically significant separation between primary (complete) and secondary (incomplete) burials (Table 5.2).[2]

---

[1] This study did not include rattlesnake specimens because the bone size and type (mainly vertebrae) were unsuited for isotope analysis. In addition, as most isotope studies have been conducted on mammals, there is little information about how serpentine body physiology affects the isotopic values.

[2] Warinner and Tuross (2009) demonstrated differences in bone-enamel offset whereby $\delta^{13}C_{carbonate-enamel}$ values are enriched by 2.3‰. In all figures and tables, tooth values were corrected to bone.

TABLE 5.1
Carbonate and Collagen Sampling Strategy for Each Context and Animal Type

		Felid		Canid		Eagle		Leporid		Total	
		Carbonate	Collagen	Carbonate	Collagen	Carbonate	Collagen	Carbonate	Collagen	Carbonate	Collagen
Burial 2	Bone	2/6	3/6	0/1	1/1	9/9	9/9	2/5	1/5	13/21	14/21
	Tooth	4/4	—	2/2	—	—	—	—	—	6/6	—
	Total	6/10	3/6	2/3	1/1	9/9	9/9	2/5	1/5	19/27	14/21
Burial 6	Bone	9/12	8/12	4/8	5/8	14/15	14/15	4/4	4/4	31/39	31/39
	Tooth	13/13	—	8/8	—	—	—	1/1	—	22/22	—
	Total	22/25	8/12	12/16	5/8	14/15	14/15	5/5	4/4	53/61	31/39
Burial 3	Bone	2/5	1/5	0/9	0/9	—	—	—	—	2/14	1/14
	Tooth	6/6	—	8/8	—	—	—	—	—	14/14	—
	Total	8/11	1/5	8/17	0/9	—	—	—	—	16/28	1/14
Burial 5	Bone	0/6	0/6	1/2	0/2	0/1	0/1	—	—	1/9	0/9
	Tooth	8/8	—	3/3	—	—	—	—	—	11/11	—
	Total	8/14	0/6	4/5	0/2	0/1	0/1	—	—	12/20	0/9
Total	Bone	13/29	12/29	5/20	6/20	23/25	23/25	6/9	5/9	47/83	46/83
	Tooth	31/31	—	21/21	—	—	—	1/1	—	53/53	—
	Total	44/60	12/29	26/41	6/20	23/25	23/25	7/10	5/9	100/136	46/83

Numbers represent the quantity of samples that passed the diagenesis test over the total.

TABLE 5.2a

Descriptive Statistics for Complete versus Incomplete Specimens

	$^{13}C_{carbonate}$	$^{13}C_{collagen}$	$^{15}N_{collagen}$
Complete (37 carbonate, 34 collagen)			
Average	−6.1	−13.6	7.7
SD	2.4	2.8	1.9
Range	−13.1 to −1.6	−17.4 to −6.1	3.4 to 11.8
Incomplete (42 carbonate, 18 collagen)			
Average	−12.2	−15.8	7.3
SD	3.9	2.7	1.1
Range	−17.8 to −4.4	−19.5 to −11.1	5.8 to 9.2

SD = standard deviation.

TABLE 5.2b

Descriptive Statistics by Animal

	$^{13}C_{carbonate}$	$^{13}C_{collagen}$	$^{15}N_{collagen}$
Felid (29 carbonate, 15 collagen)			
Average	−10.9	−13.7	8.1
SD	5.0	4.0	1.6
Range	−17.8 to −2.7	−17.8 to −6.1	6 to 11.8
Canid (18 carbonate, 7 collagen)			
Average	−12.6	−15.9	7.4
SD	3.4	3.8	1.9
Range	−15.7 to −4.3	−19.5 to −9.8	6 to 10.9
Eagle (24 carbonate, 24 collagen)			
Average	−6.2	−14.2	7.9
SD	1.5	1.9	1.2
Range	−8.9 to −2.8	−17.4 to −11.1	5.2 to 9.5
Leporid (7 carbonate, 5 collagen)			
Average	−6.6	−15.2	5.4
SD	1.3	1.5	1.4
Range	−9.3 to −5.3	−16.7 to −12.8	3.4 to 6.9

SD = standard deviation.

Incomplete $\delta^{13}C_{carbonate}$ values were significantly more enriched ($p < 0.001$)[3] than complete skeletons (Figure 5.2a). The semi-complete leporid remains in the stomach content of the sacrificed carnivores were likely consumed whole and were considered within the "complete" category. Leporid isotopic values plotted within the expected range of their consumers (Figure 5.2b). Complete skeletons with $\delta^{13}C_{carbonate}$ values as enriched as −2.7‰ reflect the carnivores consumed up to 79% C_4-based products (PC_4),[4] indicative of an artificial diet. In contrast, $\delta^{13}C_{carbonate}$ values of secondary deposits ranged from samples indicative of a "wild" absolute C_3 reliance to samples revealing up to 64% C_4-based diets in line with a captive population.

$\delta^{13}C_{carbonate}$ variation was not standardized across species (Table 5.2b). Felids expressed the highest degree of variation (5‰ standard deviation [SD]), exhibiting some of the highest and lowest $\delta^{13}C_{carbonate}$ values. Primary and secondary eagle deposits were isotopically indistinguishable, with very tight distribution (1.5‰ SD). The latter pattern concurs with the zooarchaeological evidence of secondary eagles with osteological markers of confinement (Figure 5.2b).

Collagen isotope data had similar outcomes; complete skeletons exhibited significantly more enriched $\delta^{13}C_{collagen}$ ($p < 0.001$) and $\delta^{15}N$ ($p < 0.005$) values than secondary burials (Figure 5.3). Complete animals were consuming more C_4-based resources and more meat protein (B in Figure 5.1). Unlike eagle primary and secondary samples that were isotopically indistinguishable, canid and felid populations displayed pronounced differences by burial type (Figure 5.3a). Despite differences between complete and incomplete specimens, a small proportion of secondary burials (six eagles, two felids, and one canid) had $\delta^{13}C_{collagen}$ values within 1 SD of the mean of complete values (above −16.4‰). This suggests that among prepared faunal paraphernalia, some animals (mainly eagles) were likely also habitually fed artificial diets despite evidence of postmortem manipulation of the corpse.

As $\delta^{15}N_{collagen}$ values closely track the trophic level of the consumer, it exhibited significantly less variation. Leporids (average 5.3‰) ranged predictably a trophic level lower than predators (average 7.4‰–8.1‰) (Figure 5.3b). Increased C_4 input (enriched $\delta^{13}C_{collagen}$ values) correlated with $\delta^{15}N$ enrichment ($R^2 = 0.5167$), implying a positive relationship between artificial food consumption and degree of carnivory. As agricultural practices significantly affect $\delta^{15}N_{collagen}$ values (Bateman

---

[3] All statistical significance was evaluated utilizing the student t-test assuming a type two, two-tailed normal distribution.

[4] Calculated following Schwarcz (1991) as $PC_4 = ((\delta_3 - (\delta_b - \Delta))/(\delta_4 - \delta_3)) \times 100$, where δ_3 is the $\delta^{13}C_{apatite}$ value of C_3 foods (−25‰); δ_4 is the $\delta^{13}C_{apatite}$ value of C_4 foods (−9‰); δ_b is the measured $\delta^{13}C_{apatite}$ value of sample; and Δ is the 9.7‰ diet-apatite spacing. While there will be variations in baseline values, it provides a rough estimate of the proportion of C_4-based products consumed by the organism.

144 ANIMAL MATTER

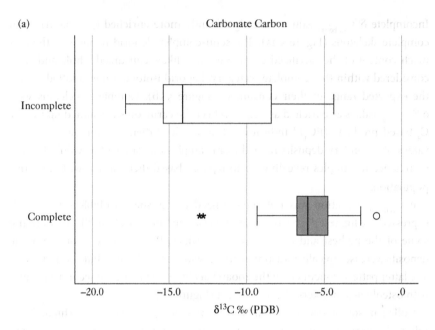

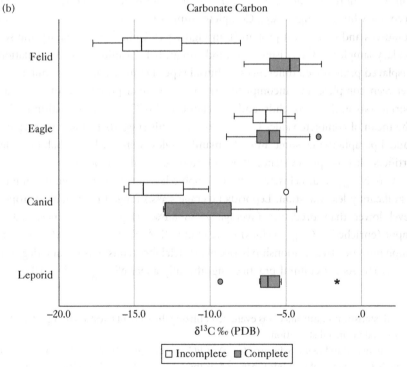

FIGURE 5.2
Box plot of bone $\delta^{13}C_{carbonate}$ values of all animals by (a) burial type (complete/incomplete) and by (b) animal and burial type.

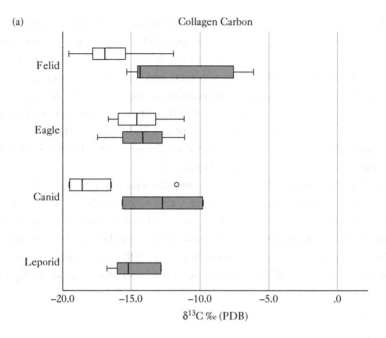

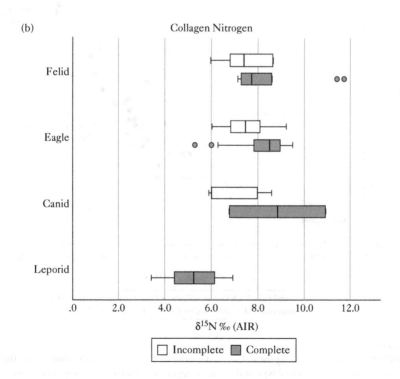

FIGURE 5.3
Box plot of (a) $\delta^{13}C_{collagen}$ and (b) $\delta^{15}N_{collagen}$ values for each animal by burial type (complete/incomplete).

et al. 2005; Warinner et al. 2013), C_4 enrichment due to the incorporation of intensively cultivated maize may have also contributed to this pattern. This correlation was strongest among complete carnivore bones ($R^2 = 0.7404$) in comparison to both incomplete carnivores ($R^2 = 0.5323$) and leporid ($R^2 = 0.1474$) remains. Consequently, lower $\delta^{15}N$ values were recorded among many carnivores with correspondingly lower $\delta^{13}C_{collagen}$ values, rejecting the hypothesis that captivity may lead to increased levels of omnivory (C in Figure 5.1). The $\delta^{15}N_{collagen}$ values of two felids stood as outliers with excessively high values almost another trophic level higher than the rest of the felid population (Figure 5.3b).

The Teotihuacan data were plotted onto the simple carbon model following Kellner and Schoeninger (2007) (Figure 5.4). Except for the incomplete eagles, most of the incomplete animal's isotope values fell along or near the C_3 protein line (white markers). An incomplete felid outlier was above the C_4/marine protein line at the extreme of the 100% C_3 non-protein portion of the diet (Figure 5.4, white diamond on extreme left). If this specimen reflects a "wild" diet, it seems the C_4 signal

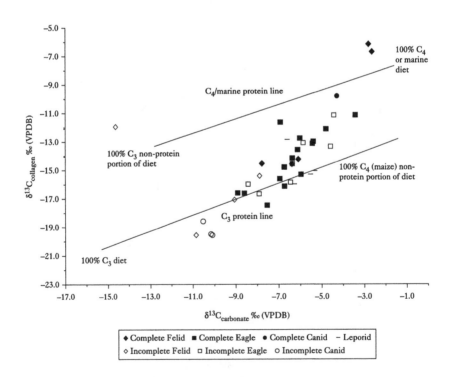

FIGURE 5.4
Simple carbon model plotting the $\delta^{13}C_{carbonate}$ (x-axis) and $\delta^{13}C_{collagen}$ (y-axis) values onto the two regression lines by burial type and animal category (Kellner and Schoeninger 2007).

found among incomplete felids with mixed diets originates from the total diet, not the protein source itself.

In comparison, a substantial proportion of the complete specimens fell between the two regression lines, distributed from the mid to upper region of the 100% C_4 non-protein diet line. Two complete felids displayed incredibly high signals, indicating complete reliance on C_4/marine protein and total diet (two filled diamonds in upper right, Figure 5.4). Later, we will return to these two samples, E.1818 and E.1984. Leporid values continued to reflect the isotopic values of their primary consumers. Unlike the incomplete specimens, the complete burials signaled that C_4 input originated from a combination of the total diet and the protein source. The leporid isotopic signature indicates a primarily C_3 protein source but with a high C_4 total diet. Such maize-stuffed rabbits account for the carnivores' high C_4-protein values.

A discriminant function analysis of the Teotihuacan samples was also plotted against the multivariate model (Froehle et al. 2012). Figure 5.5 confirms the

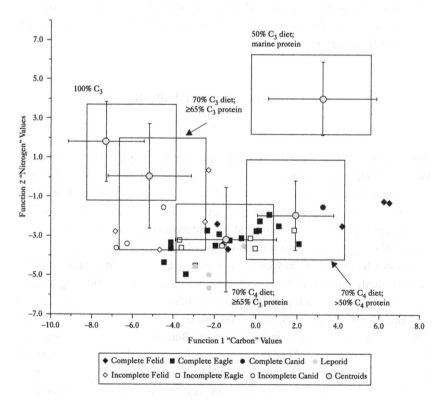

FIGURE 5.5
Multivariate model parameters (Froehle et al. 2012) plotted against complete, incomplete, and leporid Teotihuacan samples.

overall patterns discussed in the simple carbon model, with most incomplete specimens (white markers) distributed within two clusters: 70% C_3 diet with ≥65% C_3 protein and 70% C_4 diet with ≥65% C_3 protein. The three exceptions of secondary deposits that fell within the 70% C_4 diet with >50% C_4 protein model were of eagles.

Complete specimens (black markers) were primarily distributed either in the range of 70% C_4 diet with >50% C_4 protein or 70% C_4 diet with >65% C_3 protein, and only a few complete eagle samples spilled into the 70% C_3 diet with >65% C_3 protein range. Two complete felids plotted in the 70% C_4 diet with >65% C_3 protein range, and lagomorph specimens were exclusively in this range. The same two complete felid outliers (E.1818 and E.1984) indicated exceptionally high values above any multivariate models. Marine/freshwater contributions to the diet were excluded as a source of high nitrogen and carbon values. The multivariate model recorded two potential captive populations: one in which overall diet was majority C_4, but their protein was still primarily composed of C_3 sources (leporids, complete and incomplete eagles, and some complete felids), and a more exclusive population where C_4 resources comprised the majority of the whole diet and protein sources (complete felids, canids, and eagles).

Intra-Species Isotopic Patterns

Felids

Table 5.3 plots Moon Pyramid felid isotopic values alongside two comparative datasets: modern felid samples from C_3 and C_4 ecosystems reported in interregional studies that provide natural baselines of known vegetation (Kelly 2000; Schoeninger and DeNiro 1984) and a Teotihuacan puma sample reported from Teopancazco apartment compound (Morales Puente et al. 2012: Table XI.6).

Felid $\delta^{13}C_{carbonate}$ values had a bimodal distribution extending from −17.8‰ to −2.7‰, which signifies PC_4 ranged from 0% to as high as 79%. This variation can be attributed to the differences between complete versus incomplete felids (Figure 5.2b). The $\delta^{13}C_{carbonate}$ values of complete felids were significantly more enriched ($p < 0.001$), averaging −6.2‰ ± 1.7‰ (1σ), while incomplete animals had a mean of −13.6‰ ± 3.2‰ (1σ). Three incomplete individuals from Burial 6 had moderately enriched $\delta^{13}C_{carbonate}$ values above 1 SD of the mean, which suggests that though incomplete felids were based dominantly or even exclusively on C_3-based diets, a few incorporated varying degrees of C_4-based resources into their diet (PC_4 above 39%). In contrast, all complete felids relied on various quantities of C_4-based resources ($PC_4 = 47\%–79\%$).

TABLE 5.3

Descriptive Statistics of Felid Collagen and Carbonate Results

	$^{13}C_{carbonate}$	$^{13}C_{collagen}$	$^{15}N_{collagen}$
MP Felid Complete (9 carbonate, 9 collagen)			
Average	−6.2	−12.0	8.6
SD	1.7	3.9	1.8
Range	−7.8 to −2.7	−15.3 to −6.1	7.1 to 11.8
MP Felid Incomplete (20 carbonate, 6 collagen)			
Average	−13.6	−16.4	7.5
SD	3.2	2.6	1.1
Range	−17.8 to −7.6	−19.5 to −11.9	6.0 to 8.7
Sun Pyramid (1 carbonate, 1 collagen)[1]			
Puma skull	−7.6	−17.8	6.8
Teopancazco (1 collagen)[2]			
Puma bone		−19.8	7.1
Modern Felids in C_3 ecosystems (4 collagen)[3*]			
C3 Puma[4]		−16.1	7.6
Average		−17.0	8.0
SD		2.8	1.6
Range		−20.9 to −14.3	6.2 to 10.0
Modern Felids in C_4 ecosystems (3 collagen)[3*]			
Average		−7.0	10.0
SD		3.7	0.2
Range		−4.2 to −1.2	9.8 to 10.2

MP: Moon Pyramid (this study). Comparative data summarized from 1. Sugiyama et al. 2015: Table S1; 2. Morales Puente et al. 2012: Table XI.6; 3. Kelly 2000: Table A2; and 4. Schoeninger and DeNiro 1984: Table 1. *Modern samples corrected for industrial effect.

Published $\delta^{13}C_{carbonate}$ values of a puma skull from the Sun Pyramid Offering 2 and isolated specimen from Teopancazco (−7.6‰ and −11.7‰)[5] were within the expected range obtained from Moon Pyramid secondary burials. The latter specimen originated from a neighborhood center within Teotihuacan, an economic hub for trade and artisanship (Manzanilla 2017). The isotopic composition of the primary burials from the Moon Pyramid was thus substantially different from other,

---

[5] The Teopancazco puma tooth sample reported as −9.4‰ was corrected based on Warinner and Tuross (2009) bone-enamel offset whereby $\delta^{13}C_{carbonate-enamel}$ values are enriched by 2.3‰.

150 ANIMAL MATTER

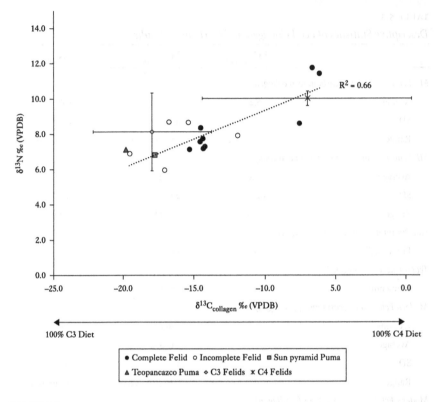

FIGURE 5.6
Felid $\delta^{15}N$ and $\delta^{13}C_{collagen}$ values of Moon Pyramid complete and incomplete samples, a puma from Teopancazco (Morales Puente et al. 2012: Table XI.6), and modern felids in C_3 and C_4 based habitats (Kelly 2000: Table A2).

presumably more wild, felid populations represented by secondary remains from the Moon Pyramid, the Sun Pyramid, and the Teopancazco apartment compound.

The complete and incomplete felid collagen samples (like the carbonates) also clustered into two populations, with primary burials with significantly ($p < 0.05$) enriched $\delta^{13}C_{collagen}$ values averaging −12.0‰ ± 3.9‰ (1σ). In contrast, secondary burials had a mean of −16.4‰ ± 2.6‰ (1σ) (Figure 5.6). Collagen isotopic ratios from Teotihuacan were likewise compared to wild pumas and other felids reported in the literature (Table 5.3). A puma from Southern California with $\delta^{13}C_{collagen}$ value of −17.6‰ (or −16.1‰ after adjustment due to industrial effect, all modern values are reported post correction)[6] and $\delta^{15}N_{collagen}$ of 7.6‰

---

[6] The industrial effect is caused by the differences in atmospheric CO^2 in modern versus preindustrial periods due to the burning of fossil fuels (Keeling 1979). Thus, all modern samples compared to archaeological materials were adjusted positively by 1.5‰.

(Schoeninger and DeNiro 1984: Table 1) was within expected range as wild felids inhabiting C_3 based ecosystems (bobcat, lynx, and tiger) (Kelly 2000: Table A2). In comparison, felids from C_4 vegetation zones like the leopard, the lion, and the cheetah exhibited much more positive $\delta^{13}C_{collagen}$ and $\delta^{15}N_{collagen}$ values (Kelly 2000: Table A2). The Teotihuacan felid (pumas and jaguars) samples were distributed across the entire modern felid range from C_3- and C_4-based habitats. $\delta^{13}C_{collagen}$ values spanned −19.5‰ to −6.1‰ and $\delta^{15}N_{collagen}$ values ranged from 6‰ to 11.8‰. Anthropogenic diets seem to alter the organism's diet considerably more than the range of variation encompassed by vegetation and climatic factors.

Plotting the isotopic averages of felids with C_3- and C_4-based diets and their respective error bars (± 2σ) alongside the archaeological felid samples, three complete felids fell within the $\delta^{13}C_{collagen}$ values expected for C_4 habitats (Figure 5.6). These three felids correspond to specimens with zooarchaeological indicators of captivity (Chapter 4); the puma caged in Burial 2 (E.143), a puma from Burial 6 with pathologies on its femur, pelvis, and cranium (E.1818, see Chapter 6 for more detail), and another complete puma from Burial 6 with fused left upper limb (E.1984). In comparison, the secondary and other primary felids tended to be distributed within samples from C_3 habitats. The Sun Pyramid and Teopancazco compound collagen results are within the expected range for felids in C_3-based habitats and the incomplete felids from the Moon Pyramid. The isotopic data substantiate the hypothesis that animals who expressed health issues due to prolonged confinement (disease, trauma, and nutrition) correlated with the highest levels of alteration in their diet. However, the lack of such pathological data did not necessarily exclude the possibility of fundamental dietary shifts reflective of various degrees of anthropomorphic diets alluding to human cohabitation.

The significant variation observed in the $\delta^{15}N$ values is more complex to interpret. The $\delta^{15}N_{collagen}$ values represent at least two trophic levels that extend between 11.8‰ and 6‰, with the lowest values surprisingly low for an exclusive carnivore. There were no significant differences between primary and secondary $\delta^{15}N_{collagen}$ values ($p = 0.25$). A strong positive correlation ($R^2 = 0.66$) between $\delta^{13}C_{collagen}$ and $\delta^{15}N_{collagen}$ values confirms the simple and multivariate dietary models that characterize anthropogenic diets were composed of high C_4-based protein sources. Since the dietary models excluded marine/freshwater products as the contributor to these high $\delta^{13}C_{collagen}$ and $\delta^{15}N_{collagen}$ values, what omnivorous protein resource with almost 100% C_4 diets were these three felids consuming? We will return to this question in Chapter 6 when describing the biography of the puma, E.1818.

Canids

Poor preservation compromised the interpretive potential of canid isotopic results of complete individuals ($n = 3$). Table 5.4 presents canid descriptive statistics. The majority of the canid $\delta^{13}C_{carbonate}$ values ranged between −16‰ and −10‰, with one complete canid outlier (−4.3‰) (Figure 5.7). The PC_4 of this primary canid from Burial 6 (E.2199) equals roughly 69%, very high for a natural diet. The $\delta^{13}C_{carbonate}$ value was roughly equivalent to a prepared wolf cranium found in Offering 2 of the Sun Pyramid (E.209) (Sugiyama et al. 2015) and two dog teeth excavated from the Teopancazco apartment compound (Morales Puente et al. 2012: Table XI.6). Dogs are usually good proxies to human diets as scavengers of human waste and their high C_4 (maize) input ($\delta^{13}C_{carbonate}$ −3.1‰ and −4.2‰)[7] confirms this expectation. Thus, the

TABLE 5.4
Descriptive Statistics of Canid Collagen and Carbonate Results

	$^{13}C_{carbonate}$	$^{13}C_{collagen}$	$^{15}N_{collagen}$
MP Canid Complete (3 carbonate, 2 collagen)			
Average	−10.1	−12.7	8.9
SD	5.0	4.1	2.9
Range	−13.1 to −4.3	−15.6 to −9.8	6.8 to 10.9
MP Canid Incomplete (15 carbonate, 5 collagen)			
Average	−13.2	−17.1	6.9
SD	−3.0	3.3	1.3
Range	−15.7 to −5	−19.5 to −11.7	5.8 to 8.6
Sun Pyramid (1 carbonate, 1 collagen)[1]			
Wolf head	−5.0	−11.7	8.6
Teopancazco (2 carbonate, 2 collagen)[2]			
Dog 1	−3.1	−7.5	10.8
Dog 2	−4.2	−7.6	9.1
Modern Wolf (1 collagen)[3*]			
Wolf		−19.1	9.9

MP: Moon Pyramid (this study). Comparative data summarized from (1) Sugiyama et al. 2015; (2) Morales Puente et al. 2012: Table XI.6; and 3. Kelly 2000: Table A2. *Modern samples corrected for industrial effect.

[7] With tooth correction, see footnote 2.

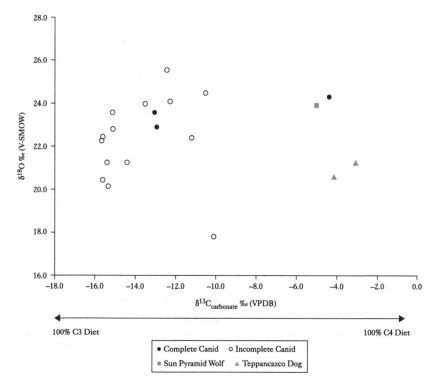

FIGURE 5.7
Canid $\delta^{18}O$ and $\delta^{13}C_{carbonate}$ values for Moon Pyramid complete and incomplete samples, Sun Pyramid wolf (Sugiyama et al. 2015), and Teopancazco dog tooth (Morales Puente et al. 2012: Table XI.6).

complete wolf from Burial 6 consumed C_4-based diets comparable to those of known domesticates. Interestingly, the prepared wolf cranium from the Sun Pyramid resulted in values higher than any incomplete specimens from the Moon Pyramid, indicative of a more anthropogenic diet. Two complete wolves from the Moon Pyramid, E.213.1 from Burial 2 and E.1636.2 from Burial 5, resulted in low $\delta^{13}C_{carbonate}$ values signaling a primarily C_3-based diet comparable to incomplete canids.

While I refrain from making conclusions from the $\delta^{18}O$ ratios in this book (see Sugiyama et al. 2015), I want to mention they were reasonably consistent, ranging between 20‰ and 26‰, except for one outlier whose $\delta^{18}O$ value was 17.8‰. Even the two canids with enriched $\delta^{13}C_{carbonate}$ values had similar $\delta^{18}O$ ranges, suggesting a relatively homogenous local group. Other species analyzed from the Moon Pyramid had much greater variability.

Canid $\delta^{13}C_{collagen}$ value range was extensive (−19.5‰ to −9.8‰) while the $\delta^{15}N$ values were more confined (6‰ to 10.9‰) (Figure 5.8). The small sample size and

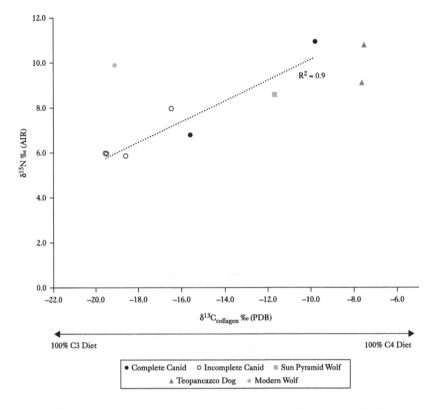

FIGURE 5.8
Canid $\delta^{15}N$ and $\delta^{13}C_{collagen}$ values of Moon Pyramid complete and incomplete samples, Teopancazco dog (Morales Puente et al. 2012: Table XI.6), Sun Pyramid wolf (Sugiyama et al. 2015), and a modern wolf from a C_3-based habitat (Kelly 2000: Table A2).

skewed representation (no samples from Burials 3 and 5) precluded recognizing statistically significant patterns. The $\delta^{13}C_{collagen}$ results from Teotihuacan canids span the entire range of possible diets, with some specimens indicating complete C_3-based diets while others signaled heavy reliance on C_4 resources (Figure 5.8). $\delta^{15}N$ values represented varying degrees of omnivory and carnivory.

A wild wolf mandible from Alaska from a dominantly C_3-based environment provided a modern comparative baseline ($\delta^{13}C_{collagen}$ −19.1‰,[8] $\delta^{15}N$ 9.9‰) (Kelly 2000). Several incomplete canids plotted near the $\delta^{13}C_{collagen}$ value of this wild specimen. One Moon Pyramid complete canid sample aligned more closely with the isotope values of a wolf skull from the Sun Pyramid Offering 2 and two dogs from the Teopancazco apartment compound, both of which presented very high $\delta^{13}C_{collagen}$ (−11.7‰

---

[8] Post correction of industrial effect, see footnote 6.

to −7.5‰) and $\delta^{15}N$ (8.6‰ to 10.8‰) values (Morales Puente et al. 2012: Table XI.6; Sugiyama et al. 2015). Surprisingly, some of the Moon Pyramid wolves exhibited $\delta^{15}N$ values lower than the Teopancazco dog samples. The positive correlation between the $\delta^{13}C_{collagen}$ and $\delta^{15}N$ ratio ($R^2 = 0.9$) indicates that increasing trophic levels coincide with greater C_4 dependence, confirming the conclusions of the multivariate model that the C_4 signal originated from the protein source itself (Figure 5.5).

Eagles

Eagle $\delta^{13}C_{carbonate}$ values reflected a relatively homogeneous population with the lowest SD (1.5‰) and enriched $\delta^{13}C_{carbonate}$ values ranging between −8.9‰ and −2.8‰ (PC_4 40%–78%) (Table 5.2b). Remarkably, all eagles, even those reflecting the lowest $\delta^{13}C_{carbonate}$ values, had over 40% C_4-based diets. Secondary eagle deposits could not be isotopically distinguished from primary burials, probably because both sacrificed and prepared eagles were drawn from the same managed population that consumed C_4-based diets.

In contrast to the relatively homogenous $\delta^{13}C_{carbonate}$ values, eagle $\delta^{18}O$ values were the most variable of all animals from the Moon Pyramid assemblage (18.5‰ to 30.5‰). This may reflect their extended home ranges as well as the varied source populations. In addition, eagles have only been spotted to drink water directly in captivity (Watson 2010). As standing water evaporates, it modifies $\delta^{18}O$ values, which could also contribute to this variation. More data on the local water isotope values in this region and how eagle physiology affects oxygen isotope values are necessary to interpret these results.

Eagle collagen isotope results averaged −14.2‰ ± 1.9‰ (1 σ) for $\delta^{13}C_{collagen}$ and 7.9‰ ± 1.2‰ (1 σ) for $\delta^{15}N$ (Figure 5.9). Like the carbonate dataset, the $\delta^{13}C_{collagen}$ and $\delta^{15}N$ values had no significant differences between primary and secondary burials. Unfortunately, no suitable comparative materials were available for eagle populations that can help distinguish the Teotihuacan sample from a "wild" signature. The closest modern baseline was a rough-legged hawk (*Buteo lagopus*) from Southern California that consumes a C_3-based trophic chain reported $\delta^{13}C_{collagen}$ value of −15.4‰ and $\delta^{15}N$ value of 6.8‰ (triangle, Figure 5.9) (Schoeninger and DeNiro 1984). Likewise, a complete eagle sacrificed in Offering 2 of the Sun Pyramid (square, Figure 5.9) fell squarely within the Moon Pyramid collagen isotope variation range. A more robust comparative sample is required to explain the Teotihuacan eagle variation.

Like the canid results, there was a positive correlation between the $\delta^{13}C_{collagen}$ and $\delta^{15}N$ distribution ($R^2 = 0.7$). Unlike the felids, there was no statistical difference between primary and secondary deposits. This is in accordance with the zooarchaeological dataset of secondary deposits that also contained pathological

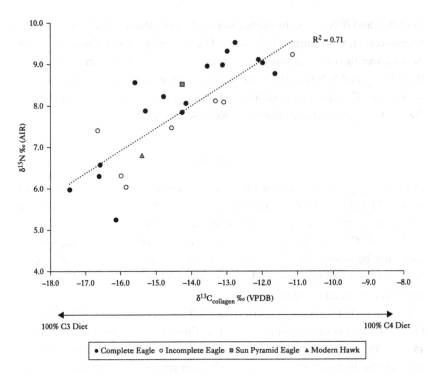

FIGURE 5.9
Eagle $\delta^{15}N$ and $\delta^{13}C_{collagen}$ values of Moon Pyramid complete and incomplete samples, and a modern hawk from a C_3-based habitat (Kelley 2000: Table A2).

indicators of confinement. Thus, I conclude that primary and secondary eagles originated from the same population of managed raptors kept within city confines with varying residency periods.

Leporidae

Isotopic data of leporid remains from Teotihuacan published by Somerville et al. (2016, 2017) provide robust comparative data to interpret the Moon Pyramid offering contexts. The authors analyzed materials from not only the Moon Pyramid fill but also two apartment compounds within Teotihuacan (Teopancazco and Oztoyahualco), as well as two post-Teotihuacan assemblages (Puerta 5 and Cuevas). In addition, their modern leporid samples from the Basin of Mexico provide a baseline for the area. One leporid specimen from the Sun Pyramid Offering 2, found in the stomach of a sacrificed golden eagle, provides an additional data point for an offering context (Sugiyama et al. 2015). Somerville et al. (2017: 91) conclude that C_4/CAM consumption increased during the growth of the city (in chronological order, Moon Pyramid fill: 1–450 CE; Teopancazco: 200–550 CE; and Oztoyahualco: 350–550

CE) and decreased during the Epiclassic (Puerta 5, 600–1150 CE) and Postclassic (Cuevas 1150–1500 CE) periods. The authors argue that the Teotihuacanos practiced a combination of captive raising (especially at Oztoyohualco, where archaeological evidence also supports more specialized rearing practices) and garden-hunting crop-raiding leporids (see also Sugiyama et al. 2017).

Leporid descriptive statistics are summarized in Table 5.5. I chart the distribution of the Moon Pyramid offering assemblage analyzed in this study alongside

TABLE 5.5
Descriptive Statistics of Leporid Collagen and Carbonate Results

	$^{13}C_{carbonate}$	$^{13}C_{collagen}$	$^{15}N_{collagen}$
MP Burials (7 carbonate, 5 collagen)			
Average	−6.6	−15.2	5.4
SD	1.3	1.5	1.4
Range	−9.3 to −5.3	−16.7 to −12.8	3.4 to 6.9
Sun Pyramid (1 carbonate, 1 collagen)[1]			
Sylvilagus	−1.6	−12.8	4.4
MP Fill (54 carbonate, 49 collagen)[2]			
Average	−8.6	−16.3	5
SD	2.5	3	2.3
Teopancazco (20 carbonate, 18 collagen)[2]			
Average	−6.9	−15.1	6.7
SD	1.4	2	2.3
Oztoyahualco (16 carbonate, 17 collagen)[2]			
Average	−5.8	−14.1	5.2
SD	2	3.3	1.5
Puerta 5 (25 carbonate, 16 collagen)[2]			
Average	−6.9	−15.8	4.7
SD	2	3.1	2.1
Cuevas (12 carbonate, 12 collagen)[2]			
Average	−8.7	−16.3	6.1
SD	1.9	2.6	2.6
Modern Leporids (13 carbonate, 12 collagen)[2]*			
Average	−12.4	−17.8	4.4
SD	1.8	2	2.5

MP: Moon Pyramid, MP burials (this study). Comparative data summarized from 1. Sugiyama et al. 2015, and 2. Somerville et al. 2016, 2017. *Modern samples corrected for industrial effects by Somerville et al. 2017.

the comparative data points in a simple carbon model following Somerville et al. (2017) (Figure 5.10). All leporid materials analyzed from the Moon Pyramid offerings pertain to the stomach contents of sacrificed carnivores. The $\delta^{13}C_{carbonate}$ distribution ranged from −9.3‰ to −5.3‰, corresponding to PC_4 values extending from 38% to 63%. All samples plotted within the comparative leporid data range. Four of the five were within the distribution of Oztoyohualco's captive raised leporids. The highest $\delta^{13}C_{carbonate}$ value (−1.6‰) pertains to a rabbit found in the stomach content of a sacrificed eagle from the Sun Pyramid's Offering 2 (E.211.2, square in Figure 5.10). Similar to the comparative datasets, all the samples fell along the C_3 protein line.

As rabbits and hares could be foraging along the edges of milpas as synanthropists, varying degrees of C_4 plants may be incorporated into a leporid's diet due to garden hunting. However, the consistent evidence of elevated PC_4

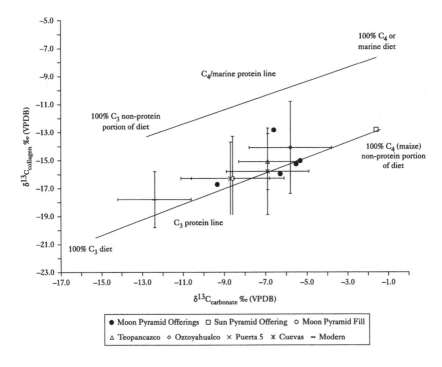

FIGURE 5.10
Simple carbon model plotting leporid $\delta^{13}C_{carbonate}$ and $\delta^{13}C_{collagen}$ values from Moon Pyramid offerings, alongside average and 1σ values from the Sun Pyramid Offering 2 (Sugiyama et al. 2015), Moon Pyramid Fill, Teopancazco, Puerta 5, cuevas, and modern samples from the Basin of Mexico (Somerville et al. 2016, 2017).

across various contexts throughout Teotihuacan and the abundance of leporids in the zooarchaeological record suggests reliance on leporids as a staple protein source that likely included intentional animal rearing, though the scale of this operation is still undetermined (Sugiyama et al. 2017). Sustaining exclusive carnivores selected for ritual sacrifice for prolonged periods would have required a reliable meat staple. Leporids are well adapted to urban settings and likely provided a key C_4-dominant protein source that sustained the carnivores in captivity.

Life Histories of Teeth and Bones

We can retrieve aspects of the life history of an animal by comparing isotopic data of teeth enamel and bones, each of which captures the paleodiet at different moments throughout the organism's life. Such a life history approach can help pinpoint the length of captivity (Sugiyama et al. 2022). Table 5.6 summarizes the descriptive statistics of $\delta^{13}C_{carbonate}$ tooth enamel to bone offset from the same individual. Figure 5.11 plots the two values for each type of animal for complete and incomplete specimens. A positive offset suggests that tooth values (reflecting infancy) were more enriched than bone (white dot above or more positive than black dot, Figure 5.11), indicating a decrease in C_4 resources over the lifespan of the organism. A negative

TABLE 5.6

$\delta^{13}C_{carbonate}$ Tooth to Bone Offset Data for Canids, Felids, and Leporids

		N	Ave T-B Offset	SD	Range	Ave Direction of Offset
Canid						
	Complete	1	1.0	—	—	1.0
	Incomplete	14	1.5	0.9	0.3–2.7	−0.2
Felid						
	Complete	8	1.5	1.0	0.3–2.8	0.7
	Incomplete	12	1.3	1.0	0.1–3.4	−0.3
Leporid						
	Stomach content	1	0.1	—	—	0.1
Total		36	1.6	1.5	0.1–8.2	0.0

Ave = average, T = tooth, B = bone, SD = standard deviation.

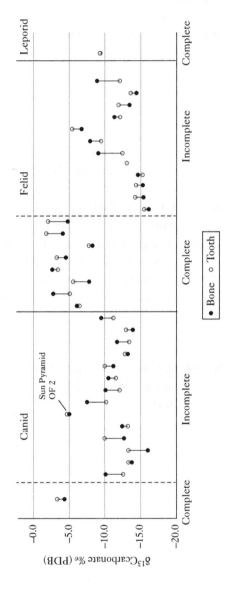

FIGURE 5.11
$\delta^{13}C_{carbonate}$ values of tooth (early) and bone (late) from same individuals for canids, felids, and leporids divided by complete and incomplete individuals. OF 2 = Offering 2.

offset indicates tooth values were more depleted than bone (black dot above white dot), reflecting increased C_4 input. As enamel carbonate is naturally more enriched than bone carbonate by roughly 2.3‰ (Warinner and Tuross 2009), if the animal's diet were consistent throughout the individual's lifespan, we would expect a positive 2.3‰ tooth-bone offset.

Here, we will test the four hypotheses stated at the beginning of this chapter (Figure 5.1). (H_0) Hunted wild animals would have relatively low $\delta^{13}C_{carbonate}$ value, with enamel 2.3‰ more enriched than the bone, indicative of natural tooth-bone offset. ($H_{1/2}$). Capture and artificial feeding after the first set of teeth have erupted would be reflected by a negative offset, whereby bone would be more positive than teeth despite the 2.3‰ positive tooth-bone offset. The difference between H_1 and H_2 depended on the degree of omnivory (reflected most directly in the nitrogen values), which we cannot assess with carbonate results. (H_3) An animal raised in captivity early in life (before forming adult dentition) would exhibit enriched tooth and bone $\delta^{13}C_{carbonate}$ values, with teeth 2.3‰ more enriched than the bone. As the zooarchaeological and isotopic evidence for captivity varied significantly between complete (primary) and incomplete (secondary) burials, I examined the results by animal and burial type.

Only one complete canid had a tooth and bone sample that passed the diagenesis test.[9] E.2199, from Burial 6, indicated relatively high C_4 input. Accounting for the 2.3‰ tooth-bone offset and enriched enamel (−3.3‰) and bone (−4.3‰) $\delta^{13}C_{carbonate}$ values, this individual corresponds to H_3; by the time the wolf's first inferior molar was being formed (four to five months old), it was already consuming a relatively high degree of C_4 dietary input. This trend continued until the organism's death. E.2199 expressed one of the highest nitrogen values among the canids (10.9‰), and its location within the multivariate model fits squarely within the 70% C_4 diet and 50% C_4 protein region (Figure 5.5, black circle). Only felids exhibited more elevated nitrogen and carbon (carbonate and collagen) values than this individual. High degrees of carnivory of E.2199 indicate these high $\delta^{13}C$ values originate from C_4-fed game like the leporids found in the stomachs of sacrificed animals.

Incomplete canid isotope results were highly variable. Some samples had expected positive offsets circa 2.3 (2.7‰, $n = 2$) that align with H_0, while others showed a more negative trend ($n = 7$). The average direction of the offset was

---

[9] A recent diagenesis study produced a preservation index of processed bone C/P 0.05–0.32 and IRSF values of bone 2.5–4.3, while processed enamel recommended values of C/P were 0.08–0.2 and IRSF of 3.1–4.0 (France et al. 2020: Table 6). These values were utilized for this life history approach, which allowed us to increase the sample size.

slightly negative. Samples with the highest negative T-B offset between −1.8 to −2.6 (indicating a substantial increase in C_4 resources) consisted of bone $\delta^{13}C$ values 1 SD above the mean (−13.2‰ ± 3‰, $n = 5$). These wolves likely entered captivity after forming their adult dentition, confirming instances of H_1 and H_2 also existed. A cranium found in Offering 2 of the Sun Pyramid exhibited tooth (−4.7‰) and bone (−5.0‰) $\delta^{13}C_{carbonate}$ values well above all other incomplete specimens (Figure 5.11, OF2 Sun Pyramid). In this rare instance, a canid secondary specimen documented an H_3 scenario of early captivity (since dentition was forming).

Complete felids generally exhibited higher $\delta^{13}C_{carbonate}$ values on both teeth and bone than the incomplete specimens, with a general positive offset that agrees with H_3, that cubs were brought into the city confines before teeth formation, resulting in values within the general expected 2.3‰ offset. The multivariate model confirms that C_4-based resources contributed to their protein source as well as the total diet. In the case of E.1984, there is a −2.3‰ tooth-bone offset; in a few instances, animals were introduced into the city confines later in life ($H_{1/2}$). In this case, the $\delta^{13}C_{carbonate}$ value of the third superior incisor (−6.0‰) and the maxillary Pm4 (−5.1‰) can be compared with the cranium (−2.8‰) from the same individual. As incisors develop first (around five-and-a-half months) while premolars form after eight months (Currier 1983), and the bone remodels consistently throughout the organism's life, the isotopes capture a gradual increase in C_4 resources throughout its lifespan. As E.1984 (and most primary burials) were relatively young, in this case, eighteen months old, these dietary changes occurred relatively quickly.

Incomplete felid $\delta^{13}C_{carbonate}$ values were more heterogeneous, though the majority displayed fairly consistent bone and teeth values that coincide with a wild population ($n = 8$) (H_0). A few samples ($n = 4$) signaled an unnaturally high C_4 intake (1 SD above average incomplete −13.6‰ ± 3.2‰). Of these, two examples stand out as having significantly negative tooth-bone offsets above −3.0‰ (E.2245 and E.1500), indicating a substantial increase in C_4 intake later in life. Bone values (−9.1‰ and −8.8‰, respectively) suggest transitioning into a more C_3-C_4 mixed diet. Unfortunately, these samples did not have corresponding collagen preservation to distinguish if $H_{1/2}$ was a more appropriate model of artificial feeding. The remaining two cases likely result from an H_3 scenario of captivity from a young age.

Only one leporid sample permitted a life-history approach. This leporid sample from Burial 2 expressed one of the lowest $\delta^{13}C_{carbonate}$ values (−9.3‰ bone) with minimal teeth-bone offset. More samples will be necessary to apply a life-history approach to leporid captivity.

A prominent C_4 dietary change will be reflected in an organism's isotopes only when there is a drastic dietary shift during confinement alongside a prolonged confinement period. The temporal span necessary for an isotopic shift varies by the organism and remodeling rates of the bone in question. The life-history approach has documented instances of both sustained wild (H_0), sustained captive (H_3), and gradual changes in the diet of the organism ($H_{1/2}$) for both primary and secondary burials. Extrapolating the data to the general trend observed in the simple and multivariate models, burial type and species-specific tactics for captivity were at play at Teotihuacan.

Primary burials tended to have more homogeneity in both the isotopic composition of the group and paleopathological indicators that explicitly show a relational link among artificial feeding and trauma, disease, and surface modifications. Artificial diets were primarily composed of C_4-based protein sources, likely maize-fed leporids bred within the city confines (complete canids, felids, and some eagles) (B, Figure 5.1), or non-protein C_4 resources caused by direct consumption of maize (leporids, eagles) (C, Figure 5.1).

Secondary remains, on the other hand, are generally composed of a more heterogeneous population with relatively high proportions of wild-hunted individuals. However, the life-history analysis exposed some of the diverse adjustments made even among canid and felid secondary remains, where some may have consumed C_4-based resources later in life ($H_{1/2}$) or from an early age (H_3). Reconstructing biographies of each primary and secondary agent was the only way to capture this variation.

Though eagles were excluded from this life-history approach as they lack teeth, it is worth mentioning that they were the only population with no apparent isotopic distinction between primary and secondary deposits. This supports the zooarchaeological evidence of pathological evidence of captivity among the skeletons prepared postmortem. Luckily, in this case, we can use the zooarchaeological evidence to trace the biographies of these individuals in the subsequent chapter.

CHAPTER 6

ANIMAL BIOGRAPHIES

CORPOREAL ANIMAL FORMS WITHIN THE dedicatory caches are the primary dataset that led to this journey into dedicatory spectacles at Teotihuacan. Here, I integrate the zooarchaeological (Chapter 4) and isotopic (Chapter 5) data to reconstruct ancient human–animal dynamics of specific taxa by narrating animal biographies of key persons participating in the ritual spectacle. This approach accentuates how corporeal animal forms provide an entry into the experiential narratives of human–animal interactions during capture, confinement, and ritual performance. Detailed lifeways of captivity, including the sometimes menacing and challenging relationships, are structurally engrained into the chemistry and morphology of the corporeal animal forms.

I begin with a summary of the zooarchaeological and isotopic patterns documented on primary and secondary remains, and then introduce in-depth biographies of four animal persons. These reveal specific decision nodes in the coordination of the ritual process, including the archaeological markers used to capture how human and animal matter came into direct confrontation. I then use a detailed account of the Aztec Toxcatl festival to argue that corporeal animal forms underwent a similar transformation as the human captive that became the ritualized body of the deity Tezcatlipoca himself. I argue that human–animal intercorporeal encounters during the ritualization process "set apart" or consecrated wild carnivores into ritualized bodies of master guardian animals, positioning themselves as mediators of Teotihuacan's sovereignty formations (Chapter 7).

Primary Corporeal Animal Forms

The in-depth descriptions of each animal informed how and why each actor was chosen for sacrifice. I have shown how animal biology, physiology, and behavior are not only instrumental to the zooarchaeological methodology (e.g., age and sex designation) but can also directly inform animal vitalities that shaped ancient human–animal dynamics. Many surface modifications indicated long-term sustained human–animal interactions, including violent mediation of these ferocious carnivores before and during the ritual spectacle.

The pathological traces of animal captivity tell of the difficulties and sometimes even mishaps of taming the fiercest animals for sacrifice. Bone surfaces and their chemistry feature a staggering abundance of broken limbs, disease, dietary changes, and intentional efforts to facilitate handling. The practicalities and difficulties in acquiring prescribed numbers of live carnivores for the ritual were etched into the faunal record. Primary and secondary burials displayed distinct age and sex distributions, indicative of the behind-the-scenes decisions weighed by the practices and perils of maintaining felids, wolves, eagles, and rattlesnakes alive for ritual display. Young animals were preferred for sacrifice because they were easier to acquire and tame. In the case of eagles, perhaps due to mishaps, secondary burials were most likely caught in preparation for the ritual event, kept in confinement, and processed extensively (possibly even by a taxidermist) to participate in the ritual performance as intact bodies. Many primary burials, chiefly from Burials 2 and 6, were buried alive. Consistent evidence of feeding rabbits/hares to multiple sacrificed animals indicates this was part of a ritual protocol across species and contexts (rattlesnakes were fed smaller rodents).

I have corroborated the zooarchaeological evidence with isotope data. Differential dietary patterns among habituated felids, canids, and eagles for sacrifice affirm captivity led to artificial diets distinct from their wild counterparts. Paleodietary isotope models and life history reconstructions demonstrated sacrificed carnivores were often captured as cubs/chicks, fed a C_4-enriched diet, likely through indirect consumption of C_4-fed rabbits/hares, for the majority of their young lives.

Secondary Corporeal Animal Forms

Secondary corporeal animal forms comprised a more diverse population, represented by varying ages, preparation techniques, and pathological and dietary patterns. Element and cutmark distribution identified two general preparation techniques among felids and canids; the skulls were either minimally modified to preserve the entire skull, including the cranial-mandibular joint, or extensive modification left only the snout and the frontal section of the mandible intact. While there was some variation, overall, Burials 2 and 6 favored the former pattern, retaining the skull relatively complete, while Burials 3 and 5 tended to be processed more extensively.

Skulls in Burials 2 and 6 would have been bare, with no pelts attached. Green bone fractures on some skulls indicate that extraction of secondary products such as the skin, meat, and other soft tissue occurred soon after the organism's death. Extensive cutmarks likewise trace pelt removal while the meat and muscles remain intact. The cluster of isolated paw bones (phalanges) signal pelts participated alongside prepared skulls. Skulls from Burials 3 and 5 exhibited fewer surface modifications, exacerbated by poor preservation conditions that restricted the determination of processing procedures and the timing of interventions. Nonetheless, we cannot ignore apparent differences in cutmark distribution and scarcity of neurocranium fragments.

Mesoamerican dignitaries and warriors are often depicted adorned in animal pelts, the paws and/or claws (the third phalange) of the beast still attached. Felid, canid, and eagle paraphernalia were highly prized goods worn only by the bravest warriors, rulers, and high priests (Chapter 3). Felid warriors marching into battle on the murals at Teotihuacan may be representing humans transformed into ferocious beasts through embodying felid regalia. These lavish skulls and other secondary animal products accompanied sacrificed animals. At times, perhaps only the skulls were deposited, whereby the processed pelts likely adorned the ritual practitioners, warriors, and state officials who participated in the ritual spectacle. In this case, it would intimately entangle animal matter with ritual practitioners, creating an active site for animal politics to be vividly displayed. In others, pelts either accompanied the skulls or were placed as another corporeal animal form that is often invisible in archaeological records. In the following sections, I narrate four osteobiographies: a primary puma, a secondary eagle, a primary canid, and a primary rattlesnake in service of exploring these dynamics.

Animal Biography #1: Primary Puma, E.1818

E.1818 provides the most concrete evidence of a felid habituated to city life. This young female, about eighteen months of age, lay on the western sector of Burial 6 with her extremities bound (Plate 13a). She was probably captured as a cub and experienced a nonfatal injury on her right lower limb at this time or during confinement. Her femoral head was dislodged, and her deformed acetabular joint reflects each painful limping stride taken during the rest of her life (Plate 13b). Such an injury would have been fatal for this solitary predator in the wild. Nevertheless, remodeling around the femoral shaft and the obliquely deformed acetabulum indicates she survived the injury (Plate 13c). Slight remodeling around a blow to the back of her head likewise suggests this was not a perimortem trauma but one inflicted during confinement (Plate 13d).

The puma's poor oral health also recounts a life of hardship. Extensive wearing on her mesial dentition caused the loss of her first and second incisors (Plate 13e). The filled alveolar cavity reveals a prolonged period of tooth loss before meeting her fate. As felids do not regularly utilize their incisors for consumption or hunting, it merits considering plausible causes. Her canines are also abnormally worn for her young age (comparable to a seven-to-nine year old) (Gay and Best 1996). In contrast, her carnassial teeth utilized for food processing look healthy and exhibit very little wear. Abnormal stress during long-term confinement manifests through pacing, head bobbing, suckling on the tail and toes, and fur plucking among wild tigers in modern zoological parks (Pitsko 2003). Obsessive gnawing is also a sign of stress, and gnawing on restrictive devices like a cage (e.g., the wooden cage found in Burial 2) could lead to the described pathologies and abnormal tooth wear patterns.

Another indication of captivity was derived from her stomach cavity, which contains residue of a last meal before the ritual slaughter. The uniformity of the diet among sacrificed felids, canids, and eagles, mainly consisting of either rabbits or hares (Chapter 4, Microfauna: Stomach Contents), suggests intentional ritual feeding in anticipation of sacrifice. Among E.1818's stomach contents were two fairly complete rabbits and an unidentified avian bone. Mixed discolored (burnt) elements are direct evidence of artificial feeding of cooked foodstuff despite the puma's specialized feeding habits.

So how long was E.1818 maintained in captivity? A tooth (permanent maxillary third premolar) and bone (metatarsal II) were sampled for isotopic analysis. $\delta^{13}C_{apatite}$ values were −5.1‰ (after teeth-bone correction) and −2.7‰, respectively, corresponding to roughly 64% and 79% C_4 dietary input. Tooth isotope values reflect diet during tooth formation. Unfortunately, tooth eruption sequences are only published for pumas up to eight months of age, when their permanent incisors and canines appear, and their premolars are still deciduous (Currier 1979). By two years of age, the animal's permanent dentition is established (Gay and Best 1996). Based on tooth eruption sequences of lynx (six months) (Crowe 1975: Table 2) and leopard (eight to ten months) (Stander 1997: Table 1), the puma's premolars likely form just after eight months of age. By this age, over half of E.1818's diet was already based on C_4-based resources. Further samples of even earlier forming teeth are necessary to distinguish between carnivores bred in captivity versus those caught during early infancy. There is no evidence of adult pumas being kept in captivity to breed alongside these young individuals. Given the logistical hardships of successful captive breeding of highly territorial felids, pumas were likely not bred in captivity at Teotihuacan.

In the urban center, acquiring the 1.2–1.4 kg/day of requisite meat for this specialized carnivore would have carried logistical hardships. What were they fed? E.1818's bone isotope sample was one of two outliers with exceptionally high $\delta^{13}C_{carbonate}$, $\delta^{13}C_{collagen}$, and $\delta^{14}N_{collagen}$ values. Her elevated C_4/marine protein and C_4 total dietary signal in the simple carbon model (Figure 5.4, dark diamond upper right) and placement well outside the 70% C_4 diet, >50% C_4 protein spectrum in the multivariate model (Figure 5.5) indicate that both her protein sources and overall diet were comprised almost exclusively of C_4 resources. Given the high nitrogen value (a trophic level higher than all other felid samples), E.1818's primary meat source was an omnivorous (though not marine) resource that consumed maize and maize-fed protein.

Only two possible candidates fit this description: the oldest domesticate, the dog, or humans. As mentioned, dogs consume human waste and are often indistinguishable from their owners (Allitt et al. 2008). In Mesoamerica, they were fattened for consumption on a maize-based diet and certainly would have been available in the city center. By Aztec and colonial times, the town of Acolman specialized in dog breeding, producing surplus for sale at the marketplace for food and sacrifice (Durán 1971: 278). However, at Teotihuacan, it seems dogs did not comprise a vital protein source, as they contributed only 11% of the total MNI of zooarchaeological remains from the city (Sugiyama et al. 2017).

Interestingly, the latter hypothesis of pumas consuming human tissue is referenced in Teotihuacan mural art, which renders pumas and jaguars consuming trilobed human hearts (Figure 3.3). Headrick (2007: 84) has interpreted such scenes as humans shown in the guise of their naguals, indicating acts of ritual cannibalism. Whether this was a metaphoric expression or a mnemonic device to recall historical event(s) is an interesting question. What we can say is that Bernardo Díaz de Castillo, a Spanish conquistador, described the animals encountered in Moctezuma's House of Beasts in the following manner:

> *They give them as food deer and fowls, dogs and other things which they are used to hunt, and I have heard it said that they feed them on the bodies of Indians who have been sacrificed . . . they saw open the chest with stone knives and hasten to tear out the palpitating heart and blood, and offer it to their Idols, in whose name the sacrifice is made. Then they cut open the thighs, arms and head and eat the former at feasts and banquets, and the head they hang up on some beams, and the body of the man sacrificed is not eaten but given to these fierce animals.* (Díaz del Castillo 2003: 213)

What happens when we take animal matter (and the evidence derived from it) seriously? Isotope evidence will not be able to tease apart the two hypotheses. However, the chemical signature in the bones reflects a sustained consumption pattern across the duration of E.1818's young life in captivity, a pattern experienced by at least its companion E.1984. I suspect both dogs and human tissues were consumed, the latter to display felid power to the public, and the former a more practical solution to obtain the high demand for daily dietary protein. Additional primary felids also incorporated more C_4-based herbivores into their diet, likely consuming high frequencies of corn-stuffed rabbits/hares, among other possible animals (turkeys, quails, waterfowl).

Animal Biography #2: Secondary Eagle, E.2246

E.2246's remains recount a complex biography lurid with both pathological indicators of captivity alongside surface modifications of postmortem manipulation of the corpse (Plate 14). This male eagle of adult stature lay by the northern wall of Burial 6, adjacent to the pile of decapitated humans (Figure 6.1). Two pathologies were observed. Both tarsometatarsi had an infection that caused extensive bone remodeling along the medial shaft (Plate 14d), identical to the two primary eagles discussed in Chapter 4, likely the result of a tethered lifestyle. Remodeling on his left distal humeral epicondyle reveals an injury/infection on the wing along this critical humeral-ulna joint (Plate 14f). Such an injury, while nonfatal, could have made flight difficult until recovery. Bone isotope data provide additional support for captivity, with elevated degrees of C_4 food resources expressed in both carbon carbonate (−5.9‰) and collagen (−13.1‰) results, alongside a relatively high nitrogen value (8.1‰). Generally, eagles deposited secondarily into the cache had

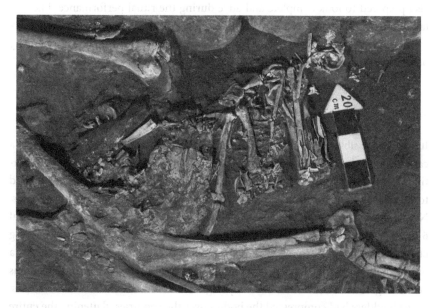

FIGURE 6.1
Eagle E.2246 from Burial 6 along northern wall. © Moon Pyramid Project.

isotope values just as elevated as their primary counterparts. In essence, pathological and isotopic indicators of captivity on several secondary eagles paralleled primary burials, indicating histories of prolonged captivity among some secondary raptors.

Although E.2246's complete and articulated skeleton led excavators to identify him as a primary burial, zooarchaeological analysis revealed postmortem manipulation of the corporeal animal form. Practitioners extracted the encephalic tissue through a cranial opening along the occipital region (Plate 14a). Light cutmarks were placed throughout the skeleton, including along the shaft close to the epiphysis of both femurs (Plate 14c, e) and the left tibiotarsus (lower hind limb). A circular perforation penetrating the left furculum on the scapular tuberosity (shoulder area) and the proximal end of the left tibiotarsus (Plate 14b, g) also indicate extensive manipulation. Though the right fulcrum was fragmented, both sides likely contained the same perforation to maintain skeletal integrity at the shoulder girdle. This eagle may have also been wrapped or stuffed, as fibers (though very degraded) were found adhered onto the skeleton, including the keel, both femurs, left tibiotarsus, both carpometacarpi, vertebrae, and mandible.

Abundant surface modifications and the undisturbed articulated position suggest that practitioners took steps to preserve skeletal integrity even after the organism's death. Though skeletal representation differed from that of a taxidermically prepared eagle (E.2139) introduced in Chapter 4, I suspect E.2246 was also prepared to look complete and alive during the ritual performance. Like the taxidermically prepared eagle, several secondary remains relay that early experimentation of captive maintenance of eagles was met with difficulties requiring postmortem remediations.

Animal Biography #3: Primary Wolf, E.2199

It was impossible to reconstruct a similarly detailed life history account of a canid due to the limited quantity of primary burials ($n = 3$), the poor preservation, and the relatively low frequency of surface modifications. Alterations tended to be restricted to postmortem cutmarks and breakages on secondary remains. No pathologies were recorded. A female wolf, E.2199, was excavated from Burial 6 among the pile of primary burials in the southwestern corner of the offering chamber. She lay to rest on her right side, with her extremities superimposed in a bound configuration (Figure 6.2). No information about the surface modifications could be gathered due to the extremely degraded condition of the faunal remains. Large boulders had compressed the bodies over the centuries, flattening the entire area and requiring archaeologists to extract body segments as consolidated blocks.

FIGURE 6.2
Complete wolf E.2199 from Burial 6. © Moon Pyramid Project.

The third and fourth premolar length and width did not confirm initial identification as a possible dog-wolf hybrid, and she is designated as a possible wolf until further analysis. The combination of a complete permanent dentition and unfused long bones determined she was a juvenile.

Pathological markers of captivity on the canid skeleton were absent among primary and secondary remains. Dogs are the domesticated counterparts of wolves, and thus, wolves are more adaptable to human settlements than specialized carnivores selected for sacrifice. As it was unclear if the absence of pathologies on the canid assemblage was due to poor surface visibility, the adaptability of the canid biology/behavior to human settlement, or the lack of captivity among the canid population, isotopic data helped tease apart these different scenarios.

E.2199's enriched carbon isotope ratio ($-4.3‰$ $\delta^{13}C_{carbonate}$) contrasted sharply with two primary canid isotope values from Burial 5 and 2 ($\delta^{13}C_{carbonate}$ average $-13‰$), representing a mixed but primarily C_3-based diet. E.2199's $\delta^{13}C_{carbonate}$ values on her mandibular first molar ($\delta^{13}C_{carbonate}$ $-3.3‰$) and tibia ($-4.3‰$) were comparable to values reported for a domesticated dog sampled from a residential context. By at least four to five months when the permanent first molar was forming (Blanco Padilla, Rodríguez Galicia, et al. 2009), the canid was already consuming an artificial diet.

Unlike felids that require expansive terrain and are highly territorial, wolves form packs, are locally available, and have higher encounter rates as they prey on domesticated animals and secondary browsers attracted to nearby milpas. They were likely more predictable and accessible for capture and hunting. The low frequency of its use as primary burials and, contrastingly, frequent deposition as secondary corporeal animal forms implied wolf symbolism and usage patterns differed from the more explicit restricted access observed among felid and eagle counterparts. It is perhaps not surprising to find instances like E.2199, where humans readily adopted a wolf into the human settlement as they are amiable to domestication.

Animal Biography #4: Primary Rattlesnake, E.1494

As isotope work on snakes has yet to be completed, I base this life history reconstruction on zooarchaeological data. A rattlesnake in the eastern sector of Burial 5, E.1494, provides a glimpse of its life in captivity because it is one of the only relatively complete skeletons with a pathology (Plate 15). Two mid-trunk vertebrae were fused, in keeping with colonial sources that detail the methods of capturing poisonous live serpents:

> And when it is taken, in order to be caught, it is beaten with a stick, a willow. And to be speedy, it is caught with fine tobacco. He who wishes to take it rubs fine tobacco in his hands; then also he throws it at [the serpent]. Especially if the fine tobacco enters its mouth, this serpent then stretches out stupefied; it moves no more. Thus, he simply takes it up with his hand. This happens with all serpents; they are stupefied by fine tobacco. (Sahagún 1963: 76)

Serpents captured alive would have their fangs extracted and placed in a vase. Rattlesnakes killed with a stick had their head and tail removed, ready to be skinned and consumed (Aguilera 1985: 74). The rattlesnake E.1037 uncovered from the middle of a smashed ceramic vessel implies ceramic or organic containers were used for rattlesnake transport, such as the basket containing a heap of rattlesnakes discovered in Burial 6.

Rattlesnakes seem to have also adhered to the same ritualization process, wherein consuming an ultimate meal may have been a strategic part of the procession. E. 1494 was one of four rattlesnakes from Burial 5 still digesting a feast of two rodents (*Peromyscus* sp.) in its ribcage. Digestion slows the rattlesnake's movement, which likely had the added benefit during transport.

The Ritualization Process: The Toxcatl Festival

As Turner (1977) explained, sacrifices are not events but processes, and I argue that, in this case, the process began with the encounter with the wild animal. In this section, I utilize the Toxcatl festival, an Aztec human sacrificial rite, as a comparative model to interpret the consecration process, how a sacrificial subject was "set apart" and sacralized into the ultimate ritualized body. Patton (2006) examines animal sacrifice across various religious texts to argue that the selection process begins when the victim is perfected or beautified, as only the flawless are apt to reach a state of deathlessness, becoming "like the gods." Carrasco's (1991) description of the Toxcatl festival begins with a male warrior captive undergoing a selection process a year prior to his sacrifice who will embody the perfect archetype of *teteo imixiptlahuan*, a deity "impersonator" (*hombre-dios* in Spanish), in this case of the god Tezcatlipoca. Though this term is often translated as "impersonator," given the discussion of relational ontologies that regard embodiments encompassed transformations of fully becoming (localized ensoulments), not metaphoric representations (Bassett 2015), I utilize the Nahuatl terminology to support the divine presence of Tezcatlipoca was experienced through the captive's corporeal presence. The Florentine codex states very detailed criteria for the god's "human form"; the idealized, perfected body was to have "no flaw, who had no [bodily] defects, who had no blemish, who had no mark" (Sahagún 1951: 68).

Once the victim is selected, their social identity is transformed through corporeal acts. The *teteo imixiptlahuan* lives as the god Tezcatlipoca within the city for a year. Receiving official training in Aztec arts (music, poetry, etc.) and indulging in the greatest carnal and material luxuries (food, women, goods, etc.), he embodies this new identity, ostentatiously displayed as he is fêted throughout the empire (Carrasco 1991). As his processual route wound through the city from center to periphery and back to the ceremonial core, the *teteo imixiptlahuan* bridged the boundaries between center and periphery, serving as a wobbling pivot that ritualized the entire landscape. Daily interpersonal interactions between the *teteo imixiptlahuan* and the whole of Aztec society consecrated the selected warrior's corporeal manifestation into Tezcaltipoca (Carrasco 1991).

According to Patton (2006), the chosen subject displays a "fiction of willingness" during such acts. At least in theory, they should never be divested of their agency/free will. Being selected as a *teteo imixiptlahuan* had its advantages, not only during godly livelihood but also because divine immortality brought benefits to the family. Allegedly, he would voluntarily walk up the steps of the main temple of the city center. There, his heart was extracted, he was beheaded, and his skull was placed on the *tzompantli* or skull rack (Sahagún 1951). Nevertheless, other sources recount that the willingness of sacrificial subjects varied greatly (Carrasco 1991, 2008), and there were apparent social pressures.

In the case of animal sacrifice in ancient Greek *thusia* and ancient Israelite *qorban 'olah* rituals, Patton (2006) explains that the animal's free-willed consent was performed by sprinkling water upon the heads, making the animals appear to nod in assent. Like sacrifice, several authors explain acceptance as an essential precondition of hunting. The prey species, or the master of animals that controls them, must consent to the terms of the hunt or selected fate (Brown and Emery 2008; Hill 2011). The Ainu would likewise explain that the *kamuy* spirit presented itself to the Ainu through embodying the bear (Kimura 1999).

The embodiment of *teteo imixiptlahuan* as god makes us consider the social implications of the subject's corporeal form. The ensoulment and embodiment process of the subject results in death, not of the sacrificial human body, but of the god himself (López Austin 1973, 1988: 376–377). The care of the sacrificial subject's corpse, as the embodied deity is reverently brought down from the temple platform, and the veneration of the skull in the ceremonial center as part of the *tzompantli*, all demonstrate an emphasis on the corporeal form as a material expression recording the negotiated rights and obligations generated through corporeal interactions with the divine personage.

Reviewing the analysis of the Toxcatl festival by Carrasco (1991), the hierophantic transformation of a warrior captive into *teteo imixiptlahuan* was the process by which the public set apart the human captive as the ultimate sacrificial entity, the deity Tezcatlipoca. Similarly, I interpret animal sacrifice as the process by which human–animal eco-contracts are experienced, embodied, and materialized through interpersonal encounters with corporeal animal forms. An animal, or group of animals, presents themselves with agency, purpose, identity, and metaphysical standing (see Chapter 1) and engages in sometimes innovative ways with human communities. Their corporeal manifestations during residency at Teotihuacan, like the public display of *teteo imixiptlahuan*'s engagements in the capital and periphery of the Aztec Empire, were the means of establishing interpersonal contact with the public that led to their divine transformation from a generic wild predator into the ultimate ritualized body for sacrifice.

Co-Producing Ritualized Bodies: Animal Sacrifice at Teotihuacan

The biographies of corporeal animal forms and a review of the Toxcatl festival highlight that the ritual performance was part of a longer ritualization process. I define four stages in the ritualization of corporeal animal forms at Teotihuacan: acquisition, management, postmortem manipulation, and sacrifice and/or deposition.

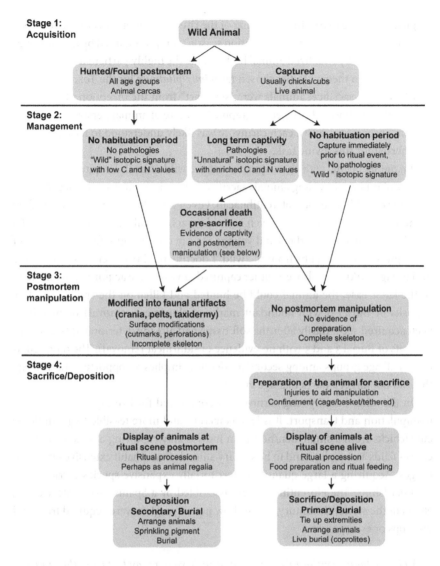

FIGURE 6.3
Four stages of the ritualization process and archaeological signatures.

Figure 6.3 outlines each stage, the specific human–animal interactions, and the archaeological/isotope data utilized to sustain these interpretations for primary and secondary remains.

The patterned distribution of cosmologically significant numbers of apex predators of a particular sex indicates a strategic selection process with many months of planning and coordination in anticipation of the grand ritual performance. This preplanning stage marks the beginning of the ritualization process whereby the selection process (taxa, age, sex, acquisition season) was preordained by the meanings to be embodied by ritualized animal bodies. Like the highly particular criterion applied (at least in theory) to the chosen *teteo imixiptlahuan* for the Toxcatl festival a year before his sacrifice, animals were "set apart" from the inception of the grand sacrificial plan. If we take the ethnographic literature of animal personhood in this selection process seriously, each carnivore was likely understood to have presented him/herself for this divine task.

The model begins with the acquisition of the wild animal. Despite the high frequency of infant and young animals sacrificed, there is no direct evidence of active breeding of wild carnivores at Teotihuacan. Given the difficulty of captive breeding of these specialized carnivores (even in modern zoological parks) and the lack of a breeding population (mothers and young), we can only account for the practice of live capture of chicks/cubs from the wild. I documented two scenarios during the initial stage: wild animals were either captured alive or were acquired postmortem. In the latter case, the animal could be hunted and killed on the spot (secondary deposits of Burial 6 with abundant marks of skin/meat removal) or may have been acquired secondarily after the soft tissue had already deteriorated (secondary deposits of Burial 3 and 5 with no evidence of skin/meat removal). The representation of all age groups among secondary deposits implies an opportunistic strategy that did not target a particular age group.

On the other hand, young carnivores were favored for live capture to facilitate manipulation and transport. It is less dangerous and more feasible to get multiple cubs/chicks from a single den/nest than individually capturing adults who, in the case of felids and eagles, tend to be solitary animals that inhabit extensive territorial ranges. Acquiring a large quantity of territorially expansive species carries logistical hardships. The Florentine Codex, assembled by a Spanish friar interviewing elders in the sixteenth century, details how nesting eaglets were acquired from cliff outcrops or escarpments.

> *And they hunt them in this way: so that their young may be taken, the hunter places a palm-leaf or solid reed basket on his head. When the eagle becomes angry, it sets out to seize the palm-leaf basket; it carries it off. Very high it carries it. From there it drops it, thinking it is the hunter. When [the eagle] has released it, then it comes thundering down on it. But the hunter has meanwhile removed its young far away.* (Sahagún 1963: 42)

Hunting parties at Teotihuacan could likewise be scheduled to appropriate breeding seasons for each species to strategically acquire multiple young cubs/chicks. As mentioned in Chapter 3, ethnographic data from US Southwest communities likewise assume similar strategies. More genetic data may help refine this issue for Teotihuacan samples.

The second stage captures the period of direct human contact with the live animal. The wild animal may have been seized immediately before its deposition with no habituation period—in which case no pathological or dietary indicators would be discernible—or in anticipation of the ritual. This latter scenario would arise when a sizeable predetermined number of animals needed to be sacrificed at once, requiring timely acquisition due to the restricted distribution of the species (e.g., felids and eagles). Capture and captivity may result in injuries, such as a blow to the head or fractured extremities, that are registered in the zooarchaeological record. These pathologies are telling of some of the stringent and dangerous encounters with captive carnivores faced by their handlers. Nutritional and behavioral stress markers are also symptoms of captivity. Enriched $\delta^{13}C$ and $\delta^{15}N$ values from their teeth and bones also detected a dietary shift to artificial foodstuff. This management period allows select individuals (like the governing elite) to establish a novel and exclusive relationship with some of the most powerful entities on the landscape.

Like the *teteo imixiptlahuan*, these animals would be prominently integrated into Teotihuacan society as they were heard, seen, and vividly experienced as residents. The sacrificed spider monkey's life history at Plaza of the Columns calculated the captive period extended at least two years (Sugiyama et al. 2022). Like the Aztecs who showcased their imperial prowess to their Spanish visitors by touring their impressive menagerie, visitors, residents, animal caretakers, and governing officials alike would have felt the presence of these animals at Teotihuacan in myriad ways. Interpersonal bonds, such as naming the animal, and familiarity with their personalities, gender, and other vitalities, would form during this period. Differential access to develop direct interpersonal bonds with these potent corporeal animal forms carried substantive affects to social positionality.

In the third stage of postmortem manipulation, animals that occasionally died during their habitation period, as well as those acquired postmortem, were prepared. In the former case, practitioners quickly processed animal carcasses to preserve skeletal integrity and prevent decomposition. Secondary burials of eagles in Burial 6 exhibited both zooarchaeological markers of captivity alongside evidence of explicit postmortem manipulation. Perhaps these are the telling signs of mishaps during initial experimentation with live capture of eagles at an unprecedented scale. Interestingly, as will be described in more detail in Chapter 7, the sex of the eagles continued to be remembered even after death as an integral component defining personhood.

Fresh skeletons were prepared by extracting the soft tissue from the braincase and removing the pelt, feathers, and other secondary products. Abundant cutmarks, perforations, and changes in element distribution indicated methods for maintaining skeletal integrity (including taxidermy) among the eagles. Pelt production left deep grooves along the phalanges during the strenuous task of separating the skin from the paws, leaving just the second and third phalanges in place. While some skulls showed extensive cutmarks suggesting pelt extraction preceded deposition, others lacked surface modifications and displayed weathering patterns supportive of acquisition post decomposition and minimal intervention.

In the final stage of the sacrifice and/or deposition, animals would enter the ritual scene either alive (to be sacrificed) or postmortem as faunal artifacts. Various preparatory steps were necessary for the live animal, including intentional injuries to aid manipulation and transport (usually to animals not already tamed) and some method to confine their movement (rattlesnakes in a basket or ceramic vessel, mammals in cages or with binding of their extremities).

Both live animals and their secondary products were likely lavishly displayed in a ritual procession along the Avenue of the Dead to their final resting place (Chapter 8). Secondary animal products may have splendidly adorned the ritual practitioners who exhibited diverse high-luxury goods (shells, greenstone, obsidian, etc.).

Live animals were likely the centerpiece of the procession alongside human sacrifices. Practitioners likely ritually fed many of the carnivores in anticipation of their emplacement into the pyramid. Just as the lion's feeding is a popular attraction in modern zoos, preparation and feeding rabbits and hares (or rodents for the rattlesnake) would have been a spectacle highlighting their prowess and carnivorous qualities. As there is evidence of rabbit/hare taming and management at Teotihuacan (Somerville et al. 2016), this would have been an abundant and reliable foodstuff to use in sacrificial rituals. As rabbits are closely associated with the moon (Stone and Zender 2011: 199), their close affinity with the Moon Goddess may have added to their designated participation in sacrifices at the Moon Pyramid.[1] The ultimate feast likely preceded the ascent of the selected animals, supposedly willingly, to their final resting place in the same fate the *teteo imixiptlahuan* courageously walked up the temple steps to meet his destiny.

We can imagine two degrees of participation: the general public that observed the lavish procession of the ritual entourage to the Moon Pyramid, and a more exclusive group that directly witnessed the final deposition and burial. In this more restricted setting, primary burials were carefully placed alongside diverse ritual accuterments into a specific meaningful pattern following the prescribed

---

[1] Rabbits were also consumed by eagles sacrificed in the Sun Pyramid (Nawa Sugiyama et al. 2013) and inside Offering D4 at Plaza of the Columns Complex (Sugiyama et al. 2022), so rabbit feeding was not restricted to the Moon Pyramid sacrifices.

quantity, orientation, and sex of the animal. Still alive, their extremities were tied to restrict movement from their designated spatial configuration. Coprolites in the cages of Burial 2 attest the animals entered the scene alive, awaiting their fate as other offerings were being arranged. Ritual practitioners likewise arranged secondary deposits in a symbolic layout, and sometimes sprinkled red pigment over their bodies.

This reconstruction of the ritualization process accentuates the material traces of human–animal encounters: initial contact and physical interaction while the animal was alive, as well as the long-term planning, management, and preparation during their transformation into a ritualized body. It also highlights the complex realities of coordinating a ritual spectacle. During the procession of eighteen eagles screeching and flapping their wings, tethered tightly by their caretakers, would the crowd notice a few still taxidermically prepared eagles? These snapshots of ancient ritual performances enliven the event to me; they showcase the realities and complications of orchestrating the ritual performance that help us relate to people from the past (see Chapter 8). As Evans-Pritchard (1967) famously recorded in his ethnography of Nuer religion, a cucumber is substituted when you do not have a sacred cow to sacrifice, but that does not diminish the ritual outcome. If the eagle you have carefully raised for the ritual event dies a few days before the spectacle, you do what is needed to make sure there are the eighteen eagles necessary for the ritual slaughter, whether dead or alive.

Negotiated attributes included species selection, the appropriate number of each species, prey choice for ritual feeding, and even the age and sex of the animals chosen to participate in the ritual. It would have necessitated a slew of caregivers who interacted daily with the animals and implies that city dwellers would have seen, heard, and experienced the animals to differing degrees. The conquistador Hernan Cortés (1971) described three hundred attendees caring for the birds in Moctezuma's aviary. Encounters with these beasts left a lasting emotionally charged impression, as one conquistador describes, "the infernal noise when the lions and tigers roared and the jackals and foxes howled and the serpents hissed, it was horrible to listen to and it seemed like a hell" (Diaz del Castillo 2003: 213). All of these factors were negotiated based on the animal's cosmological significance, the meanings attributed to each dedicatory ritual, and specific logistical issues of animal availability and biology. The interpersonal relationships established during confinement at Teotihuacan would have altered the perception of these animals as divine persons distinct from their wild counterparts. Just as the physical manifestation of the *teteo imixiptlahuan* as he learned the arts and lived a godly existence was instrumental to his transformation into Tezcatlipoca, the presence of these carnivores in the city would have established a distinct social identity and positionality, co-produced by the entanglements of human and nonhuman persons, into ultimate ritualized bodies.

The prolonged and complex human–animal encounters established during this ritualization process fueled meaningful and impactful interpersonal interactions at every stage. The hunters who first established contact with these powerful beings, the caregivers who fed and managed their daily needs, the populace who would have heard their screeches and roars during confinement, maybe even witnessed feedings, and the participants who stood witness to their ultimate act of sacrifice embodied a new form of human–animal relationship, one in which the Teotihuacan state assumed a strategically distinct positionality to these powerful predators. I further this argument in the next chapter, explaining how animal matter, as ritualized bodies mediated placemaking at the Moon Pyramid.

CHAPTER 7

ANIMALS INHABITING THE *ALTEPETL*

IN THE PREVIOUS CHAPTER, I reconstructed the ritualization process of key animal actors through detailed animal osteobiographies. Both sacrificed animals and their by-products established complex relationships with Teotihuacan's inhabitants as they were seen, heard, used, and experienced in confinement, as well as during the dedicatory act itself. I have introduced animal matter as active persons—sentient beings with social positionality that often relate to the order of the cosmos—and how the governing elite vividly displayed their newly established relationships with these potentate beings during state ritualized performances. In this chapter, I use the specific decision nodes highlighted in these reconstructions to decipher the underlying meanings of these key actors and how they directly contributed to placemaking, transforming the Moon Pyramid into the *altepetl* of Teotihuacan.

I begin this chapter by summarizing the species diversity, spatial patterning, and seasonality data for each dedicatory cache in chronological order. I then interpret how corporeal animal forms participated in the Moon Pyramid's ritualized co-production. As the Teotihuacan state conceived Burials 2 and 6 as a pair during the fourth building phase, I consider how they planned both offerings in unison despite their execution at two separate moments. I thus conceptualize the long transformation process from a wild carnivore into a ritualized body as two performances within the same ritualization process.

Building 4's construction demarcated when Teotihuacan elites directly controlled highly restricted, symbolically charged predators for the first time. There is a reason why the earliest evidence of systematic handling of apex predators for ritual usage in Mesoamerica coincided with the development of a dominant state ideology vividly ingrained into the monumental landscape. Interpersonal encounters with these potent beings consecrated these animal persons into master guardian animals and empowered delegates of the Teotihuacan state.

In this analysis, I understand pyramids as mountains and particularly focus on the function of the *altepetl*, the watery hill, in the ceremonial landscape (Chapter 2). The dedicatory caches materialized a novel cosmogram that was the very means by which placemaking occurred. Live animals and their physical remains carefully embedded into the nucleus of Building 4 animated this dirt mound into a differentiated landscape where the *altepetl* stood as an embodiment of sovereignty.

Subsequent offertory complexes (Burial 3 and 5) reflect diachronic changes in animal matter usage and roles as the Moon Pyramid continued to be remodeled. Novel entanglements with human corporeal forms demonstrate that animal matter increasingly interacted with specific groups and individuals of the Teotihuacan state. In each context, human-corporeal animal form interactions transformed animal matter into empowered ritualized bodies intimately entangled with sovereignty formations at Teotihuacan.

Building 4: Burial 2

Teotihuacan ritual specialists embedded conspicuous references to their cosmogram in the earliest dedicatory caches (Burials 2 and 6) at the Moon Pyramid during the first city-wide monumental construction program during the Ceremonial Monuments period (Chapter 2). These two caches represent the most comprehensive evidence of animals' active and central role in state ritualized activities, with ubiquitous evidence of physical encounters with potentate animals in captivity. Burial 2 contained eighteen sacrificial victims, while Burial 6 included thirty-three primary deposits. In addition to the formidable labor required for construction, a total MNI of 117 animals from these two contexts portrays an unprecedented coordination feat during the development of Building 4. The zooarchaeological and isotopic datasets indicate that Teotihuacan state personnel captured and confined apex animals in preparation for these two dedicatory acts and habituated them to city life. In addition, artisans elaborated these carnivores into ritual paraphernalia.

Burials 2 and 6 are located inside Building 4, the former along the bedrock layer marking the initiation of the construction and the latter as the monument elevated toward the sky. Lopez Luján and Sugiyama (2017) discussed the parallels between the two offerings, confirming that they were designed as a cohesive unit that materialized the Moon Pyramid's role within the Teotihuacan cosmogram.

Species Diversity and Abundance

Burial 2 included ten species distributed among eleven genera (Table 3.1). Nine complete golden eagles constituted the most abundant species. Secondary remains of other birds, mainly raptors, including the great horned owl, hawk, common raven, and prairie falcon contributed to species diversity. These birds were primarily represented by their extremities, especially wings that would have retained their magnificent feathers. Remains of small game found in the stomach content and/or fill included hares, rabbits, and rodents.

The post holes confining two pumas and a Mexican wolf indicate these animals were buried alive. The coprolites preserved within the cages also support this scenario. Four infant or juvenile felid crania were also deposited in the dedicatory chamber. Their young age only permitted confirmation that at least one was of a puma.

At least six rattlesnakes, represented by many vertebrae, ribs, and six pairs of mandibles, were placed near the center. These rattlesnakes were confined to one area, so they may have been in an organic container, perhaps a bag or basket that deteriorated, like the miraculously preserved circular basket from Burial 6.

Spatial Patterning

Animal and other nonhuman persons strategically oriented the ritual space. The eagles were distributed at the center and roughly along axial and inter-axial loci (Plate 4). Similarly, five Tlaloc jars lay in the intercardinal corners and center of the cache. The two prominent celestial beings, the sun (eagle) and celestial waters (Tlaloc), were paired. However, some animals were noticeably out of place—for example, eagle E.309 settled by the caged wolf skeleton. Most likely, judging from the presence of the other three eagles found on the corners of the cache, the raptor was meant to be placed on the southwestern corner. Though tethered, the animals were buried alive and could have shifted from their original placement. The caged wolf is also roughly, though not precisely, placed along the north-south axis. Despite these exceptions, the animals marked cardinal and inter-cardinal points and the core, which resembles Burial 6's spatial arrangement.

Two sets of nine bifacial knives were likewise placed in a radial pattern, marking the cardinal and intercardinal directions around two central greenstone figurines (not unlike Burial 6). The number of obsidian bifaces and primary fauna coincides. Eighteen obsidian bifaces and sacrificed animals (three caged animals, six rattlesnakes, and nine eagles) oriented the spatiotemporal axes. Eighteen represents the layers of the upperworld and underworld, as well as the number of months in the 360-day calendric cycle (Sugiyama and López Luján 2007). Eighteen was a consistent potent number also emphasized in Burial 6.

Though there is a more apparent pattern of sexual division of space in Burial 6 (see later), the pairing of male/female, though less consistent, is worth mentioning in Burial 2. The two superimposed cages included a male and a female puma paired into the northern sector. In the southern sector, a caged male wolf lay near a female eagle, pairing male and female animals. A single human male sat along the eastern wall with his hands tied behind his back. Like Burial 6, the sacrificed human's position seems secondary (in the perimeter with no apparent pattern) to the rest of the offering assemblage.

Seasonality

A primary eagle and wolf provide valuable insight into the timing of the ritual event. Burial 2 was the only context with sacrificed eaglets. Eagle chicks tend to be under-represented because they grow at an exceptional pace, reaching adult size by three months. On the flip side, the presence of a young individual provides an opportunity for a tight seasonality designation. At least one infant/juvenile and three possible juvenile eagles in Burial 2 indicate that the ritual happened when they were roughly two months old. Because eaglets hatch between April and early May, internment is estimated to have occurred sometime between June and July.

A juvenile wolf from the same context somewhat contradicted this seasonal designation. Wolves generally go into heat in the winter and have a two-month gestation period, with births occurring in the spring (February–April) (Blanco Padilla, Rodríguez Galicia, et al. 2009). The six-to-nine-month age designation of E.213 places the ritual between August and January. However, wolf breeding patterns depend on prey availability and are much more variable than an eagle's. Its domesticated form, the dog, breeds year-round. Thus, I relied more heavily on eagle age calculations with more restricted breeding seasons and age estimates to conclude that the burial likely occurred from the summer to late summer (June–August) during the rainy season.

Building 4: Burial 6

Burial 6 represents the most abundant evidence of animal mass sacrifice and animal by-products playing a central role in state-sponsored rituals at Teotihuacan (MNI: 75) (Table 3.1). After Burial 2's deposition at the base, Burial 6 was produced when this same monument reached approximately 15 m high. Many complete animals were superimposed in the southwest corner (Plate 5). An interesting parallel exists between the overlapping complete animals sacrificed at the southwest corner and the piled human skeletal remains on the northwest corner of the cache.

Species Diversity and Abundance

Species representation (eleven species distributed among nine genera) (Table 3.1) and the layout of Burial 6 mirror that of Burial 2 with slight variations. Eighteen golden eagles comprised the most abundant species, which included primary and secondary burials. The fill matrix also included the bobwhite quail and the inca dove.

Though most of the canids were represented by the wolf, there were also two coyote skulls. The possibility of a hybrid between a wolf and a dog is pending further analysis. While wolf-dog (even coyote) hybrids have been identified among the canid maxillary pendants at the FSP (Valadez Azúa et al. 2002a, 2002b), a complete coyote skeleton has not been identified from other ritual contexts during the Teotihuacan occupation. There were primary and secondary deposits of puma and jaguar, though confirmation of the latter, given the young age of the skeletons, is pending.

Abundant rattlesnakes were constrained inside a circular basket at roughly the center of the dedicatory cache (Plate 5, blue). An MRI of the basket revealed approximately eighteen serpents. Species found in the stomach content of complete carnivores included the desert and eastern cottontails. Several bones of a Mexican gray squirrel also pertain to the fill matrix.

Spatial Patterning

The considerable size of the offertory chamber (5 m^2) left some areas, like the central-southern region, with few or no artifacts. Just north of the center was a large concentration of offerings, including Tlaloc vessels, large pyrite disks, obsidian eccentrics, and two complete humans (Sugiyama and López Luján 2007). Most striking was the heap of beheaded human sacrificial victims piled along the northern wall. In contrast to the superimposed human corpses, animal remains were more evenly distributed throughout the chamber (Plate 5).

Ritual practitioners began by incising two circles intercepted by lines drawn in cardinal and inter-cardinal directions onto the ground (Sugiyama and López Luján 2006b). Paired obsidian bifaces and eccentrics overlay each line. A pyrite disc shielded these radiating obsidian artifacts, and a mosaic figurine stood atop the disc. Like the lithic artifacts, the eagles were also deposited in pairs along these axial lines according to spatial syntax.

Like Burial 2, animal clusters were positioned at cardinal and inter-cardinal sectors and the centroid (Plate 16a). Each cluster contained a pair of eagles and variable numbers of canid/felid skulls and complete bodies; usually one canid and one felid skull, with a primary burial of a canid or felid (this last component varied significantly). For example, the cluster in the southwestern corner of the cache included two primary eagles, a complete canid, two complete felids, and one canid cranium. While primary eagles were distributed homogeneously throughout the chamber, most complete canid and felid skeletons were in the western sector; only one complete felid skeleton (E.1991) was in the east.

I also recognized an apparent spatial division according to the animal's sex. The Teotihuacanos seem to have preferentially placed male skeletons in the eastern sector of the chamber while females were deposited in the western half (Plate 16a). This pattern largely holds for eagles, felids, and canids that could be sexed, with a few exceptions that I discuss later. It was particularly stunning that both primary ($n = 5$) and secondary ($n = 6$) eagle internments were generally accurately sexed and placed in their corresponding east/west sectors because eagles are not only difficult to age but also notoriously challenging to sex. Modern biologists ran a multicomponent analysis to determine which measurements are most effective for sexing modern golden eagles—the hallux length and cranial length (Harmata and Montopoli 2013), both measurements that are unfortunately hard to take with fragmentary and disarticulated archaeological samples. Biologists either visually confirmed body position during copulation or ran a DNA test to determine the sex of the raptor to conduct the subsequent bone measurement study. I used statistics of greatest proximal breadth and length ratios (Figure 3.9) compared to sexed eagle measurements from McKusick (2001: Table 9). Teotihuacan ritual specialists who deposited these raptors according to sex did not utilize such analytical methods. They must have distinguished male and female eagles by general body size and watching their actions, particularly during courtship, copulation, and incubation. Sex determination would have required direct observation of live eagles, and for secondary deposits, its sex needed to be remembered for proper placement into the cache.

We must, however, acknowledge that there are several exceptions to this general pattern. One canid cranium, E.2194, was identified as female, even though it was in the northeast corner. While prepared canid/felid skulls generally followed the sex division (E.1941 and E.1959), most of the sexed skeletons were primary burials. It is likely that for prepared canid skeletons such as E.2194 that were extensively processed and secondarily deposited into the chamber, sex was not classified or remembered postmortem by the Teotihuacanos. Another possibility is that I misidentified this relatively young adult, one to two years of age, due to its smaller size and age. More recently, Singleton and colleagues (2023) conducted genetic testing of the eagle population that helped confirm the original sex designations of fifteen individuals, altering the designation of four individuals. With these new sex designations, three primary eagles (Element 1888, 2200, and 2070) deposited in the western sector disrupt the overwhelming pattern of male/female and east/west division.

At first, I was admittedly disappointed and considered removing mention of this pattern in this manuscript. However, as discussed with the evidence of taxidermy, such "adjustments" made in ritual spectacles portray the reality that past rituals are as imperfect as today. I believe that eighteen out of twenty-two sexed corporeal animal forms (primary and secondary burials) distributed according to sex divisions is a significant pattern (82%) that conveys intentionality. More likely, the three eagles and a secondary canid skull represent exceptions mediated through substitutions in the same vein as the prepared eagle bodies (see Chapter 6). It would be quite a feat for the Teotihuacan state to control the necessary symbolic number of sacrificial victims alive of a desired sex (half male, half female), and the burial data show this goal was almost, but not quite achieved through minor substitutions. The question is, who would notice? Perhaps not even the great orchestrator of ritual (the ruler), as he was no biologist and likely not the direct caretaker of the eagles to be able to sex them. If the Teotihuacan public charged animals to divide the place into male and female counterparts, would the biological sex of a few animals, which cannot easily be visually differentiated, lead to a failed ritual?

What is clear is that sexual designations for eagles were achieved through observation in confinement, which explains why prepared eagles (and not mammals) contained a combination of pathological indicators of disease and extensive cutmarks. In addition, the isotopic signatures of primary and secondary eagles were indistinguishable. We may even suggest it is because eagles' particular vitalities (biologically tricky to sex and expedient growth patterns) invited human-animal cohabitation to an extent undocumented among other secondary animal forms. Each eagle likely had established identities (perhaps given names like modern pets) including a sex designation that was important to its social positionality that influenced the selection process.

Seasonality

One primary felid, between six and eight months old, allowed for a seasonality estimate for Burial 6. Felids' long birth cycle extends from April to September, placing the ritual sometime between September and April. Mesoamerica's calendric cycle split the year between the wet and dry seasons; the dry season corresponds roughly to the dates after the summer monsoons are completed, and the sun is in the Southern Hemisphere until April. Thus, the seasonality designation of Burial 6 overlaps most considerably during the dry season.

Building 5: Burial 3

In Burial 3, three sacrificed humans lay extended, oriented north-south with their hands tied behind the back, while a fourth individual (3-D) was seated to the north on a fiber mat (Plate 6). This offering contained the lowest species diversity, with only three identified species: wolves, pumas, and hawks (Table 3.1). This cache exhibited the most significant quantity of canid paraphernalia from any single context. Wolf corporeal forms were a particularly salient component of this offering, totaling likely eighteen wolves. Notably, eagles and rattlesnakes were absent despite their persistent presence in other dedicatory contexts.

As Burial 3 lacked primary burials, there is no seasonality designation, and the deteriorated remains permitted only limited sex designations. Corporeal animal forms were haphazardly scattered around the heads and feet of the sacrificial victims. Wolf skulls tended to have a wider distribution, with many placed near the head of sacrificed humans (eastern sector). In contrast, felid skulls were restricted near the feet of the sacrificial victims (western sector). The only exception was E.597.3, the frontal portion of a puma's mandible, mixed with two wolf crania on the southeastern corner by the head of Individual 3-A. Hawk remains were also restricted to the western sector by the feet of the sacrificial victims.

As explained in Chapter 2, osteological and isotopic results suggest these human victims were war captives, all male (Spence and Pereira 2007; White et al. 2007). This close association among warriors, sacrifice, canids, and state militarism expressed by canid skull usage in Burial 3 parallels the entangled associations between canid maxillary pendants adorning war captives with the FSP (Chapter 2). Canid corporeal forms likely signified the social identities of these humans as emblematic of warriors and of Teotihuacan military prowess. The shift from animals participating in placemaking (Building 4) versus animals contributing to human group identity is noticeable.

Building 5 to 6 Transition: Burial 5

The subsequent offertory complex's animal usage pattern presented a similar shift to that described for Burial 3. Burial 5 contained some unique species, including the deer mouse— found in the serpent's stomach content—and a spider monkey forelimb. The latter was an exceptional find, as this species is nonlocal and transported from southern tropical regions. Recent reports of a spider monkey sacrifice at Plaza of the Columns Complex suggest this exotic and charismatic animal may have been involved in a highly strategic diplomatic

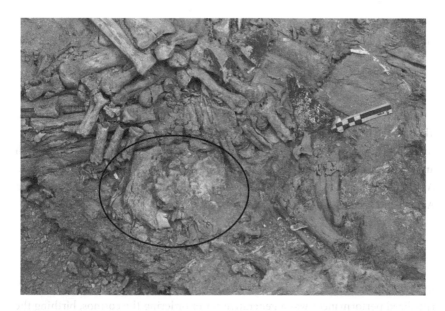

FIGURE 7.1
Puma skull E.1500 in the hands of Individual 5-B. © Moon Pyramid Project.

gift exchange with the Maya (Sugiyama et al. 2022). Most animals were secondary deposits except rattlesnakes (*n* = 9), a wolf, a raven, an eagle, and a puma deposited whole (Plate 7).

The avian and mammalian primary deposits are directly associated with the three sacrificed humans. Next to Individual 5-C lay a wolf, in front of Individual 5-B lay a puma on its side, and in front of Individual 5-A an eagle and a raven were found juxtaposed as a pair. Individuals 5-C and 5-A held a canid and a felid cranium, respectively, in their hands (Figure 7.1). Each had a high concentration of canid and felid skulls/claws scattered nearby. The crow and the eagle laid to rest in front of individual 5-A would have represented the duality of day/night, as the eagle carries strong associations with the sun (Aguilera 1985: 63–64) while the crow reflects darkness or the night sky.

The nine rattlesnakes, again not a coincidental number, represented the most abundant sacrificed subject in this context. Yet the three seated humans had their backs to eight serpents clustered along the eastern section where there was the highest density of offertory objects, most notably a greenstone figurine. Serpent E.1037 was isolated in a broken ceramic bowl placed in front of the two southern sacrificial victims (Individuals 5-A, 5-B). The other rattlesnakes were probably transported in additional organic containers or baskets, like that found in Burial 6. Excavators uncovered isolated elements of different mammalian and avian species in the eastern sector of the dedicatory cache (spider monkey, three hawks, and three doves/pigeons).

Seasonality

I used a juvenile wolf, between six and nine months old, to calculate seasonality. Though relying on a wolf age designation is risky because they can breed year-round during periods of prey abundance, this was the only primary burial with an age designation. If this wolf was born in the spring, during the February to April natural breeding season, Burial 5 would have taken place sometime between August and January, amid the dry season.

Co-producing the *Altepetl*: Building 4

In this section I argue that the participation of animal matter in Burial 2 and 6's ritualized performances was a generative act of ordering the cosmos, birthing the Moon Pyramid into the *altepetl* of Teotihuacan. Both contexts followed similar spatial syntax emphasizing cardinal and inter-cardinal directionality and quantitative patterning of fauna. The cosmologically significant number eighteen figures prominently among corporeal animal forms and diverse offertory objects. In Burial 6, with a few exceptions, the animals followed prescribed sex-based positions; males tended to be placed in the eastern sector while females favored the west.

The dedicatory acts took place in complementary seasons. Burial 2 occurred during the summer to late summer (June–August) during the wet season, while Burial 6 was executed sometime between September and April in the dry season. Burials 2 and 6 represented the two seminal seasons in the agricultural cycle, the wet and dry seasons.

Intentional decisions of when, who, how many, and how to arrange corporeal animal forms inform the underlying significance of the offertory spectacle. In turn, decisions were heavily affected by the biology, behavior, and co-participation of corporeal animal forms. The animals embodied codified numerals and directionalities that transformed them into material expressions of time and space; as an assemblage, their corporeal presence co-constituted a cosmogram. I argue that the two burials functioned as a unit to orient the ritual space in horizontal and vertical dimensions (Figure 7.2). East (or right) was associated with males, while females represented the west (or left) along the horizontal plane. There was also a dual division of the upper and lower sectors of the monument, the upper (Burial 6) emphasizing the dry, celestial sphere, while the monument's base (Burial 2) signified wetness placed directly on the bedrock.

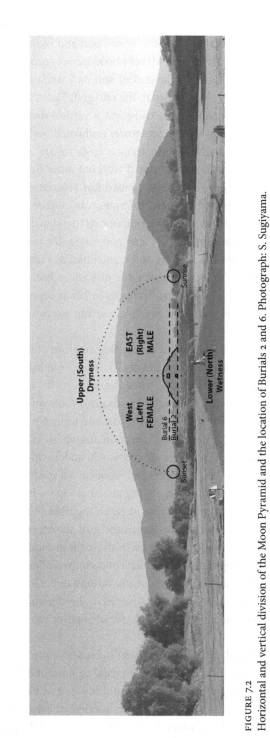

FIGURE 7.2
Horizontal and vertical division of the Moon Pyramid and the location of Burials 2 and 6. Photograph: S. Sugiyama.

Complementary oppositions are a central component of Mesoamerican cosmovision effectively ingrained into the symbolism and layout of monumental works. For example, the Aztec Templo Mayor also materially expressed duality: the southern temple was dedicated to the god of sun and warfare, Huitzilopochtli, while the northern temple corresponded to the rain god, Tlaloc (López Austin and López Luján 2009). At the same time, there was a vertical division between the base platform, where tellurian serpent sculptures undulated, and the upper sectors inhabited by celestial beings (Matos Moctezuma 1986: 70–71). At Templo Mayor, the southern-superior zones were associated with hot astral bodies and dryness, while the northern-superior aspects represented hot vegetation and humidness. Complementary values divided southern-inferior areas associated with cold vegetation and dryness from the northern-inferior aspects that signaled cold vegetation and humidity (López Austin and López Luján 2009: 481). The two eagles sacrificed in Offering 125 substantiated these rules and regulations, as a male eagle with gold bangles was placed to the south, expressing the masculine, hot, celestial world. In opposition, the female eagle adorned with copper bells was deposited to the north, alluding to the dark underworld that is a cold, earthly, wet, and feminine sphere (López Luján et al. 2022).

Various ethnographies decode the directional symbolism of indigenous groups who track the sun's movement through the sky. The east (or right) is associated with the rise of the male sun every morning, while the west (or left) manifests the transition to the female moon during sunset (Gossen 1979). Cora myths recount a dual origin between men who originated from the east and women who came from the west (Lumholtz 1945: 500). There is a connection among males, celestial spheres, and heat, while females are associated with the earth, underworld, and cold.

Gossen (1979) describes these directional associations in the daily life of the Chamula. Their houses, for example, are organized around a hearth, and spatial regulations divide males and boys to sit and eat to the right of the hearth (facing the interior from the front door) while women and girls place themselves to the left. Males typically sit in tiny chairs that raise them above the ground and wear sandals to separate them from the ground to complement their masculine heat. Conversely, women sit on the ground and walk barefoot, providing a direct link to the feminine and cold earth. This dichotomy is also manifested in the church, as all major male saints march right (counterclockwise) while female figures move left (clockwise) around the atrium.

The north is associated with the wet season because the sun's northern trajectory along the eastern horizon (between the vernal equinox and the summer solstice) marks the beginning of the wet season and the start of the annual growing cycle (Gossen 1979). In contrast, the sun moves southward between the autumnal equinox and the winter solstice when the days are shorter and the growing season ends. Thus, the south is often associated with the dry season, the underworld, and nighttime.

López Austin's (1993: 170–171) description of Nahua beliefs demonstrates similar celestial division to north/south and east/west. For Nahua communities, the south, or above, symbolizes life because the sun runs chiefly to the south while the north, or below, is associated with death and the underworld. At the same time, the east is considered masculine and the west feminine because warriors slain during combat reside in the eastern sky while women who died in childbirth reside in the western sky.

Maya ceramics and stelae convey similar conceptions of the left/right division. Central figures, usually superior ritual and political leaders and men, were more likely to face the right and use their right hand, exemplifying the right's affiliation with masculinity, power, and the sacred (Palka 2002). In contrast, the left consistently alluded to femininity, subordination, and the profane. In this manner, directional concepts of left/right (west/east) and upper/lower (south/north) governed where people stood, which way they faced, how individuals moved within a space, and the daily actions of persons.

In the case of Burials 2 and 6, corporeal animal forms vividly expressed and embodied these rules and regulations that oriented the ritual scene. The animals were positioned along cardinal points, unlike the human sacrificial victims that were either scarce (Burial 2) or heaped at the northwestern corner (Burial 6). In the case of Burial 6, they also expressed a gendered directionality. Males were generally placed to the east (right), emphasizing a direct connection to masculine, solar, celestial, and warfare. Females were positioned to the west in reference to female, lunar, underworld, and earth/fertility.

At the same time, the two dedication rituals were conducted during very different seasons, probably intentionally, to represent the agricultural cycle. At the base, the dedicatory ritual for Burial 2 was planned during the wet season because lower (or north) represents the earth, cold, and humidity. The upper chamber, Burial 6, was offered during the dry season as the upper (or southern) sphere was associated with the heavens, heat, and dryness. The dedicatory theatrical event, both its timing and placement of the animals, were key in performing and experiencing the cosmos. It solidified the monument in vertical and horizontal space as a meaning-laden *place* on the ceremonial landscape.

So what was the meaning of this highly codified place? Because the sacrificial victims were the main protagonists that oriented the ritual space, they hold the key to unlocking this question. In their comprehensive description, López Austin and López Lujan (2009) define several functions of the *altepetl*: as an axis mundi; as a point of access to the heavenly bodies; mountain of wealth; refuge for flora and fauna; home of the patron god; origin place for humans; source of power, authority, and order; and as a dwelling of the dead. The mountains controlled vital life sources (water, lightning, thunder, clouds), where ancestral spirits, patron deities, and animals resided (see summary in Chapter 2). In this context, it is significant that the mountain is where animals, particularly the master guardian, dwelled.

The zooarchaeological evidence from the Moon Pyramid demonstrated that the animals were probably in vivo deposits. All the primary animal remains from Burial 6 had their extremities joined, presumably bound to restrict movement. Burial 2, with its caged pumas and a wolf, provides conclusive evidence that these animals entered the ritual scene alive. This is significant because for the audience that participated in the dedicatory act, many of the animals considered master guardian animals actively reside within the *altepetl*. This is why I chose to apply a definition that does not stress the kill as the central component of sacrifice but their consecration process for a specific purpose (Chapter 1).

I cannot help but juxtapose these animals buried alive within the Moon Pyramid with the aforementioned ethnohistoric source of the Fiesta del Volcán (Chapter 2), wherein a giant papier-mâché volcano replica housed live deer, peccaries, tapirs, coatis, and other creatures in its artificial mountain (Hill 1992: 1–6). Like the artificial volcano, the Moon Pyramid was an *altepetl* that housed powerful predators intimately tied to their community.

The master guardian animals that reside at the core of the monument helped directionally (cardinality and east-west sex division) and temporally (calendric numerals and seasonality) orient the ceremonial landscape. The ritualization process "set apart" or consecrated corporeal animal forms into ritualized bodies with personhood as master guardian animals in the same vein as a warrior captive became Tezcatlipoca and reoriented the connection between center and periphery in the Aztec imperial landscape (Carrasco 1991; see discussion in Chapter 6). These corporeal animal forms, habituated through captivity within the city confines, developed interpersonal relationships with Teotihuacan governing officials, visitors, and residents to an unprecedented degree, becoming part of the public just as the Teotihuacan state was establishing an innovative form of sovereignty. The procession of these corporeal animal forms into the nucleus of the Moon Pyramid co-produced an *altepetl* into being.

Maintenance and Change, Durability of the *Altepetl*: Burials 3 and 5

Once the Moon Pyramid was animated as the *altepetl* on the landscape, the monument persisted as an active place continuously remodeled, maintained, and visited. I interpret the archaeological traces of building modifications and associated ritualized actions as the material manifestations of a nascent, and always on the verge of becoming, personhood of the Moon Pyramid. They physically reflect the fluid, transformative, and emergent capacity of sovereignty formations at Teotihuacan, wherein animal matter has taken a decidedly distinct form of participation. Burial 3 was embedded along the base during the fifth construction phase, while Burial 5 was placed between Building 5's termination and Building 6's construction (Chapter 2). Although offerings continued to include corporeal animal forms, there were evident changes in human–animal interactions from the patterns in Building 4 mentioned earlier. I argue that these changes reflect a shift in the social positionality of animal matter, which became related to groups and individuals within Teotihuacan society.

Spatial regulations of corporeal animal forms in Buildings 5 and 6 seem to be dictated by the layout of the human sacrificial victims, not by cardinality and temporality, as was observed in Building 4. In these two later deposits, species distribution adhered closely to human actors that coordinated spatial syntax; in Burial 3, the animals index the social identity of a group of humans (likely warriors), while in Burial 5, each animal type seems to be intimately entangled with specific human forms seated cross-legged in authoritative positions. There is also a relative scarcity of complete sacrificial animals in later deposits. Burial 3 lacked primary burials, while Burial 5 only included four large predators and nine serpents as primary deposits. So what do these changes in animal usage convey about their social positionality as potential mediators of Teotihuacan sovereignty?

At the base of Building 5, Burial 3 lavishly instated the power of state militarism through the sacrifice of four warriors identified by war accouterments (projectile points) and the scattering of empowered corporeal animal forms, especially canid skulls, around their heads and bodies. Though much more modest, this deposit has a faint resemblance to the FSP warriors, some of whom wore canid maxillary pendants emblazoned on their chests. Empowered animals, like canids, were military delegates elaborately depicted throughout the city, and the Teotihuacan state ostentatiously paraded canid corporeal animal forms in state ritualized performances to solidify this novel relationship.

Burial 5 marked the termination of Building 5 and the consecration of Building 6. By the fourth century CE, during Burial 5's dedication (Teotihuacan Expansion phase, Chapter 2), the Teotihuacan state had not only established itself as a powerful entity but also had a far-reaching military presence within the Basin of Mexico and abroad (Hirth et al. 2020). To apply relational ontologies seriously, we must rely on ritual and spatial syntax to understand relationalities between potential persons (Chapter 1). In the case of Burial 5, I posit that the most prominent ritualized body that centers the entire cache is not an animal nor a human but a greenstone anthropomorphic figurine (Plate 7). Three sacrificed humans sit as though guarding the greenstone figure. What if we consider the greenstone figurine—the spatial

FIGURE 7.3
Greenstone figurine seated cross-legged adorned with greenstone accouterments from Burial 5. © Moon Pyramid Project.

centroid of the cache—not as an object but as a powerful being with personhood surrounded by riches and protected or served by human and animal persons?

Spatial syntax reveals at least three distinctions among the human forms. Like the sacrificed victims, the greenstone figurine sat cross-legged, splendidly adorned with two sets of nine greenstone beads and earspools, paralleling two sacrificed individuals (Figure 7.3; Sugiyama 2017d). Of particular note is the rectangular pendant that may be drawing on, but not identical to, the pendants emblazoned as Maya royal insignia that decorated Individuals 5-A and 5-B. The greenstone figurine was likely male due to body position (seated), form (no anatomical indicators), and rich ritual attire that differed from female figurines in other burial contexts (personal communication by S. Sugiyama 2020). The highest quantity and quality of offerings are assembled near the figurine. In comparison, the offerings directly related to the human sacrifices was primarily composed of corporeal animal forms, with their backs to the greenstone figurine and its associated assemblage. Each human form was proximal to a concentration of a specific animal type scattered to the north (canid, Individual 5-C), south (felid, Individual 5-B), west (crow/eagle, Individual 5-A), and east (rattlesnake/felid, greenstone figurine) (Plate 7). These animals seem to provide yet another layer of protection for the greenstone figurine.

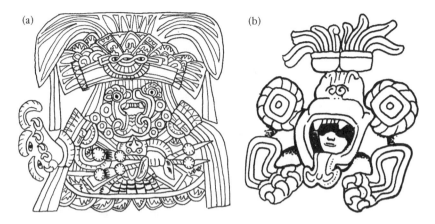

FIGURE 7.4
Feline war serpent iconography, feline head with serpentine bifurcated tongue: (a) mural from Tepantitla Teotihuacan and (b) ceramic censer lid of Teotihuacan warrior wearing a war serpent helmet from Xico. Drawing courtesy of K. Taube (a) Miller 1973: Fig. 193, (b) from Taube 2000: Fig. 10.11b.

Although repeatedly found in the Moon Pyramid caches, rattlesnakes are archaeologically rare. Eight rattlesnakes were scattered by the greenstone figurine and the general eastern section (Plate 7 in yellow). Fiber-like substances, likely a mat (a supreme status symbol), were also found in this region and under Individuals 5-A and 5-B. Puma cranial elements were also found scattered alongside the serpents throughout this eastern section. Here, I note that felids with bifurcated tongues of a rattlesnake are prevalent in the mural and ceramic iconography at Teotihuacan (Figure 7.4). Taube (2012) has attributed this multispecies representation to the feline war serpent. Like the commingling of deer mandibles and crocodilian dentition birthed the chimeric Maya mythological figure of the Starry-Deer crocodile into tangible corporeal animal form at Copan (Sugiyama et al. 2019; Chapter 1), it is possible the commingling of rattlesnake with puma crania similarly brought the feline war serpent into being at the Moon Pyramid.

This scatter of rattlesnakes reminds me of an image from the Florentine codex (Sahagún 1963: 81) that describes *coapetlatl* or *petlacoatl* as a serpentine mat that signals either a bad omen or a destined ruler (Figure 7.5). The patterned distribution of thirteen serpents in the Aztec period Offering R has been interpreted as a serpentine mat (Valentin Maldonado 1999: 112–113). While the data do not allow us to reconstruct the form of these arranged rattlesnakes, what is essential is that serpents, especially as mats, were emblems of rulership.

At the FSP, the Feathered Serpent is the delegate that brought the insignia of rulership to Teotihuacan (Sugiyama 2005). With the added charge of puma skulls (and

FIGURE 7.5
Coapetlatl or *Petlacoatl*, a serpentine mat. From Sahagún (1577: fol.84r). Photograph: World Digital Library.

the possible link to the feline war serpent), the greenstone figurine was likely the highest-ranking individual within the dedicatory cache that centered and directed the distribution of other offerings, including the placement of the three human sacrifices and corresponding corporeal animal forms.

The animal remains alone cannot resolve the social identity of the sacrificed individuals from Burial 5. What can be inferred is that the sacrificed humans were likely non-Teotihuacan in origin (both because of isotope results and associated Maya-style artifacts), and the spatial arrangement suggests a potent animal (alongside other matter) mediated the social positionality of the humans. They differed from cases of human sacrifice at Teotihuacan in body position (seated with hands in front, not behind their backs) and adornment (imported greenstone artifacts) closely associated with Maya rulership (Sugiyama and López Luján 2006b). Two individuals (5-A, 5-B) seated side by side seem to be of similar rank based on identical greenstone adornments. They are associated with the eagle/crow and felid, respectively, which were also considered emblems of power and prestige. A third individual (5-C) sitting slightly to the north holds a third positionality that is not necessarily of lesser rank to the former. Grasping a canid skull in his hands, this third individual was likely associated with the canid military order referenced in Burial 3. The elaborate greenstone assemblage (though lacking royal insignia) places him as a high military official distinct from the four individuals in Burial 3.

It is worth mentioning again the close association between specific, influential individuals and animal mediators referenced in the thin orange bowl excavated by Sigvald Linné (1942: 170–174, Figure 128) at Las Colinas, Calpulalpan, Tlaxcala (Chapter 2, Figure 2.2). Like Burial 5, there is no consensus on the identity of the personages associated with a distinct companion—a tassel headdress, a Feathered Serpent, a bird, and a canid—and whether they are of heterarchical distinction or if a central authority leads them.

I suspect the individuals depicted in the vessel and sacrificed human forms in Burial 5 include a leading agent, likely of a royal station. His eminent positionality is signaled by the tassel headdress (Calpulalpan vessel) and greenstone figurine (Burial 5), respectively, and is accompanied by high elites with perhaps other forms of authority (religious, administrative, and/or military) in service of the leading figure. At least one held a military rank, indexed by the canids. Burials 5-A and 5-B were distinguished by their nonlocal accouterments, though positioned alongside familiar local fauna traditionally tied to Teotihuacan sovereignty.

The subtle inclusion of a spider monkey arm in this context is intriguing, given the precedent of spider monkey diplomacy (dating to fifty to one hundred years prior to Burial 5), where a captive spider monkey was likely given to the central administrative complex of Plaza of the Columns (Sugiyama et al. 2022). It seems part of Teotihuacan's success was derived from authority recognized by regional and pan-regional relationships expressed through its ability to negotiate, trade, and conquer these areas (Sugiyama and Sugiyama 2020). Command over foreign diplomats directly expressed in Burial 5 by the sacrifice of two individuals explicitly marked by Maya royal insignia would have substantiated Teotihuacan's domain over these relationships.

In Burials 3 and 5, corporeal animal forms not only embodied general notions of power and prestige but also indexed specific rankings of royal and other forms of authority of the Teotihuacan state. In a society as complex as Teotihuacan, the public (human and nonhuman) constantly negotiated various sources of authority through inter-elite, royal-elite, and community engagement. Corporeal animal forms were likely at the forefront of embodying these power dynamics at play in state ritual spectacles where they were manipulated, owned, displayed, and continued to be central persons in Teotihuacan's sociopolitical landscape.

Finally, as was the case with Burials 2 and 6, the location of the offering dictated in what season the ceremony should take place. Unfortunately for Burial 3, the absence of primary deposits prohibited seasonal reconstruction, but Burial 5 most likely occurred between August and January during the dry season. The seasonality of Burial 5's placement on the summit of Building 5 during the construction of Building 6 confirms the association of the monument's pinnacle with notions of dryness, heat, and the celestial. Following the spatial syntax established in Building 4, Burial 5 emphasized this division between the wet and dry, lower and upper. Human and nonhuman participants in the ritual production of *place* maintained some aspects, such as spatioempral regulations (timing and cardinality), while modifying others, such as the specific form of human–animal dynamics.

Animal Politics in Sovereignty Formations

Following Bauer and Kosiba (2016), I have defined politics as processes where social differences are established through the collective public, oriented toward a "problem" (Chapter 3). In this case, the public entailed the active participation of animals, humans, and other nonhuman persons in the ritualized co-production of the Moon Pyramid at Teotihuacan. Now I ask, how did animal matter engage in the politics of sovereignty formations at Teotihuacan?

In 2015, I experienced animal politics at the forefront of sovereignty formations as I watched the military march of the Mexican Independence on September 16, where uniformed soldiers marched with large raptors–including golden eagles–tethered to their arms along Reforma Avenue in downtown Mexico City (Plate 16b). These golden eagles—likely highly tamed and trained, judging by their experienced serenity despite the blasting trumpets, drums, and crowds—mediated Mexican national identity as they stood majestically on the militants' arms, reinforcing their appearance emblazoned on the national flag. Its processional participation as an intimate and influential member of the public indicated to me how human–animal participation in state-choreographed rituals was part of the co-production and maintenance of the Mexican nation-state. That is, animal matter and animal politics go hand in hand with sovereignty formations.

In the case of ancient indigenous ontologies, I have discussed animals as socially differentiated within hierarchical structures and how some, like the apex predators analyzed in this volume, are heavily engaged in animal politics as persons (Chapter 3). Many indigenous communities recognize a dominant species. For example, a pelican presides over lake birds while the jaguar looms over wild animals as a direct consultant of ancestor gods (Holland 1964: 304; López Austin 1993: 158). At the same time, an individual within a species is the chief or father; the

Takawiru is the chief of buzzards among the Yaquis of Arizona (Giddings 1959: 68), or the chief of deer inhabits the interior of the mountains (Lumholtz 1945: 302). López Austin (1993: 158) further mentions the Códice Florentino documents that dominant species, like the jaguar, held political titles such as *tecpilli, tlazopilli, pilli, tlatoani,* and *achcuauhtli.* Animal classificatory systems result from the relational disposition of human and nonhuman persons in the landscape, negotiated through direct interpersonal, often corporeal, interaction.

State personnel embed themselves into this classification system by displaying direct corporeal contact with prominent species that reside in the highest echelon. Postclassical rulers have regularly drawn upon the *altepetl* for their political backing, as access to control vital life sources stored deep within the sacred mountain was crucial for governing the community under its protection (Hirth 2003; López Austin and López Luján 2009). The sacred mountain materialized in the pyramids (itself stratified to reach the heavens) was organized by the hierarchically arranged animals that resided within, wherein interpersonal interactions displayed during these rituals authenticated the negotiated ecological order. By the Aztec period, the *altepetl* not only represented hierarchies but also served as a social integrating unit that entangled the political structure of divine kingship with the supporting human communities and territories (Hirth 2003; López Austin and López Luján 2009; see also Chapter 2). This study argues that the sociality of the *altepetl* as the very means of social integration and sovereignty was materialized effectively into the ceremonial landscape during Teotihuacan's Ceremonial Monuments period. But, as McAnany rightfully argues, "authority cannot exist in a vacuum; rather it must be materialized in inherited and labor-intensive items and performed through ritual practice" (2008: 220).

This is why reconstructing human–animal interactions as manifested in ritualized performances is an effective avenue for recording the formation and maintenance of an enigmatic form of sovereignty at Teotihuacan. State-sponsored spectacles solidified newly rising dominance over the entire social landscape with the public. Animal matter played a central role in hunting rituals, royal rites, feasts, seasonal ceremonies, and dedicatory rituals around the globe (Brown and Emery 2008; Fiskesjö 2001; Goepfert 2012; Sugiyama et al. 2019; Yuan and Flad 2005). Teotihuacan was no exception, as animal matter visually displayed human dominance over some of the most potent agents on the landscape at a scale unprecedented in Mesoamerica, comparable only to later Aztec cases of animal sacrifice (López Luján et al. 2014; López Luján and Matos Moctezuma 2022; Polaco 1991). The ritual spectacle, understood within the process of placemaking, was how a web of interpersonal relationships with live animals and other corporeal animal forms materialized explicit negotiations of power and authority. It was how the public experienced sovereignty formations at Teotihuacan.

Interpreting these ritualized acts as a performance allows us to focus on the ritual's material correlates, including the socialities of the participants, their corporlalities, and their setting; attributes that are retrievable in the archaeological record (Inomata and Coben 2006a). As such, a performative approach to ritual enables interpreting the dialogue of meaning and intra-action—in this case, the construction of carnivores as empowered persons directly contributing to sovereignty formations. The relational ontological approach applied to the study of corporeal animal forms enlivens the physicality of interactions among humans, animals, *altepetl*, and other persons (like the greenstone figurine from Burial 5) to the forefront of investigation.

I have traced the transformation of powerful animals into master guardians of Teotihuacan through detailed osteobiographical reconstructions of the ritualization process, including how potentate animals were physically captured, managed, tamed, and deposited. These physical encounters seize the moment and context wherein humans and animals dramatically altered their social positionality. This study provided a methodology to reconstruct this relationship (zooarchaeology and isotopes combined with iconography and animal biology/behavior), and applied a relational ontological framework to disentangle the social actors and processes at play during sovereignty formations. What I found was dynamic narratives of the struggles, mishaps, and hidden transcripts of managing some of the most dangerous carnivores in the landscape. Animal vitalities, such as the eagle's unique biology, captivated Teotihuacan state officials and caused them to adjust their ritual performance.

Physical capture and management of wild animals would have revolutionized the social landscape, as some individuals who controlled these top predators–most likely equivalent to the master of animals–elevated themselves above these creatures. Haraway's assertion was correct: animals are not just "good to eat" and "good to think" (Lévi-Strauss 1966; see also Tambiah 1969), but especially "here to live with" (Haraway 2003: 5). In the case of Teotihuacan, we must understand human manipulation over some of the animals—traditionally regarded as powerful entities that controlled the natural landscape and the mediums through which communication to deities, spirits and ancestors occurred—would have had explicit implications to gaining a source of authority previously undocumented in the area.

It is no coincidence that the earliest evidence of animal management and the spectacular participation of these beasts in state-level ritual performances coincide with one of the most ambitious placemaking enterprises in Mesoamerica. It is contemporaneous with the Ceremonial Monuments period when the Teotihuacan state coordinated the erection of the three major pyramids. At the Moon Pyramid, corporeal animal forms; the governing Teotihuacan elite who coordinated the ritual; the city's population that built and participated in the grand ritual display; and the sacrificed humans all participated in the ritualized production of a sacred place, the *altepetl* of Teotihuacan born during Building 4's construction. The dedicatory theatrical event, in both its timing and how the animals were placed within the burial environment, was key in performing and experiencing the cosmos as materialized in the monument. Animal matter engaged in meaningful (often hierarchical) social relations as part of the public and oriented ritualized landscapes, capable of birthing an *altepetl* from an earthen mound by their residence within it.

The framework of sovereignty formations recognizes that the sociopolitical landscape was a nascent, polyvalent, and negotiated process reflected through adjustments to their material engagements. Subsequent construction phases at the Moon Pyramid continued to engage with animal matter during dedicatory rituals in Burials 3 and 5. Evidence for captivity, while present, was much scarcer in later deposits because the number of sacrificed animals was very minimal, and disarticulated heads were more likely to have been acquired from the wild. Perhaps, once it was established that powerful animals reside in the monument, new mediators of sovereignty were introduced onto the stage—this time human forms were linked to place. During the Urban Renewal period, Burial 3 materialized the entanglement of a group of sacrificial victims with canid corporeal forms and implements of war. A coherent group identity was indexed here through corporeal animal forms directly related to state militarism.

Burial 5 marks a distinct transitional phase to the Teotihuacan Expansion period, observed through reforms on major monumental structures (concealment of the FSP) and public-administrative structures at the city's core (see Chapter 2). The corporeal animal forms, once again, embodied such changes in the governance structure wherein their positionality seems to have shifted vis-à-vis specific, influential human and nonhuman persons. The life histories and burial attire of the three sacrificed humans suggest that their identity was derived from their foreign and elite status (two were likely of foreign and royal station). The centralizing agent, a greenstone figurine, seems to have prominent relational positionality to human and animal corporeal forms. The ultimate regal animal, the rattlesnake (as manifested by the Feathered Serpent), is entangled with this greenstone figurine's ultimate authority through sacrifice. The matter of corporeal animal forms directly substantiated the process of imperial formations (sensu Stoler 2008) as Teotihuacan's footprint in Mesoamerica was about to reach its maximum extent. As a portable export good, I suspect the Calpulalpan bowl amplified this impact as mnemonic referents to broadcast to a broader public the interpersonal eco-contracts embodied by human and nonhuman persons in the bowl's ritual scene. From this perspective, apex predators expressed in Teotihuacan art that proliferates the city allowed the public to reengage with and constantly remind them of the socialites of animal matter in daily praxis. Corporeal animal forms and their representations encompassed the tactile animal matter that allowed the public to interact with Teotihuacan sovereignty.

In this manner, the Moon Pyramid as the *altepetl* was maintained and reexperienced through connected histories, memories, and identities reimagined and reformulated throughout the city's occupation. Teotihuacan's imperial formations materialized an entangled landscape activated by interpersonal relationships among humans, animal matter (especially corporeal animal forms), and nonhuman persons. Animal matter was an active participant in the processes of placemaking and sovereignty during elaborate ritualized performances at Teotihuacan.

CHAPTER 8

EPILOGUE: A THICK DESCRIPTION OF BURIAL 6

. . . cosmovisions are not perfect. They have contradictions, lapses, exceptions, absurdities, duplicates, and patches. Fortunately, they are not the same for all members of society. They are constructions with which human beings try to adjust themselves dialectically to the present. (López Austin 1993: 165)

THIS CHAPTER IS AN experimental one. It is a personal attempt to bring the experiential narrative of the participant-observer to the forefront of our understanding of the past. It is a fight against the "othering" of the past, against an unfortunate tendency for the cipher of research convention to reduce the living voices of its subjects—already distorted by temporal separation—to little more than tabulations of a fragmentary archaeological record (see also Boutin 2011). This is not a criticism of the necessarily quantitative manner by which rigorous support for findings is established (and which this author endorses without reservation), but a recognition that it dissolves the individual and intuitively relatable experience of the past into siloed aggregations by regularity and pattern. Individual experience is thus challenging to reconstitute from such data, as doing so entails a certain amount of speculative scaffolding. Researchers have, therefore, been reluctant to undertake interpretative yet rigorously supported narratives of the corporeal and highly codified actions of the past.

Though we may never be able to witness the behaviors of past peoples directly, I believe it is possible to create for Teotihuacan a "thick description" of the sort Geertz (1973) composed from field notes of an epic exchange between his informant Cohen and the Berbers, Jews, and French in Morocco. Yes, I argue that the contextually contingent distinction between a wink and an eye twitch can and should be read through the archaeological record. Even such minimal expressions as these can encode significant cultural value, and if this value is accorded sufficient substance through sustained repetition, it can be materialized and thus distinguishable in the archaeological record.

A ritual performance explicitly materializes social values with the objective of substantiating them through controlled repetition, distribution, and representation. Using detailed experiential narratives of the visual, auditory, and tactile engagement of ritualized bodies helps identify decision nodes that shape ritual syntax by which archaeologists can better understand the past through the interrelated meanings of its rules, motivations, and restrictions (see Chapter 6). In particular, the state spectacle offers a singularly rich cultural seam from which to mine an archaeologically informed thick description. The well-preserved primary context of the offerings permitted me to unpack, with tight spatiotemporal control, detailed animal biographies recorded in the discrete processes by which corporeal animal forms transformed into ritualized bodies (sensu Bell 1992) in Chapter 6.

In this chapter, I bring full circle a performative approach of ritual by integrating all the datasets—zooarchaeological, isotopic, iconographic, biological, ethnographic, historical, and theoretical discourse of corporeal animal forms—into a narrative centered on the perspective of a Teotihuacano experiencing the dedicatory act as a participant-observer. Of course, whereas the ethnographer has access to the testimony of living memory, the archaeologist is concerned with events that sleep beneath centuries of stratigraphy. Even the richest and most rigorously validated archaeological datasets anchor the past but sparsely, sketching it in fragmented constellations of cultural material and environmental traces of human activity. The vast expanse of meaning that interconnects these islands of material data must be first analyzed and then mapped for us to relate to the lived experiences of the people who created them (Hodder 2012).

We can explore these spaces using methodologies customarily found in the ethnographer's toolkit, such as the thick description. With proper methodological provisions for differing primary resources, the thick description can be adapted into a powerful tool by which archaeologists may encompass an angular skeleton of disjointed data in an organic connectome of sensual, tangible, and emotional responses to the physical apprehension of a ritualized performance.

As continuous refinement of reconstruction techniques at the macroscopic, microscopic, and chemical levels has improved the resolution and dimensional depth of each archaeological find, so, too, should we strive to better observe past ritualized acts, interpret their meanings, and detail how they impacted the social memory of the culture in which they formed. I am hopeful that this thick description of Burial 6 will help inspire and encourage more researchers to consider using this multilayered approach to navigate their readers through the experience of past ritual performances.

Creating this narrative was fulfilling. It forced me to move beyond the charts and tables of data generated by my rigorous methodologies to color the past with realistic scenarios, actors, and raw emotions. It forced me to confront the effervescence (Durkheim 2001), the strong emotive responses within a community, necessary to solidify messages into the social memories of participants, like Stone-Rabbit and his daughter Four-Petal-Flower, whom you will meet later. It demonstrates how the public embodies and participates in sovereignty formations through state-choreographed interpersonal encounters in the ritual theater. I found fuller truth in López Austin's astute observation, for it is precisely the very imperfections in these reconstructions that serve to humanize the past. Many a wink and grimaced "adjustment" were detected, some which otherwise passed unnoticed, which thickened the reality of ritual spectacle at Teotihuacan.

Burial 6: A Thick Description

Stone-Rabbit[1] propped a leg on a small cairn he had piled near the corner of the Moon Pyramid plaza and rubbed a calloused palm over his stiffening calves. He'd been standing in this spot since daybreak and now the sun was almost directly overhead, crowning a cloudless blue vault of mid-third-century CE sky. This vantage point, just opposite the plaza from the base of the half-completed monument, he knew to be ideal for taking in the entire scene about to unfold, but his burly stonemason's frame was unaccustomed to standing idle for so long. Still, the fatigue only catalyzed the anticipation building within him and indeed all around him. Though all was cool and still when he entered the plaza just after sunrise, it had become a thrumming churn of voices and colors, of swirling scents and spirits. It seemed as though the entire city had swarmed into every last niche of public space in the neatly imbricated grid of streets and structures that radiate from this sacred place, the ceremonial core of Teotihuacan. Stone-Rabbit was pleased with his chosen post, for he did not want to miss what everyone had come to see: the grand *tlatoani* (lord) of Teotihuacan presiding over a mass sacrificial ceremony in the dedication of the Moon Pyramid.[2]

---

[1] Each character informs this thick description based on individual perspectives and interpretations built from personal experiences. I chose an immigrant stonemason as my primary informant to illustrate how state ritual performances were the mechanism that integrated a multiethnic population to abide by a vivid and consistent form of cultural expression (see Chapter 2). I demonstrate how the participation of Stone-Rabbit and his daughter in the ritual performance made them embody a renowned sense of place as residents who live protected by the *altepetl*. His name, Stone-Rabbit, was taken from a sculpture discovered at the site of Oztoyahualco, a typical middle-class apartment complex in the city (Valadez Azúa 1993) like the one Stone-Rabbit and his family may have settled into.

[2] There is still no resolution if Teotihuacan was ruled autocratically or through some form of co-governance (Manzanilla 2001; Sugiyama 2005). Though I agree that it remains an open question, this narration is based on the scenario of autocratic rulership due to the hierarchical nature of Burial 5's human/figurine sacrifices and the interpretation by Millon

This spectacle would have personal significance for Stone-Rabbit, who knew the pyramid literally from the inside out. Not long ago, he first joined the massive construction crew which would toil unceasingly to encase a modest earthen mound within the base of the substantially larger pyramid rising at the plaza's north end. He reflected on his family's new life here; the day he surprised them with the announcement that he intended to bring them to this city to escape increasingly unfavorable living conditions in their home village. He had heard talk of surging demand for robust and reliable laborers at Teotihuacan from cousins who often traveled to that famed city to trade in stoneware and whose sudden prosperity lent credibility to their tales.[3] They persuaded Stone-Rabbit to accompany them on their next excursion northward from their homelands in the southern region of the Basin of Mexico. "It is not a long journey, a couple days to get there," they said, "if you don't like it, you can come right back with us; all we ask is you help us carry our supplies." What they did not say, he noted with some irritation, was that their next departure would be at the height of the rainy season, and progress would be a slog through powerful downpours and floods of snowmelt coming off the smoking peaks at the eastern edge of the valley. But all was forgiven the moment he entered the outskirts of the city, where he encountered a shuffling caravan of porters, each bearing a tidy stack of dressed stone. All robust workers like himself—and so many! He reckoned that there were more people in this one line of laborers than in his entire home village.

He followed the procession up to a broad hummock opening on a cavernous grotto, from the depths of which rang the rhythmic *chink-chink* of stone mallets on bedrock.[4] A flurry of bronzed arms bustled within, quarrying for building material. Here and there, a glimpse of brilliant color would flash through the haze beyond the far edge of the site, where a handful of rather conspicuously attired figures were engaged in discussion. There seemed to be no end of work to be done, and the astonishing scale of the place made Stone-Rabbit's chest pound hot and his shoulders go limp, though he felt neither tired nor afraid. Instead, this surge of sensation pushed him over a hump of conflict that nagged him the whole journey here; about how foolish it was to consider uprooting one's family from the village of

---

(1988a) of the Calpulalpan bowl (Chapters 2 and 7; see, however, Manzanilla 2001). Note that I use Nahuatl terms throughout the narrative. We still do not know the lingua franca at Teotihuacan, and Nahuatl is one likely hypothesis proposed by Whittaker (2021).

[3] Many immigrants (from the greater Basin of Mexico and beyond) continued to hold ties with their kin, contributing a steady stream of foreign goods and in-migration (Manzanilla 2017).

[4] For details about the sourcing of building materials and construction logistics see Barba et al. (1990) and Murakami (2010).

their ancestors on the strength of a few fulsome rumors about a legendary city. The prospect before him vanquished these doubts as glad certainty swelled within his chest at the thought of how handsomely he, a simple countryside laborer, would be able to provide for his family all the rest of his days. A few hours of asking around confirmed that work crews were being marshaled for an enormous project to commence very soon with great ceremony. He hastened back to his village to prepare his household for the news that they would soon join him here.

Only a few moons had passed since Stone-Rabbit and his crew received an order to begin grading flat the irregular surface of a massive quadrangular fundament they had compiled from countless basketfuls of bedrock and soil. This platform, which now rose roughly 18 Teotihuacan Measurement Units[5] (TMU; about 15 m) above the ever-present haze stirred by the hubbub of a busy city, would serve as the base of a central rectangular chamber about the size of a large room.[6] Rumors flared as the crew laid each course of stone along the chamber's walls. They were confident it would house sacrifices and precious gifts to be offered in the upcoming mass dedicatory event.

Stone-Rabbit was fortunate to arrive at Teotihuacan just a couple of weeks before the previous spectacle, where construction commenced with auspicious offerings deposited at bedrock level (Burial 2).[7] Though he wasn't able to get as close to the action as he would have liked, he never forgot the delighted faces of his fellow crewmates when the parade of marvels drew close enough to make out a magnificent array of nine eagles and the glowering visages of three powerful beasts pacing in shadowy cages. Teotihuacan was like nothing else he'd ever seen, and he was proud to know his hands contributed to its grandeur.[8]

---

[5] S. Sugiyama (2010) has argued that the TMU, measuring roughly 83 cm, was applied to engineer this highly codified cityscape based on cosmologically significant numbers related to astronomical events (e.g., 18 months, 260-day lunar calendar). I have converted metric units to TMUs when discussing lengths to convey an emic perspective.

[6] 6 × 5.5 TMU, or 4 × 4.5 m.

[7] The temporal separation between Burial 2 and Burial 6's dedication rituals has yet to be determined. Seasonality calculations place Burial 2 between June and August (wet season) and Burial 6 between September and April (dry season) (Chapter 7). Murakami (2015: Table 3) calculates that the Moon Pyramid's Building 4 required 826,160 person-days and estimates a range of between one-third to a little over a year for completion. As explained in Chapter 7, both events were likely planned sequentially as part of the same ritualization process, and it is plausible that Stone-Rabbit could have experienced both within the period of settling into the city. Here, I portray his reaction to Burial 2 as an outsider just arriving in the city and contrast this with his active participation in the ritual at Burial 6.

[8] Despite his immigrant status, Stone-Rabbit's physical involvement in building the stage for this mass sacrificial event has led him to participate in the placemaking of the *altepetl*,

He wondered aloud what the upcoming dedicatory ritual would be like. Maguey-Spine,[9] an excitable crewmate he had befriended shortly after arriving, exclaimed, "Brother, I heard this offering's going to be even more spectacular than the previous. I mean, look at the size of this chamber!" Maguey-Spine leered comically while gesturing toward his neck in a thrusting motion, adding in a low voice, "Just imagine how many are gonna get it this time!" He went on and on about how his relatives had already begun traveling to the city to see the dedication for themselves. They, too, had heard that their local *tlatoani* would be a distinguished participant.[10] Stone-Rabbit teased Maguey-Spine, chuckling that he might have to feed his guests *nopal* spines since their neighborhood butcher recently confessed he had little rabbit meat left to sell, claiming that "ever since the lord's pets took a liking to them, their handlers clear all my stock every market day."[11] With a grim shake of his head and bringing his voice to a whisper, he replied, "Oh no, my brother, rumor has it they dine off those poor war captives, and they are just keeping a few for the dedication ceremony."[12]

Stone-Rabbit wanted his inquisitive eldest daughter, Four-Petal-Flower,[13] to see for herself that his father's tales of awesome beasts under the control of the Teotihuacan lord were true. On those nights when the cool highland breeze would draw distant screeching echoes and infernal roars[14] to their ears, he would remind

embodying the messages broadcast in the ritual. Production is thus physical, corporeal, and ritualized (Monaghan 1998; Chapter 2).

[9] Maguey-Spine's name is based on a series of glyphs painted on the floor of La Ventilla apartment complex (Cabrera Castro 2006b: Figure 6). Though the Teotihuacan script remains undeciphered, it is clear some elements of writing were present in the city (Taube 2011).

[10] Ritual spectacles were not restricted to residents but were opportunities for Teotihuacan to strengthen relations with foreign economic and political partners and attract immigrants. Locals and foreigners from all echelons of society would have participated.

[11] Speculation and curiosity about these ferocious animals would dominate the gossip and small talk of a populace eager to know more about their presence in the city. Given the evidence of rabbit management at the household level (Somerville et al. 2016, 2017), they were likely protein staples traded in the marketplace (Sugiyama et al. 2017).

[12] Human flesh as a possible food source for the carnivores is presented as a rumor because it is impossible to verify if dogs, humans, or both account for the high nitrogen and carbon values of several sacrificed victims (Chapter 6). Regardless, sowing the seeds of these predatory characteristics vividly into the social memories of the populace was successfully carried through mural iconography and daily gossip like that portrayed in this scene.

[13] Four-Petal-Flower iconography is prevalent in murals, architecture, and portable art at Teotihuacan.

[14] For Stone-Rabbit, the visceral experience of hearing these exotic animals' vocalizations would have been comparable to that of the Spanish conquistadors who visited Moctezuma's menagerie many centuries later (Díaz de Castillo 2003).

her, "One day you will meet the master spirits who dwell in the *altepetl*,[15] the protectors who will march into our city.[16] Though fearsome, it is they who ensure our food and water are plenty and safeguard us from harm." As the day of the ceremony approached, these sounds became increasingly frequent during Stone-Rabbit's walk home from the construction site. During a consult with the architectural chief at the Sun Pyramid complex, he had to pass uncomfortably close to an array of pumas carved from stone. Each terrible maw was poised in mid-snap at a trilobed bundle of human hearts positioned before it.[17] Yet they looked exactly as they should—dreadful and unsettling as the snarls that gave him quite a start when he accompanied Maguey-Spine to peek at the captive pumas with his friend, who delivered food to their cages.[18]

Stone-Rabbit directed his gaze southward where the Avenue of the Dead, level and straight as a sunbeam, stretched toward the verdant slopes. Each ornate temple structure flanking its broad span teemed with a glittering caparison of spectators that draped into the masses below, giving the impression of a battle among many ant hills (Figure 2.7).[19] Numerous tendrils of smoke issued from smudges smoldering in incense burners lining a low platform in the center of the plaza, suffusing the air with an invigorating tang. The rhythmic jingle of *ayoyotes* (ankle shell shakers) punctuated the frolicking stomps of *danzantes* (dancers) gyrating to drums and chants and churning eddies of dust and incense into the wan midday haze.[20] Vendors and artisans orbit the spaces opened by performers, seizing the

[15] In this case, referring to Cerro Gordo as the natural mountain after which the Moon Pyramid is modeled.

[16] These apex predators are depicted throughout the city as protagonists marching in military uniform, performing essential agricultural and ritual acts (Chapter 3).

[17] As described in Chapter 2, the large felid balustrades found by the Sun Pyramid Project were likely crafted around the same time or in close succession as the Moon Pyramid's Building 4 (Sarabia González and Núñez Redón 2017).

[18] I suggest that apex predators' residency within the city affected the public's daily praxis beyond the ritual event, facilitating both choreographed public and spontaneous private instances of human–animal encounters.

[19] This description is inspired by my experience at the site during the Spring Equinox (Chapter 2). Given the lower population density of Mesoamerica, fewer people attended these rituals. However, the impression of confronting a mass of people would have been comparatively impactful, given the different baselines in populations throughout the rest of Mesoamerica. Murakami (2014) estimates roughly 35,000 people at roughly .46 persons/m^2 (Inomata 2006) would have stood in the Moon Plaza, and Cowgill (1983) argues the entire Teotihuacan population (100,000) was able to gather in the Great Plaza of the Ciudadela.

[20] This scene was inspired by my experience attending a Huichol ritual, wherein "dancing" was characterized as "feeling the earth." The circular pathway of the sandals pounding the earth kicked up the dirt, creating centripetal energy among us. Though the Moon Plaza

opportunity to entice a captivated audience parched by the gritty heat with food and drink. Others worked the avenue with figurines and the city's renowned obsidian crafts.[21] The long wait was starting to overwhelm Four-Petal-Flower. She tried hard to emulate her father's impassive calm, but at seven solar cycles her reservoir of patience could no longer quench hours of overstimulation and the sweaty press of the crowd. A much older boy inadvertently blocked her view of a performance, provoking a disrespectful snap had her father not directed the youths' attention to a ripple of excitement spreading their way.

The river of bodies swelling the Avenue of the Dead was parting as a vanguard of officials cleared the way for the main procession to advance. The dancing stopped, and the roil of the crowd eased into an expectant simmer. Warriors bearing intricately carved feathered shell trumpets the size of large papayas emerged from the porticos of the temples lining the avenue.[22] On a signal, each descended their station to form a line running the length of the passage cleared along the avenue. There was an instant of frozen silence, followed by a long and hallow trumpet call so far off that Stone-Rabbit could not be sure he had really heard it. A higher note joined, followed by a lower one, and then many more tumbled in; each player's call solidifying the mass of the rest until the whole valley was fixed in a standing wave of sound. In the Moon Pyramid Plaza, the final player brought the call to a close, and the procession departed the Citadel to begin its stately advance toward the plaza.[23]

Four-Petal-Flower found this wait even harder to endure. With the performers now silent, there was nothing to distract from her imprisonment in what amounted to a shrinking oubliette of compressed bodies, which, given her diminutive stature,

would have been plastered white, limiting the quantity of dust, I wanted to convey the drums, stomping, and embodied energy generated through the circular pathway of the dancers.

[21] The role of vendors is taken from the current experience of entering the archaeological park as a tourist, detailed in Chapter 2. Though there is little information regarding the marketplace and how much the state controlled the exchange of goods, large gatherings like this would have generated immense economic opportunities. It is essential to recognize the ritual economy (Wells and McAnany 2008) of spectacle that would lead to disseminating Teotihuacan portable objects (obsidian, candeleros, etc.) in many sites throughout Mesoamerica.

[22] Iconography on the Temple of the Feathered Trumpets, located southwest of the Moon Plaza, inspired this description. Large spiral shells (*Pleuroploca gigantea*) modified into trumpets found in the dedication caches of the Moon Pyramid (Sugiyama 2004) were likely utilized in these rituals.

[23] Evans (2015), among others, has described Teotihuacan as a processual landscape, especially the choreographed experience of walking along the Avenue of the Dead, as narrated in Chapter 2.

furnished a rather disagreeable view. She beseeched Stone-Rabbit for an escape atop his stout shoulders. "When they have passed the Sun Pyramid, little one. Not much to see until then." When they noticed a distant glint of green meandering above the sea of heads and jubilant arms, Stone-Rabbit hoisted up a much-relieved child. It wouldn't be long now.

It was from this advantaged position that Four-Petal-Flower observed the procession as it neared the terminus of the avenue. She didn't understand the meanings of the sacred movements it traced, only that something wonderful bobbed and swished to and fro as it came nearer. A mass that, at first, suggested a copse of reeds flexing in a swift current soon resolved into a splendid cluster of improbably large and brilliant feathers. Was that the head of an animal she saw crouching within? The party entered the plaza. In the clearing, Four-Petal-Flower could catch the full profile of the men whose arrival was announced by their fabulous headgear. She let out a yelp of excitement that nearly toppled her from Stone-Rabbit's shoulders. So many questions!

Her father immediately identified the leader of the procession as the grand *tlatoani*; there was no mistaking the bold black rings of the Storm God emphasizing his deep-set eyes, nor the dazzling tasseled headdress that elevated the ruler's naturally prominent stature nearly two full heads above his entourage.[24] The pendulous greenstone necklace draped across his chest matched a pair of equally outsized ear spools that nearly reached his shoulders and glowed translucent in the radiant afternoon sun. A cascade of beaded shells along the hem of his tunic issued peals of rainfall-like clings with every motion. Four-Petal-Flower was impressed by the mass tuft of feathers that leaped so high from his headdress. Every few steps, the *tlatoani* withdrew a handful of seeds from a rattlesnake-tail pouch he carried before him, which he scattered to mark his path. His thighs were wrapped in a handsome jaguar-pelted loin cloth. Four-Petal-Flower prodded her father to move closer. All wanted a glimpse of this living legend who could singlehandedly command the rise of a human-made mountain from the earth.

The ruler signaled a pose as the procession approached an imposing monolith atop the elevated altar in the middle of the Moon Plaza. The now slightly tilted sunbeam accentuated deep grooves crosscutting the natural crevasses of the andesite boulder that traced the contours of a female figure that stood towering over the ruler.[25] Her robust build was softened by an ornate *quechquemitl* blouse and

---

[24] This procession scene was inspired by the iconography on the Calpulalpan thin-orange bowl described in Chapters 2 and 7 (Figure 2.2) with additional details of body accouterments worn by individuals sacrificed in Burial 5 or depicted in the mural art.

[25] Two female monoliths have been found in the Moon Pyramid Complex. The larger figure was found behind an adjacent structure in the southwestern corner of the plaza (Monolith 1), and a second heavily eroded block is currently positioned in front of a central

accentuated with prominent quadrangular and tubular beads weighing across her chest.[26] Anticipating her question, Stone-Rabbit whispered, "The Earth Goddess,[27] they will make offerings to her, spread the seeds for her, as she will allow our maize to grow." The ruler directed two servants to approach. They carried a wooden platform sustaining a sizeable circular basket, which they set down on the ruler's left side. The basket twitched softly as though alive, evoking gasps from those who were alert enough to notice. At the edge of the clearing nearest the basket, a woman bade her companions to hush, "Listen! Something makes a sound there!" The murmuring receded, permitting the petrifying noises issuing from within to be heard by the wider gathering. Stone-Rabbit, who tended his family's *milpa* in childhood, instantly recognized the hostile alarm of a threatened rattlesnake. One staccato twitch became several, and as with the crescendo of trumpets, a cacophony of individual rasps merged into an undifferentiated rush that sounded to Four-Petal-Flower like raindrops driven thick into palapa rooftops before an approaching storm.[28] "How many could possibly be in there?" "What's alive in the basket *teta*?"[29] "What's that noise?"[30]

---

altar in the Moon Plaza (Monolith 2, described in this narrative). Though I acknowledge Monolith 2 in the narrative, the exact date of manufacture remains unresolved. López Luján (2017) has argued Monolith 1 stood at the apex of the Moon Pyramid and Monolith 2's original provenience was on the plaza's central altar. A female figurine uncovered in Burial 2 suggests the Moon Pyramid's personhood linked to a female earthly figure was already established by Building 4's construction (López Luján and Sugiyama 2017).

[26] The Moon Plaza monolith (Monolith 2) measures 198 × 151 × 143 cm and weighs about 6,000 kg in its highly eroded state, though it would have likely stood closer to the dimensions of Monolith 1 (319 × 165 × 165 cm) (López Luján 2017: 60).

[27] The two monoliths have been identified as Mountain, Earth, Water, or Great Goddess (López Luján 2017; Pasztory 1997: 87–89) connected with the moon (Sugiyama 2017c). Paulinyi (2006) rightfully criticizes the oversimplification of calling every female deity the Great Goddess. Here I refer to this figure as the Earth Goddess, though the proper name for each female figure remains to be verified.

[28] Rattlesnakes are associated with the rainy season precisely because their proliferation presages the start of the rains, and their rattles sound like raindrops (Chapter 3).

[29] "Father" in Nahuatl.

[30] Each participant possessed various degrees of experience and esoteric knowledge. The priest and animal handler know the symbolism and exact number of rattlesnakes in the basket ($n = 18$), the construction worker's familiarity with the ritual caches and upbringing in the milpas led him to infer the contents of the basket, and the daughter who remains mystified but nonetheless knows by the serious and reverent behavior of her elders that there's something very important concealed within the basket. Despite differing levels of understanding, everyone's physical presence in that space bound them into the collective experience.

The ruler acknowledged the offering with handfuls of seeds, snail shells, and greenstone beads cast in cardinal directions before the Earth Goddess and then motioned for the procession to advance.[31] Two paces behind him, a stern-looking man led an entourage in single file. His face was framed under a stylized jaguar helmet, while a long jaguar pelt fell down his back.[32] Large greenstone beads dangled across his chest, and like the ruler, his ears were maximally distended by the generous weight and circumference of ear spools crafted from this same precious material. His stride was accentuated by a hefty serpentine mosaic figurine affixed to a wooden upright, which he bore before him.[33] Being arranged in corporeal forms of the jaguar identified him as the master priest rumored to possess vision so acute it could penetrate one's soul and manipulate their *nagual* (animal companion) during the blackest night.[34] Stone-Rabbit shuddered at the dreadful sight of him and instructed Four-Petal-Flower to look away from his eyes, though there was little risk of this as the man's focus never shifted from the Earth Goddess whom he steadily approached.

Affixed to each of the three members of the entourage was a rattlesnake tail pouch like the one carried by the preceding officiant. From this, each member in turn produced handfuls of precious riches and noble crop seeds which were scattered about in the same manner accompanied by a droning incantation, to augment the path of sustenance marked by the ruler. Upon completing the seed scattering, the priest intensified his eye contact with the Earth Goddess, slowly raising the mosaic figurine into the full embrace of the sun, leveling it before her view, and continued chanting. Stone Rabbit squinted against the glare to better make out the delicate placement of each greenstone piece. Her red shell lips seemed to faintly smile down in acknowledgment of her fate, and he responded with a smile of his own.[35]

---

[31] Though no excavations document offerings scattered near the female monolith, tunnel excavations in the Moon Pyramid have recorded small snail shells cast along the path to the dedicatory chamber. The Calpulalpan bowl (Figure 2.2) and mural art convey priestly figures scattering seeds, greenstone beads, and shells onto the fertile earth.

[32] The description of the priest's attire was inspired by a mural painting of two individuals conducting seed scattering in felid regalia from the Teopancazco apartment complex.

[33] In Burial 6 a greenstone mosaic figurine stood atop a pyrite disc (Filloy Nadal et al. 2006). There is no explicit sex identifier, and I have left this unspecified in the narrative. Given that another figurine also found atop a pyrite disc in Burial 2 was female, I suspect this mosaic figurine was also female.

[34] The jaguar's acute night vision was associated with their ability to see in the dark underworld and peer into people's souls (see Chapter 3).

[35] I attempt to convey the mosaic figurine's animacy. Inter-corporeal relations with the public endowed her personhood. She was also sacrificed, perhaps willingly, in Burial 6.

Following in the precise steps of the master priest was a man whose heavy-heeled footfalls were less measured, but no less confident. His left hand presented a wolf skull, his waist was neatly wrapped in a sumptuous wolf pelt, and his head was encased in a wolf-pelt helmet to complete the canid motif. Dangling over his otherwise bare back was a *tezcacuitlapilli* (a reflective disc with slate backing worn by warriors) that sent brilliant solar sprites flashing across the crowd with each step. His right arm bore an *atlatl* (spear-thrower), a bundle of darts, and a feathered shield. A catenary of human maxillary pendants adorned his chest.[36] Four-Petal-Flower squealed at the sight of this fabled warrior-chief, *Tlacochcalcatl* (keeper of the house of darts),[37] who led scores of victorious battles. On the walk to the plaza, she told her father tales that *Tlacochcalcatl*'s men had recently returned with so many captives the grand *tlatoani* ran out of space to detain them as they awaited sacrifice.

The wolf-warrior was followed by the final member of the entourage, whose headgear sported the same eagle feather accouterments as the ruler but with an added thematic charge in the form of a live golden eagle tethered to his right arm. Sensing a cool shift in the afternoon air, the raptor fussily reoriented itself and unfurled its wings wide to rest on the passing currents. His handler, knowing the astonishing impression that an eagle at full flourish can make on those who have never seen such a magnificent creature close-up, elevated his right arm skyward so all can get a better view. The sun caught the sharp contours of its beak, fringing it in brilliant translucence. It let out a series of piercing cries that reported strangely from the angular monuments surrounding the plaza and seemed to emanate from everywhere at once. The crowd hushed in awe and a flash of uncertainty quivered in Stone-Rabbit's chest. His daughter, however, kept up a running patter of whispered commentary on various details of interest to herself, such as the stoutness of the cuff that kept the man's wrist and forearm from being skewered in the grip of powerful talons and black hallux.[38]

---

[36] Warrior costumes are reconstructed based on depictions of warriors rendered in Teotihuacan and abroad. I also base descriptions on burial accouterments worn by sacrificial victims from the FSP that included over 150 pieces of *tezcacuitlapilli* and human maxillary pendants (made of real human bones, shell imitations, and canid bones) (see Chapter 2; Sugiyama 2005).

[37] *Tlacochcalcatl* was the title of a high-ranking military officer during the Aztec period, which García-Des Lauriers (2008) argued can be traced back to Teotihuacan times.

[38] I draw attention to the eagle's sharp talons because evidence of trauma on the tendons illustrates injury to weaken these perilous weapons. I suspect the audience did not know about these injuries and would have remained awestruck to see humans handling these ferocious beings.

The bird had become agitated from the crowd's attention and the stress of constantly steadying itself during the processional walk, and so began to flap its wings and test its tether. The eagle's handler tensed his perch arm as firm as a tree branch and stealthily fished a ribbon of meat from a blood-sodden pouch hanging just below his *tezcacuitlapilli*. With a practiced flick, he swung the sinewy treat right into the gaping beak above his head, keeping his fingers well outside the range of its bite. The soothing taste of fresh meat both relaxed the eagle and presented yet another remarkable novelty for a curious youngster to observe. Four-Petal-Flower watched intently as the bird settled back onto its mount, closed its wings, and blinking and tilting its head backward, negotiated the entire dripping mass into its gullet with a ferocious satisfaction.[39] The becalming of the eagle offered his handler a chance to perform the same ritualized seed scattering as his concelebrants. The girl asked her father why the man took an extra moment to circulate the seeds he drew from his rattlesnake pouch in his hand that was bloodied from proffering the meat. "The fluid that gives life," his father explained, "he must feed to the seeds in that manner before releasing them to the soil before the Earth Goddess."[40]

Members of the procession continued to file into the plaza, where they began staging into groups that would perform the upcoming ritual. Ruler and retinue steadily continued to ascend steps that scaled the first corpus of the unfinished structure while the eagle handler stepped aside on the raised altar, awaiting the subsequent group to pass by. One by one, their silhouettes disappeared beyond the limb where the stair met the graded platform. Behind them, troupes of dancers and performers split off from the procession, beating out stirring rhythms and whirling in a highly choreographed promenade.

Soldiers in full warrior dress followed suit, marking time with synchronized stomps. They were equipped uniformly: feathered helmets, shell necklaces that clung with each step, a *tezcacuitlapilli*, and a broad belt from which several feathers depended. They carried round shields tufted with eagle plumage and a brace of *atlatl* darts on their left arm. Each displayed offertory objects soaring high on their raised right hand. One army unit was led by a warrior wearing a puma cranium headdress; its coat cascaded in gold and amber down his back. The men under his

---

[39] Alongside semi-complete rabbit/hare remains were partial elements of birds and other small game in the stomach content. Perhaps these were little treats used to distract the animals during this long and likely exhausting procession.

[40] Blood was considered a vital energy source and was offered in dedicatory acts, though soil chemical data is needed to trace such acts (see, e.g., Barba et al. 1996).

command carried bundles of wolf, jaguar, and puma pelts.[41] Several men carried bare skulls of these felids and wolves soaring high above their heads. Four-Petal-Flower leaned closer to inspect the pearlescent canines that propped the mouths agape despite the swaying display of the skulls: "*Teta*, are those the skulls of the pumas and jaguars? Why look at their huge teeth, I bet they can pierce right through our bones!"

Stone-Rabbit had never seen such a prominent force in one place.[42] The crowd was backed into the margins of the plaza to make space as row after row of warriors marched in from the avenue. Those laden with bounties of obsidian, ceramic, shell, and greenstone scaled the temple steps and sank out of view as the ruler and his company had done earlier. They would proceed to the superior *tlatoani*, who would oversee the deposition of these offerings. Last to cross the plaza were a dozen listless figures whose ashen faces cast a pall over their entrance. Bound to one another by ropes and restraints, their leaden feet made a disorderly shuffle along the path of seed cast by elites who awaited them above. They were enclosed by a formation of guards that pressed them together like a human palisade, prodding them along while confining their movement. Though these prisoners were dressed in warrior regalia, some were foreign designs suggesting they had been captured in battle and marked for sacrifice. Four-Petal-Flower tightened her grip on Stone-Rabbit's shoulders. She bent low by her father's cheek and asked, "*Teta*, are they the chosen ones?" Making no effort to turn toward his daughter, her father summoned the most paternal tone he could muster and replied, "Yes, *teichpuch*,[43] yes."

Father and daughter were abruptly jolted from their contemplation of this miserable tableaux by an undignified yelp from the middle of the plaza. There, they discovered several groups of men had been bearing cages up the short stairway of the central platform. One of the men was thrown off balance while dodging a swipe from a very irate puma occupying the cage on his back.[44] Regaining his composure, he cautiously repositioned himself under the corner of the cage. Though his right

---

[41] I provide detailed descriptions of secondary animal accouterments in Chapter 4, including bare crania, crania with attached pelts, and others represented by only the pelt (as recorded by clusters of phalanges).

[42] Inomata (2014) has described the importance of display and performance in Maya warfare. The annual military march along Reforma Avenue the day after the Mexican Independence demonstrates this to be true even today. I suspect that Teotihuacan warfare was also theatrically displayed in state rituals.

[43] "Daughter" in Nahuatl.

[44] Evidence of trauma on the animals was likely to restrain mobility of these dangerous predators. In a tight cage like this one (modeled after Burial 2's evidence), it is unlikely the audience would have noticed one of the pumas (E.1818) was limping (Chapter 6).

shoulder was now striped with a trickle of blood, he was relieved that the cage had not crashed open and released the outraged predator into the plaza. The eagle handler calmly approached the tottering cage and rapped its corner post with a baton, causing the big cat to recoil from the edge. The bearers hastily deposited their cargo near the center of the altar where others soon joined it. Three more pumas, a jaguar cub, and a wolf were arranged around the eagle handler in a circle.

He summoned an assistant bearing a large sack squirming with creatures that Four-Petal-Flower correctly guessed were rabbits. Stone-Rabbit, who knew what was about to happen, leaned forward without realizing he was doing so. Sensing the tension, Four-Petal-Flower grabbed fistfuls of her father's hair and lurched forward, almost toppling them. The eagle handler stuffed a terrified rabbit between the bars of the central cage. The puma set upon its entrapped quarry with the fierce claws and sharp canines of a predator par excellence.[45] "Next!" At this simple command, a second puma cage is hauled to center stage. Crouched in anticipation, the beast within fixed its dilated pupils on a furry commotion emerging from the open end of the sack, its tail steadily undulating right and left. It pounced at the corner of the cage as a second rabbit was pushed through the posts. It might have caught the hand doing the pushing were it not for the eagle handler's practiced reflexes. Stone-Rabbit's heart beat fast. Squeal and snatch were followed by splattering blood and a dull crunch of shattering bone as the predator ripped into the rabbit's plump torso. A dark red liquid trailed from the cage onto the altar floor, staining the brilliant white plaster. Noticing that his daughter had released his hair, he turned to examine her reaction. Four-Petal-Flower's jaw was clenched fast, her eyes saccade in horrified fascination at the scene being imprinted into her young spirit. Snarls gave way to a sibilance of tooth on bone and smacking of lips as the two pumas preoccupied themselves with this final feast prior to their fateful ascent onto the pyramid.

The cage bearers lift each animal slowly, taking pains to avoid provoking them unnecessarily during their passage across the plaza and up the pyramid face. As Stone-Rabbit wonders how the men will scale such a steeply inclined staircase

---

[45] My recent experience observing a live cheetah feeding illustrated these as an active theatrical event that brings crowds in awe and astonishment. Ritual practitioners likely programmed regular feedings during captivity and the final ritual feast before sacrifice for public observation. Witnessing the predator's prowess would have created shared heightened emotive experiences engrained into the social memories of the participants. Parts of a second rabbit consumed by the puma E.1818 exhibited evidence of burning, likely cooked foodstuff. This may have been a preemptive meal to calm the puma's hunger before embarking on the procession, but it is not described in this scene because the evidence of burning was not consistent. Two pumas and two eagles ate rabbits from Burial 6 (Chapter 4).

without dropping the unwieldy cages, Four-Petal-Flower's gaze is transfixed by the finale of the procession, which has now assembled nearby. He feels his daughter's legs straining, raising herself higher on his shoulders. He could not see what had caught her attention, but as it was rumored that eighteen eagles were being prepared for this ceremony and they had thus far seen only one, he simply asked, "Are there more eagles? How many do you see?" The girl answered in a stammer because she had never been so close to one eagle, let alone this many. A train of handlers ascended toward the platform, each with a perfect specimen flapping and pacing on their right arm.[46] This was led by a man who was cloaked in an eagle's cape, whose outstretched arms flapped akimbo every few steps as if to create the currents that stirred the eagles from their handlers' arms.[47] When they joined the master eagle handler, their number was indeed eighteen altogether. As Four-Petal-Flower excitedly classified each bird's various cries and movements, Stone-Rabbit (who could now see them as they crested the stairs) noticed something peculiar. One of the birds did not pace, cry, or turn in any direction but straight ahead. Its expansive wings were held in a constant spread, which it would wriggle in response to some kind of touch its handler applied to its back. "I did not expect," he thought, "to see an eagle tolerate such manipulation by a man."[48] Stone-Rabbit pondered what this might mean as a call went out to bring two of the finest eagles to the edge of the central platform. "Ahh! *Teta*, they're going to feed them, too!"

The eagle handler had planned every movement of his companion's final meal. First, its leg tether was slightly loosened, and a little more length was spooled out. An assistant prepared to place a rabbit near the edge of the platform within sight of those gathered in the plaza below. The eagle, conditioned after months of training to associate this activity with the appearance of a delicious meal, bounded from its arm perch. A couple of light flaps lofted it in position over its target without

---

[46] I observed the military parade for the Mexican Independence on September 16, 2015, where military personnel marched with golden eagles perched on their arms (Plate 16b). Here I am trying to reconstruct the emotions I felt observing this impressive line-up of golden eagles participating in nation-building, much as Stone Rabbit would have experienced these majestic figures as mediators of the Teotihuacan state.

[47] E.2239 consisted of wing and foot bones, likely reflecting a feathered cape or some extensively processed eagle paraphernalia. Such corporeal animal forms provided tactile, embodied experiences of human–animal intra-action during ritual co-participation.

[48] My interpretation of the taxidermically prepared eagles exemplifies a Geertzian "wink." We know that not all eagles were alive at the offering. However, they were likely *perceived* to be alive by the public, and only a few select individuals would have known or noticed the truth. This moment of differentiated experiences within the same ritual illustrates the messy imperfections of ritual action in the past. Immediately, I thought of Evans-Pritchard's (1967) point of substituting a goat or a cucumber for a cow when resources were unavailable.

reaching the end of the tether. It expected the rabbit would try to escape toward the plaza, for a semicircle of officiants blocked any other exit. These stern men flinched instinctively as a fury of wing and claw descended upon the rabbit, pinning it down to be savagely dismantled by a hungry beak.[49]

Though Stone-Rabbit's plan had secured an excellent view of the Moon Plaza itself, a ground-level angle would inevitably conceal much of what was taking place on the raised platform. His daughter kept her father abreast of the action as best she could from her advantaged viewpoint a couple of heads above. She recounted how the feeding ritual was the same for both eagles and had great fun thinking of names, such as Left-Claw or Ear-Beak, for each bird's tactic to arrest the flight of its prey. For a long time, he could only see a pair of pointy beaks jabbing the air above the platform edge, indicating the birds were still gulping down remnants of their prizes. The handlers bent down to cinch the leg tethers again, and the eagles alighted to their arms. All headed away from the platform edge and toward the party of celebrants gathered out of sight near the center. Stone-Rabbit relaxed his posture and sank flat on his feet, which had gone numb from being on tiptoe since the procession entered the plaza. His calves burned, and there had been no spare moment to rub them. No matter. He had finally seen with his own eyes that his favorite animal, the eagle, truly represented all that was majestic and honorable in a powerful predator.

Stone-Rabbit closed his eyes and tried to picture what was happening above in the offertory chamber he knew so well. After the thrill of warriors flooding the plaza, opulent treasures carried high on the pyramid steps, and the eagles and the near calamity of a puma running loose in the crowd, a deferential hush had now come to settle in place. Everyone was suddenly mindful of the gravity of what was to come next. A sliver of shadow darkened the plaza's western edge when the captives entered; now it stretched almost across the blood-stained central platform. "Smoke! I see smoke up there, *teta*. More is coming!" Stone-Rabbit told his daughter that the priests must have begun the final stage of the dedication, which entailed a great deal of fragrant herbs and incense.

Wisps of smoke from scores of censers placed around the chamber mingled as they rose, drifting like a phalanx of wraiths over the plaza. The apparition carried propitiations from the unseen officiants below, whispers which soon drowned in a swell of desperate ululations and defiant curses before the climax of sacrifice was abruptly terminated in a volley of dull, sickening thuds. Hungry growls from the

---

[49] This reconstruction is partly based on my observation of a raptor demonstration. Given the uniformity in the rabbits in the eagle's stomachs, I reconstruct this feeding to be an integral part of the ritual process that was displayed to the public.

felids and wolf tumble down to the crowd as the waning daylight turned amber and vermillion. Unlike her father, Four-Petal-Flower had never seen a sacrificial dedication before and was perplexed by the frightful screams she had just heard. "*Teta*, what's happened to those men?" Her father thought it best to be oblique for the moment and save the topic for their walk home when there was time to explain the meaning of these acts more thoroughly. "Do you hear the creatures, *teichpuch*? They smell the blood that was spilled from those captives. They want to taste it." This reply seemed to placate his child, who was slowly emerging from the thrall of novelty and stimulation and had been wanting to ask about food anyway.

Just then, a stunning howl blasted from the steps of the Moon Pyramid, where the trumpet corps had stealthily reassembled during the captive sacrifice. The chorus of chanters and percussionists joined in from new posts along the length of the avenue. Stone-Rabbit knew the purpose of this signal was, in part, to help cover the unseemly scrapes, thumps, and crew commands that accompanied the frenzied loading and dumping of many basketfuls of earth necessary to refill the chamber and vouchsafe the offerings within. Stone-Rabbit whispers to his daughter, "They have begun sealing the inner chamber." The sound also covered something else. The animals, largely silent as they were deposited in vivo accompanying the treasures and the lifeless corpses of the captives, were mounting a futile protest of their entombment with yowls and screeches and frenetic gnawing at the tethers that held them in place.[50] One by one their cries were snuffed by the rising fill of earth. Four-Petal-Flower tugs hard at her father's shoulders, trying to understand what is happening, "*Teta*, the animals are alive?" His father had practiced his answer to this inevitable question. "Yes, *teichpuch*, the animal spirits reside within this mountain. They will live there for as long as this great city stands. We will continue to honor them, and they will continue to protect us."

When the whimpering struggles of the last creature could no longer be heard, the trumpeters were dismissed, and the ruler's entourage began their long retracement down the Avenue of the Dead. The work of chamber-filling would continue well past sunset. The return procession was a much more perfunctory affair than the advance. The animals were gone and the march of their vacant cages left a hefty void in Stone Rabbit's chest. The warriors who had deposited so many gifts and treasures in the chamber had little to carry home but their armaments. Several had even given their own pelt attire up to the chamber, and their bare shoulders seemed diminished as they slowly retraced their steps. Stone-Rabbit was entranced by the

---

[50] Unlike Burial 2, there was no evidence of cages in Burial 6. The animals were ultimately deposited with their extremities bound. Some may have been affixed to the two large wooden poles uncovered in Burial 6.

elongated shadow figures dragging their feet that raked across the plaza onto the platform steps. Their silhouettes became lost among the darkening mountain range as they worked their way toward the Ciudadela. The shambolic troupe of captives who had been dispatched with the rest of the offerings did make a gruesome return, of a sort. All but two of the victims' disembodied heads were arranged on a wooden plinth that accompanied the ruler and his entourage.[51] Rivulets of blood flowed from each victim's severed neck, leaving a trail of speckled crimson on the ground below. The revelers lining the processional route were polarized at the sight of their frozen, agonized faces. Some could not bear to look; others could not look away. Stone-Rabbit was concerned for his daughter, whose few years may not have readied her for such a shock. Though clearly shaken by what she saw, she was mainly trying to keep her focus on the wolf-warrior's steady and dignified march as the nearby boy was attempting to tease her by making grotesque imitations of the heads on the plinth.

As the last rank of warriors passed by, the processional corridor melted away behind them. The plaza and the avenue beyond resumed their role as bustling interchanges of commerce and gossip at the heart of the Teotihuacan state. Breathless accounts of the spectacle were shared as people caught up on quotidian chores and errands that had been sidelined by the day's events. The crowds disbanded in the fading twilight, as people headed off to the celebratory feasts and family reunions across the city. Stone-Rabbit recalled how the pyramid's chief engineer boasted of his invitation to an exclusive gathering in the Plaza of the Columns, with many foreign dignitaries and the royal retinue in attendance.[52] After setting Four-Petal-Flower back on her own feet, they started their long walk home down the Avenue of the Dead. The routine commute took on fresh significance for Stone-Rabbit now that he was witness to its consecration by the grand *tlatoani* himself. He felt viscerally present for the first time since he arrived in the city, as though a thick, invisible garment that insulated his senses had now been removed. Energizing sounds

---

[51] Ten humans in Burial 6 were decapitated. It is likely human crania were curated for other purposes. Moon Pyramid's Burial 4 uncovered seventeen severed heads (and an eighteenth individual represented by the atlas vertebra) (Spence and Pereira 2007), and human maxillary pendants adorned warriors in the FSP (Sugiyama 2005).

[52] Rituals that attracted foreign dignitaries and curious travelers would not conclude with the public spectacle but continue providing crucial social networking opportunities via more exclusionary "after parties," including large state-regulated feasts. A massive deposit of local and foreign wares and foodstuff uncovered at the Plaza of the Columns captures how governing elites executed foreign diplomacy through feasting and gift exchange (Sugiyama, Fash, et al. 2020).

of merrymaking, dancing, and erudite discussion were issued from every fire-lit doorway and patio they passed.

Four-Petal-Flower, who had gone uncharacteristically quiet for most of the walk home, suddenly stopped in her tracks, turned to her father, and asked, "*Teta*, you'll finish building the mountain so the animals can protect us, will you?" Stone-Rabbit beamed as he replied, "Yes, I am certain we will."

The pyramids of Teotihuacan cast a panoptic gaze across the city, anchoring a supremely ritualized landscape codified through the spectacle of state ceremony. Animal matter embedded within these sacred places constituted sentient persons by which earthen mounds were animated into the *altepetl*. Teotihuacan, with a footprint embossed into the terrain of Central Mexico and fingerprints on the entire Classic Mesoamerican era, remains a marvel of depth and complexity wherein animal matter was intimately and physically entangled through ritual, placemaking, and sovereignty formations.

APPENDIX

TABLE A1

Summary of Faunal Data from the Feathered Serpent Pyramid (Counts Are in MNI)

		Sec 8	Sec 8/9	Sec 13	Sec 13/8	Sec 14	Sec 14/9	Total	Notes
Aves									
Aquila chrysaetos	Golden eagle	-	-	-	-	-	1	1	Sec 14/9, Unidad 1/91, Layer CVII-B.14, E.374. No NISP reported.
Actitis macularius	Spotted sandpiper	-	1	-	-	-	-	1	NISP 1 from fill.
Buteo sp.	Hawk	-	-	1	-	-	1	2	Sec 13, B.1, NISP 12. Sec 14/9, B.14, E.877, no NISP reported.
Mammalia									
Bassariscus astutus	Ring-tailed cat	-	-	1	-	-	-	1	Mummified in ancient tunnel fill.
Canis sp.	Canid	-	-	-	-	1	-	1	Incisor
C. lupus baileyi	Mexican grey wolf	-	-	-	1	-	-	1	Sec 13/8, B.14, Front C, Layer XC-VII, E.534, caranium and mand.
C. familiaris*	Dog	1	5	-	-	-	-	6	Sec 8, Front C, B.4, E.112 and 117, painted and modified. Sec 8/9, Front C, B.2, E.49, dog cranium, E.50 frag left maxilla, E.52 frag maxilla, and two maxillae (E.146, 51, 49, or 50, and E.103, 128, or 134). Total MNI 6.
Puma concolor	Puma	1	-	-	1	-	1	3	Sec 8, Unidad 100, Cuadro 8, Fosa 3, B.4, Layer LXXIII (disturbed), mand. and maxilla. Sec 8/9, deciduous tooth. Sec 14/9, B.14, young puma, E.294, 534, 622, 710, 797.

(continued)

TABLE A1
Continued

		Sec 8	Sec 8/9	Sec 13	Sec 13/8	Sec 14	Sec 14/9	Total	Notes
Lepus sp.	Hare	-	1	1	-	-	-	2	Sec 8/9 NISP 2, Sec 13, *Lepus callotis*, NISP 1.
Sylvilagus sp.	Cottontail	1	-	-	-	-	2	3	NISP 4 vertebrae from Unidad 100, Cuadro 87, Fosa 3, Layer LXXIIF.
S. cunicularius	Mexican cottontail	-	1	1	-	-	-	2	Sec 9 NISP 1. Sec 13, NISP 5, MNI is likely 1.
S. audubonii	Desert cottontail	-	1	-	-	-	-	1	Sec 8 y9, Fosa1, B.2, Frente C, Layer XXIX (relleno).
S. floridanus	Eastern cottontail	1	2	-	1	-	-	4	Sec 8, mummified leg in ancient tunnel. Sec 8/9, NISP 5. Sec 13/8, NISP 2.
Odocoileus virginianus	White-tailed deer	1	1	1	-	1	1	5	Sec 8 pelvis and sacrum. Sec 8/9 worked bone. Sec 13 NISP 3 (E..6). Sec 14, NISP 1, prox tibia. Sec 14/9, 1 phalange.
O. hemionus	Mule deer	-	-	2	-	-	-	2	Sec 13, NISP 5 (E.6), NISP 1 (E.12).
Pappogeomys tylorhinus	Smoky pocket gopher	-	-	1	-	-	-	1	Sec 13, cranium and mandible in ancient tunnel fill.
Peromyscus maniculatus	North Amer. deer mouse	-	-	-	-	-	1	1	
P. melanophrys	Plateau mouse	-	-	-	1	-	-	1	NISP 10.

P. difficilis	Southern rock deer mouse	-	-	1	-	1	NISP 2.
P. truei	Pinyon mouse	-	-	3	-	3	NISP 7.
Spermophilus variegatus	Rock squirrel	-	-	-	1	1	
Sceloporus torquatus	Torquate lizard	1	1	1	-	1	Ent. 14, mand. and premaxila.
UNID Mammal		1	-	-	1	3	Sec 8, B.14, Sec 13, E.12, Sec 14, all worked bone.
Reptiles							
Crotalus sp.	Rattlesnake	3	-	-	1	4	Sec 8, Unidad 100, Cuadro 87F, Layer LXXIII, B.2. Sec 14/9, Unidad 1/91, Layer CVII, B.14, E.827, vert.
Dermatemys mawii	Central Amer. river turtle	-	-	-	1	1	Turtle carapace frag in fill.
Anura/Lacertidae	Frog/lizard	1	-	-	-	1	
TOTAL		10	12	9	9	53	

* Canid maxillae identified by Álvarez and Ocaña (1993) as MNI of 6 have been reanalyzed by Valádez Azúa et al. (2002) as 14 MNI comprised of various canid species.

Shading denotes species also present in the Moon Pyramid. Sec: Section, Amer.:American, E.#: Element #, B.#: Burial # , Vert: vertebrae, mand: mandible.

Source: From Álvarez and Ocaña (1993).

BIBLIOGRAPHY

Abe, Yoshiko, Curtis W. Marean, Peter J. Nilssen, Zelalem Assefa, and Elizabeth C. Stone. 2002. The Analysis of Cutmarks on Archaeofauna: A Review and Critique of Quantification Procedures, and a New Image-Analysis GIS Approach. *American Antiquity* 67(4): 1–21.

Acosta, Jorge R. 1964. *El Palacio del Quetzalpapalotl*. México, D.F.: Instituto Nacional de Antropología e Historia.

Aguilera, Carmen. 1985. *Flora y Fauna Mexicana: Mitología y Tradiciones*. México, D.F.: Editorial Everest Mexicana, S.A.

Aguilera, Carmen. 2002. Los Quetzales de Teotihuacan. In *Ideología y Política a Través de Materiales, Imágenes y Símbolos*, edited by María Elena Ruiz Gallut, pp. 399–410. Memoria de la Primera Mesa Redonda de Teotihuacan. México, D.F.: Universidad Nacional Autónoma de México, Instituto Nacional de Antropología e Historia.

Allitt, Sharon, R. Michael Stewart, and Timothy Messner. 2008. The Utility of Dog Bone (*Canis familiaris*) in Stable Isotope Studies for Investigating the Presence of Prehistoric Maize (*Zea mays* ssp. *mays*): A Preliminary Study. *North American Archaeologist* 29(3): 343–367. DOI:10.2190/NA.29.3-4.h.

Álvarez, Ticul, and Aurelio Ocaña. 1993. *Identificación de los Restos Óseos Procedentes del Templo de Quetzalcoóatl, Teotihuacán, México*. Technical Report in Archivo Técnico de la Coordinación de Arqueología, México, D.F.: Instituto Nacional de Antropologia e Historia.

Ambrose, Stanley H., and Michael J. DeNiro. 1986. The Isotopic Ecology of East African Mammals. *Oecologia* 69(3): 395–406. DOI:10.2307/4217961.

Ambrose, Stanley H., and Lynette Norr. 1993. Experimental Evidence for the Relationship of the Carbon Isotope Ratios of Whole Diet and Dietary Protein to Those of Bone Collagen and Carbonate. In *Prehistoric Human Bone: Archaeology at the Molecular Level*, edited by Joseph B. Lambert and Gisela Grupe, pp. 1–37. Berlin: Springer-Verlag.

Anderson, David G. 2000. *Identity and Ecology in Arctic Siberia: The Number One Reindeer Brigade*. Oxford Studies in Social and Cultural Anthropology. Oxford: Oxford University Press.

Angulo, Jorge V. 2006. Teotihuacán: Aspectos de la Cultura a Través de su Expresión Pictórica. In *La Pintura Mural Prehispánica en México: I Teotihuacan*, edited by Batriz de la Fuente, Vol. 2, pp. 65–186. México, D.F.: Universidad Nacional Autónoma de México, Instituto de Investigaciones Estéticas.

Armstrong, Barry L., and James B. Murphy. 1979. *The Natural History of Mexican Rattlesnakes*. Vol. 5. Lawrence: University of Kansas, Museum of Natural History.

Armstrong Oma, Kristin. 2010. Between Trust and Domination: Social Contracts Between Humans and Animals. *World Archaeology* 42(2): 175–187. DOI:10.1080/00438241003672724.

Astor-Aguilera, Miguel 2011. *Maya World of Communicating Objects: Quadripartite Crosses, Trees, and Stones*. Albuquerque: University of New Mexico Press.

Aveni, Anthony F. 2000. Out of Teotihuacan: Origins of the Celestial Canon in Mesoamerica. In *Mesoamerica's Classic Heritage: From Teotihuacan to the Aztecs*, edited by Davíd Carrasco, Lindsay Jones, and Scott Sessions, pp. 253–268. Boulder: University Press of Colorado.

Aveni, Anthony F., and H. Hartung. 1986. *Maya City Planning and the Calendar*. Vol. 76, pt. 7. Transactions of the American Philosophical Society. Philadelphia: American Philosophical Society.

Aveni, Anthony F., Horst Hartung, and Beth Buckingham. 1978. The Pecked Cross Symbol in Ancient Mesoamerica. *Science* 202(4365): 267–279.

Barad, Karen. 2007. *Meeting the Universe Halfway: Quantum Physics and the Entanglement of Matter and Meaning*. Durham, NC: Duke University Press.

Barba, Luis, Linda R. Manzanilla Naim, René Chávez, Luis Flores, and Arturo Jorge Arzate. 1990. Caves and Tunnels at Teotihuacan, Mexico: A Geological Phenomenon of Archaeological Interest. In *Archaeological Geology of North America*, edited by Norman P. Lasca and Jack Donahue, Centennial special Vol. 4: pp. 431–438. Boulder, CO: Geological Society of America.

Barba, Luis A., Agustín Ortiz, Karl F. Link, Leonardo López Luján, and Luz Lazos. 1996. Chemical Analysis of Residues in Floors and the Reconstruction of Ritual Activities at the Templo Mayor, Mexico. In *Archaeological Chemistry: Organic, Inorganic, and Biochemical Analysis*, edited by Mary Virginia Orna, 625: pp. 139–156. ACS Symposium Series. Washington, DC: American Chemical Society.

Bassett, Molly H. 2015. *The Fate of Earthly Things: Aztec Gods and God-Bodies*. 1st ed. Recovering Languages and Literacies of the Americas. Austin: University of Texas Press.

Basso, Keith H. 1996. *Wisdom Sits in Places: Landscape and Language Among the Western Apache*. Albuquerque: University of New Mexico Press.

Bateman, Alison S., Simon D. Kelly, and Timothy D. Jickells. 2005. Nitrogen Isotope Relationships between Crops and Fertilizer: Implications for Using Nitrogen Isotope Analysis as an Indicator of Agricultural Regime. *Journal of Agricultural and Food Chemistry* 53(14): 5760–5765. DOI:10.1021/jf050374h.

Batres, Leopoldo. 1906. *Teotihuacan: Memoria que Presenta Leopoldo Batres*. México, D.F.: Imprenta de Fidencio S. Soria.
Bauer, Andrew M., and Steve Kosiba. 2016. How Things Act: An Archaeology of Materials in Political Life. *Journal of Social Archaeology* 16(2): 115–141. DOI:10.1177/1469605316641244.
Bell, Catherine. 1992. *Ritual Theory, Ritual Practice*. Oxford: Oxford University Press.
Bell, Catherine. 1997. *Ritual Perspective and Dimensions*. Oxford: Oxford University Press.
Bell, Catherine. 2005. Ritual [Further Considerations]. In *Encyclopedia of Religion*, 2nd ed., edited by Lindsay Jones, Vol. 11: pp. 7848–7856. Detroit, MI: Macmillan.
Bennett, Jane. 2010. *Vibrant Matter: A Political Ecology of Things*. A John Hope Franklin Center Book. Durham, NC: Duke University Press.
Benson, Elizabeth P., ed. 1972. *The Cult of the Feline: A Conference in Pre-Columbian Iconography*. Washington, DC: Dumbarton Oakes Research Library and Collection.
Bernal, Ignacio. 1963. *Teotihuacán: Descubrimientos, Reconstrucciones*. México, D.F.: Instituto Nacional de Antropología e Historia.
Bernal-Garcia, Maria Elena. 1993. Carving Mountains in a Blue/Green Bowl: Mythological Urban Planning in Mesoamerica. Unpublished PhD diss., University of Texas at Austin.
Berrin, Kathleen, ed. 1988. *Feathered Serpents and Flowering Trees: Reconstructing the Murals of Teotihuacán*. San Francisco: Fine Arts Museums of San Francisco. Distributed by University of Washington Press.
Betts, Matthew, Susan Blair, and David Black. 2012. Perspectivism, Mortuary Symbolism, and Human-Shark Relationships on the Maritime Peninsula. *American Antiquity* 77(4): 621–645. DOI:10.7183/0002-7316.77.4.621.
Bird-David, Nurit. 1999. "Animism" Revisited: Personhood, Environment, and Relational Epistemology. *Current Anthropology* 40(S1): S67–S91.
Blanco Padilla, Alicia, Gilberto Pérez Roldán, Bernardo Rodríguez Galicia, Nawa Sugiyama, Fabiola Torres, and Raúl Valadez Azúa. 2009. El Zoológico de Moctezuma ¿Mito o Realidad? *AMMVEPE* 20(2): 29–39.
Blanco Padilla, Alicia, Bernardo Rodríguez Galicia, and Raúl Valadez Azúa. 2007. El Lobo Mexicano (*Canis lupus baileyi*) en el Contexto Cultural Prehispánico: Las Fuentes Escritas. *AMMVEPE* 18(3): 68–76.
Blanco Padilla, Alicia, Bernardo Rodríguez Galicia, and Raúl Valadez Azúa. 2009. *Estudio de los Cánidos Arqueológicos del México Prehispánico*. 1. Textos básicos y manuales. Instituto Nacional de Antropología e Historia, Universidad Nacional Autónoma de México. México, D. F.: Instituto de Investigaciones Antropológicas.
Bloch, Leigh. 2020. Animate Earth, Settler Ruins: Mound Landscapes and Decolonial Futures in the Native South. *Cultural Anthropology* 35(4): 516–545. DOI:10.14506/ca35.4.02.
Bourdieu, Pierre. 1977. *Outline of a Theory of Practice*. Cambridge: Cambridge University Press.
Boutin, Alexis T. 2011. Crafting a Bioarchaeology of Personhood: Osteobiographical Narratives from Alalakh. In *Breathing New Life into the Evidence of Death: Contemporary Approaches to Bioarchaeology*, edited by Aubrey Baadsgaard, Alexis T. Boutin, and Jane E. Buikstra, pp. 109–133. Santa Fe, NM: School of American Research Press.

Bove, Frederick J., and Sonia Madrano Busto. 2003. Teotihuacan, Militarism, and Pacific Guatemala. In *The Maya and Teotihuacan: Reinterpreting Early Classic Interaction*, edited by Geoffrey E. Braswell, pp. 45–79. Austin: University of Texas.

Bradley, Richard. 1998. *The Significance of Monuments: On the Shaping of Human Experience in Neolithic and Bronze Age Europe*. London: Routledge.

Brady, James E., and Wendy Ashmore. 1999. Mountains, Caves, Water: Ideational Landscapes of the Ancient Maya. In *Archaeologies of Landscape: Contemporary Perspectives*, edited by Wendy Ashmore and Arthur Bernard Knapp, pp. 124–145. Malden, MA: Blackwell.

Braswell, Geoffrey E., ed. 2003. *The Maya and Teotihuacan: Reinterpreting Early Classic Interaction*. Austin: University of Texas Press.

Bray, Tamara L. 2018. Partnering with Pots: The Work of Objects in the Imperial Inca Project. *Cambridge Archaeological Journal* 28(2): 243–257. DOI:10.1017/S0959774317000828.

Brightman, Marc, Vanessa Elisa Grotti, and Olga Ulturgasheva, eds. 2012. *Animism in Rainforest and Tundra: Personhood, Animals, Plants and Things in Contemporary Amazonia and Siberia*. New York: Berghahn Books.

Brisbin, I. Lehir Jr., and C. Kenyon Wagner 1970. Some Health Problems Associated with the Maintenance of American Kestrels *(Falco sparverius)* in Captivity. *International Zoo Yearbook* 10(1):29–30.

Broda, Johanna. 1988. Templo Mayor as Ritual Space. In *The Great Temple of Tenochtitlan: Center and Periphery in the Aztec World*, edited by Johanna Broda, Davíd Carrasco, and Eduardo Matos Moctezuma, pp. 61–123. Berkeley: University of California Press.

Broda, Johanna. 1989. Geografía, Clima y Observación de la Naturaleza en la Mesoamérica Prehispánica. In *Las Máscaras de la Cueva de Santa Ana Teloxtoc*, edited by Ernesto Vargas, 105: pp. 35–51. Serie antropológica. Universidad Nacional Autónoma de México, México, D.F.

Brown, Linda A., and Kitty F. Emery. 2008. Negotiations with the Animate Forest: Hunting Shrines in the Guatemalan Highlands. *Journal of Archaeological Method and Theory* 15(4): 300–337.

Brown, Linda A., and William H. Walker. 2008. Prologue: Archaeology, Animism and Non-human Agents. *Journal of Archaeological Method and Theory* 15(4): 297–299.

Brück, Joanna, and Melissa Goodman. 1999. *Making Places in the Prehistoric World: Themes in Settlement Archaeology*. London: UCL Press.

Busatta, Sandra. 2007. Good to Think: Animals and Power. *Antrocom* 4(1): 3–11.

Cabrera Castro, Rubén. 1998. La Serpiente Emplumada y el Jaguar Como Símbolo del Control Político en Teotihuacan. In *Historia Comparativa de las Religiones*, edited by Henry Karol Kocyba and Yólotl González Torres, pp. 197–220. México, D.F.: Instituto Nacional de Antropología e Historia.

Cabrera Castro, Rubén. 2006a. Atetelco. In *La Pintura Mural Prehispánica en México, I Teotihuacan*, edited by Beatriz de la Fuente, Vol.1: pp. 203–258. México, D.F.: Universidad Nacional Autónoma de México, Instituto de Investigaciones Estéticas.

Cabrera Castro, Rubén. 2006b. Caracteres Glíficos Teotihuacanos en un Piso de La Ventilla. In *La Pintura Mural Prehispánica en México, I Teotihuacan*, edited by Beatriz de la Fuente, Vol. 2: pp. 401–427. México, D.F.: Universidad Nacional Autónoma de México, Instituto de Investigaciones Estéticas.

Cabrera Castro, Rubén, and Oralia Cabrera. 1991. El Proyecto Templo de Quetzalcoatl: Planteamientos Generales y Resultados Preliminares. *Arqueología* 6: 19–31.

Cabrera Castro, Rubén, Ignacio Rodriguez G., and Noel Morelos G., eds. 1982a. *Memoria del Proyecto Arqueológico Teotihuacán 80-82*. Colección Científica 132. México, D.F.: Instituto Nacional de Antropología e Historia.

Cabrera Castro, Rubén, Ignacio Rodriguez G., and Noel Morelos G., eds. 1982b. *Teotihuacan 80-82: Primeros resultados*. México, D.F.: Instituto Nacional de Antropología e Historia.

Cabrera Castro, Rubén, Saburo Sugiyama, and George L. Cowgill. 1991. The Templo de Quetzalcoatl Project at Teotihuacan. *Ancient Mesoamerica* 2: 77–92.

Cabrera Cortés, Mercedes Oralia. 2011. Craft Production and Socio-Economic Marginality: Living on the Periphery of Urban Teotihuacan. Unpublished PhD diss., Arizona State University.

Carballo, David M. 2007. Implements of State Power: Weaponry and Martially Themed Obsidian Production Near the Moon Pyramid, Teotihuacan. *Ancient Mesoamerica* 18: 173–190.

Carballo, David M. 2013. The Social Organization of Craft Production and Interregional Exchange at Teotihuacan. In *Merchants, Markets, and Exchange in the Pre-Columbian World*, edited by Kenneth G. Hirth and Joanne Pillsbury, pp. 113–140. Washington, DC: Dumbarton Oaks Research Library and Collection.

Carballo, David M. 2016. *Urbanization and Religion in Ancient Central Mexico*. Oxford: Oxford University Press.

Carballo, David M. 2020. Power, Politics, and Governance at Teotihuacan. In *Teotihuacan: The World Beyond the City*, edited by Kenneth G. Hirth, David M. Carballo, and Barbara Arroyo, pp. 57–96. Washington, DC: Dumbarton Oaks Research Library and Collection.

Careta, M. A. Nicolás. 2001. *Fauna Mexica: Naturaleza y Simbolismo*. Leiden, Netherlands: Research School CNWS, Leiden University.

Carrasco, Davíd. 1988. Myth, Cosmic Terror, and the Templo Mayor. In *The Great Temple of Tenochtitlan: Center and Periphery in the Aztec World*, edited by Johanna Broda, Davíd Carrasco, and Eduardo Matos Moctezuma, pp. 124–162. Berkeley: University of California Press.

Carrasco, Davíd. 1991. The Sacrifice of Tezcatlipoca: To Change Place. In *To Change Place: Aztec Ceremonial Landscapes*, edited by Davíd Carrasco, pp. 31–57. Niwor: University Press of Colorado.

Carrasco, Davíd. 2000. *Quetzalcoatl and the Irony of Empire: Myths and Prophecies in the Aztec Tradition*. Rev. Boulder: University Press of Colorado.

Carrasco, Davíd. 2005. Sacrifice [Further Considerations]. In *Encyclopedia of Religion*, edited by Lindsay Jones, pp. 8008–8010. Detroit, MI: Macmillan.

Carrasco, Davíd. 2008. Human Sacrifice/Dept Payments from the Aztec Point of View. In *The History of the Conquest of New Spain by Bernal Díaz del Castillo*, edited by Davíd Carrasco, pp. 458–465. Albuquerque: University of New Mexico Press.

Carter, Jeffrey. 2003. *Understanding Religious Sacrifice: A Reader*. Controversies in the Study of Religion. London: Continuum.
Chávez Balderas, Ximena, Diana K. Moreiras Reynaga, Fred J. Longstaffe, Leonardo López Luján, Sarah H. Hendricks, and Robert K. Wayne. 2022. Los Lobos de Tenochtitlan: Identificación, Cautiverio y Uso Ritual. In *Los Animales y el Recinto Sagrado de Tenochtitlan*, edited by Leonardo López Luján and Eduardo Matos Moctezuma, pp. 101–125. Primera edición. Ciudad de México: El Colegio Nacional.
Chen, Mel Y. 2012. *Animacies: Biopolitics, Racial Mattering, and Queer Affect*. Durham and London: Duke University Press.
Clayton, Sarah C. 2005. Interregional Relationships in Mesoamerica: Interpreting Maya Ceramics at Teotihuacan. *Latin American Antiquity* 16(4): 427–448.
Clayton, Sarah C. 2009. Ritual Diversity and Social Identities: A Study of Mortuary Behaviors at Teotihuacan Unpublished. PhD diss., Arizona State University.
Clutton-Brock, Juliet. 1989. A Dog and a Donkey Excavated at Tell Brak. *Iraq* 51: 217–224.
Clutton-Brock, Juliet. 1994. The Unnatural World: Behavioural Aspects of Humans and Animals in the Process of Domestication. In *Animals and Human Society: Changing Perspectives*, edited by Aubrey Manning and James Serpell, pp. 23–35. London: Routledge.
Coe, Michael D. 1972. Olmec Jaguars and Olmec Kings. In *The Cult of the Feline, A Conference in Pre-Columbian Iconography*, edited by Elizabeth P. Benson, pp. 1–18. Washington, DC: Dumbarton Oakes Research Library and Collection.
Conneller, Chantal. 2004. Becoming Deer: Corporeal Transformations at Star Carr. *Archaeological Dialogues* 11(1): 37–56. DOI:10.1017/S1380203804001357.
Cortés, Hernán. 1971. *Cartas de Relación*. 6th ed. Vol. 7. México, D.F.: Editorial Porrua.
Costin, Cathy Lynne, ed. 2016. *Making Value, Making Meaning: Techné in the Pre-Columbian World*. Washington, DC: Dumbarton Oakes Research Library and Collection.
Cowgill, George L. 1983. Rulership and the Ciudadela: Political Inferences from Teotihuacan Architecture. In *Civilization in the Ancient Americas*, edited by Richard M. Leventhal and Alan L. Kolata, pp. 313–343. Cambridge, MA: University of New Mexico Press and Peabody Museum of Archaeology and Ethnology.
Cowgill, George L. 2004. Origins and Development of Urbanism: Archaeological Perspectives. *Annual Review of Anthropology* 33: 525–549.
Cowgill, George L. 2008. An Update on Teotihuacan. *Antiquity* 82: 962–975.
Cowgill, George L. 2015. *Ancient Teotihuacan: Early Urbanism in Central Mexico*. Cambridge: Cambridge University Press.
Crowe, Douglass M. 1975. Aspects of Ageing, Growth, and Reproduction of Bobcats from Wyoming. *Journal of Mammalogy* 56(1):177–198.
Currier, Mary Jean P. 1979. An Age Estimation Technique and Some Normal Blood Values for Mountain Lions (*Felis concolor*). Unpublished PhD diss., Colorado State University.
Currier, Mary Jean P. 1983. Felis concolor. *Mammalian Species* 200: 1–7.
Delwiche, Constant C., and Pieter L. Steyn. 1970. Nitrogen Isotope Fractionation in Soils and Microbial Reactions. *Environmental Science & Technology* 4(11): 929–935. DOI:10.1021/es60046a004.

DeMarrais, Elizabeth. 2004. Materialization of Culture. In *Rethinking Materiality: The Engagement of Mind with the Material World*, edited by Elizabeth DeMarrais, Chris Gosden, and Colin Renfrew, pp. 11–22. Cambridge: McDonald Institute for Archaeological Research. Distributed by Oxbow Books.

DeMarrais, Elizabeth, Luis Jaime Castillo, and Timothy Earle. 1996. Ideology, Materialization, and Power Strategies. *Current Anthropology* 37(1): 15–31.

DeMarrais, Elizabeth, Chris Gosden, and Colin Renfrew, eds. 2004. *Rethinking Materiality: The Engagement of Mind with the Material World*. McDonald Institute Monographs. Cambridge: McDonald Institute for Archaeological Research. Distributed by Oxbow Books.

DeNiro, Michael J, and Samuel Epstein. 1978. Influence of Diet on the Distribution of Carbon Isotopes in Animals. *Geochimica et cosmochimica acta* 42(5): 495–506.

Department of the Interior. 2015. Endangered and Threatened Wildlife and Plants; Endangered Status for the Mexican Wolf Fish and Wildlife Service. *Federal Register* 80(11): 2488–2512.

Descola, Philippe. 2012. Beyond Nature and Culture: The Traffic of Souls. Translated by Janet Lloyd. *HAU: Journal of Ethnographic Theory* 2(1): 473–500. DOI:10.14318/hau2.1.021.

Di Peso, Charles C., John B. Rinaldo, and Gloria J. Fenner. 1974. *Casas Grandes: A Fallen Trading Center of the Gran Chichimeca*. 1st ed. Vol. 8. Dragoon and Flagstaff, AZ: Amerind Foundation/Northland Press.

Díaz del Castillo, Bernal. 2003. *The Discovery and Conquest of Mexico, 1517–1521*. Translated by A. P. Maudslay. Cambridge: Da Capo Press.

Dornan, Jennifer. 2007. Beyond Belief: Religious Experience, Ritual, and Cultural Neuro-phenomenology in the Interpretation of Past Religious Systems. *Cambridge Archaeological Journal* 14(1): 25–36.

Douglas, Mary. 1957. Animals in Lele Religious Symbolism. *Journal of the International African Institute* 27(1): 46–58.

Drucker, R. David. 1977. A Solar Orientation Framework for Teotihuacan. In *Los Procesos de Cambio en Mesoamerica y Areas Circunvecinas*, pp. 277–284. XV Mesa Redonda II. Sociedad Mexicana de Antropología, Universidad de Guanajuato, México.

Durán, Diego. 1971. *Book of the Gods and Rites and The Ancient Calendar*. Translated by Fernando Horcasitas. [1st]. Vol. 102. The Civilization of the American Indian series. Norman: University of Oklahoma Press.

Durkheim, Émile. 2001. *The Elementary Forms of Religious Life*. Oxford: Oxford University Press.

Earle, Timothy. 2001. Institutionalization of Chiefdoms: Why Landscapes Are Built. In *From Leaders to Rulers*, edited by Jonathan Haas, pp. 105–124. New York: Kluwer.

Elizalde Mendez, Israel. 2017. El Cautiverio de Animales en Tenochtitlan: Un Estudio a Través de los Restos Óseos Recuperados en las Ofrendas del Templo Mayor. Unpublished BA thesis, Escula Nacional de Antropología e Historia.

Elizalde Mendez, Israel. 2022. La Fauna del Emperador en el Vivario de Tenochtitlan. In *Los Animales y el Recinto Sagrado de Tenochtitlan*, edited by Leonardo López Luján and

Eduardo Matos Moctezuma, pp. 81–99. Primera edición. Ciudad de México: El Colegio Nacional.

Emery, Kitty F., Lori E. Wright, and Henry Schwarcz. 2000. Isotopic Analysis of Ancient Deer Bone: Biotic Stability in Collapse Period Maya Land-use. *Journal of Archaeological Science* 27(6): 537–550. DOI:10.1006/jasc.1999.0491.

Emmons, Louise H. 1987. Comparative Feeding Ecology of Felids in a Neotropical Rainforest. *Behavioral Ecology and Sociobiology* 20(4): 271–283.

Evans, Susan Toby. 2015. Procesiones en Teotihuacan Agua y Tierra. *Arqueologia Mexicana* 22(131): 48–53.

Evans, Susan Toby. 2016. Location and Orientation of Teotihuacan, Mexico: Water Worship and Processional Space. *Occasional Papers in Anthropology at Penn State* 33: 52–121.

Evans, Susan Toby, and Deborah L. Nichols. 2016. Water Temples and Civic Engineering at Teotihuacan, Mexico. In *Human Adaptation in Ancient Mesoamerica: Empirical Approaches to Mesoamerican Archaeology*, edited by Nancy Gonlin and Kirk D. French, pp. 25–61. Boulder: University Press of Colorado.

Evans-Pritchard, E. E. 1967. *Nuer Religion*. Oxford: Clarendon Press,.

Fash, William L., and Barbara W. Fash. 1996. Building a World-View: Visual Communication in Classic Maya Architecture. *RES: Anthropology and Aesthetics* 29/30: 127–147. DOI:10.2307/20166946.

Fash, William L., and Leonardo López Luján, eds. 2009. *The Art of Urbanism: How Mesoamerican Kingdoms Represented Themselves in Architecture and Imagery*. Washington, DC: Dumbarton Oaks Research Library and Collection.

Fash, William L., Alexandre Tokovinine, and Barbara W. Fash. 2009. The House of New Fire at Teotihuacan and its Legacy in Mesoamerica. In *The Art of Urbanism: How Mesoamerican Kingdoms Represented Themselves in Architecture and Imagery*, edited by William L. Fash and Leonardo López Luján, pp. 201–229. Washington, DC: Dumbarton Oaks Research Library and Collection.

Fausto, Carlos. 2012. Too Many Owners: Mastery and Ownership in Amazonia. In *Animism in Rainforest and Tundra: Personhood, Animals, Plants and Things in Contemporary Amazonia and Siberia*, edited by Marc Brightman, Vanessa Elisa Grotti, and Olga Ulturgasheva, pp. 29–47. New York: Berghahn Books.

Fewkes, J. Walter. 1900. Property-Right in Eagles Among the Hopi. *American Anthropologist* 2(4): 690–707. DOI:10.1525/aa.1900.2.4.02a00070.

Fikes, Jay C. 1985. Huichol Indian Identity and Adaptation: Ritual, Shamanism, Ecology. Unpublished PhD diss., University of Michigan.

Filloy Nadal, Laura, Maria Eugenia Gumi, and Yuki Watanabe. 2006. La Restauracion de una Figura Antropomorfa Teotihuacana de Mosaico de Serpentina. In *Sacrificios de Consagración en la Pirámide de la Luna*, edited by Saburo Sugiyama and Leonardo López Luján, pp. 61–78. México, D.F.: Instituo Nacional de Antropología e Historia, Museo de Templo Mayor, Arizona State University.

Fischer, Albert. 2007. Computerized Bone Templates as the Basis of a Practical Procedure to Record and Analyze Graphical Zooarchaeological Data. *Revista Electrónica de Arqueología PUCP* 2(1):1–10.

Fiskesjö, Magnus. 2001. Rising from Blood-Stained Fields: Royal Hunting and State Formation in Shang China. *Bulletin of the Museum of Far Eastern Antiquities* 73: 48–191.

Fogelin, Lars. 2007. The Archaeology of Religious Ritual. *Annual Review of Anthropology* 36: 55–71.

Fogelin, Lars. 2008. Introduction: Methods for the Archaeology of Religion. In *Religion, Archaeology, and the Material World*, edited by Lars Fogelin, 36: pp. 1–14. Center for Archaeological Investigations. Carbondale: Southern Illinois University Carbondale.

Foucault, Michel. 1980. *Power/Knowledge: Selected Interviews and Other Writings, 1972–1977*. Translated by Colin Gordon. 1st American. New York: Pantheon Books.

Fowles, Severin M. 2013. *An Archaeology of Doings: Secularism and the Study of Pueblo Religion*. 1st ed. Santa Fe: School for Advanced Research Press.

France, Christine A. M., Nawa Sugiyama, and Esther Aguayo. 2020. Establishing a Preservation Index for Bone, Dentin, and Enamel Bioapatite Mineral Using ATR-FTIR. *Journal of Archaeological Science: Reports* 33: 102551. DOI:10.1016/j.jasrep.2020.102551.

Freidel, David A., Hector L. Escobedo, and Stanley P. Guenter. 2007. A Crossroads of Conquerors: Waka' and Gordon Willey's "Rehearsal for the Collapse" Hypothesis. In *Gordon R. Willey and American Archaeology: Contemporary Perspectives*, edited by Jeremy A. Sabloff and William Leonard Fash, pp. 187–208. Norman: University of Oklahoma Press.

Freidel, David A., Olivia C. Navarro-Farr, Michelle E. Rich, Juan Carlos Meléndez, Juan Carlos Pérez, Griselda Pérez Robles, and Mary Kate Kelly. 2023. Classic Maya Mirror Conjurors of Waka', Guatemala. *Ancient Mesoamerica*: 1–23. DOI:10.1017/S0956536122000141.

Freidel, David A., and Linda Schele. 1989. Dead Kings and Living Temples: Dedication and Termination Rituals Among the Ancient Maya. In *Word and Image in Maya Culture: Explorations in Language, Writing, and Representation*, edited by William F. Hanks and Don Stephen Rice, pp. 223–243. Salt Lake City: University of Utah Press.

Fritts, Steven H., Robert O. Stephenson, Robert D. Hays, and Luigi Boitani. 2003. Wolves and Humans. In *Wolves: Behavior, Ecology and Conservation*, edited by L. David Mech and Luigi Boitani, pp. 289–316. Chicago: University of Chicago Press.

Froehle, A. W., C. M. Kellner, and M. J. Schoeninger. 2010. FOCUS: Effect of Diet and Protein Source on Carbon Stable Isotope Ratios in Collagen: Follow up to Warinner and Tuross (2009). *Journal of Archaeological Science* 37(10): 2662–2670. DOI:10.1016/j.jas.2010.06.003.

Froehle, A. W., C. M. Kellner, and M. J. Schoeninger. 2012. Multivariate Carbon and Nitrogen Stable Isotope Model for the Reconstruction of Prehistoric Human Diet. *American Journal of Physical Anthropology* 147(3): 352–369. DOI:10.1002/ajpa.21651.

Fuente, Beatriz de la, ed. 1995a. *La Pintura Mural Prehispánica en México, I Teotihuacan*. Vol. V.1. México, D.F.: Universidad Nacional Autónoma de México, Instituto de Investigaciones Estéticas.

Fuente, Beatriz de la. 1995b. Zona 4: Animales Mitológicos. In *La Pintura Mural Prehispánica en México, I Teotihuacan*, edited by Beatriz de la Fuente, Vol. 1: pp. 92–101. México, D.F.: Universidad Nacional Autónoma de México, Instituto de Investigaciones Estéticas.

Fuente, Beatriz de la. 1995c. Zone 3: Gran Puma. In *La Pintura Mural Prehispánica en México, I Teotihuacan*, edited by Beatriz de la Fuente, Vol. 1: pp. 83–85. México, D.F.: Universidad Nacional Autónoma de México, Instituto de Investigaciones Estéticas.

Furst, Peter T. 1968. The Olmec Were-Jaguar Motif in the Light of Ethnographic Reality. In *Dumbarton Oaks Conference on the Olmec*, edited by Elizabeth P. Benson, pp. 143–175. Washington, DC: Dumbarton Oaks Research Library and Collection.

Gamio, Manuel. 1922. *La Poblacion del Valle de Teotihuacan*. Vol. I. México, D.F.: Dirección de Talleres Graficos de la Secretaría de Fomento.

García-Des Lauriers, Claudia. 2008. The House of Darts: The Classic Period Origins of the Tlacochcalco. *Mesoamerican Voices* 3: 35–52.

García-Des Lauriers, Claudia, and Tatsuya Murakami, eds. 2022. *Teotihuacan and Early Classic Mesoamerica: Multiscalar Perspectives on Power, Identity, and Interregional Relations*. Boulder: University Press of Colorado.

Garza, Mercedes de la. 2001. La Serpiente en la Religión Maya. In *Animales y Plantas en la Cosmovisión Mesoamericana*, edited by Yólotl González Torres, pp. 145–157. México, D.F.: Plaza y Valdés Editores: Instituto Nacional de Antropología e Historia: Sociedad Mexicana para el Estudio de las Religiones.

Gay, Samantha W., and Troy L. Best. 1996. Age-Related Variation in Skulls of the Puma (*Puma concolor*). *Journal of Mammalogy* 77(1): 191–198.

Gazzola, Julie. 2009. Características Arquitectónicas de Algunas Construcciones de Fases Tempranas en Teotihuacán. *Arqueología* 42: 216–233.

Gazzola, Julie. 2017. Reappraising Architectural Processes at the Ciudadela Through Recent Evidence. In *Teotihuacan: City of Water, City of Fire*, edited by Matthew Robb, pp. 38–47. San Francisco, CA: Fine Arts Museum of San Francisco in association with University of California Press.

Gazzola, Julie, and Sergio Gómez. 2020. La Relación Entre las Élites de Teotihuacán y las de las Tierras Altas Mayas Durante el Primer Siglo de Nuestra Era en Teotihuacan y el Área Maya. In *Memorias del XXXIII Simposio de Investigaciones Arqueológicas en Guatemala*, edited by Bárbara Arroyo, Luis Méndez Salinas, and Gloria Ajú Álvarez, pp. 45–60. Ciudad de Guatemala: Museo Nacional de Arqueología y Etnología, Ministro de Cultura y Deportes, Instituto de Antropología e Historia, Asociación Tikal.

Geertz, Clifford. 1973. *The Interpretation of Cultures*. 1st ed. New York: Basic Books.

Giddings, Ruth Warner. 1959. *Yaqui Myths and Legends*. Vol. 2. Anthropological Papers of the University of Arizona. Tucson: University of Arizona.

Gifford-Gonzalez, Diane. 2018. *An Introduction to Zooarchaeology*. Cham, Switzerland: Springer.

Goepfert, Nicolas. 2012. New Zooarchaeologial and Funerary Perspectives on Mochica Culture (A.D. 100–800), Peru. *Journal of Field Archaeology* 37(2): 104–120.

Gómez Chávez, Sergio. 2002. Presencia del Occidente de México en Teotihuacan. Aproximaciones a la Política e Ideología. In *Ideología y Política a Través de Materiales, Imágenes y Símbolos*, edited by María Elena Ruiz Gallut, pp. 563–626. México, D.F.: Memoria de la Primera Mesa Redonda de Teotihuacan. Universidad Nacional Autónoma de México Instituto Nacional de Antropología e Historia.

Gómez Chávez, Sergio. 2013. The Exploration of the Tunnel Under the Feathered Serpent Temple at Teotihuacan. First Results. In *Constructing, Deconstructing, and Reconstructing Social Identity- 2,000 years of Monumentality in Teotihuacan and Cholula, Mexico*, edited by Saburo Sugiyama, Shigeru Kabata, Tomoko Taniguchi, and Etsuko Niwa, pp. 11–18. Aichi, Japan: Cultural Symbiosis Research Institute, Aichi Prefectural University.

Gómez Chávez, Sergio. 2017. The Underworld at Teotihuacan: The Sacred Cave Under the Feathered Serpent Pyramid. In *Teotihuacan: City of Water, City of Fire*, edited by Matthew Robb, pp. 48–55. San Francisco, CA: Fine Arts Museum of San Francisco in association with University of California Press.

Gompper, Matthew. 2002. The Ecology of Northeast Coyotes: Current Knowledge and Priorities for Future Research. *Wildlife Conservation Society Working Paper* 17: 1–48.

Gordon, Seton. 1955. *The Golden Eagle: King of Birds*. London: Collins.

Gossen, Gary H. 1975. Animal Souls and Human Destiny in Chamula. *Man* 10(3): 448–461.

Gossen, Gary H. 1979. Temporal and Spatial Equivalents in Chamula Ritual Symbolism. In *Reader in Comparative Religion: An Anthropological Approach*, edited by William A. Lessa and Evon Z. Vogt, pp. 116–129. 4th ed. New York: Harper & Row.

Gossen, Gary H. 1994. From Olmecs to Zapatistas: A Once and Future History of Souls. *American Anthropologist* 96(3): 553–570.

Grigione, M. M., P. Beier, R. A. Hopkins, D. Neal, W. D. Padley, C. M. Schonewald, and M. L. Johnson. 2002. Ecological and Allometric Determinants of Home-range Size for Mountain Lions (*Puma concolor*). *Animal Conservation* 5: 317–324.

Grove, David C. 1972. Olmec Felines in Highland Central Mexico. In *The Cult of the Feline, A Conference in Pre-Columbian Iconography*, edited by Elizabeth P. Benson, pp. 153–164. Washington, DC: Dumbarton Oakes Research Library and Collection.

Grube, Nikolai, and Sergio Gómez Chávez. 2017. Preliminary Iconographic Study of the Shell Trumpets from the Tlalocan Project. In *Teotihuacan: City of Water, City of Fire*, edited by Matthew Robb, p. 248. San Francisco, CA: Fine Arts Museum of San Francisco in association with Univ of California Press.

Hall, E. Raymond. 1981. *The Mammals of North America*. Vol. I. New York: Wiley.

Hallowell, A. Irving. 2002. Ojibwa Ontology, Behavior, and World View. In *Readings in Indigenous Religions*, edited by Graham Harvey, pp. 17–49. London: Continuum.

Hamerton-Kelly, Robert. 1987. *Violent Origins: Walter Burkert, René Girard and Jonathan Z. Smith on Ritual Killing and Cultural Formation*. Stanford, CA: Stanford University Press.

Haraway, Donna Jeanne. 2003. *The Companion Species Manifesto: Dogs, People, and Significant Otherness*. Paradigm 8. Chicago: Prickly Paradigm Press.

Hargrave, Lyndon Lane. 1970. *Mexican Macaws: Comparative Osteology and Survey of Remains from the Southwest*. Vol. 20. Tucson: Anthropological Papers of the University of Arizona. University of Arizona Press.

Harmata, Al, and George Montopoli. 2013. Morphometric Sex Determination of North American Golden Eagles. *Journal of Raptor Research* 47(2): 108–116. DOI:10.3356/jrr-12-28.1.

Harrison-Buck, Eleanor. 2018. Relational Matters of Being: Personhood and Agency in Archaeology. In *Relational Identities and Other-than-Human Agency in Archaeology*, edited by Julia A. Hendon and Eleanor Harrison-Buck, pp. 263–282. Boulder: University Press of Colorado.

Harrison-Buck, Eleanor, and David A. Freidel. 2021. Reassessing Shamanism and Animism in the Art and Archaeology of Ancient Mesoamerica. *Religions* 12(6): 394. DOI:10.3390/rel12060394.

Harrison-Buck, Eleanor, and Julia A. Hendon. 2018. An Introduction to Relational Personhood and Other-than-Human Agency in Archaeology. In *Relational Identities and Other-Than-Human Agency in Archaeology*, edited by Julia A. Hendon and Eleanor Harrison-Buck, pp. 3–28. Boulder: University Press of Colorado.

Headrick, Annabeth. 2007. *The Teotihuacan Trinity: The Sociopolitical Structure of an Ancient Mesoamerican City*. 1st ed. William & Bettye Nowlin Series in Art, History, and Culture of the Western Hemisphere. Austin: University of Texas Press.

Heffelfinger, James R., Ronald M. Nowak, and David Paetkau. 2017. Clarifying Historical Range to Aid Recovery of the Mexican Wolf. *The Journal of Wildlife Management* 81(5): 766–777. DOI:10.1002/jwmg.21252.

Helmke, Christophe, and Jesper Nielsen. 2014. If Mountains Could Speak: Ancient Toponyms recorded at Teotihuacan, Mexico. *Contributions in New World Archaeology* 7: 73–112.

Hendon, Julia A., and Eleanor Harrison-Buck. 2018. *Relational Identities and Other-than-Human Agency in Archaeology*. Boulder: University Press of Colorado.

Henninger, Joseph. 2005. Sacrifice. In *Encyclopedia of Religion*, edited by Lindsay Jones, pp. 7997–8008. Detroit, MI: Macmillan.

Herron, Gary B., Craig A. Mortimore, and Marcus S. Rawlings.1985. *Nevada Raptors: Their Biology and Management*. Vol. 8. Department of Wildlife Biological Bulletin. Reno: Nevada Department of Wildlife.

Heyden, Doris. 1975. An Interpretation of the Cave Underneath the Pyramid of the Sun in Teotihuacan, Mexico. *American Antiquity* 40(2): 131–147.

Heyden, Doris. 1981. Caves, Gods, and Mythos: World-View and Planning in Teotihuacan. In *Mesoamerican Sites and World-Views*, edited by Elizabeth P. Benson, pp. 1–35. Washington, DC: Dumbarton Oaks Research Library and Collections.

Hidalgo Mihart, Mircea, Lisette Cantú Salazar, Alberto González Romero, and Carlos A. López González. 2004. Historical and Present Distribution of Coyote (*Canis latrans*) in Mexico and Central America. *Journal of Biogeography* 31: 2025–2038.

Hill, Erica. 2000. The Contextual Analysis of Animal Interments and Ritual Practice in Southwestern North America. *Kiva* 65(4): 361–398.

Hill, Erica. 2011. Animals as Agents: Hunting Ritual and Relational Ontologies in Prehistoric Alaska and Chukotka. *Cambridge Archaeological Journal* 21(3): 407–426. DOI:10.1017/S0959774311000448.

Hill, Erica. 2013. Archaeology and Animal Persons: Toward a Prehistory of Human-Animal Relations. *Environment and Society: Advances in Research* 4: 117–136.

Hill, Erica. 2018. Personhood and Agency in Eskimo Interactions with the Other-than-Human. In *Relational Identities and Other-Than-Human Agency in Archaeology*, edited by Julia A. Hendon and Eleanor Harrison-Buck, pp. 29–50. Boulder: University Press of Colorado.

Hill, Robert M. 1992. *Colonial Cakchiquels: Highland Maya Adaptations to Spanish Rule, 1600-1700*. Case Studies in Cultural Anthropology. Fort Worth, TX: Harcourt Brace Jovanovich.

Hirsch, Eric, and Michael O'Hanlon, eds. 1995. *The Anthropology of Landscape: Perspectives on Place and Space*. Oxford Studies in Social and Cultural Anthropology. Oxford: Oxford University Press.

Hirth, Kenneth G. 2003. The Altepetl and Urban Structure in Prehispanic Mesoamerica. In *El Urbanismo en Mesoamérica: Urbanism in Mesoamerica*, edited by William T. Sanders, Alba Guadalupe Mastache de Escobar, and Robert H. Cobean, pp. 57–84. México D.F.: Instituto Nacional de Antropología e Historia.

Hirth, Kenneth G. 2020. Teotihuacan Economy from the Inside-Out. In *Teotihuacan: The World Beyond the City*, edited by Kenneth G. Hirth, David M. Carballo, and Barbara Arroyo, pp. 97–136. Washington, DC: Dumbarton Oakes Research Library and Collection.

Hirth, Kenneth G., David M. Carballo, and Barbara Arroyo, eds. 2020. *Teotihuacan: The World Beyond the City*. Washington, DC: Dumbarton Oakes Research Library and Collection.

Hockett, Bryan Scott. 1996. Corroded, Thinned and Polished Bones Created by Golden Eagles (*Aquila chrysaetos*): Taphonomic Implications for Archaeological Interpretations. *Journal of Archaeological Science* 23: 587–591.

Hodder, Ian. 2012. *Entangled: An Archaeology of the Relationships Between Humans and Things*. Hoboken, NJ: John Wiley & Sons.

Hofman, Courtney A., Karissa S. Hughes, and Robin R. Singleton. 2023. Análisis Paleogenómico de Restos de Cánidos de Teotihuacan. In *Proyecto Complejo Plaza de las Columnas, Teotihuacan, Informe Parcial de la Sexta Temporada (2022)*, edited by Nawa Sugiyama, Saburo Sugiyama, and Luis Rogelio Rivero Chong, pp. 583–598. Mexico City, Mexico: Technical Report in Archivo Técnico de la Coordinación de Arqueología, Instituto Nacional de Antropologia e Historia.

Holland, William R. 1964. Contemporary Tzotzil Cosmological Concepts as a Basis for Interpreting Prehistoric Maya Civilization. *American Antiquity* 29(3): 301–306.

Houston, Stephen D., ed. 1998. *Function and Meaning in Classic Maya Architecture: A Symposium at Dumbarton Oaks, 7th and 8th October 1994*. Washington, DC: Dumbarton Oaks Research Library and Collection.

Houston, Stephen, Edwin Román Ramírez, Thomas G. Garrison, David Stuart, Héctor Escobedo Ayala, and Pamela Rosales. 2021. A Teotihuacan Complex at the Classic Maya City of Tikal, Guatemala. *Antiquity* 95(384):e32, 1–9. DOI:10.15184/aqy.2021.140, accessed May 20, 2022.

Houston, Stephen D., David Stuart, and Karl A. Taube. 2006. *The Memory of Bones: Body, Being, and Experience Among the Classic Maya*. 1st ed. Joe R. and Teresa Lozano Long Series in Latin American and Latino Art and Culture. Austin: University of Texas Press.

Howell, Steve N. G., and Sophie Webb. 1995. *A Guide to the Birds of Mexico and Northern Central America*. Oxford: Oxford University Press.

Hruby, Zachary X. 2007. Ritualized Chipped-Stone Production at Piedras Negras, Guatemala. Edited by Zachary X. Hruby, Rowan K. Flad, and Gwen Patrice Bennett. *Rethinking Craft Specialization in Complex Societies: Archeological Analyses of the Social Meaning of Production* 17: 68–87. Archeological Papers of the American Anthropological Association.

Hubert, Henri, and Marcel Mauss. 1964. *Sacrifice: Its Nature and Function.* Chicago: University of Chicago Press.

Hunn, Eugene. 1982. The Utilitarian Factor in Folk Biological Classification. *American Anthropologist* 84(4): 830–847.

Ikram, Salima. 2005. *Divine Creatures: Animal Mummies in Ancient Egypt.* Cairo: American University in Cairo Press.

Ingold, Tim. 1986. *The Appropriation of Nature: Essays on Human Ecology and Social Relations.* Manchester, UK: Manchester University Press.

Ingold, Tim. 1988a. Introduction. In *What Is an Animal?*, edited by Tim Ingold, pp. 1–16. London: Unwin Hyman.

Ingold, Tim, ed. 1988b. *What Is an Animal?* London: Unwin Hyman.

Ingold, Tim. 2006. Rethinking the Animate, Re-animating Thought. *Ethnos* 71(1): 9–20. DOI:10.1080/00141840600603111.

Ingold, Tim. 2013. *Making: Anthropology, Archaeology, Art and Architecture.* London: Routledge.

Inomata, Takeshi. 2001. The Power and Ideology of Artistic Creation: Elite Craft Specialists in Classic Maya Society. *Current Anthropology* 42(3): 321–349.

Inomata, Takeshi. 2006. Plazas, Performers, and Spectators: Political Theaters of the Classic Maya. *Current Anthropology* 47(5): 805–842.

Inomata, Takeshi. 2014. War, Violence, and Society in the Maya Lowlands. In *Embattled Bodies, Embattled Places: War in Pre-Columbian Mesoamerica and the Andes*, edited by Andrew K. Scherer and John W. Verano, pp. 25–56. Washington, DC: Dumbarton Oaks Research Library and Collection.

Inomata, Takeshi, and Lawrence S. Coben. 2006a. Overture: An Invitation to the Archaeological Theater. In *Archaeology of Performance: Theaters of Power, Community, and Politics*, edited by Takeshi Inomata and Lawrence S. Coben, pp. 11–44. Lanham, MD: Altamira Press.

Inomata, Takeshi, and Lawrence S. Coben, eds. 2006b. *Archaeology of Performance: Theaters of Power, Community, and Politics.* Lanham, MD: Altamira Press.

Inomata, Takeshi, and Stephen D. Houston, eds. 2000. *Royal Courts of the Ancient Maya.* Boulder, CO: Westview Press.

Insoll, Timothy. 2004. *Archaeology, Ritual, Religion.* Themes in Archaeology. London: Routledge.

Isidro Luna, Xóchitl. 2007. Estudio Morfológico del Cráneo del Jaguar (*Panthera onca*) de México. Unpublished BA thesis, Universidad Nacional Autónoma de México.

Jackson, Hartley H. T. 1951. Classification of the Races of the Coyote. In *The Clever Coyote*, edited by Stanley P. Young and Harthley H. T. Jackson, pp. 227–341. Harrisburg, VA: The Stackpole Company.

Jones, Andrew. 1998. Where Eagles Dare: Landscape, Animals and the Neolithic of Orkney. *Journal of Material Culture* 3(2): 301–324.

Joyce, Arthur A. 2020. Assembling the City: Monte Alban as a Mountain of Creation and Sustenance. In *New Materialisms Ancient Urbanisms*, edited by Timothy R. Pauketat and Susan M. Alt, pp. 65–93. Abingdon, Oxon: Routledge.

Joyce, Rosemary A. 1992. Ideology in Action: Classic Maya Ritual Practice. In *Ancient Images, Ancient Thought: The Archaeology of Ideology*, edited by A. Sean Goldsmith, Sandra Garvie, David Selin, and Jeannette Smith, pp. 497–505. Proceedings of the Twenty-third Annual Conference of the Archaeological Association of the University of Calgary. Calgary: University of Calgary Archaeological Association.

Joyce, Rosemary A. 2005. Archaeology of the Body. *Annual Review of Anthropology* 34(1): 139–158. DOI:10.1146/annurev.anthro.33.070203.143729.

Keane, Webb. 2018. Killing Animals: On the Violence of Sacrifice, the Hunt and the Butcher. *Anthropology of this Century* 22:1 –5.

Keeling, Charles D. 1979. The Suess Effect: 13Carbon-14Carbon Interrelations. *Environment International* 2(4): 229–300. DOI:10.1016/0160-4120(79)90005-9.

Kelley, David H. 1955. Quetzalcoatl and His Coyote Origins. *El Mexico Antiguo, Revista Internacional de Arqueologia, Etnologia, Folklore, Prehistoria, Historia Antigua y Linguistica Mexicanas* VIII: 397–413.

Kellner, Corina M., and Margaret J. Schoeninger. 2007. A Simple Carbon Isotope Model for Reconstructing Prehistoric Human Diet. *American Journal of Physical Anthropology* 133: 1112–1127.

Kelly, Jeffrey F. 2000. Stable Isotopes of Carbon and Nitrogen in the Study of Avian and Mammalian Trophic Ecology. *Canadian Journal of Zoology* 78(1): 1–27. DOI:10.1139/z99-165.

Kertzer, David I. 1991. The Role of Ritual in State-Formation. In *Religious Regimes and State-Formation: Perspective from European Ethnology*, edited by Eric R. Wolf, pp. 85–103. Albany: State University of New York Press.

Khatchadourian, Lori, 2016. *Imperial Matter Ancient Persia and the Archaeology of Empires*. Oakland: University of California Press.

Kimura, Takeshi. 1999. Bearing the "Bare Facts" of Ritual: A Critique of Jonathan Z. Smith's Study of the Bear Ceremony Based on a Study of the Ainu Iyomante. *Numen* 46(1): 88–114. DOI:10.2307/3270292.

Knapp, Arthur Bernard, and Wendy Ashmore. 1999. Archaeological Landscapes: Constructed, Conceptualized, Ideational. In *Archaeologies of Landscape: Contemporary Perspectives*, edited by Wendy Ashmore and Arthur Bernard Knapp, pp. 1–30. Malden, MA: Blackwell.

Kowalski, Jeff K. 1999. Natural Order, Social Order, Political Legitimacy, and the Sacred City: The Architecture of Teotihuacan. In *Mesoamerican Architecture as a Cultural Symbol*, edited by Jeff K. Kowalski, pp. 76–109. Oxford: Oxford University Press.

Krueger, Harold W., and Charles H. Sullivan. 1984. Models for Carbon Isotope Fractionation Between Diet and Bone. *Stable Isotopes in Nutrition* 258: 205–220.

Kubler, George. 1972. Jaguars in the Valley of Mexico. In *The Cult of the Feline*, edited by Elizabeth P. Benson, pp. 19–49. Washington, DC: Dumbarton Oaks Research Library and Collections.

Kyriakidis, Evangelos, ed. 2007a. *The Archaeology of Ritual*. Vol. 3. Cotsen Advanced Seminars. Los Angeles: Cotsen Institute of Archaeology, University of California, Los Angeles.

Kyriakidis, Evangelos, 2007b. Archaeologies of Ritual. In *The Archaeology of Ritual*, edited by Evangelos Kyriakidis, pp. 289–308. Los Angeles: Cotsen Institute of Archaeology, University of California, Los Angeles.

LaDuke, Thomas C. 1991. The Fossil Snakes of Pit 91, Rancho La. Brea, California. *Contributions in Science* 424:1–28.

Latour, Bruno. 2000. The Berlin Key of How to Do Words with Things. In *Matter, Materiality, and Modern Culture*, edited by Paul Graves-Brown, pp. 10–21. London: Routledge.

Latour, Bruno. 2005. *Reassembling the Social an Introduction to Actor-Network-Theory*. Clarendon Lectures in Management Studies. Oxford: Oxford University Press.

Leach, Edmund. 1964. Anthropological Aspects of Language: Animal Categories and Verbal Abuse. In *New Directions in the Study of Language*, edited by Eric H. Lenneberg, pp. 23–63. Cambridge, MA: The Massachusetts Institute of Technology Press.

Leopold, Starker A. 1972. *Wildlife of Mexico: The Game Birds and Mammals*. Los Angeles: University of California Press, Berkeley.

Lévi-Strauss, Claude. 1955. The Structural Study of Myth. *The Journal of American Folklore* 68(270): 428–444.

Lévi-Strauss, Claude. 1966. *The Savage Mind*. The Nature of Human Society Series. Chicago: University of Chicago Press.

Linné, Sigvald. 1942. *Mexican Highland Cultures: Archaeological Researches at Teotihuacan, Calpulalpan and Chalchicomula in 1934/35*. 7. Lund, Sweden: The Ethnographical Museum of Sweden, Stockholm.

Lipe, William D., R. Kyle Bocinsky, Brian S. Chisholm, Robin Lyle, David M. Dove, R. G. Matson, Elizabeth Jarvis, Kathleen Judd, and Brian M. Kemp. 2016. Cultural and Genetic Contexts for Early Turkey Domestication in the Northern Southwest. *American Antiquity* 81(1): 97–113.

López Austin, Alfredo. 1973. *Hombre-Dios: Religión y Política en el Mundo Náhuatl*. 1st. ed. Serie de cultura nahuatl. Monografías, 15. México, D.F.: Universidad Nacional Autónoma de México, Instituto de Investigaciones Históricas.

López Austin, Alfredo. 1988. *The Human Body and Ideology: Concepts of the Ancient Nahuas*. Vol. 1. Salt Lake City: University of Utah Press.

López Austin, Alfredo. 1993. *The Myths of the Opossum: Pathways of Mesoamerican Mythology*. 1st ed. Albuquerque: University of New Mexico Press.

López Austin, Alfredo, and Leonardo López Luján. 2009. *Monte Sagrado: Templo Mayor*. México, D.F.: Instituto Nacional de Antropología e Historia, Universidad Nacional Autónoma de México.

López Austin, Alfredo, Leonardo López Luján, and Saburo Sugiyama. 1991. The Temple of Quetzalcoatl at Teotihuacan: Its Possible Ideological Significance. *Ancient Mesoamerica* 2: 93–105.

López Luján, Leonardo. 2005. *The Offerings of the Templo Mayor of Tenochtitlan*. Albuquerque: University of New Mexico Press.

López Luján, Leonardo. 2017. Life After Death in Teotihuacan: The Moon Plaza's Monoliths in Colonial and Modern Mexico. In *Visual Culture of the Ancient Americas: Contemporary Perspectives*, edited by Andrew Finegold and Ellen Hoobler, pp. 59–74. Norman: University of Oklahoma Press.

López Luján, Leonardo, Alejandra Aguirre Molina, and Israel Elizalde Mendez. 2022. Vestidos para Matar: Animales Ataviados en las Ofrendas del Recinto Sagrado de Tenochtitlan. In *Los Animales y el Recinto Sagrado de Tenochtitlan*, edited by Leonardo López Luján and Eduardo Matos Moctezuma, pp. 183–225. Ciudad de México, México: El Colegio Nacional.

López Luján, Leonardo, Ximena Chávez Balderas, Zúñiga-Arellano, Alejandra Aguirre Molina, and Norma Valentín Maldonado. 2012. Un Portal al Inframundo: Ofrendas de Animales Sepultadas al Pie del Templo Mayor de Tenochtitlan. *Estudios de Cultura Náhuatl* 44: 9–40.

López Luján, Leonardo, Ximena Chávez Balderas, Zúñiga-Arellano, Alejandra Aguirre Molina, and Norma Valentín Maldonado. 2014. Entering the Underworld: Animal Offerings at the Foot of the Great Temple of Tenochtitlan. In *Animals and Inequality in the Ancient World*, edited by Sue Ann McCarty and Benjamin Arbuckle, pp. 33–61. Boulder: University Press of Colorado.

López Luján, Leonardo, and Eduardo Matos Moctezuma. 2022. *Los Animales y el Recinto Sagrado de Tenochtitlan*. Primera edición. Ciudad de México, México: El Colegio Nacional.

López Luján, Leonardo, and Guilhem Olivier. 2010. *El Sacrificio Humano en la Tradición Religiosa Mesoamericana*. México, D.F.: Instituto Nacional de Antropología e Historia, Universidad Nacional Autónoma de México.

López Luján, Leonardo, and Saburo Sugiyama. 2017. The Ritual Deposits in the Moon Pyramid at Teotihuacan. In *Teotihuacan: City of Water, City of Fire*, edited by Matthew Robb, pp. 82–89. San Francisco: Fine Arts Museum of San Francisco in association with University of California Press.

Losey, Robert J., Vladimir I. Bazaliiskii, Sandra Garvie-Lok, Mietje Germonpré, Jennifer A. Leonard, Andrew L. Allen, M. Anne Katzenberg, and Mikhail V. Sablin. 2011. Canids as Persons: Early Neolithic Dog and Wolf Burials, Cis-Baikal, Siberia. *Journal of Anthropological Archaeology* 30(2): 174–189. DOI:10.1016/j.jaa.2011.01.001.

Losey, Robert J., Vladimir I. Bazaliiskii, Angela R. Lieverse, Andrea Waters-Rist, Kate Faccia, and Andrzej W. Weber. 2013. The Bear-able Likeness of Being: Ursine Remains at the Shamanka II Cemetery, Lake Baikal, Siberia. In *Relational Archaeologies: Humans, Animals, Things*, edited by Christopher M. Watts, pp. 65–96. London: Routledge.

Lumholtz, Carl. 1945. *El México Desconocido: Cinco Años de Exploración entre las Tribus de la Sierra Madre Occidental, en la Tierra Caliente de Tepic y Jalisco, y entre los Tarascos de Michoacán*. Ed. ilustrada. Vol. V.I. México, D.F.: Publicaciones Herrerias.

Manzanilla, Linda. 1997. Teotihuacan: Urban Archetype, Cosmic Model. In *Emergence and Change in Early Urban Societies*, edited by Linda Manzanilla, pp. 109–168. New York: Plenum Press.

Manzanilla, Linda R. 2001. Gobierno Corporativo en Teotihuacan: Una Revisión del Concepto "Palacio" Aplicado a la Gran Urbe Prehispánica. *Anales de Antropología* 35: 157–190.

Manzanilla, Linda R., ed. 2017. *Multiethnicity and Migration at Teopancazco: Investigations of a Teotihuacan Neighborhood Center*. Gainesville: University Press of Florida.

Manzanilla, Linda R., Luis Barba, René Chávez, Andrés Tejero, Gerardo Cifuentes, and Nayeli Peralta. 1994. Caves and Geophysics: An Approximation to the Underworld of Teotihuacan, Mexico. *Archaeometry* 36(1): 141–157.

Marcus, Joyce. 2020. Maya Usurpers. In *A Forest of History: The Maya after the Emergence of Divine Kingship*, edited by Travis W. Stanton and M. Kathryn Brown, pp. 49–66. Louisville: University Press of Colorado.

Marean, Curtis W., Yoshiko Abe, Peter J. Nilssen, and Elizabeth C. Stone. 2001. Estimating the Minimum Number of Skeletal Elements (MNE) in Zooarchaeology: A Review and a New Image-Analysis GIS Approach. *American Antiquity* 66(2): 333–348.

Matos Moctezuma, Eduardo. 1986. *Vida y Muerte en el Templo Mayor*. 1a ed. Ediciones Océano, Mexico, D.F. 1995 *La Pirámide del Sol, Teotihuacán: Antología*. México, D.F.: Artes de México.

Matos Moctezuma, Eduardo. 1999. The Templo Mayor of Tenochtitlan: Cosmic Center of the Aztec Universe. In *Mesoamerican Architecture as a Cultural Symbol*, edited by Jeff K. Kowalski, pp. 199–219. Oxford: Oxford University Press.

McAnany, Patricia Ann. 1998. Ancestors and the Classic Maya Built Environment. In *Function and Meaning in Classic Maya Architecture: A Symposium at Dumbarton Oaks, 7th and 8th October 1994*, edited by Stephen D. Houston, pp. 271–298. Washington, DC: Dumbarton Oaks Research Library and Collection.

McAnany, Patricia Ann. 2008. Shaping Social Difference: Political and Ritual Economy of Classic Maya Royal Courts. In *Dimensions of Ritual Economy*, edited by E. Christian Wells and Patricia Ann McAnany, vol. 27: pp. 219–247. Research in Economic Anthropology. Bingley, UK: JAI Press.

McAnany, Patricia Ann, and E. Christian Wells. 2008. Toward a Theory of Ritual Economy. In *Dimensions of Ritual Economy*, edited by E. Christian Wells and Patricia Ann McAnany, v. 27: pp. 1–16. Research in Economic Anthropology. Bingley, UK: JAI Press.

McClung de Tapia, Emily, and Nawa Sugiyama. 2012. Conservando la Diversidad Biocultural de México: El Uso de Algunas Plantas y Animales en el Pasado y Presente. *Arqueología Mexicana* XIX(114): 20–25.

McKusick, Charmion R. 2001. *Southwest Birds of Sacrifice*. The Arizona Archaeologist. Globe: Arizona Archaeological Society.

McNiven, Ian J. 2010. Navigating the Human-Animal Divide: Marine Mammal Hunters and Rituals of Sensory Allurement. *World Archaeology* 42(2): 215–230.

Mech, L. David, and Luigi Boitani. 2003. Wolf Social Ecology. In *Wolves: Behavior, Ecology, and Conservation*, edited by L. David Mech and Luigi Boitani, pp. 1–34. Chicago: University of Chicago Press.

van der Merwe, Nikolaas J. 1982. Carbon Isotopes, Photosynthesis, and Archaeology: Different Pathways of Photosynthesis Cause Characteristic Changes in Carbon Isotope Ratios that Make Possible the Study of Prehistoric Human Diets. *American Scientist* 70(6): 596–606. DOI:10.2307/27851731.

van der Merwe, Nikolaas J., and Donald H. Avery. 1987. Science and Magic in African Technology: Traditional Iron Smelting in Malawi. *Africa: Journal of the International African Institute* 57(2): 143–172.

Meskell, Lynn. 2008. The Nature of the Beast: Curating Animals and Ancestors at Çatalhöyük. *World Archaeology* 40(3): 373–389.

Miller, Arthur G. 1967. The Birds of Quetzalpapalotl. *Ethnos* 1–4: 5–17.

Miller, Arthur G. 1973. *The Mural Painting of Teotihuacán*. Washington, DC: Dumbarton Oaks.

Miller, Mary, and Karl Taube. 1993. *An Illustrated Dictionary of The Gods and Symbols of Ancient Mexico and the Maya*. London: Thames & Hudson.

Millon, Clara. 1973. Painting, Writing, and Polity in Teotihuacan, Mexico. *American Antiquity* 38(3): 294–314.

Millon, Clara. 1988a. A Reexamination of the Teotihuacan Tassel Headdress Insignia. In *Feathered Serpents and Flowering Trees: Reconstructing the Murals of Teotihuacan*, edited by Kathleen Berrin, pp. 114–134. Seattle: Fine Arts Museum of San Francisco.

Millon, Clara. 1988b. Coyote with Sacrificial Knife. In *Feathered Serpents and Flowering Trees: Reconstructing the Murals of Teotihuacan*, edited by Kathleen Berrin, pp. 207–217. Seattle: Fine Arts Museum of San Francisco.

Millon, Clara. 1988c. Coyotes and Deer. In *Feathered Serpents and Flowering Trees: Reconstructing the Murals of Teotihuacan*, edited by Kathleen Berrin, pp. 219–221. Seattle: Fine Arts Museum of San Francisco.

Millon, René. 1960. The Beginnings of Teotihuacan. *American Antiquity* 26(1): 1–10.

Millon, René. 1981. Teotihuacan: City, State, and Civilization. In *Supplement to the Handbook of Middle American Indians*, edited by Jeremy A. Sabloff, 1: pp. 198–243. Austin: University of Texas Press.

Millon, René. 1992. Teotihuacan Studies: From 1950 to 1990 and Beyond. In *Art, Ideology, and the City of Teotihuacan: A Symposium at Dumbarton Oaks, 8th and 9th October 1988*, edited by Janet Catherine Berlo, pp. 339–429. Washington, DC: Dumbarton Oaks Research Library and Collection.

Millon, René, and Bruce Drewitt. 1961. Earlier Structures within the Pyramid of the Sun at Teotihuacan. *American Antiquity* 26(3): 371–380.

Millon, René, Bruce Drewitt, and James A. Bennyhoff. 1965. The Pyramid of the Sun at Teotihuacán: 1959 Investigations. *Transactions of the American Philosophical Society* 55(6): 5–93.

Mills, Barbara J., and William H. Walker. 2008. *Memory Work: Archaeologies of Material Practices*. School for Advanced Research Advanced Seminar Series. Santa Fe, NM: School for Advanced Research Press.

Monaghan, John. 1998. Dedication: Ritual or Production? In *The Sowing and the Dawning: Termination, Dedication, and Transformation in the Archaeological and Ethnographic Record of Mesoamerica*, edited by Shirley Boteler Mock, pp. 47–52. Albuquerque: University of New Mexico Press.

Montiel, Lisa M. 2010. Teotihuacan Imperialism in the Yautepec Valley, Morelos. Unpublished PhD diss., State University of New York at Albany.

Montserrat Morales-Mejía, Fabiola, Joaquín Arroyo-Cabrales, and Oscar J. Polaco. 2010. Estudio Comparativo de Algunos Elementos de las Extremidades Anteriores y Posteriores y Piezas Dentales de Puma (*Puma concolor*) y Jaguar (*Panthera onca*). *TIP Revista Especializada en Ciencias Químico-Biológicas* 13(2): 73–90.

Moore, Jerry D. 1996a. The Archaeology of Plazas and the Proxemics of Ritual: Three Andean Traditions. *American Anthropologist* 98(4): 789–802. DOI:10.2307/681886.

Moore, Jerry D. 1996b *Architecture and Power in the Ancient Andes: The Archaeology of Public Buildings*. New studies in archaeology. Cambridge: Cambridge University Press.

Morales Puente, Pedro, Edith Cienfuegos Alvarado, Linda R. Manzanilla, and Francisco Javier Otero Trujano. 2012. Estudio de la Paleodieta Empleando Isótopos Estables de los Elementos Carbono, Oxígeno y Nitrógeno en Restos Humanos y de Fauna Encontrados en el Barrio Teotihuacano de Teopancazco. In *Estudios Arqueométricos del Centro de Barrio de Teopancazco en Teotihuacan*, edited by Linda R Manzanilla, pp. 347–423. México, D.F.: Instituto de Investigaciones Antropológicas, UNAM.

Morley, Iain, and Colin Renfrew, eds. 2010. *The Archaeology of Measurement: Comprehending Heaven, Earth and Time in Ancient Societies*. Cambridge: Cambridge University Press.

Motta, Ana Paula, and Martin Porr. 2023. The Jaguar Gaze: Is It Possible to Decolonise Human-Animal Relationships Through Archaeology? In *Decolonising Animals*, edited by Rick De Vos, pp. 185-218. Sydney: Sydney University Press.

Murakami, Tatsuya. 2010. Power Relations and Urban Landscape Formation: A Study of Construction Labor and Resources at Teotihuacan. Unpublished PhD diss., Arizona State University.

Murakami, Tatsuya. 2014. Social Identities, Power Relations, and Urban Transformations: Politics of Plaza Construction at Teotihuacan. In *Mesoamerican Plazas: Arenas of Community and Power*, edited by Kenichiro Tsukamoto and Takeshi Inomata, pp. 34–49. Tucson: University of Arizona Press.

Murakami, Tatsuya. 2015. Replicative Construction Experiments at Teotihuacan, Mexico: Assessing the Duration and Timing of Monumental Construction. *Journal of Field Archaeology* 40(3): 263–282. DOI:10.1179/2042458214Y.0000000008.

Murakami, Tatsuya. 2019. Labor Mobilization and Cooperation for Urban Construction: Building Apartment Compounds at Teotihuacan. *Latin American Antiquity* 30(4): 741–759.

Nado, Kristin L., Natalya Zolotova, and Kelly J. Knudson. 2017. Paleodietary Analysis of the Sacrificial Victims from the Feathered Serpent Pyramid, Teotihuacan. *Archaeological and Anthropological Sciences* 9: 117–132. DOI:10.1007/s12520-016-0420-2.

Nichols, Deborah L. 2015. Teotihuacan. *Journal of Archaeological Research* 24(1): 1–74. DOI:10.1007/s10814-015-9085-0.

Nicholson, Henry B. 1955. Moctezuma's Zoo. *Pacific Discovery* 4(8): 3–11.

Nielsen, Jesper, and Christophe Helmke. 2008. Spearthrower Owl Hill: A Toponym at Atetelco, Teotihuacan. *Latin American Antiquity* 19(4): 459–474.

Noguera, Eduardo. 1935. Antecedentes y Relaciones de la Cultura Teotihuacana. *El Mexico Antiguo* 3(5–8): 3–90.

Olivier, Guilhem. 2004. *Tezcatlipoca: Burlas y Metamorfosis de un Dios Azteca*. Translated by Tatiana Sule. México, D.F.: Fondo de Cultura Económica.
Olivier, Guilhem, ed. 2016. *Artes de Mexico*. Special edition on Jaguar. Vol. 121. Mexico City, Mexico: Artes de Mexico.
Ortíz, Ponciano, and Maria del Carmen Rodríguez. 2006. The Sacred Hill of El Manatí: A Preliminary Discussion of the Site's Ritual Paraphernalia. In *Olmec Art and Archaeology in Mesoamerica: Social Complexity in the Formative Period*, edited by John E. Clark and Mary Pye, pp. 75–94. Studies in the History of Art, 58. Washington, DC: National Gallery of Art.
Ortner, Sherry B. 1973. On Key Symbols. *American Anthropologist* 75: 1338–1346.
Palka, Joel W. 2002. Left/Right Symbolism and the Body in Ancient Maya Iconography and Culture. *Latin American Antiquity* 13(4): 419–443.
Parkin, David. 1992. Ritual as Spatial Direction and Bodily Division. In *Understanding Rituals*, edited by Daniel de Coppet, pp. 11–25. London: Routledge.
Parsons, Jeffrey R. 2006. The Aquatic Component of Aztec Subsistence: Hunters, Fishers, and Collectors in an Urbanized Society. In *Arqueología e Historia del Centro de México: Homenaje a Eduardo Matos Moctezuma*, edited by Leonardo López Luján, Davíd Carrasco, and Lourdes Cué, pp. 241–256. México, D.F.: Instituto Nacional de Antropología e Historia.
Parsons, Jeffrey R. 2015. An Appraisal of Regional Surveys in the Basin of Mexico, 1960–1975. *Ancient Mesoamerica* 26(1): 183–196. DOI:10.1017/S0956536115000097.
Pasztory, Esther. 1988. Feathered Feline and Bird Border. In *Feathered Serpents and Flowering Trees: Reconstructing the Murals of Teotihuacan*, edited by Kathleen Berrin, pp. 185–193. Seattle: Fine Arts Museum of San Francisco.
Pasztory, Esther. 1997. *Teotihuacan: An Experiment in Living*. Norman: University of Oklahoma Press.
Patton, Kimberley C. 2006. Animal Sacrifice: Metaphysics of the Sublimated Victim. In *A Communion of Subjects: Animals in Religion, Science, and Ethics*, edited by Paul Waldau and Kimberley C. Patton, pp. 391–405. New York: Columbia University Press.
Paulinyi, Zoltán, 2006. The "Great Goddess" of Teotihuacan: Fiction or Reality? *Ancient Mesoamerica* 17(1): 1–15.
Pérez, José R. 1935 Exploración del Tunel de la Pirámide del Sol. *El Mexico Antiguo* 3(5–8): 91–95.
Pilaar Birch, Suzanne E. 2013. Stable Isotopes in Zooarchaeology: An Introduction. *Archaeological and Anthropological Sciences* 5(2): 81–83. DOI:10.1007/s12520-013-0126-7.
Pinzón Castaño, Carlos Ernesto. 2002. El Chamán y Sus dos Anillos. In *Rostros Culturales de la Fauna: Las Relaciones Entre los Humanos y los Animales en el Contexto Colombiano*, edited by Astrid Ulloa, pp. 57–71. Instituto Columbiano de Antropología e Historia, Fundación Natura, Columbia.
Pitarch Ramón, Pedro. 2010. *The Jaguar and the Priest: An Ethnography of Tzeltal Souls*. 1st ed. The Linda Schele Series in Maya and Pre-Columbian Studies. Austin: University of Texas Press.
Pitsko, Leigh Elizabeth. 2003. Wild Tigers in Captivity: A Study of the Effects of the Captive Environment on Tiger Behavior. Unpublished MS thesis, Virginia Polytechnic Institute and State University.

Plank, Shannon E. 2004. *Maya Dwellings in Hieroglyphs and Archaeology: An Integrative Approach to Ancient Architecture and Spatial Cognition.* Vol. 1324. BAR International Series. Oxford: John and Erica Hedges.

Pohl, Mary D. 1977. Hunting in the Maya Village of San Antonio, Rio Hondo, Orange Walk District, Belize. *Journal of Belizean Affairs* 5:52–63.

Pohl, Mary D. 1991. Women, Animal Rearing, and Social Status: The Case of the Formative Period Maya of Central America. In *The Archaeology of Gender*, edited by Dale Walde and Noreen D. Willows, pp. 392–399. Proceedings of the Twenty-Second Annual Conference of the Archaeological Association of the University of Calgary. Calgary: University of Calgary Archaeological Association.

Polaco, Oscar J., ed. 1991. *La Fauna en el Templo Mayor.* Colección Divulgación. Asociación de Amigos del Templo Mayor. México, D.F.: Instituto Nacional de Antropología e Historia.

Polaco, Oscar J., ed. 2004. The Ritual Fauna of the Moon Pyramid. In *Voyage to the Center of the Moon Pyramid: Recent Discoveries in Teotihuacan*, edited by Saburo Sugiyama, pp. 40–42. Mexico, D.F.: Arizona State University, Instituto Nacional de Antropologia e Historia.

Quezada Ramírez, Osiris, Norma Valentín Maldonado, and Amaranta Argüelles Echevarría. 2010. Taxidermia y Cautiverio de Águilas en Tenochtitlan. *Arqueología Mexicana* XVII(105): 18–23.

Rabinowitz, A. R., and B. G. Nottingham Jr. 1986. Ecology and Behaviour of the Jaguar (*Panthera onca*) in Belize, Central America. *Journal of Zoology London A* 210: 149–159.

Ramamoorthy, T. P., Robert Bye, Antonio Lot, and John Fa, eds. 1993. *Biological Diversity of Mexico: Origins and Distribution.* Symposium on the Biological Diversity of Mexico. New York: Oxford University Press.

Ramírez, Susan E. 2005. *To Feed and Be Fed: The Cosmological Bases of Authority and Identity in the Andes.* Stanford, CA: Stanford University Press.

Ramírez-Bautista, Aurelio, Uriel Hernández-Salinas, Uri Omar García-Vázquez, Adrian Leyte-Manrique, and Luis Canseco-Márquez. 2009. *Herpetofauna del Valle de México: Diversidad y Conservación.* Hidalgo, Mexico: Universidad Autónoma del Estado de Hidalgo.

Rapoport, Amos. 1994. Spatial Organization and the Built Environment. In *Companion Encyclopedia of Anthropology*, edited by Tim Ingold, pp. 460–502. London: Routledge.

Rappaport, Roy A. 1979. *Ecology, Meaning, and Religion.* Richmond, CA: North Atlantic Books.

Rawlings, Tiffany A., and Jonathan C. Driver. 2010. Paleodiet of Domestic Turkey, Shields Pueblo (5MT3807), Colorado: Isotopic Analysis and its Implications for Care of a Household Domesticate. *Journal of Archaeological Science* 37(10): 2433–2441.

Reese-Taylor, Kathryn, Rex Koontz, and Annabeth Headrick, eds. 2001. *Landscape and Power in Ancient Mesoamerica.* Boulder, CO: Westview Press.

Reichel-Dolmatoff, Gerardo. 1975. *The Shaman and the Jaguar: A Study of Narcotic Drugs Among the Indians of Colombia.* Philadelphia: Temple University Press.

Reina, Ruben E. 1967. Milpas and Milperos: Implications for Prehistoric Times. *American Anthropologist* 69(1):1–20. DOI:10.2307/670482.

Reitz, Elizabeth J., and Elizabeth S. Wing. 2004. *Zooarchaeology*. Cambridge Manuals in Archaeology. Cambridge: Cambridge University Press.
Renfrew, Colin. 2007. The Archaeology of Ritual, of Cult, and of Religion. In *The Archaeology of Ritual*, edited by Evangelos Kyriakidis, pp. 109–122. Los Angeles: Cotsen Institute of Archaeology, University of California.
Renfrew, Colin, and Ezra B. W. Zubrow, eds. 1994. *The Ancient Mind: Elements of Cognitive Archaeology*. New directions in archaeology. Cambridge: Cambridge University Press.
Robb, Matthew H. 2007. The Spatial Logic of Zacuala, Teotihuacan. In *Proceedings, 6th International Space Syntax Symposium*, 2007:62. Citeseer, Istanbul.
Robb, Matthew H. 2017. Vessel with Procession of Figures and Animals, 550–650. In *Teotihuacan: City of Water, City of Fire*, edited by Matthew Robb, pp. 212. San Francisco: Fine Arts Museum of San Francisco in association with University of California Press.
Rodríguez Galicia, Bernardo. 2000. Estudio Morfologico y Morfometrico, Craneal y Dental, de Perros (*Canis familiaris*) y Lobos (*Canis lupus*); Hallados en Teotihuacan y su Aplicacion en la Arqueozoologia. Unpublished BA thesis, Universidad Nacional Autonoma de México.
Rodríguez Galicia, Bernardo. 2006. El Uso Diferencial del Recurso Fáunico en Teopancazco, Teotihuacan, y su Importancia en las Áreas de Actividad. Unpublished MA thesis, Universidad Nacional Autónoma de México.
Rodríguez Galicia, Bernardo. 2010. Captura, Preparación y Uso Diferencial de la Ictiofauna Encontrada en el Sitio Arqueológico de Teopancazco, Teotihuacan. Unpublished PhD diss., Universidad Nacional Autónoma de México.
Rodríguez Galicia, Bernardo, and Raúl Valadez Azúa. 2013. Vestigios del Recurso Costero en el Sitio Arqueológico de Teopancazco, Teotihuacan, Estado de México. *Revista Española de Antropología Americana* 43(1): 9–29.
Rosa, Carlos Leonardo de la, and Claudia C. Nocke. 2000. *A Guide to the Carnivores of Central America: Natural History, Ecology, and Conservation*. 1st ed. Austin: University of Texas Press.
Ruiz de Alarcón, Hernando. 1984. *Treatise on the Heathen Superstitions that Today Live Among the Indians Native to this New Spain, 1629*. Translated by Ross Hassig. 1st ed. Vol. 164. The Civilization of the American Indian Series. Norman: University of Oklahoma Press.
Russell, Nerissa. 2012a. Hunting Sacrifice at Neolithic Çatalhöyük. In *Sacred Killing: The Archaeology of Sacrifice in the Ancient Near East*, edited by Anne Porter and Glenn M. Schwartz, pp. 79–95. Winona Lake, IN: Eisenbrauns.
Russell, Nerissa. 2012b. *Social Zooarchaeology: Humans and Animals in Prehistory*. Cambridge: Cambridge University Press.
Sahagún, Bernardino de XVI. *Historia Universal de las Cosas de la Nueva España: Repartida en Doze Libros: en Lengua Mexicana y Española*. Real Academia de la Historia, Ms. 9/5524, Biblioteca Digital Real Academia de la Historia. https://bibliotecadigital.rah.es/es/consulta/registro.do?control = RAH20150000019.
Sahagún, Bernardino de S. 1577. *Historia General de las Cosas de Nueva España, Libro undecimo que es Bosque, jardin, vergel de lengua Mexican, 1577*. Biblioteca Medicea

Laurenziana, Med. Palat. 220, fol. 84r: detail, World Digital Library. Retrieved from the Library of Congress, www.loc.gov/item/2021667856.

Sahagún, Bernardino de S. 1951. *Florentine Codex. Book 2-The Ceremonies*. Translated by Arthur J. O. Anderson and Charles E. Dibble. Vol. Number 14, Part III. School of American Research Monographs. Salt Lake City: University of Utah Press.

Sahagún, Bernardino de S. 1956. *Historia General de las Cosas de Nueva España*. México, D.F.: Porrúa.

Sahagún, Bernardino de S. 1963. *Florentine Codex. Book 11-Earthy Things*. Translated by Charles E. Dibble. Santa Fe, NM: The School of American Research and the University of Utah.

Sanders, William T., ed. 1965. *The Cultural Ecology of the Teotihuacan Valley: A Preliminary Report of the Results of the Teotihuacan Valley Project*. University Park: Pennsylvania State University.

Sanders, William T. 2000. The Natural Environment and 20th Century Occupation of the Teotihuacan Valley. In *The Teotihuacan Valley Project Final Report: The Aztec Period Occupation of the Valley Part 1*, edited by Susan T. Evans and William T. Sanders, 5: pp. 5–57. Occasional Papers in Anthropology. University Park: Department of Anthropology, Pennsylvania State University.

Sanders, William T. 2008. Prestige, Power and Wealth: A Perspective Based on Residential Architecture at Teotihuacan. In *El Urbanismo en Mesoamérica = Urbanism in Mesoamerica*, edited by Alba Guadalupe Mastache de Escobar, Robert H. Cobean, Ángel García Cook, and Kenneth G. Hirth, 2: pp. 113–131. México D.F.: Instituto Nacional de Antropología e Historia.

Sanders, William T., and Susan Toby Evans. 2006. Rulership and Palaces at Teotihuacan. In *Palaces and Power in the Americas: From Peru to the Northwest Coast*, edited by Jessica Joyce Christie and Patricia Joan Sarro, pp. 256–284. 1st ed. Austin: University of Texas Press.

Sanders, William T., Jeffrey R. Parsons, and Robert S. Santley. 1979. *The Basin of Mexico: Ecological Processes in the Evolution of a Civilization*. Studies in Archaeology. New York: Academic Press.

Sarabia González, Alejandro. 2002. *Trabajos de Consolidación y Mantenimiento en la Base de la Plataforma Adosada de la Pirámide del Sol, Teotihuacán México. Unidad de Salvamento Arqueológico Teotihuacán: Informe Técnico 2000 VI*. México, D.F.: Technical Report in Archivo Técnico de la Coordinación de Arqueología, Instituto Nacional de Antropologia e Historia.

Sarabia González, Alejandro. 2008. Más de Cien Años de Exploraciones en la Pirámide del Sol. *Arqueología Mexicana* XVI(92): 18–23.

Sarabia González, Alejandro, and Nelly Zoé Núñez Redón. 2017. The Sun Pyramid Architectural Complex in Teotihuacan: Vestiges of Worship and Veneration. In *Teotihuacan: City of Water, City of Fire*, edited by Matthew Robb, pp. 62–67. San Francisco, CA: Fine Arts Museum of San Francisco in association with Univ of California Press.

Saunders, Nicholas J. 1989. *People of the Jaguar: The Living Spirit of Ancient America*. London: Souvenir Press.

Saunders, Nicholas J. 1990. Tezcatlipoca: Jaguar Metaphors and the Aztec Mirror of Nature. In *Signifying Animals: Human Meaning in the Natural World*, edited by Roy G. Willis, 16: pp. 159–177. One World Archaeology. London: Unwin Hyman.

Saunders, Nicholas J. 1994. Predators of Culture: Jaguar Symbolism and Mesoamerican Elites. *World Archaeology* 26(1): 104–117.

Schlesinger, Victoria. 2001. *Animals and Plants of the Ancient Maya: A Guide*. 1st ed. Austin: University of Texas Press.

Schmidt, Peter R. 2009. Tropes, Materiality, and Ritual Embodiment of African Iron Smelting Furnaces as Human Figures. *Journal of Archaeological Method and Theory* 16(3): 262–282. DOI:10.1007/s10816-009-9065-0.

Schoeninger, Margaret J. 2009. Stable Isotope Evidence for the Adoption of Maize Agriculture. *Current Anthropology* 50(5): 633–640.

Schoeninger, Margaret J., and Michael J. DeNiro. 1984. Nitrogen and Carbon Isotopic Composition of Bone Collagen from Marine and Terrestrial Animals. *Geochimica et Cosmochimica Acta* 48(4): 625–639. DOI:10.1016/0016-7037(84)90091-7.

Schwarcz, Henry P. 1991. Some Theoretical Aspects of Isotope Paleodiet Studies. *Journal of Archaeological Science* 18(3): 261–275. DOI:10.1016/0305-4403(91)90065-W.

Schwartz, Christopher W., Andrew D. Somerville, Ben A. Nelson, and Kelly J. Knudson. 2021. Investigating pre-Hispanic Scarlet Macaw Origins Through Radiogenic Strontium Isotope Analysis at Paquimé in Chihuahua, Mexico. *Journal of Anthropological Archaeology* 61: 101256. DOI:10.1016/j.jaa.2020.101256.

Schwartz, Glenn M. 2017. The Archaeological Study of Sacrifice. *Annual Review of Anthropology* 46(1): 223–240.

Seler, Eduard. 1986. *Plano Jeoglífico de Santiago Guevea*. Colección de Disertaciones sobre Lenguas y Arqueologías Americanas. México, D.F.: Imprenta Madero S.A.

Seler, Eduard. 2004. *Las Imágenes de Animales en los Manuscritos Mexicanos y Maya*. México, D.F.: Casa Juan Pablos.

Serjeantson, Dale. 2009. *Birds*. Cambridge Manuals in Archaeology. New York: Cambridge University Press.

Seymour, Kevin L. 1989. *Panthera onca. Mammalian Species* 340: 1–9.

Sharpe, Ashley E., Kitty F. Emery, Takeshi Inomata, Daniela Triadan, George D. Kamenov, and John Krigbaum. 2018. Earliest Isotopic Evidence in the Maya Region for Animal Management and Long-Distance Trade at the Site of Ceibal, Guatemala. *Proceedings of the National Academy of Sciences* 115(14): 3605–3610. DOI:10.1073/pnas.1713880115.

Shipton, Parker. 2014. Trusting and Transcending: Sacrifice at the Source of the Nile. *Current Anthropology* 55(S9): S51–S61. DOI:10.1086/676593.

Singleton, Robin R., Nawa Sugiyama, Megan Judkins, Ron Van den Bussche, and Courtney A. Hofman. 2023. Animal Management and Sacrificial Power: Using Ancient Genomics to Study Golden Eagle (*Aquila chrysaetos*) Sacrifice in Teotihuacan. Paper presented at the International Society for Biomolecular Archaeology meeting, Boise, Idaho.

Sload, Rebecca. 2015. When Was the Sun Pyramid Built? Maintaining the Status Quo at Teotihuacan, Mexico. *Latin American Antiquity* 26(2): 221–241.

Smith, Adam T. 2003. *The Political Landscape: Constellations of Authority in Early Complex Polities*. Berkeley: University of California Press.

Smith, Bruce N., and Samuel Epstein. 1971. Two Categories of 13C/12C Ratios for Higher Plants. *Plant Physiology* 47(3): 380–384.

Smith, Jonathan Z. 1980. The Bare Facts of Ritual. *History of Religions* 20(1/2): 112–127.

Smith, Jonathan Z. 1987a. The Domestication of Sacrifice. In *Violent Origins: Walter Burkert, René Girard and Jonathan Z. Smith on Ritual Killing and Cultural Formation*, edited by Robert Hamerton-Kelly, pp. 191–205. Stanford, CA: Stanford University Press.

Smith, Jonathan Z. 1987b. *To Take Place: Toward Theory in Ritual*. Chicago Studies in the History of Judaism. Chicago: University of Chicago Press.

Smith, Michael E., and Lisa Montiel. 2001. The Archaeological Study of Empires and Imperialism in Pre-Hispanic Central Mexico. *Journal of Anthropological Archaeology* 20: 245–284.

Somerville, Andrew D., Mikael Fauvelle, and Andrew W. Froehle. 2013. Applying New Approaches to Modeling Diet and Status: Isotopic Evidence for Commoner Resiliency and Elite Variability in the Classic Maya Lowlands. *Journal of Archaeological Science* 40(3): 1539–1553. DOI:10.1016/j.jas.2012.10.029.

Somerville, Andrew D., Ben A. Nelson, and Kelly J. Knudson. 2010. Isotopic Investigation of Pre-Hispanic Macaw Breeding in Northwest Mexico. *Journal of Anthropological Archaeology* 29: 125–135.

Somerville, Andrew D, and Nawa Sugiyama. 2021. Why Were New World Rabbits Not Domesticated? *Animal Frontiers* 11(3): 62–68. DOI:10.1093/af/vfab026.

Somerville, Andrew D., Nawa Sugiyama, Linda R. Manzanilla, and Margaret J. Schoeninger. 2016. Animal Management at the Ancient Metropolis of Teotihuacan, Mexico: Stable Isotope Analysis of Leporid (Cottontail and Jackrabbit) Bone Mineral. *PLoS ONE* 11(8): e0159982. DOI:10.1371/journal.pone.0159982.

Somerville, Andrew D., Nawa Sugiyama, Linda R. Manzanilla, and Margaret J. Schoeninger. 2017. Leporid Management and Specialized Food Production at Teotihuacan: Stable Isotope Data from Cottontail and Jackrabbit Bone Collagen. *Archaeological and Anthropological Sciences* 9: 83–97. DOI:10.1007/s12520-016-0420-2.

Speller, Camilla F., Brian M. Kemp, Scott D. Wyatt, Cara Monroe, William D. Lipe, Ursula M. Arndt, and Dongya Y. Yang. 2010. Ancient Mitochondrial DNA Analysis Reveals Complexity of Indigenous North American Turkey Domestication. *Proceedings of the National Academy of Sciences* 107(7): 2807–2812.

Spence, Michael W, and Luis Manuel Gamboa Cabezas. 1999. Mortuary Practices and Social Adaptation in the Tlailotlacan Enclave. In *Prácticas Funerarias en la Ciudad de los Dioses: Los Enterramientos Humanos de la Antigua Teotihuacan*, edited by Linda R. Manzanilla and Carlos Serrano Sánchez, pp. 173–201. México, D.F.: Instituto de Investigaciones Antropológicas, Universidad Nacional Autónoma de México.

Spence, Michael W., and Grégory Pereira. 2007. The Human Skeletal Remains of the Moon Pyramid, Teotihuacan. *Ancient Mesoamerica* 18: 147–157.

Spence, Michael W., Christine D. White, Fred J. Longstaffe, and Kimberley R. Law. 2004. Victims of the Victims: Human Trophies Worn by Sacrificed Soldiers from the Feathered Serpent Pyramid, Teotihuacan. *Ancient Mesoamerica* 15(1): 1–15.

Šprajc, Ivan. 2000. Astronomical Alignments at Teotihuacan, Mexico. *Latin American Antiquity* 11(4): 403–415.

Starbuck, David R. 1975. Man-Animal Relationships in Pre-Columbian Central Mexico. Unpublished PhD diss., Yale University.

Starbuck, David R. 1987. Faunal Evidence for the Teotihuacan Subsistence Base. In *Teotihuacan, Nuevos Datos, Nuevas Síntesis, Nuevos Problemas*, edited by Emily McClung de Tapia and Evelyn Childs Rattray, pp. 75–90. México, D.F.: Universidad Nacional Autónoma de México.

Steenberg, Judie. 1981. Captive Breeding of American Golden Eagles at Topeka Zoo between 1969 and 1976. *International Zoo Yearbook* 21(1): 109–115. DOI:10.1111/j.1748-1090.1981.tb01960.x.

Stehlik, Josef. 1971. Breeding Jaguars at Ostrava Zoo. *International Zoo Yearbook* 11(1): 116–118. DOI:10.1111/j.1748-1090.1971.tb01871.x.

Stoler, Ann Laura. 2008. Imperial Debris: Reflections on Ruins and Ruination. *Cultural Anthropology* 23(2): 191–219. DOI:10.1111/j.1548-1360.2008.00007.x.

Stone, Andrea Joyce, and Marc Zender. 2011. *Reading Maya Art: A Hieroglyphic Guide to Ancient Maya Painting and Sculpture*. New York: Thames & Hudson.

Storey, Rebecca. 1992. *Life and Death in the Ancient City of Teotihuacan: A Modern Paleodemographic Synthesis*. Tuscaloosa: University of Alabama Press.

Storey, Rebecca. 2006. Mortality Through Time in an Impoverished Residence of the Precolumbian City of Teotihuacan: A Paleodemographic View. In *Urbanism in the Preindustrial World: Cross-Cultural Approaches*, edited by Glenn R. Storey, pp. 277–294. Tuscaloosa: University of Alabama Press.

Stross, Brian. 1998. Seven Ingredients in Mesoamerican Ensoulment: Dedication and Termination in Tenejapa. In *The Sowing and the Dawning: Termination, Dedication, and Transformation in the Archaeological and Ethnographic Record of Mesoamerica*, edited by Shirley Boteler Mock, pp. 31–39. Albuquerque: University of New Mexico Press.

Stuart, David. 1997. The Hills Are Alive: Sacred Mountains in the Maya Cosmos. *Symbols* Spring: 15–17.

Stuart, David. 1998. "The Fire Enters His House": Architecture and Ritual in Classic Maya Texts. In *Function and Meaning in Classic Maya Architecture*, edited by Stephen D. Houston, pp. 373–425. Washington, DC: Dumbarton Oaks Research Library and Collection.

Stuart, David. 2000. "The Arrival of Strangers": Teotihuacan and Tollan in Classic Maya History. In *Mesoamerica's Classic Heritage: From Teotihuacan to the Aztecs*, edited by Davíd Carrasco, Lindsay Jones, and Scott Sessions, pp. 465–514. Boulder: University Press of Colorado.

Stuart, David. 2024. Spearthrower Owl: A Teotihuacan Ruler in Maya History. Washington D.C: Dumbarton Oaks Research Library and Collection.

Sugiyama, Nawa. 2014. Animals and Sacred Mountains: How Ritualized Performances Materialized State-Ideologies at Teotihuacan, Mexico. Unpublished PhD diss., Harvard University.

Sugiyama, Nawa. 2016. La Noche y el Día en Teotihuacan. *Artes de México* 121: 30–35.

Sugiyama, Nawa. 2023. Revisiting "Mesoamerica's Classic Heritage": Updates from Teotihuacan. In *When East Meets West, Volumes I and II: Chichen Itza, Tula, and the Postclassic Mesoamerican world*, edited by Travis W. Stanton, Karl A. Taube, Jeremy D. Coltman, and Nelda I. Marengo Camacho, pp. 33–40. Oxford: BAR.

Sugiyama, Nawa, William L. Fash, Barbara W. Fash, and Saburo Sugiyama. 2020. The Maya at Teotihuacan? New Insights into Teotihuacan-Maya Interactions from Plaza of the Columns Complex. In *Teotihuacan: The World Beyond the City*, edited by Kenneth G. Hirth, David M. Carballo, and Barbara Arroyo, pp. 139–171. Washington, DC: Dumbarton Oaks Research Library and Collection.

Sugiyama, Nawa, William L. Fash, and Christine A. M. France. 2018. Jaguar and Puma Captivity and Trade Among the Maya: Stable Isotope Data from Copan, Honduras. *PLOS ONE* 13(9): e0202958. DOI:10.1371/journal.pone.0202958.

Sugiyama, Nawa, William L. Fash, and Christine A. M. France. 2019. Creating the Cosmos, Reifying Power: A Zooarchaeological Investigation of Corporal Animal Forms in the Copan Valley. *Cambridge Archaeological Journal* 29(3): 407–426.

Sugiyama, Nawa, María Fernanda Martínez-Polanco, Christine A. M. France, and Richard G. Cooke. 2020. Domesticated Landscapes of the Neotropics: Isotope Signatures of Human-Animal Relationships in Pre-Columbian Panama. *Journal of Anthropological Archaeology* 59: 101195. DOI:10.1016/j.jaa.2020.101195.

Sugiyama, Nawa, and Andrew D. Somerville. 2017. Feeding Teotihuacan: Integrating Approaches to Studying Food and Foodways of the Ancient Metropolis. *Archaeological and Anthropological Sciences* 9(1) :1–10. DOI:https://doi.org/10.1007/s12520-016-0419-8.

Sugiyama, Nawa, Andrew D. Somerville, and Margaret J. Schoeninger. 2015. Stable Isotopes and Zooarchaeology at Teotihuacan, Mexico Reveal Earliest Evidence of Wild Carnivore Management in Mesoamerica. *PLOS ONE* 10(9): e0135635. DOI:10.1371/journal.pone.0135635.

Sugiyama, Nawa, and Saburo Sugiyama. 2007. From Dedication Burials to Murals: Re-Interpreting the Teotihuacan Animal Imagery. Unpublished Paper presented at the 72nd Annual Society for American Archaeology Conference. Austin.

Sugiyama, Nawa, Saburo Sugiyama, Clarissa Cagnato, Christine A. M. France, Atsushi Iriki, Karissa S. Hughes, Robin R. Singleton, Erin Thornton, and Courtney A. Hofman. 2022. Earliest Evidence of Primate Captivity and Translocation Supports Gift Diplomacy Between Teotihuacan and the Maya. *Proceedings of the National Academy of Sciences* 119(47): e2212431119. DOI:10.1073/pnas.2212431119.

Sugiyama, Nawa, Saburo Sugiyama, Tanya Catignani, Adrian S. Z. Chase, and Juan C. Fernandez-Diaz. 2021. Humans as Geomorphic Agents: Lidar Detection of the Past, Present and Future of the Teotihuacan Valley, Mexico. *PLOS ONE* 16(9): e0257550. DOI:10.1371/journal.pone.0257550.

Sugiyama, Nawa, Saburo Sugiyama, Verónica Ortega Cabrera, and William Fash. 2016. ¿Artistas Mayas en Teotihuacan? *Arqueologia Mexicana* XXIV(142): 8.

Sugiyama, Nawa, Saburo Sugiyama, and Alejandro Sarabia G. 2013. Inside the Sun Pyramid at Teotihuacan, Mexico: 2008-2011 Excavations and Preliminary Results. *Latin American Antiquity* 24(4): 403–432.

Sugiyama, Nawa, Saburo Sugiyama, and Alejandro Sarabia G. 2018. Revisiting the Sun Pyramid Ceramic and Radiocarbon dates from Teotihuacan: Comment on Sload. *Latin American Antiquity* 29(2): 398–400. DOI:10.1017/laq.2017.68.

Sugiyama, Nawa, Raúl Valadez Azúa, and Bernardo Rodríguez Galicia. 2017. Faunal Acquisition, Maintenance, and Consumption: How the Teotihuacanos Got their Meat. *Archaeological and Anthropological Sciences* 9(1): 61–81. DOI:10.1007/s12520-016-0387-z.

Sugiyama, Saburo. 1993. Worldview Materialized in Teotihuacan, Mexico. *Latin American Antiquity* 4(2): 103–129.

Sugiyama, Saburo. 1998a. Termination Programs and Prehistoric Looting at the Feathered Serpent Pyramid in Teotihuacan, Mexico. In *The Sowing and the Dawning: Termination, Dedication, and Transformation in the Archaeological and Ethnographic Record of Mesoamerica*, edited by Shirley Boteler Mock, pp. 147–164. Albuquerque: University of New Mexico Press.

Sugiyama, Saburo. 1998b. Cronología de Sucesos Ocurridos en el Templo de Quetzalcóatl, Teotihuacán. In *Los Ritmos de Cambio en Teotihuacán*, edited by Rosa Brambila and Rubén Cabrera, pp. 167–184. México, D.F.: Instituto Nacional de Antropología e Historia.

Sugiyama, Saburo. 2000. Teotihuacan as an Origin for Postclassic Feathered Serpent Symbolism. In *Mesoamerica's Classic Heritage: From Teotihuacan to the Aztecs*, edited by Davíd Carrasco, Lindsay Jones, and Scott Sessions, pp. 117–144. Boulder: University Press of Colorado.

Sugiyama, Saburo, ed. 2004. *Voyage to the Center of the Moon Pyramid: Recent Discoveries in Teotihuacan*. México, D.F.: Arizona State University and Instituto Nacional de Antropología e Historia.

Sugiyama, Saburo. 2005. *Human Sacrifice, Militarism, and Rulership: Materialization of State Ideology at the Feathered Serpent Pyramid, Teotihuacan*. Cambridge: Cambridge University Press.

Sugiyama, Saburo. 2010. Teotihuacan City Layout as a Cosmogram: Preliminary Results of the 2007 Measurement Unit Study. In *The Archaeology of Measurement: Comprehending Heaven, Earth and Time in Ancient Societies*, edited by Iain Morley and Colin Renfrew, pp. 130–149. New York: Cambridge University Press.

Sugiyama, Saburo. 2013. Creation and Transformation of Monuments in the Ancient City of Teotihuacan. In *Constructing, Deconstructing, and Reconstructing Social Identity— 2,000 Years of Monumentality in Teotihuacan and Cholula, Mexico*, edited by Saburo Sugiyama, Shigeru Kabata, Tomoko Taniguchi, and Etsuko Niwa, pp. 1–10. Aichi, Japan: Cultural Symbiosis Research Institute, Aichi Prefectural University.

Sugiyama, Saburo. 2017a. Teotihuacan: Planned City with Cosmic Pyramids. In *Teotihuacan: City of Water, City of Fire*, edited by Matthew Robb, pp. 28–37. San Francisco, CA: Fine Arts Museum of San Francisco in association with University of California Press.

Sugiyama, Saburo. 2017b. Feathered Serpent Pyramid at Teotihuacan: Monumentality and Sacrificial Burials. In *Teotihuacan: City of Water, City of Fire*, edited by Matthew Robb, pp. 56–61. San Francisco, CA: Fine Arts Museum of San Francisco in association with University of California Press.

Sugiyama, Saburo. 2017c. Teotihuacan: Planned City with Cosmic Pyramids. In *Teotihuacan: City of Water, City of Fire*, edited by Matthew Robb, pp. 28–37. San Francisco, CA: Fine Arts Museum of San Francisco in association with University of California Press.

Sugiyama, Saburo. 2017d. 115 Seated Figurine and Miniature Pectoral, 300-350. In *Teotihuacan: City of Water, City of Fire*, edited by Matthew Robb, pp. 318. San Francisco, CA: Fine Arts Museum of San Francisco in association with University of California Press.
Sugiyama, Saburo, and Ruben Cabrera Castro. 2000. El Proyecto Pirámide de la Luna: Algunos Resultados de la Segunda Temporada 1999. *Arqueología* 23(2): 161–172.
Sugiyama, Saburo, and Ruben Cabrera Castro. 2007. The Moon Pyramid Project and the Teotihuacan State Polity. *Ancient Mesoamerica* 18: 109–125.
Sugiyama, Saburo, and Ruben Cabrera Castro. 2017. Moon Pyramid and the Ancient State of Teotihuacan. In *Teotihuacan: City of Water, City of Fire*, edited by Matthew Robb, pp. 74–81. San Francisco, CA: Fine Arts Museum of San Francisco in association with University of California Press.
Sugiyama, Saburo, Shigeru Kabata, Tomoko Taniguchi, and Etsuko Niwa, eds. 2013. *Constructing, Deconstructing, and Reconstructing Social Identity- 2,000 years of Monumentality in Teotihuacan and Cholula, Mexico*. Aichi, Japan: Cultural Symbiosis Research Institute, Aichi Prefectural University.
Sugiyama, Saburo, and Leonardo López Luján, eds. 2006a. *Sacrificios de Consagración en la Pirámide de la Luna*. México, D.F.: Instituto Nacional de Antropología e Historia, Museo de Templo Mayor, Arizona State University.
Sugiyama, Saburo, and Leonardo López Luján, eds. 2006b. Simbolismo y Función de los Entierros Dedicatorios de la Pirámide de la Luna en Teotihuacan. In *Arqueología e Historia del Centro de México: Homenaje a Eduardo Matos Moctezuma*, edited by Leonardo López Luján, Davíd Carrasco, and Lourdes Cué, pp. 131–151. México, D.F.: Instituto Nacional de Antropología e Historia.
Sugiyama, Saburo, and Leonardo López Luján, eds. 2007. Dedicatory Burial/Offering Complexes at the Moon Pyramid, Teotihuacan: A Preliminary Report of 1998–2004 Exploration. *Ancient Mesoamerica* 18: 127–146.
Sugiyama, Saburo, and Nawa Sugiyama. 2020. Interactions Between Ancient Teotihuacan and the Maya World. In *The Maya World*, edited by Scott R. Hutson and Traci Ardren, pp. 689–708. New York: Routledge.
Sugiyama, Saburo, and Nawa Sugiyama. 2021. Monumental Cityscape and Polity at Teotihuacan. In *Mesoamerican Archaeology: Theory and Practice*, 2nd ed., edited by Julia A. Hendon, Lisa Overholtzer, and Rosemary A. Joyce, pp. 98–128. Hoboken, NJ: Wiley-Blackwell.
Tambiah, Stanley J. 1969. Animals Are Good to Think and Good to Prohibit. *Ethnology* 8(4): 423–459.
Tambiah, Stanley J. 1981. *A Performative Approach to Ritual*. Radcliffe-Brown lecture in social anthropology. London: British Academy.
Tambiah, Stanley J. 1985. *Culture, Thought, and Social Action: An Anthropological Perspective*. Cambridge, MA: Harvard University Press.
Taube, Karl A. 1986. The Teotihuacan Cave of Origin: The Iconography and Architecture of Emergence Mythology in Mesoamerica and the American Southwest. *RES: Anthropology and Aesthetics* 12: 51–82.
Taube, Karl A. 1992. The Temple of Quetzalcoatl and the Cult of Sacred War at Teotihuacan. *RES: Anthropology and Aesthetics* 21: 53–87. DOI:10.1086/RESv21n1ms20166842.

Taube, Karl A. 1996. The Rainmaker: The Olmec and Their Contribution to Mesoamerican Belief and Ritual. In *The Olmec World: Ritual and Rulership*, edited by Michael D. Coe, Richard A. Diehl, David A. Freidel, Peter T. Furst, F. Kent III Reilly, Linda Schele, Carolyn E. Tate, and Karl A. Taube, pp. 82–103. Princeton, NJ: Art Museum, Princeton University; In association with Harry N. Abrams.

Taube, Karl 2000. The Turquoise Hearth: Fire, Self-Sacrifice, and the Central Mexican Cult of War. In *Mesoamerica's Classic Heritage: From Teotihuacan to the Aztecs*, edited by David Carrasco, Lindsay Jones, and Scott Sessions, pp. 269–340. University Press of Colorado, Boulder, Colorado.

Taube, Karl A. 2003. Ancient and Contemporary Maya Conceptions About Field and Forest. In *The Lowland Maya Area: Three Millennia at the Human-Wildland Interface*, edited by Arturo Gómez-Pompa, Michael F. Allen, Scott L. Fedick, and Juan J. Jiménez-Osornio, pp. 461–492. Binghamton, NY: Food Products Press.

Taube, Karl A. 2011. Teotihuacan and the Development of Writing in Early Classic Central Mexico. In *Their Way of Writing: Scripts, Signs, and Pictographies in Pre-Columbian America*, edited by Elizabeth Hill Boone and Gary Urton, pp. 77–109. Dumbarton Oaks Pre-Columbian symposia and colloquia. Washington, DC: Dumbarton Oaks Research Library and Collection.

Taube, Karl A. 2012. The Symbolism of Turquoise in Ancient Mesoamerica. In *Turquoise in Mexico and North America: Science, Conservation, Culture and Collections*, edited by J. C. H. King, Max Carocci, Caroline Cartwright, and Colin McEwan, pp. 117–134. London: Archetype Publications.

Taylor, Mark C., ed. 1998. Religion, Religions, Religious. In *Critical Terms for Religious Studies*, pp. 269–284. Chicago: University of Chicago Press.

Tilley, Christopher Y. 1994. *A Phenomenology of Landscape: Places, Paths, and Monuments*. Explorations in Anthropology. Oxford: Berg.

Tobriner, Stephen. 1972. The Fertile Mountain: An Investigation of Cerro Gordo's Importance to the Town Plan and Iconography of Teotihuacan. In *Teotihuacán: XI Mesa Redonda*, edited by Alberto Ruz Lhuillier, pp. 103–115. México, D.F.: Sociedad Mexicana de Antropología.

Todd, Zoe. 2014. Fish Pluralities: Human-Animal Relations and Sites of Engagement in Paulatuuq, Arctic Canada. *Études/Inuit/Studies* 38(1/2): 217–238.

Todd, Zoe. 2016. An Indigenous Feminist's Take on the Ontological Turn: 'Ontology' Is Just Another Word for Colonialism. *Journal of Historical Sociology* 29(1): 4–22. DOI:10.1111/johs.12124.

Townsend, Richard Fraser. 1982. Pyramid and Sacred Mountain. *Annals of the New York Academy of Sciences* 385(1): 37–62. DOI:10.1111/j.1749-6632.1982.tb34258.x.

Tsukamoto, Kenichiro, and Takeshi Inomata. 2014. *Mesoamerican Plazas: Arenas of Community and Power*. Tucson: University of Arizona Press.

Turner, Victor. 1977. Sacrifice as Quintessential Process Prophylaxis or Abandonment? *History of Religions* 16(3): 189–215.

Turner, Victor. 1986. *The Anthropology of Performance*. 1st ed. Preface by Richard Schechner. New York: PAJ Publications.

Ulloa, Astrid, ed. 2002. *Rostros Culturales de la Fauna: Las Relaciones Entre los Humanos y los Animales en el Contexto Colombiano*. Bogota, Instituto Columbiano de Antropología e Historia, Fundación Natural.

Urton, Gary, ed. 1985. *Animal Myths and Metaphors in South America*. Salt Lake City: University of Utah Press.
Vaillant, George C. 1932. Stratigraphical Research in Central Mexico. *Proceedings of the National Academy of Sciences* 18(7): 487–490.
Valadez Azúa, Raúl. 1992. Impacto del Recurso Faunístico en la Sociedad Teotihuacana. Unpublished PhD diss., Universidad Nacional Autónoma de Mexico.
Valadez Azúa, Raúl. 1993. Microfósiles Faunísticos. In *Anatomía de un Conjunto Residencial Teotihuacano en Oztoyahualco*, edited by Linda Manzanilla, II: pp. 729–831. México, D.F.: Instituto de Investigaciones Antropológicas, Universidad Nacional Autónoma de México.
Valadez Azúa, Raúl. 2003. *La Domesticación Animal*. Mexico, D.F.: Universidad Nacional Autónoma de México, Instituto de Investigaciones Antropológicas.
Valadez Azúa, Raúl, and Bernardo Rodríguez Galicia. 2009. Arqueofauna de Vertebrados de las Cuevas. In *El Inframundo de Teotihuacan: Ocupaciones Post-Teotihuacanas en Los Túneles al Este de la Pirámide del Sol*, edited by Linda R. Manzanilla Naim, II: El Ambiente y el Hombre: Arqueofauna de los Túneles de Teotihuacan, pp. 47–300. Volume coordinator Raúl Valadez. México, D.F.: El Colegio Nacional.
Valadez Azúa, Raúl, Bernardo Rodríguez Galicia, Rubén Cabrera Castro, George Cowgill, and Saburo Sugiyama. 2002a. Híbridos de Lobos y Perros (Tercer acto): Hallazgos en la Pirámide de Quetzalcóatl de la Antigua Ciudad de Teotihuacan (Primeros de dos partes). *AMMVEPE* 13(5): 165–176.
Valadez Azúa, Raúl, Bernardo Rodríguez Galicia, Rubén Cabrera Castro, George Cowgill, and Saburo Sugiyama. 2002b. Híbridos de Lobos y Perros (Tercer acto): Hallazgos en la Pirámide de Quetzalcóatl de la Antigua Ciudad de Teotihuacan (Segunda y última de dos partes). *AMMVEPE* 13(6): 219–231.
Valadez, Susana Eger. 1996. Wolf Power and Interspecies Communication in Huichol Shamanism. In *People of the Peyote: Huichol Indian History, Religion, and Survival*, edited by Stacy B. Schaefer and Peter T. Furst, pp. 267–305. 1st ed. Albuquerque: University of New Mexico Press.
Valentín Maldonado, Norma. 1999. Los Restos de Serpientes de la Ofrenda R del Templo Mayor de Tenochtitlan. *Arqueología* 22: 107–114.
Valentín Maldonado, Norma. 2018. Preparación Taxidérmica para las Oblaciones del Templo Mayor de Tenochtitlan. In *Arqueología de la Producción*, edited by Emiliano Ricardo Melgar Tísoc and Linda Manzanilla, pp. 251–266. Primera edición. Colección arqueología. Serie Logos. Ciudad de México: Secretaría de Cultura, Instituto Nacional de Antropología e Historia, UNAM.
Valeri, Valerio. 1985. *Kingship and Sacrifice: Ritual and Society in Ancient Hawaii*. Chicago: University of Chicago Press.
VanPool, Christine S. 2009. The Signs of the Sacred: Identifying Shamans Using Archaeological Evidence. *Journal of Anthropological Archaeology* 28: 177–190.
Viveiros de Castro, Eduardo. 1998. Cosmological Deixis and Amerindian Perspectivism. *The Journal of the Royal Anthropological Institute* 4(3): 469–488. DOI:10.2307/3034157.
Vogt, Evon Z. 1981. Some Aspects of the Sacred Geography of Highland Chiapas. In *Mesoamerican Sites and World-Views: A Conference at Dumbarton Oaks, October 16th*

and 17th, 1976, edited by Elizabeth P. Benson, pp. 119–138. Washington, DC: Dumbarton Oaks Research Library and Collections, Trustees for Harvard University,

Vogt, Evon Z. 1983. Ancient and Contemporary Maya Settlement Patterns: A New Look from the Chiapas Highlands. In *Prehistoric Settlement Patterns: Essays in Honor of Gordon R. Willey*, 1st ed., edited by Evon Zartman Vogt and Richard M. Leventhal, pp. 89–114. Albuquerque: University of New Mexico Press; Cambridge, MA: Peabody Museum of Archaeology and Ethnology.

Vogt, Evon Z. 1998. Zinacanteco Dedication and Termination Rituals. In *The Sowing and the Dawning: Termination, Dedication, and Transformation in the Archaeological and Ethnographic Record of Mesoamerica*, edited by Shirley Boteler Mock, pp. 21–30. Albuquerque: University of New Mexico Press.

Vogt, Evon Z., and David Stuart. 2005. Some Notes on Ritual Caves Among the Ancient and Modern Maya. In *In the Maw of the Earth Monster: Mesoamerican Ritual Cave Use*, edited by James E. Brady and Keith M. Prufer, pp. 155–185. Austin: University of Texas Press.

Von Den Drisch, Angela. 1976. *A Guide to the Measurement of Animal Bones from Archaeological Sites*. Cambridge, MA: Peabody Museum of Archaeology and Ethnology, Harvard University.

Von Winning, Hasso. 1948. The Teotihuacan Owl-and-Weapon Symbol and Its Association with "Serpent Head X" at Kaminaljuyu. *American Antiquity* 14(2): 129–132.

Wacquant, Loïc J. D. 1992. Toward a Social Praxeology: The Structure and Logic of Bourdieu's Sociology. In *An Invitation to Reflexive Sociology*, edited by Pierre Bourdieu and Loïc J. D. Wacquant, pp. 1–59. Chicago: University of Chicago Press.

Walker, Karen. 2003. An Illustrated Guide to Trunk Vertebrae of Cottonmouth (*Agkistrodon piscivorus*) and Diamondback Rattlesnake (*Crotalus adamanteus*) in Florida. *Bulletin of the Florida Museum of Natural History* 44(1): 91–100.

Warinner, Christina, Nelly Robles Garcia, and Noreen Tuross. 2013. Maize, Beans and the Floral Isotopic Diversity of Highland Oaxaca, Mexico. *Journal of Archaeological Science* 40(2): 868–873. DOI:10.1016/j.jas.2012.07.003.

Warinner, Christina, and Noreen Tuross. 2009. Alkaline Cooking and Stable Isotope Tissue-Diet Spacing in Swine: Archaeological Implications. *Journal of Archaeological Science* 36: 1690–1697.

Watson, Jeff. 2010. *The Golden Eagle*. 2nd ed. New Haven, CT: Yale University Press.

Watts, Christopher M., ed. 2013. *Relational Archaeologies: Human, Animals, Things*. London: Routledge.

Watts, Vanessa. 2013. Indigenous Place-Thought and Agency Amongst Humans and Non Humans (First Woman and Sky Woman Go on a European World Tour!). *Decolonization: Indigeneity, Education & Society* 2(1): 20–34.

Wells, E. Christian, and Patricia Ann McAnany. 2008. *Dimensions of Ritual Economy*. 1st ed. Vol. 27. Research in Economic Anthropology. Bingley, UK: JAI Press.

Wheatley, Paul. 1971. *The Pivot of the Four Quarters; A Preliminary Enquiry into the Origins and Character of the Ancient Chinese City*. Chicago: Aldine.

Wheeler, Brian K., and William S. Clark. 1995. *A Photographic Guide to North American Raptors*. London: Academic Press.

White, Christine D. 2004. Stable Isotopes and the Human-Animal Interface in Maya Biosocial and Environmental Systems. *Archaeofauna* 13: 183–198.

White, Christine D., Mary E. D. Pohl, Henry P. Schwarcz, and Fred J. Longstaffe. 2001. Isotopic Evidence for Maya Patterns of Deer and Dog Use at Preclassic Colha. *Journal of Archaeological Science* 28: 89–107.

White, Christine D., Douglas Price, and Fred J. Longstaffe. 2007. Residential Histories of the Human Sacrifices at the Moon Pyramid, Teotihuacan: Evidence from Oxygen and Strontium Isotopes. *Ancient Mesoamerica* 18: 159–172.

White, Christine D., Henry P. Schwarcz, Mary Pohl, and Fred J. Longstaffe. 2004. Feast, Field, and Forest: Deer and Dog Diets at Lagartero, Tikal, and Copán. In *Maya Zooarchaeology: New Directions in Method and Theory*, edited by Kitty F. Emery, pp. 141–158. Los Angeles: Costen Institute of Archaeology, University of California.

White, Christine D., Michael W. Spence, Fred J. Longstaffe, and Hilary Stuart-Williams. 2002. Geographic Identities of the Sacrificial Victims from the Feathered Serpent Pyramid, Teotihuacan: Implications for the Nature of State Power. *Latin American Antiquity* 13(2): 217–236.

White, Christine D., Rebecca Storey, Fred J. Longstaffe, and Michael W. Spence. 2004. Immigration, Assimilation, and Status in the Ancient City of Teotihuacan: Stable Isotopic Evidence from Tlajinga 33. *Latin American Antiquity* 15(2): 176–198.

Whittaker, Gordon. 2021. *Deciphering Aztec Hieroglyphs: A Guide to Nahuatl Writing*. Oakland: University of California Press.

Widmer, Randolph J., and Rebecca Storey. 2017. Skeletal Health and Patterns of Animal Food Consumption at S3W1:33 (Tlajinga 33), Teotihuacan. *Archaeological and Anthropological Sciences* 9(1): 51–60. DOI:10.1007/s12520-016-0417-x.

Yoder, Cassady. 2010. Diet in Medieval Denmark: A Regional and Temporal Comparison. *Journal of Archaeological Science* 37(9): 2224–2236. DOI:10.1016/j.jas.2010.03.020.

Young, Stanley Paul, and Edward Alphonso Goldman. 1944. *The Wolves of North America*. Washington, DC: American Wildlife Institute.

Yuan, Jing, and Rowan K. Flad. 2005. New Zooarchaeological Evidence for Changes in Shang Dynasty Animal Sacrifice. *Journal of Anthropological Archaeology* 24: 252–270.

Zeder, Melinda A. 2006. Central Questions in the Domestication of Plants and Animals. *Evolutionary Anthropology* 15(3): 105–117. DOI:10.1002/evan.20101.

Zeder, Melinda A. 2015. Core Questions in Domestication Research. *Proceedings of the National Academy of Sciences* 112(11): 3191–3198. DOI:10.1073/pnas.1501711112.

Zingg, Robert M. 2004. *Huichol Mythology*. Edited by J. Fikes, P. Weigand, and A. Weigand. Tucson: University of Arizona Press.

INDEX

For the benefit of digital users, indexed terms that span two pages (e.g., 52–53) may, on occasion, appear on only one of those pages.
Figures and tables are indicated by an italic *f* and *t* following the page number.

aDNA/DNA, ix–x, 74–75, 106, 114–16, 138, 186
altepetl
   Cerro Gordo and, 44
   concept of, mountains and, 17–18, 25, 27, 51, 193–94
   co-producing, Building 4 and, 190
   cosmology and, 190, 193
   modifications to and durability of, Burials 3 and 5 and, 194
   Moon Pyramid and, 1–2, 17–18, 19–20, 25, 28, 181, 182, 190, 193, 194, 204
   ritualized production of, 202–3
   social hierarchies and, 27, 201
   in sovereignty formations, 1–2, 17–18, 27, 201, 202
Álvarez, Ticul, 38, 227*t*
animal
   artifacts, 16
   classificatory systems, 53, 54–55, 65, 66–67, 68, 69, 83–84, 200–1
   derived products, 4–5
   hierarchy, 53, 54–56, 63, 83–84
   management, 15, 30, 55–56, 96, 135, 202–3
   matter, 1, 2, 4–5, 6–7, 18, 52, 54, 56, 84, 85, 164, 166, 168–69, 181, 182, 190, 194–95, 200, 201, 203–4, 224
   See also corporeal animal forms
animal persons. *See* personhood and persons

animal politics, Plate 16, 53, 54, 56–59, 83–84, 85, 166, 200
animal sacrifice, 1–2, 13, 24, 48–49, 173, 174, 201
   co-producing ritualized bodies and, 174
   Moon Pyramid and, 14, 48–49, 178
   sex of animals, Plate 16, 187
   See also sacrifice
apex predators, 1–2, 4, 6, 10, 12, 13, 32–33, 56, 59, 84, 175–76, 181–82, 203–4, 211n.16
Astor-Aguilera, Miguel, 7
avian
   bones, 29, 30, 129–33, 130*t*, 132*f*, 189–90
   breeding, 76
   mural paintings, figures, representations, 76, 78
Aztec, 12, 16, 21, 24, 26, 56–59, 61, 67–68, 174, 194
   offerings, 118–19, 197, 201
   warrior, 61–63, 72*f*, 73, 75
   See also Templo Mayor; Tenochtitlan; Toxcatl festival; *teteo imixiptlahuan*

Basin of Mexico, 28–29, 31, 136–37, 195–96, 208
Bauer, Andrew M., 54, 200
Bell, Catherine, 13, 86, 206
Bird. *See* avian
Bird-David, Nurit, 2–3

263

bones and teeth, 3–4, 5–6, 86, 96–97
　isotopic analyses of, 159, 159t, 160f, 167–69, 171
　See also avian; canids; eagles; felids; zooarchaeology
Brown, Linda A., 3–4, 14–15
Building 4, 47, 48, 97, 181–82, 209n.7
　co-producing the *altepetl*, 190, 202–3
　See also Burial 2; Burial 6; Moon Pyramid
Building 5, 47, 49–50, 188, 194–95, 200. See also Burial 3; Moon Pyramid
Building 5 to 6 transition, 49–50, 188, *189*. See also Burial 5; Moon Pyramid
Burial 2, ix–x, Plate 4, Plate 8, 48–49, 111, 124, 182, 183, 184, 190, 193, 194. See also Building 4
Burial 3, Plate 6. See also Building 5, 49, 188, 194–95, 198–99, 203
Burial 5, Plate 7, 49–50, 122, 125, 188, 190, 194–96, 196f, 198–99, 200, 203–4. See also Building 5 to 6 transition
Burial 6, ix–x, Plate 5, Plate 8, Plate 16, 48, 49, 114–16, 124, 184, 185, 187, 190, 193, 194, 205, 206, 207. See also Building 4

Cabrera Castro, Ruben, ix, 34, 37–38, 47, 49, 50, 63, 69–73, 76
Calpulalpan, bowl, 32–33, 32f, 199, 203–4, 213n.24
canids, 67, 70f, 71f, 72f, 74f, 189f, 189
　canid maxillary pendant at FSP, 73–74, 74f, 100, 102, 185, 188, 195
　isotopic patterns of, 141t, 142t, 144f, 145f, 152, 152t, 153f, 154f, 159t, 160f, 161–62, 163, 171
　at Moon Pyramid, 67
　in primary burials, Plate 10, Plate 11, 103, 105t, 105t, 106t, 133
　in secondary burials, 106, 107f, 109f, 110f, 133
　warrior, 76, 166, 188
　zooarchaeological and biological considerations, 73, 103, 105t, 106t, 133, 171, 185–87
　See also iconography: canids; wolves and coyotes
Carrasco, Davíd, 173, 174
Çatalhöyük, 5–6, 16–17
Ceremonial landscapes, 1, 20, 26–27. See also cosmograms

Cerro Gordo Mountain, Plate 1, 17–18, 27–28, 35, 44
coapetlatl or *petlacoatl*, 197, 198f
Copan. See Maya
corporeal animal forms, 1, 4–5
　animal artifacts, 5–6, 16, 38, 56, 59
　animal sacrifices, 13, 174
　in human–animal encounters/interactions, 6, 53, 59, 164
　hunters manipulating, 3
　in orientation of ritual scene, 190, 193
　physical encounters with, 56, 61–63
　primary remains, 164, 187
　in relational ontology, 2, 12, 202
　ritualization of, 17, 174, 175f, 194
　as ritualized bodies, 13, 85, 164, 206
　in ritualized performances at Teotihuacan, 13, 32–33, 53–54, 164, 195
　secondary remains, 165, 187, 195
　spatial regulations of, human sacrificial victims and, 195, 196, 199
　at Sun Pyramid, 43–44, 63
　Teotihuacan state and, 194, 199, 203
　in Teotihuacan state rituals, 32–33, 74, 195, 199
　See also canids; felids; eagle; serpent; jaguars and pumas; wolves
Cortés, Hernan, 179–80
cosmograms, 20–21, 182, 190–93, 191f
cosmology, 7, 21, 23, 68, 175–76, 190, 193
"Coyotes and Deer" mural, 69, 70f
Cuzco, 32–33

dedication ceremonies, 24, 84, 210
dedicatory caches/chambers
　from Moon Pyramid, 47, 48, 49, 51–52, 56, 181, 182, 184, 188
dedicatory rituals, 11, 19–20, 22, 24, 28, 179–80, 193, 201, 203, 209n.7, 210
devaru, 2–3
Díaz de Castillo, Bernal, 75, 168
domestication, 15, 55–56, 172

eagles, 75, 76, 77f, 78, 80f, 84–85, 200
　acquisition and maintenance, 176, 177–78, 179
　biological considerations, 78–80, 80f, 184, 187, 202
　isotopic patterns of, 143, 144f, 145f, 148, 155, 156f, 163

at Moon Pyramid, 48–49, 56, 57t, 101f, 111,
    112t, 115f, 165
in primary burials, Plate 11, Plate 12, Plate 14,
    83, 93, 111, 116–17, 116f, 117f, 118f, 122, 133
in ritual performances, 111, 179
in secondary burials, 61–63, 119f, 119, 121f,
    122, 133
secondary eagle, E. 2246, animal biography
    of, 169f, 169
solar association, 84–85, 189
spatial patterning, Plate 4, Plate 5, Plate 16,
    183–84, 185, 186, 192, 196
at Sun Pyramid, Plate 2, Plate 3, 43–44, 78,
    157–58
taxidermy, 112t, 119, 120–22, 121f, 170, 179,
    187, 220n.48
in thick description, 209, 216, 218–21
zooarchaeological considerations, 78, 80f,
    114–16, 115f, 126t, 133, 170, 184, 185
See also avian: mural paintings
effervescence, 9, 10–11, 206–7
Emery, Kitty F., 3–4, 14–15
encultured landscapes, 2–3, 16–17, 21, 22, 25
entangled, 2–3, 84, 135, 182, 195, 201, 204
ethnography and ethnographic, 4, 7–8, 17, 61,
    67–68, 75–76, 111, 117, 179, 192, 206
Evans-Pritchard, E. E., 179, 220n.48

Fash, William L., 43
faunal assemblages, 15–16, 17, 48, 67, 73–74
feathered feline mural, 59, 60f
Feathered Serpent. *See* iconography
Feathered Serpent Pyramid (FSP), 24, 36,
    37–38, 39, 40, 84–85, 197–98
    canid maxillary pendant from, 73–74, 74f,
        100, 102, 185, 188, 195
    fauna, 63–65, 78, 83, 225t
    principal façade, 34, 36f, 37, 81
    Sun Pyramid and, 44, 48, 63
    See also iconography; Proyecto Templo de
        Quetzalcoatl (PTQ)
felids, 59, 63, 84–85, 189f, 189
    isotopic patterns of, 148, 149t, 150f, 159t,
        160f, 162, 163
    in primary burials at Moon Pyramid,
        Plate 8, Plate 13, 48–49, 87, 88t, 93f,
        94f, 94f, 95t, 133, 183, 184, 189, 194
    primary puma, E. 1818, animal biography
        of, Plate 13, 166, 218n.44, 219n.45

in secondary burials at Moon Pyramid,
    Plate 9, 96, 97f, 98f, 99f, 101f, 102f, 188,
    189f, 197
at Sun Pyramid, Plate 3, 43–44, 150–51
in thick description, 217–18, 221–22
zooarchaeological and biological
    considerations, 57t, 59, 60–61, 62f, 63,
    95t, 95–96, 133, 165, 167, 185–86, 187
    iconography; jaguars and pumas
feline war serpent, 63, 197f, 197–98
Fiesta del Volcán, 27, 194
Florentine codex, 173, 176, 197
Fogelin, Lars, 8
Fowles, Severin M., 7n.2, 10–11
FSP. *See* Feathered Serpent Pyramid

Gamio, Manuel, 29, 37, 67
Gazzola, Julie, 36, 39
Geertz, Clifford, 15, 205, 220n.48
golden eagles. *See* eagles
Gómez Chávez, Sergio, 36, 39, 50–51
Gossen, Gary H., 192
greenstone figurine, at Burial 5, 189–90, 195–
    98, 196f, 199, 203–4

habitus, 8
Hallowell, A. Irving, 2
Haraway, Donna Jeanne, 202
Harrison-Buck, Eleanor, 23–24
Headrick, Annabeth, 53, 168
Henninger, Joseph, 15
Huichol Indians, 55, 67–68, 211–12n.20
Huitzilopochtli, 21, 192
human–animal
    dynamics, 2, 5–6, 86, 135, 164–65, 200
    human sacrifice, 24, 44, 49, 173, 178, 185,
        193, 195, 196, 197–99, 202–4
    interactions/encounters, 3–4, 5, 10, 53, 54,
        55–56, 59, 135, 138–39, 164, 179, 180,
        182, 194–95
    relationships, 15, 16, 55, 180
    See also sacrifice

iconography
    canid, 68
    dog, 68–69
    Feathered Serpent, 37, 38, 81
    felid and feline, 43, 59–60, 63, 166
    jaguar and puma, 63–65, 64f

iconography (*cont.*)
  rattlesnake, 81, 82*f*, 84–85
  wolf and coyote, 68–73
  See also feathered feline mural; feline war serpent
ideology, 7–8, 20–21, 22, 181–82
Ingold, Tim, 2, 55–56
Inomata, Takeshi, 11, 218n.42
isotopic research and analysis, 37–38, 135–36, 138, 139, 140*f*, 141*t*, 142*t*, 144*f*, 145*f*, 146*f*, 147*f*, 159–61
  bones and teeth, 159, 159*t*, 160*f*, 167–69
  on canids, 141*t*, 142*t*, 144*f*, 145*f*, 152, 152*t*, 153*f*, 154*f*, 159*t*, 160*f*, 161–62, 163, 171
  on eagles, 143, 144*f*, 145*f*, 148, 155, 156*f*, 163
  on felids, 148, 149*t*, 156*f*, 159*t*, 160*f*, 162, 163
  intra-species isotopic patterns, 148
  on leporid and leporidae, 135, 140–46, 147, 156, 157*t*, 158*f*, 159*t*, 160*f*, 162–63
  multivariet model, 137–38, 147–48, 147*f*, 151, 154–55, 161, 162–63, 167–68
  as paleodietary proxies, 136
  simple carbon model, 137–38, 146–48, 146*f*, 157–58, 158*f*, 167–68
  See also life history and animal biography
Iyomante ceremony, 14

jaguars and pumas, 59, 62*f*, 64*f*, 84–85
  at FSP, 38, 225*t*
  iconography and mural art, 59–60, 63–65, 64*f*, 168
  master of the animals, 27, 55, 200–1
  in thick description, 210–11, 213, 215, 217–19, 221
  warriors, 12, 16
  See also felids
Jones, Andrew, 16–17

Kamuy, 14, 174
Kellner, Corina M., 137, 146–47
Kertzer, David I., 11
Khatchadourian, Lori, 11–12
kill, the, 14–15, 194
Kimura, Takeshi, 14
Kosiba, Steve, 54, 200

leporid and leporidae, 128, 128*t*
  isotopic patterns of, 135, 140–46, 147, 156, 157*t*, 158*f*, 159*t*, 160*f*, 162–63

  among stomach contents, 96, 126*t*, 128, 128*t*
  zooarchaeological and biological considerations, 79, 128*t*, 128
life history and animal biography, 6, 17, 56, 177
  canid, E. 2199, 103, 170–71
  eagle, E. 2246, 122
  isotopes, 159–61, 162, 163
  puma, E. 1818, 166
  rattlesnake, E. 1494, 172
Linné, Sigvald, 199
López Austin, Alfredo, 37, 193–94, 205, 206–7
López Luján, Leonardo, 182, 193–94

Maya
  archaeological, 11, 24, 80–81
  Copan, 5–6, 61–63, 135, 197
  modern, 3–4, 14–15, 54–55
  sites, 25, 61, 63, 138–39
  and Teotihuacan, 31, 34, 39, 50, 59, 78, 188–89, 196, 198–99
McAnany, Patricia Ann, 201
megaliths, 22, 46–47
Meskell, Lynn, 5, 16–17
Mexican Independence, Plate 16, 41, 200, 220n.46
Mexican national identity, 34–35, 200
microfauna, 125, 126*t*, 128*t*, 134
  rodentia among stomach contents, Plate 15, 129
  See also leporid and leporidae
Millon, Clara, 32–33, 67, 68–69
Moctezuma's House of Beasts or zoo, 1–2, 56–59, 75, 168, 179–80
Monaghan, John, 24
monumentality, 22, 51
Moon Pyramid of Teotihuacan, Plate 1, 1–2, 4–5, 6–7, 9–10, 11, 17, 44, 45*f*, 46*f*
  building phases, 47–48, 49–50
  as cosmogram, 20–21, 182, 190–93, 191*f*
  after decline of Teotihuacan state, 50
  female monoliths, 213–14n.25
  placemaking at, 19, 20, 50–51, 180, 181, 202–3
  ritualized bodies and, 180
  ritualized production of, 19–20, 48, 51, 181, 200, 202–3
  state monumentalism and, 48
  Sun Pyramid and, 35, 43–44, 46, 48, 149–50, 151, 152–53, 154–55, 157–58, 158*f*
thick description of Burial 6, 207

See also altepetl, animal sacrifice; Building 4; Building 5; Building 5 to 6 transition; Burial 2; Burial 3; Burial 5; Burial 6; dedicatory caches/chambers; human sacrifice; sovereignty formations; Teotihuacan
Moon Pyramid Plaza, 45f, 45–47
Murakami, Tatsuya, 208n.4, 209n.7, 211n.19
Mural, 26f, 26, 56–59, 60f, 63, 68–69, 70f, 73, 76, 77f, 81, 82f, 84, 166, 168, 197f, 197, 210n.12, 215n.32. *See also* iconography

nagual, 61, 168, 215
Nahua communities, 23, 75, 193
Nayaka hunter-gatherers, 2–3
new materialism, 1, 2, 4, 11, 12, 26–27
nonlocal fauna, 30
in burials, 129, 130t, 132f, 188–89

Ocaña, Aurelio, 38, 225t
Ojibwa ontology, 2
Osteobiography, *see* life history and animal biography

Paquime, 76, 79, 114
pathology, 76, 86, 114, 165
on canid, 105t, 171
captivity, 163, 165, 177
on eagle, Plate 14, 112t, 114–17, 115f, 116f, 117f, 118f, 119, 133, 169–70, 187
on felid, Plate 13, 88t, 93–95, 96, 100–2, 102f, 133, 151
on rattlesnake, 123t, 134, 172
on raven, 130t, 132f
Patton, Kimberley C., 173–74
performance theory/approach, 8. *See also* ritual performances
personhood and persons, 1, 2–3, 4–6, 12, 13, 14, 15, 17, 19, 23–24, 53, 56, 83–85, 175–76, 181, 194–96, 200–1, 215n.35, 224
animal, 2–3, 4, 5–6, 11, 18, 55–56, 164, 175–76, 181–82
placemaking, 19, 20, 56, 182
Moon Pyramid, 50–51, 52, 180, 181, 188, 202–3, 204, 224
Plaza of the Columns Complex, 78, 83, 129, 177, 178n.1, 188–89, 199, 223–24

Polaco, Oscar, 87
PPL. *See* Proyecto Pirámide de la Luna
PPS. *See* Proyecto Pirámide del Sol
procession, 32–33, 69–73, 178–79, 200, 212, 213, 217
ritual, 32, 40, 59, 178
Proyecto Arqueológico Teotihuacan, 37–38
Proyecto Pirámide de la Luna (PPL), ix, 47. *See also* Moon Pyramid
Proyecto Pirámide del Sol (PPS), 41, 43, 44, 78. *See also* Sun Pyramid
Proyecto Templo de Quetzalcoatl (PTQ), 37–38. *See also* Feathered Serpent Pyramid (FSP)
Public, the, 10, 11, 13, 54, 84, 174, 187, 194, 199, 200, 201, 203–4
Pueblo "doings," 10–11

rabbits and hares. *See* leporid and leporidae
Ramírez, Susan E., 32–33
rattlesnakes, 80, 82f, 203–4
in FSP, 38, 225t
in primary burials, Plate 12, Plate 15, 48–49, 50, 57t, 123, 123t, 129, 134, 183, 185, 189–90, 197
primary rattlesnake, E. 1494, animal biography of, 172
in thick description, 213–14, 215, 217
zooarchaeological and biological considerations, 83
See also iconography
relational ontology, 1, 2, 12, 195–96, 202
embodiments and, 173
narrative of, 17
ritualized production of monuments and, 23–24
See also corporeal animal forms
representation, 4, 12, 53, 59, 84, 197, 203–4. *See also* iconography
ritualization process, 15, 17, 65, 111, 164, 172, 173, 174–75, 180, 181, 194, 202
of corporeal animal forms, 1, 10, 174, 175f, 175–76, 179
ultimate meal, 96, 172
See also procession: ritual
ritualized bodies, 9, 10, 13, 51, 56, 85, 164, 182, 195–96, 206
co-producing, 174, 179–80
corporeal animal forms as, 13, 182, 194

ritualized production or co-production, 1, 23, 25, 200, 209–10n.8
   monumentality and, 22, 23–24
   of Moon Pyramid, 6–7, 19–20, 28, 46–47, 48, 51, 200, 202–3
   of place, 16–17, 20–21, 22, 24, 200
   of Sun Pyramid, 43
ritual performances, 1–2, 6, 8, 179
   characteristics of, 8, 17
   corporeal animal forms in, 13, 53–54, 195
   cosmology and, 8, 190
   places and, 22, 23
   social values and, 206
   in sovereignty formations, 32–33, 201–2, 204
   of Teotihuacan state, 8, 32–33, 111, 181, 195, 201, 202–3, 207n.1
rituals
   communication of meanings by, 9
   dedication, 2, 24, 193, 209n.7
   dedicatory, 11, 19–20, 22, 28, 179–80, 193, 201, 203, 210
   definitions and interpretive paradigms, 6–12
   matter and sovereignty, 11
   participants in, 9
   place and, 20, 200
   ritual experiences, 10
   setting for, 9–10
   See also ritualized bodies; ritual performances; Teotihuacan state rituals
Rodentia. *See* microfauna
Rodríguez Galicia, Bernardo, 74–75
rulership, 59, 81, 197–98, 207n.1

sacrifice, 14–15, 21, 164–65, 168, 173, 176, 179. *See also* animal sacrifice; human sacrifice; Toxcatl festival
Sarabia González, Alejandro, 41, 63, 64*f*
Schoeninger, Margaret J., ix–x, 137, 139–40, 146–47
serpent, 40, 75, 80–81, 123–24, 125, 126*t*, 172, 179–80, 192, 197
   zooarchaeological and biological considerations, 83, 123–24, 134, 185, 188–90, 195
   See also Feathered Serpent; feline war serpent; rattlesnake

Singleton, Robin R., 186–87
Smith, Jonathan Z., 14, 15
Somerville, Andrew, 139–40, 156–58
sovereignty formations, 11–12, 17, 31–32, 203, 224
   animal politics in, 85, 200
   corporeal animal forms in, 54, 63, 182, 194
   at Moon Pyramid, 1–2, 19–20
   ritualized matter and, 11
   of Teotihuacan state, 1–2, 19, 30, 52, 54, 56, 182, 194, 200, 204, 206–7
   See also altepet; ritual performances
spider monkey
   at the Moon Pyramid, 57*t*, 129, 188–89, 199
   at the Plaza of the Columns, 78, 83, 177, 188–89
stable isotopes. *See* isotopic research and analysis
Star Carr, 4–5, 16
stomach content, Plate 15, 56, 105*t*, 112*t*, 114–16, 123*t*, 125, 126*t*, 129, 134, 140–43, 157–58, 159*t*, 167, 183, 185, 188–89
structuralism, 7–8
Sugiyama, Saburo, 37–38, 43, 47
Sun Pyramid, Plate 1, 40, 42*f*, 210–11, 212–13
   FSP and, 44, 48, 63
   iconography, 63, 82*f*
   Moon Pyramid of Teotihuacan and, 35, 43–44, 46, 48, 149–50, 151, 152–53, 154–55, 157–58, 158*f*
   Offering 2, Plate 2, Plate 3, 63–65, 74, 78, 149–50, 154–55, 156–58
   ritualized production of, 43
   See also Proyecto Pirámide del Sol (PPS)

Taube, Karl A., 197
Templo Mayor, 12, 24, 67–68, 122, 192
Tenochtitlan, 12, 21, 75. *See also* Templo Mayor
Teopancazco apartment complex, 30, 63–65, 78, 83, 148, 149–50, 151
Teotihuacan
   animal politics at, 83
   animal sacrifice at, co-producing ritualized bodies and, 174
   apex predators in, 32–33
   archaeological park, 34, 51
   Avenue of the Dead in, Plate 1, 20, 27–28, 34–36, 40, 45–46, 178

biodiversity of, 29
Ceremonial Monuments period, 33–34, 44, 47, 182, 201, 202–3
chronology of, 33f
city and sovereignty, 30
Ciudadela Complex, 36, 37–38, 39, 40, 46
foodways in, 30
Great Compound, 35–36, 46
natural environment of, 28
pre-monumental, 39, 51–52
Pre-Monumental period, 33–34, 33f, 40, 44
pumas and jaguars in mural art, 168
ritualization of corporeal animal forms at, 174, 175f
thick description of, 205
Teotihuacan Expansion period, 33–34, 40, 44, 47, 51–52, 203–4
Urban Renewal period, 33–34, 40, 47, 51–52, 203
See also Cerro Gordo Mountain; Feathered Serpent Pyramid; iconography; Moon Pyramid of Teotihuacan; sovereignty formations; Teotihuacan state
Teotihuacan state, 2, 13, 19, 20, 22, 50, 195–96
animal matter in, 84, 85
apex predators in, 84, 181–82
corporeal animal forms and, 32–33, 74, 194, 195, 199, 203
faunal actors as state symbols, 56–59
felids and, 63
monumentality in, 22–23
social positionality of animals in, 53
state art of, 59, 60f
rituals, 1–2, 11, 13, 56, 74, 182, 199
rituals and place, 20
See also ritual performances; sovereignty formations
Teotihuacan-style thin-orange bowl. *See* Calpulalpan bowl
Teotihuacan Valley, 20, 28–29, 30, 44, 65, 67
teteo imixiptlahuan, 173–74, 177, 178, 179–80
Tezcatlipoca, 61, 164, 173, 174, 179–80, 194
thick description, 15, 17, 205–6
of Burial 6, 207
thing power, 4, 12, 66–67
Tilley, Christopher Y., 22
Tlaloc (Storm God), 26f, 26, 32f, 32–33, 81, 192
jars, Plate 11, 48–49, 183, 185
Toxcatl festival, 173, 175–76
Turner, Victor, 173

Valadez Azúa, Raúl, 38, 87
Vogt, Evon Z., 24
Von Winning, Hasso, 78

wolves and coyotes, 67, 70f, 71f, 72f
"Coyotes and Deer" mural, 69, 70f
iconography at Teotihuacan, 68–73
Mexican wolf, 67, 69, 71f, 73, 183
primary wolf E. 2199, 170, *171*
See also canids, iconography

Zooarchaeology, 1, 4, 86
method and data, 5–6, 7, 12, 15, 17, 29, 38, 57t, 86, 133
isotopes and, 135, 164
See also bone and teeth; canids; eagles; felids; rattlensakes

The manufacturer's authorised representative in the EU for product safety is Oxford
University Press España S.A. of El Parque Empresarial San Fernando de Henares,
Avenida de Castilla, 2 – 28830 Madrid (www.oup.es/en or product.safety@oup.com).
OUP España S.A. also acts as importer into Spain of products made by the manufacturer.

Printed in the USA/Agawam, MA
May 2, 2025

886845.010